OXFORD WORL

THE LAW COD

Patrick Olivelle is the Chair, Department of Asian Studies, at the University of Texas at Austin, where he is the Professor of Sanskrit and Indian Religions. Among his recent publications are *The Saṃnyāsa Upaniṣads* (Oxford, 1992), *The Āśrama System* (Oxford, 1993), *Rules and Regulations of Brahmanical Asceticism* (State University of New York Press, 1994), *The Early Upaniṣads: Annotated Text and Translation* (Oxford 1998), and *Dharmasūtras: Annotated Text and Translation* (Motilal Banarsidass, 2000). His translations of *Upaniṣads*, *Pañcatantra*, and *Dharmasūtras* were published in Oxford World's Classics in 1996, 1997, and 1999.

OXFORD WORLD'S CLASSICS

For over 100 years Oxford World's Classics have brought readers closer to the world's great literature. Now with over 700 titles—from the 4,000-year-old myths of Mesopotamia to the twentieth century's greatest novels—the series makes available lesser-known as well as celebrated writing.

The pocket-sized hardbacks of the early years contained introductions by Virginia Woolf, T. S. Eliot, Graham Greene, and other literary figures which enriched the experience of reading. Today the series is recognized for its fine scholarship and reliability in texts that span world literature, drama and poetry, religion, philosophy and politics. Each edition includes perceptive commentary and essential background information to meet the changing needs of readers.

OXFORD WORLD'S CLASSICS

The Law Code of Manu

A New Translation Based on the Critical Edition by

PATRICK OLIVELLE

OXFORD
UNIVERSITY PRESS

OXFORD
UNIVERSITY PRESS

Great Clarendon Street, Oxford OX2 6DP

Oxford University Press is a department of the University of Oxford.
It furthers the University's objective of excellence in research, scholarship,
and education by publishing worldwide in

Oxford New York

Auckland Bangkok Buenos Aires Cape Town Chennai
Dar es Salaam Delhi Hong Kong Istanbul Karachi Kolkata
Kuala Lumpur Madrid Melbourne Mexico City Mumbai Nairobi
São Paulo Shanghai Taipei Tokyo Toronto

Oxford is a registered trade mark of Oxford University Press
in the UK and in certain other countries

Published in the United States
by Oxford University Press Inc., New York

First published as an Oxford World's Classics paperback 2004
Reissued 2009

British Library Cataloguing in Publication Data

Data available

Library of Congress Cataloging in Publication Data

Data available

ISBN 978-0-19-955533-8

14

Typeset in Ehrhardt
by RefineCatch Limited, Bungay, Suffolk
Printed in Great Britain by
Clays Ltd, Elcograf S.p.A.

PREFACE

THE idea of producing a critical edition of Manu occurred to me ten years ago. Little did I realize then that this project would consume over ten years of my life. It started as a collaborative project between me and my colleague Richard Lariviere. Identifying, locating, and acquiring copies of over one hundred manuscripts from around the world took several years, supported by a grant from the Smithsonian Institution. Under a subsequent three-year grant from the National Endowment for the Humanities, we were able to undertake the examination and collation of the manuscripts in 1998. The first draft of the critical edition was completed in autumn 2002, and this translation is based on it.

I owe a debt of gratitude to numerous individuals and institutions without whose generosity and assistance this work would never have been completed. They will be fully acknowledged in the forthcoming critical edition. Here I want to thank the many individuals who helped me with the translation. First of all, my wife, Suman, has been a partner in the entire project. She read everything several times and caught numerous errors and typos. Several friends and colleagues read my translation, provided valuable criticism, and shared with me generously their extensive knowledge of Sanskrit and ancient India: Albrecht Wezler, Michael Witzel, Stephanie Jamison, Joel Brereton, and Madhav Deshpande. Others read my introduction and gave me valuable feedback: Richard Lariviere, Anne Feldhaus, and Gregory Schopen. To all of them a heartfelt thank you.

The 'Laws of Manu', as it has come to be called, has been translated numerous times into English and other European languages. The translation that has been used most frequently for over a century and has stood the test of time is George Bühler's, published in 1886 by Oxford University Press in the celebrated series Sacred Books of the East edited by Max Müller. A new translation by Wendy Doniger appeared in 1991. What, then, is the justification for yet another translation? All previous translations have been based on what I have called the 'vulgate', the version first printed in Calcutta in 1813. Jolly's assessment that subsequent editions 'are on the whole nothing but reprints of the two earliest Calcutta editions' (1887: v) holds good even for those published in more recent times. As I have shown in the introduction to my critical edition, the 'vulgate' is the version that has the *least* manuscript support. Mine is the first and only translation of the critical edition of the text based on the examination of over 100 manuscripts, nine commentaries, and testimonia consisting of citations in twelve medieval texts.

Finally, I thank Judith Luna for, once again, accepting a translation of mine for inclusion in the Oxford World's Classics series. It is fitting, I think, that 117 years after publishing Bühler's translation, Oxford University Press is once again bringing out a new, and hopefully improved, translation of Manu's treatise on law.

CONTENTS

ABBREVIATIONS

ABORI	*Annals of the Bhandarkar Oriental Research Institute*
AitĀ	*Aitareya Āraṇyaka*
AitB	*Aitareya Brāhmaṇa*
ALB	*Adyar Library Bulletin*
ĀnSS	Ānandāśrama Sanskrit Series
ĀpDh	*Āpastamba Dharmasūtra*
ĀpGṛ	*Āpastamba Gṛhyasūtra*
AŚ	Kauṭalya's *Arthaśāstra*
ĀśGṛ	*Āśvalāyana Gṛhyasūtra*
ĀśŚr	*Āśvalāyana Śrautasūtra*
AV	*Atharvaveda*
BāU	*Bṛhadāraṇyaka Upaniṣad*
BDh	*Baudhāyana Dharmasūtra*
ChU	*Chāndogya Upaniṣad*
GDh	*Gautama Dharmasūtra*
GobhGṛ	*Gobhila Gṛhyasūtra*
JAOS	*Journal of the American Oriental Society*
JB	*Jaiminīya Brāhmaṇa*
MBh	*Mahābhārata*
MDh	*Mānava Dharmaśāstra: The Law Code of Manu*
NSm	*Nārada Smṛti*
PārGṛ	*Pāraskara Gṛhyasūtra*
ṚV	*Ṛgveda*
ŚāṅGṛ	*Śāṅkhāyana Gṛhyasūtra*
ŚB	*Śatapatha Brāhmaṇa*
SBE	Sacred Books of the East
SV	*Sāmaveda*
TĀ	*Taittirīya Āraṇyaka*
TB	*Taittirīya Brāhmaṇa*
TS	*Taittirīya Saṃhitā*
VaDh	*Vasiṣṭha Dharmasūtra*
ViDh	*Viṣṇu Dharmasūtra* or *Viṣṇu Smṛti*
VS	*Vājasaneyi Saṃhitā* of the *White Yajurveda*
WZKSA	*Wiener Zeitschrift für die Kunde Südasiens*
YDh	*Yājñavalkya Dharmaśāstra*

BIBLIOGRAPHY

Primary Sources

Aitareya Āraṇyaka, ed. A. B. Keith (Reprint; Oxford: Clarendon Press, 1969).

Aitareya Brāhmaṇa, ed. with Sāyaṇa's commentary by Kāśīnātha Śāstrī Āgāśe. 2 vols (ĀnSS 32; Poona, 1896). Tr. A. B. Keith (Harvard Oriental Series 25; Cambridge, Mass., 1920).

Āpastamba Dharmasūtra, ed. G. Bühler, 3rd edn. (Bombay Sanskrit and Prakrit Series, 44, 50; Poona: Bhandarkar Oriental Research Institute, 1932). Ed. with Haradatta's commentary *Ujjvalā* by U. C. Pandeya (Kashi Sanskrit Series, 93; Varanasi: Chowkhamba Sanskrit Series Office, 1969). Tr. in Bühler 1879–82. Ed. and tr. Olivelle 1999.

Āpastamba Gṛhyasūtra, tr. in Oldenberg 1886–92.

Āśvalāyana Śrautasūtra, tr. in Oldenberg 1886–92.

Baudhāyana Dharmasūtra, ed. E. Hultzsch, 2nd edn. (Abhandlungen für die Kunde des Morgenlandes, 16; Leipzig, 1922). Ed. with Govinda's commentary by L. Srinivasacharya (Government Oriental Library Series, Bibliotheca Sanskrita, 34; Mysore, 1907). Ed. with Govinda's commentary by U. C. Pandeya (Kashi Sanskrit Series, 104; Varanasi: Chowkhamba Sanskrit Series Office, 1972). Tr. in Bühler 1879–82. Ed. and tr. Olivelle 1999.

Bṛhadāraṇyaka Upaniṣad, tr. in Olivelle 1996.

Chāndogya Upaniṣad, tr. in Olivelle 1996.

Dāyabhāga of Jīmūtavāhana, ed. L. Rocher (New York: Oxford University Press, 2002).

Gautama Dharmasūtra, ed. A. F. Stenzler (London: Trübner, 1876). Ed. with Haradatta's commentary by N. Talekar (ĀnSS, 61; Poona, 1966). Ed. with Maskarin's commenatry by Veda Mitra (Delhi: Veda Mitra and Sons, 1969) Tr. in Bühler 1879–82. Ed. and tr. in Olivelle 1999.

Gobhila Gṛhyasūtra, tr. in Oldenberg 1886–92.

Kauṭilya, *Arthaśāstra*, ed. and tr. in Kangle 1965–72.

Khādira Gṛhyasūtra, tr. in Oldenberg 1886–92.

Mahābhārata, ed. V. S. Sukthankar, 19 vols. (Poona: Bhandarkar Oriental Research Institute, 1927–59).

Manu Smṛti, ed. with the commentaries of Medhātithi, Sarvajñanārāyaṇa, Kullūka, Rāghavānanda, Nandana, Rāmacandra, Maṇirāma, Govindarāja, and Bhāruci, by J. H. Dave, 6 vols. (Bombay: Bharatiya Vidya Bhavan, 1972–84), Ed. with commentaries of Medhātithi, Govindarāja, Sarvajñanārāyaṇa, Kullūka, Rāghavānanda, Nandana, and

Rāmacandra by V. N. Mandlik, 3 vols. (Bombay: Ganpat Krishnaji's Press, 1886). Tr. Bühler 1886; Doniger 1991.

Nārada Smṛti, ed. and tr. with Asahāya's commentary in Lariviere 1989. Tr. Jolly 1889.

Pāṇini, *Aṣṭādhyāyī*, ed. and tr. O. Böhtlingk (Reprint, Hildesheim: Olms, 1964). Ed. and tr. S. C. Vasu, 2 vols. (Reprint; Delhi: Motilal Banarsidass, 1962). Ed. with the commentary *Kāśikā* of Vāmana and Jayāditya by B. R. Sastry and V. Sundara Sarma, 3 vols. (Hyderabad: Sanskrit Academy, 1969–76).

Pāraskara Gṛhyasūtra, tr. in Oldenberg 1886–92.

Patañjali, *Mahābhāṣya*, ed. F. Kielhorn, 3rd revised edn. by K. V. Abhyankar, 3 vols. (Poona: Bhandarkar Oriental Research Institute, 1962–72).

Ṛgveda Saṃhitā, ed. with Sāyaṇa's commentary by F. Max Müller. 6 vols. (London: W. H. Allen & Co., 1849–74). Tr. K. F. Geldner (Harvard Oriental Series 33–6; Cambridge, Mass., 1951–7).

Śāṅkhāyana Gṛhyasūtra with extracts from the commentaries of Nārāyaṇa and Rāmacandra, 2nd edn. (Sri Garib Dass Oriental Series, 42; Delhi: Sri Satguru Publications, 1987). Tr. in Oldenberg 1886–92.

Śatapatha Brāhmaṇa, ed. A. Weber (Reprint; Chowkhamba Sanskrit Series, 96; Varanasi: 1964). Tr. J. Eggeling (SBE 12, 26, 41, 43, 44; Oxford, 1882–1900).

Taittirīya, Āraṇyaka, ed. with Sāyaṇa's commentary by K. V. Abhyankar, 2 vols. (ĀnSS 36; reprint; Poona, 1967).

Taittirīya Brāhmaṇa, ed. with Sāyaṇa's commentary by Nārāyaṇa Śāstrī Goḍabole, 3 vols. (ĀnSS 37; reprint; Poona, 1979).

Taittirīya Saṃhitā, tr. A. B. Keith. 2 vols. (Harvard Oriental Series, 13, 19; Cambridge, Mass., 1914).

Vaikhānasa Smārtasūtra, ed. W. Caland, (Bibliotheca Indica, 242; Calcutta: Asiatic Society of Bengal, 1927). Tr. in Caland 1929.

Vasiṣṭha Dharmasūtra, ed. A. A. Führer, 1st edn. (Bombay: Government Central Book Depot, 1883); 3rd edn. [which appears to be a reprint of the 2nd edn. published in 1914] (Bombay Sanskrit and Prakrit Series, 23; Poona: Bhandarkar Oriental Research Institute, 1930). Ed. with Kṛṣṇapaṇḍita's commentary *Vidvanmodinī* (Benares, 1878). Tr. in Bühler 1879–82. Ed. and tr. Olivelle 1999.

Viṣṇu Smṛti, ed. with Nandapaṇḍita's commentary by V. Krishnamacharya. 2 vols. (Adyar Library Series, 93; Madras: Adyar Library and Research Centre, 1964). Tr. in Jolly 1880.

Yājñavalkya Smṛti, ed. with Vijñāneśvara's commentary by U. C. Pandey (Kashi Sanskrit Series, 178; Varanasi: Chowkhamba Sanskrit Series Office, 1967). Ed. with Viśvarūpa's commentary by T. Ganapati Sastri

(Reprint; Delhi: Munshiram Manoharlal, 1982). Ed. with Śūlapāṇi's commentary by J. R. Gharpure (Bombay, 1939). Ed. with Aparāditya's commentary. 2 vols. (ĀnSS 46, 1903–4).

Secondary Literature

Banerjee, N. V. (1980), *Studies in the Dharmaśāstra of Manu* (New Delhi: Munshiram Manoharlal).

Beaman, G. B. (1895), *On the Sources of the Dharma-Śāstras of Manu and Yājñavalkya* (Leipzig: Otto Harrassowitz).

Bodewitz, H. W. (1973), *Jaiminīya Brāhmaṇa I, 1–65: Translation and Commentary with a Study Agnihotra and Prāṇāgnihotra* (Orientalia Rheno-Traiectina, 17; Leiden: E. J. Brill).

—— (1985) 'Yama's Second Boon in the Kaṭha Upaniṣad', *WZKSA* 29: 5–26.

Bühler, G. (tr.) (1879–82). *Sacred Laws of the Āryas* [containing the Dharmasūtras of Āpastamba, Gautama, Vasiṣṭha, and Baudhāyana], 2 vols. (SBE 2, 14; Oxford: Oxford University Press).

—— (tr.) (1886), *The Laws of Manu* (SBE 25; Oxford: Oxford University Press).

Burnell, A. C. (tr.) (1884), *The Ordinances of Manu* (Reprint; New Delhi: Munshiram Manoharlal, 1995).

Caland, W. (tr.) (1929), *Vaikhānasasmārtasūtra* (Calcutta: Asiatic Society of Bengal).

Chatterjee, H. (1971), *The Law of Debt in Ancient India* (Calcutta: Sanskrit College).

—— (1972–4), *Forms of Marriage in Ancient India*, 2 vols. (Calcutta: Sanskrit Pustak Bhandar).

Dallapiccola, A. L., and Lallemant, S. Zingel-Avé (eds.) (1989), *The Sastric Tradition in the Indian Arts* (Beiträge zur Südasienforschung; Wiesbaden: Steiner).

Das, R. M. (1962), *Women in Manu and his Seven Commentators* (Bodh Gaya: Kanchana Publications).

Das, S. (1977), *Crime and Punishment in Ancient India* (New Delhi: Abinav Publications).

Dave, K. N. (1985), *Birds in Sanskrit Literature* (Delhi: Motilal Banarsidass). *See* Linke 1997.

Day, T. (1982), *The Conception of Punishment in Early Indian Literature* (Waterloo, Ontario: Wilfrid Laurier University Press).

Derrett, J. D. M. (1968), *Religion, Law, and the State in India* (New York: Free Press).

—— (1973), *Dharmaśāstra and Juridical Literature* (Wiesbaden: Harrassowitz).

Derrett, J. D. M. (1975), *Bhāruci's Commentary on the Manusmṛti* (The *Manu-śāstra-Vivaraṇa*, books 6–12;. text, translation and notes) 2 vols. (Wiesbaden: Franz Steiner).

Doniger, W. (tr.) (1991), *The Laws of Manu* (London: Penguin).

Dumont, L. (1980) [1970], *Homo Hierarchicus: The Caste System and its Implications*, tr. M. Sainsbury (revised edn.; Chicago: University of Chicago Press).

Falk, H. (2001), 'Suicidal Self-scorching in Ancient India.', in *Vidyārṇavavandanam: Essays in Honour of Asko Parpola*, ed. K. Karttunen and P. Koskikallio, pp. 131–46 (Studia Orientalia, 94; Helsinki: Finnish Oriental Society).

Fitzgerald, J. (forthcoming), *The Mahābhārata: 11 The Book of the Women, 12 The Book of Peace*, vol. 7 (Chicago: University of Chicago Press).

Hacker, P. (1959), 'Two Accounts of Cosmogony', in *Jñānamuktāvali: Commemoration Volume in Honour of Joh. Nobel*, ed. C. Vogel, pp. 77–91 (Sarasbati Vihara Series, 38; Delhi).

—— (1961), 'The Saṅkhyization of the Emanation Doctrine, Shown in a Critical Analysis of Texts', *WZKSA* 5: 75–112.

Halbfass, W. (1988), *India and Europe: An Essay in Understanding* (Albany, NY: State University of New York Press).

—— (1991), 'Homo Hierarchicus: The Conceptualization of the Varṇa System in Indian Thought', in *Tradition and Reflection*, ch. 10, pp. 347–405 (Albany, NY: State University of New York Press).

Hara, M. (1979), '*Śraddhāviveśa*', *Indologica Taurinensia*, 7: 261–73.

Heesterman, J. C. (1968), 'The Return of the Veda Scholar (samāvartana)', in *Pratidānam: Indian, Iranian and Indo-European Studies presented to Franciscus Bernardus Jacobus Kuiper on his Sixtieth Birthday*, ed. J. C. Heesterman *et al.*, 436–47 (The Hague: Mouton).

Hiltebeitel, A. (2001), *Rethinking the Mahābhārata: A Reader's Guide to the Education of the Dharma King* (Chicago: University of Chicago Press).

Hopkins, E. (1881), *The Mutual Relation of the Four Castes According to the Mānavadhamaçâstram* (Leipzig: Breitkopf and Hartell).

—— (1885), 'On the Professed Quotations from Manu Found in the Mahābhārata', *JAOS* 11: 239–75.

Huxley, A. (1996), 'When Manu met Mahāsammata', *Journal of Indian Philosophy* 24: 593–621.

Jain, M. P. (1966), *Outlines of Indian Legal History* (Bombay: Tripathi).

Jamison, S. W. (1991), *The Ravenous Hyenas and the Wounded Sun: Myth and Ritual in Ancient India* (Ithaca, NY: Cornell University Press).

—— (1996), *Sacrificed Wife/Sacrificer's Wife: Women, Ritual, and Hospitality in Ancient India* (New York: Oxford University Press).

—— (1998), 'Rhinoceros Toes: Manu 5.17–18 and the Development of the Dharma System', *JAOS* 118: 249–56.

—— (2000), 'A Sanskrit Maxim and its Ritual and Legal Applications', in *Anusantatyai: Festschrift für Johanna Narten zum 70. Geburtstag*, ed. A. Hintze and E. Tichy, Münchener Studien zur Sprachwissenschaft, Beiheft 19, pp. 111–25.

Jayaswal, K. P. (1930), *Manu and Yājñavalkya: A Comparison and a Contrast, A Treatise on the Basic Hindu Law* (Calcutta: Butterworth).

Jha, Ganganatha (1920–39), *Manusmṛti: With the 'Manubhāṣya' of Medhātithi*. 10 vols. (Reprint; Delhi: Motilal Banarsidass, 1999).

—— (1930), *Hindu Law and its Sources* (Delhi: Indian Press).

Jolly, J. (tr.) (1880), *The Institutes of Vishnu* (SBE 7; Oxford: Oxford University Press).

—— (1885), *Outlines of an History of the Hindu Law of Partition, Inheritance, and Adoption*, Tagore Law Lectures 1883 (Calcutta: Thacker, Spink, and Co.).

—— (1887), *Mānava Dharma-Śāstra: The Code of Manu* (London: Trübner).

—— (1889), *The Minor Law-Books: Nārada, Brihaspati* (SBE 33; Oxford: Clarendon Press).

Kane, P. V. (1962–75), *History of Dharmaśāstra*. 5 vols. (Poona: Bhandarkar Oriental Research Institute).

—— (n.d.), *Kātyāyanasmṛti on Vyavahāra* (Poona: Oriental Book Agency).

Kangle, R. P. (ed. and tr.) (1965–72), *Kauṭilya's Arthaśāstra*, 3 vols. (Bombay: University of Bombay).

—— (1964), 'Manu and Kauṭilya', *Indian Antiquary*, 3rd ser., 1: 48–54.

Köhler, H. W. (1973), *Śrad-dhā in der vedischen und altbuddhistischen Literature*, thesis, Göttingen, 1948, ed. K. L. Janert (Wiesbaden: Franz Steiner).

Lane, J. W. (1981), 'The Creation Account of *Manusmṛti*', *ABORI* 62: 157–68.

Lariviere, R. W, (ed. and tr.) (1989), *Nārada Smṛti.*, with Asahāya's commentary, 2 vols. (Philadelphia: South Asia Regional Studies).

—— (1997), 'Dharmaśāstra, Custom, "Real Law" and "Aprocryphal" Smṛtis', in *Recht, Staat, und Verwaltung im klassichen Indien*, ed. B. Koelver, pp. 97–110 (Wiesbaden: Franz Steiner).

Leslie, J. (1991), *Rules and Remedies in Classical Indian Law*. Panels of the VIIth World Sanskrit Conference (Leiden: Brill).

Lienhard, S. and Piovano, I. (eds.) (1977), *Lex et Litterae: Studies in Honour of Professor Oscar Botto* (Turin: Edizioni dell'Orso).
Lingat, R. (1973), *The Classical Law of India*, tr. J. D. M. Derrett (Berkeley: University of California Press).
Linke, E. (1997), 'Birds in Sanskrit Literature: Sanskrit–English Index', *Annals of the Bhandarkar Oriental Research Institute*, 78: 121–41. Word index to Dave 1985.
Malamoud, C. (1980). 'Théologie de la dette dans les Brāhmaṇa', *Puruṣārtha: Science Sociales en Asie du Sud*, 4: 39–62.
—— (1982), 'On the Rhetoric and Semantics of puruṣārtha', in *Way of Life: King, Householder, Renouncer. Essays in Honour of Louis Dumont*, ed. T. N. Madan, pp. 33–54 (New Delhi: Vikas).
Mani, V. (1975), *Purāṇic Encyclopaedia* (Delhi: Motilal Banarsidass).
O'Flaherty, W. (ed.) (1980), *Karma and Rebirth in Classical Indian Traditions* (Berkeley: University of California Press).
Oldenberg, H. (tr.) (1886–92) *The Gṛihya-Sūtras: Rules of Vedic Domestic Ceremonies* [containing the Sūtras of Śāṅkhāyana, Āśvalāyana, Pāraskara, Khādira, Gobhila, Hiraṇyakeśin, and Āpastamba] (SBE 29–30; Oxford: Oxford University Press).
Olivelle, P. (1981), 'Contributions to the Semantic History of *Saṃnyāsa*', *JAOS* 101: 265–74.
—— (1986–7), *Renunciation in Hinduism: A Medieval Debate*, 2 vols. (Vienna: Institute for Indology, University of Vienna).
—— (1993), *The Āśrama System: The History and Hermeneutics of a Religious Institution* (New York: Oxford University Press).
—— (1996), *Upaniṣads* (Oxford: Oxford University Press).
—— (1998), 'Caste and Purity: A Study in the Language of the Dharma Literature', *Contributions to Indian Sociology*, 32: 189–216.
—— (1999), *Dharmasūtras: The Law Codes of Ancient India* (Oxford: Oxford University Press).
—— (2002*a*), '*Abhakṣya* and *abhojya:* An Exploration in Dietary Language', *JAOS* 122: 345–54.
—— (2002*b*), 'Food for Thought: Dietary Regulations and Social Organization in Ancient India', 2001 Gonda Lecture (Amsterdam: Royal Netherlands Academy of Arts and Sciences).
—— (forthcoming *a*), 'Power of Words: The Ascetic Appropriation and the Semantic Evolution of *dharma*', in Peter Fluegel and Gustaaf Houtman (eds.), *Asceticism and Power in the Asian Context* (London: Curzon).
—— (forthcoming *b*), 'Manu and Gautama: A Study in Śāstric Intertextuality', in *Wilhelm Halbfass Commemoration Volume*, ed. K. Preisendanz and E. Franco (Vienna: Verlag der Österreichischen Akademie der Wissenschaften).

—— (forthcoming *c*), *Mānavadharmaśāstra: A Critical Edition with an Annotated Translation* (New York: Oxford University Press).

Rocher, L. (1969), '"Lawyers" in Classical Hindu Law', *Law and Society Review*, 3: 383–402.

—— (1993), 'Law Books in an Oral Culture: The Indian *Dharmaśāstras*', *Proceedings of the American Philosophical Society*, 137: 254–67.

—— (2002), '*Dāsadāsī*', *JAOS* 122: 374–80.

Scharfe, H. (1993), *Investigations in Kauṭalya's Manual of Political Science* (Wiesbaden: Harrassowitz).

Schmidt, H.-P. (1987), *Some Women's Rites and Rights in the Veda* (Poona: Bhandarkar Oriental Research Institute).

Sharma, R. S. (1990) [1958], *Śūdras in Ancient India: A Social History of the Lower Order Down to circa* A.D. *600*, 3rd edn. (Delhi: Motilal Banarsidass).

Shastri, H. C. (1972–4), *Forms of Marriage in Ancient India*. 2 vols. (Calcutta: Sanskrit Pustak Bhandar).

Smith, B. K. (1994), *Classifying the Universe: The Ancient Indian Varṇa System and the Origins of Caste* (New York: Oxford University Press).

Sternback, L. (1974), *The Mānava Dharmaśāstra I–III and the Bhaviṣya Purāṇa* (Varanasi: All India Kashi Raj Trust).

Stietencron, H. von (1997), 'The Non-Existence of Impurity and the Legitimation of Kings', in Lienhard and Piovano 1997, pp. 487–508.

Wezler, A. (1982), 'Manu's Omniscience: On the Interpretation of Manusmṛti II.7', in *Indology and Law: Studies in Honour of Professor J. Duncan M. Derrett*, ed. G. D. Sontheimer and P. K. Aithal, pp. 79–105, (Wiesbaden: Franz Steiner).

—— (1987), 'On the Term *antaḥsaṃjña-*', *ABORI* 58: 112–31.

—— (1991–2), 'Should the Adopted Son be a Close Relative? On the Interpretation of VaDhS 15.6 and 7', *Indologica Taurinensia*, 17–18: 359–81.

—— (1994), 'A Note on Sanskrit *brūṇa* and *bhrūṇahatyā*', in *Festschrift Klaus Bruhn*, ed. N. Balbir and J. Bautze, pp. 623–46 (Reinbek: Verlag für Orientalistische Fachpublikationen).

—— (1999), 'Über den sakramentalen Charakter des *dharma* nachsinnend', *Raum-zeitliche Vermittlung der Transzendenz*, ed. G. Oberhammer and M. Schmücker, pp. 63–113 (Vienna: Österreichischen Akademie der Wissenschaften).

Witzel, M. (1984), 'Sur le chemin du ciel', *Bulletin d'Études Indiennes*, 2: 213–79.

INTRODUCTION

The Law Code of Manu or *Mānava Dharmaśāstra* (*MDh*) is undoubtedly the most celebrated and the best known legal text from ancient India. The pre-eminent position of Manu among legal authorities was clearly established by the fifth century CE and possibly as early as the third. Sometime towards the middle of the first millennium, Bṛhaspati (Jolly 1889: 387), one of Manu's successors and himself the composer of a legal treatise, pays Manu the ultimate compliment: Manu is the authority, and any text contradicting Manu has no validity.

There was no diminishment in the fame of Manu through the next fifteen centuries right up to the time when the administration of law was taken over by the colonial power, Britain. More commentaries—nine are extant—were written on Manu than on any other legal text. All later legal texts, moreover, are in many ways dependent on him; some can be viewed as mere summaries or expansions of Manu. Even though in some areas of law—legal procedure, for example—other texts, such as those of Nārada and Kātyāyana, became prominent, Manu nevertheless remained pre-eminent throughout the long and distinguished history of legal literature during the middle ages. Medieval legal works cite Manu more frequently than any other primary text.

The fame of Manu spread outside of India at a relatively early date. The first king in the central Buddhist myth of origins is called Mahāsammata. The figure of this first king becomes identified with that of Manu in the Buddhist countries of Southeast Asia, especially Burma and Thailand, where the Buddhist law codes are ascribed to Manu.[1]

It is no surprise, then, that after the establishment of colonial rule when the administration of justice was carried out by British judges, the first text on Indian law that Sir William Jones, the great pioneer of Sanskrit studies, chose to translate into English in 1794 was the *Law Code of Manu*. Its translation opened for the first time the world

[1] For discussions of this issue, see Lingat 1973: 266–72; Steven Collins and Andrew Huxley, 'The Post-Canonical Adventures of Mahāsammata', *Journal of Indian Philosophy*, 24 (1996) 624–48.

of non-European law and religion to a Western audience. George Bühler's translation and study, which has remained the standard for over a century, appeared in the famous Oxford University Press series Sacred Books of the East in 1886. With the establishment of Indo-European linguistics and the discovery of the Sanskrit of the Vedas as one of the earliest extant members of the family of languages to which Greek, Latin, and most modern European languages belonged, there was great interest in Europe about the cultural heritage of ancient India. During the critical nineteenth century, which set the agenda for much of later scholarship on ancient India, Manu was for better or for worse the lens through which most European scholars viewed India's past. Nietzsche, for example, regarded the *MDh* as a life-affirming representation of the Aryan religion, in contrast to the nay-saying Buddhism. Passages from Manu are found in every collection of readings given to students of Indian culture, history, or religion in Western universities.

Fame invites controversy, and in India itself during the twentieth century Manu became a lightning rod for both the conservative elements of the Hindu tradition and the liberal movements intent on alleviating the plight of women and low-caste and outcaste individuals. For the latter, Manu became the symbol of oppression. His verses were cited as the source of legitimation for such oppression, even though the same or similar passages are found in other and older documents. The first conference by untouchables at Yeola under the leadership of Dr B. R. Ambedkar in 1935, in which it was resolved to reject Hinduism, passed a resolution with the title 'To the Untouchable Community: A New Message of a New Manu'. Within a month a group of young untouchable men gathered in Nasik to burn a copy of Manu ceremonially.[2] Even the prominent women's rights advocate, Madhu Kishwar, had to do battle with Manu.[3] Kishwar refers to the burning of copies of Manu in the precincts of the Rajasthan High Court on 25 March 2000, and observes: 'The protesters believed that the ancient text is the

[2] See Eleanor Zelliot, 'The Psychological Dimension of the Buddhist Movement in India', in *Religion in South Asia: Religious Conversion and Revival Movements in South Asia in Medieval and Modern Times*, ed. G. A. Oddie, (Columbia, Mo.: South Asia Books, 1977), 119–44. The burning of the *MDh* was advocated also by other reform activists, such as E. V. Ramasami: see M. R. Barnett, *The Politics of Cultural Nationalism in South India* (Princeton: Princeton University Press, 1976), 37.

[3] 'Manu and the Brits', *Hinduism Today* (January–February 2001), 56–9.

defining document of Brahmanical Hinduism, and also the key source of gender and caste oppression in India.'

In spite of all the attention, including burning, that Manu has received over the past two centuries, the study of the text itself has been neglected. More heat, literal and metaphorical, has been generated than light. Until now, even a close examination of the numerous extant manuscripts of this work, manuscripts written in nine scripts and spread all over the Indian subcontinent, has not been undertaken. My hope is that this translation, based on my forthcoming critical edition of Manu, will be of some help in understanding this controversial but important document from India's past.

The Early Legal Tradition

Manu was not the first author of a legal code in ancient India. The earliest extant codes predate Manu by two to three centuries. They were written in aphoristic prose called *sūtra*. Four such codes, commonly referred to as *Dharmasūtras*, have survived and are ascribed eponymously to Āpastamba, Gautama, Baudhāyana, and Vasiṣṭha.[4] These texts refer to other legal authorities, pointing both to a vibrant and contentious intellectual tradition and to a rich literature, much of which, unfortunately, is now lost.

Prior to Manu, however, the tradition of law centred on the term *dharma* was principally concerned with the life and activities of individuals belonging to the three upper classes—Brahmin, Kṣatriya, and Vaiśya—but principally with Brahmins. Ritual activities, especially those relating to the life cycle from conception and birth to death, played a central role in the lives of Brahmins. The concept of *dharma* encompasses rites and ritual obligations, even though by the time of the *Dharmasūtras* the term had assumed a wider meaning encompassing all that constituted proper conduct and the right way to lead one's life. The moral dimension of *dharma*, therefore, comes to the forefront in this literature.

There was another class of literature, *Gṛhyasūtras*, that dealt specifically with the ritual life of upper-class people, who were called 'twice-born' because the males of these classes underwent an initiatory rite regarded as their second birth (*MDh* 2.68, 146–8). The

[4] These codes have been translated in this series: see Olivelle 1999.

Dharmasūtras, therefore, deal primarily with proper conduct on the part of adolescents—who, after their initiation, spent many years at a teacher's house studying the Vedas and other matters relating to adult life—and especially married householders. The scheme envisaged in the 'orders of life' (*āśrama*) also became increasingly central to the organization of material in the *Dharmasūtras* thereby incorporating rules to regulate the ascetic lives of forest hermits and wandering mendicants. These topics also form the major component of Manu spanning Chapters 2–6.

The *Dharmasūtras* comprised one of the principal sources of Manu's law code. Of the four *Dharmasūtras*, however, Manu appears to have followed Gautama very closely (Olivelle forthcoming *b*). In the enumeration of the sources or root of *dharma*, for example, Manu presents a versified version of Gautama's *sūtra*, following the latter almost verbatim:

MDh 2.6	*GDh* 1.1–2
The root of *dharma* is the entire Veda, and the tradition and practice of those who know the Veda.	The root of *dharma* is the Veda, and the tradition and practice of those who know the Veda.[5]

The dependence of Manu on Gautama here is evident. No other *dharma* text has a formulation quite like this.

The sections of Manu dealing with the king, statecraft, and especially judicial procedure, however, are either absent or poorly developed in the *Dharmasūtras*. It was Manu's innovation to include these discussions in his treatise. Prior to Manu there was in all likelihood a separate expert tradition dealing with these matters, a tradition referred to as *Arthaśāstra*. The *Āpastamba Dharmasūtra*, for example, devotes 83 (6 per cent) of its 1,364 *sūtras* to statecraft and law, and the *Gautama Dharmasūtra* 115 (11.8 per cent) of its 973 *sūtras*. The *MDh*, on the other hand, allots 971 (36 per cent) of its 2,680 verses to statecraft and law, only slightly less than the section devoted to the Brahmin, which consists of 1,034 verses (38.6 per cent). The difference shrinks even further when we account for the fact that much of what is discussed in the section on the Brahmin (Chapters 2–6) applies equally to other twice-born individuals. The

[5] The way Manu modified Gautama's prose is more apparent in the original Sanskrit: from *vedo dharmamūlaṃ tadvidāṃ ca smṛtiśīle* of Gautama to the verse *vedo 'khilo dharmamūlaṃ smṛtiśīle ca tadvidām* of Manu.

MDh thus represented a watershed in the development of the expert tradition of *dharma*; it co-opted material that would have been viewed as belonging to the expert tradition of *Arthaśāstra*.

The tradition of *Arthaśāstra*, then, is a second textual source of Manu. Although only one treatise of this tradition has survived, the one ascribed to Kauṭalya (also spelled Kauṭilya), it refers to opinions of several other schools. There is a clear connection between some verses of Manu and the extant *Arthaśāstra* (*AS*).[6] It is impossible to determine on the basis of these parallels whether Manu is borrowing from the extant *Arthaśāstra* or whether both texts are dependent on earlier texts of this tradition. There is also a close parallel between the technical vocabularies of Manu and the *Arthaśāstra*.[7]

The most important influence of the *Arthaśāstra* tradition on Manu is the incorporation of the 'Grounds for Litigation' given in Chapters 8–9. Legal matters were dealt with in a disorganized manner in the *Dharmasūtras*. Hence, it is highly unlikely that the organizing of the material under eighteen grounds was accomplished within the *dharma* tradition. It is much more probable that this classification was achieved by the scholars of the *Arthaśāstra* tradition, law and legal procedure being a central focus of their labours. Manu probably borrowed this classificatory system, as well as the material presented within it, from the *Arthaśāstra* tradition. The systems in Manu and the extant *Arthaśāstra*, however, are so different from each other that it is unlikely that the former borrowed directly from the latter. The *Dharmasūtras* deal with the relationship between husband and wife, the classification of sons, and the partition of property within their sections on marriage. Manu's is the first text to include these discussions within the section on judicial procedure and litigation, clearly indicating the influence of the *Arthaśāstra* tradition.

Author and Date

Although Manu derived much of his material from earlier sources, his work is not merely an anthology. Manu gave a definite and unique structure to his work and introduced several innovations that mark

[6] See e.g. *MDh* 8.52–7 and *AŚ* 3.1.19; *MDh* 7.102 and *AŚ* 1.4.5; *MDh* 7.105 and *AŚ* 1.15.60; *MDh* 9.280 and *AŚ* 4.11.7.

[7] See below note to *MDh* 8.123.

his composition as a watershed in the history of ancient Indian legal literature.

The eponym 'Manu', of course, is not the name of the historical author of this text. The name, however, was an astute choice. The ancient vedic text *Taittirīya Saṃhitā* (2.2.10.2) records what appears to have been a proverbial saying: 'Whatever Manu has said is medicine.' Numerous legal maxims were ascribed to Manu, who must have been viewed by later generations as an ancient lawgiver. Further, Manu was regarded not just as the first human being but, at least according to one tradition, as the first king. With the rise of urban centres and large kingdoms in northern India around the middle of the first millennium BCE, the significance of royalty with regard to various aspects of social life appears to have increased. In religion, leaders of new sects and ascetic communities were given royal pedigrees, including the Buddha and the Mahāvīra, the founders of Buddhism and Jainism. 'King as teacher' is a motif in the Upaniṣads, where numerous significant doctrines are ascribed to kings. With the rise of devotional religions towards the end of the first millennium BCE, we have the figures of Rāma and Kṛṣṇa, the divine incarnations, who are kings and not Brahmins. Historically, the rise of the Maurya empire and the overwhelming presence of Aśoka and his imperial reforms in the third century BCE must have loomed large. That a treatise on law (*dharma*) with universal application should have been ascribed not just to any king but to the first king, therefore, should come as no surprise. The clear intent was to make the work more authoritative by connecting it to both the sage responsible for the famous proverbial sayings and to the first king of humankind. The historical and political reasons for the writing of this text, to which we shall return, make this ascription even more significant.

The *MDh* (1.58) presents a textual history of itself, ascribing the original treatise to the Creator—the Imperishable One (1.57) and the Self-existent (1.3, 6)—identified as Brahmā (1.11). The view that the Creator should have produced a text for the governance of his creatures is found also in other texts. In the *Mahābhārata* (12.59.29), Bhīṣma recounts the beginning of the world, when everything was perfect and laws were unnecessary. When things began to deteriorate, however, the Creator composed a treatise in one thousand chapters dealing with the three areas of human enterprise: Law (*dharma*),

Polity (*artha*), and Pleasure (*kāma*). According to the *MDh*, the Creator taught the treatise he had composed to his son, Manu, and he in turn taught it to his pupils, including Bhr̥gu. It is Bhr̥gu who becomes the spokesman and recites the treatise to the gathered seers. Tradition thus presents the extant version of the *MDh* as the edition (*saṃhitā*) proclaimed by Bhr̥gu.

Later tradition picks up on the theme of *saṃhitā* in the sense of editions and abridgements of the original text of Manu. At the very beginning of the *Nārada Smr̥ti* (*NSm*), a legal treatise composed several centuries after the *MDh*, it is said that Manu created a text containing 1,080 chapters and 100,000 verses. Nārada abridged it to 12,000 verses; the latter underwent further and repeated abridgements. The tradition that the original composition of Manu was subjected to repeated editorial revisions and abridgements appears to have been old.

A close examination of the *MDh* and its exquisite structure (see below p. xxvii), however, makes it abundantly clear that the text ascribed to Bhr̥gu is not an edition or version of a pre-existing text but an original composition written by a single individual. The kind of deep structure, so subtle yet so clear, makes it impossible to have been composed either through unconscious accumulation or through a series of editorial interventions spanning long intervals of time. This was conceived and put together by a single individual with extraordinary ability and a systematic mind.

I have used 'Manu' here as a shorthand term for the historical author of this law code. The name of this author is unknown, as are any details of his life: his date, his geographical location, influences that may have shaped his life and thought, and a host of biographical questions that would shed light on the text itself. The most we can say is that he was a learned Brahmin from somewhere in northern India. Some of the socio-political influences that shaped his thought and that perhaps motivated the writing of the book, however, may at least be surmised by looking at the possible date of its composition.

The relative chronology of the *MDh* has widespread scholarly consensus. The *MDh* was undoubtedly composed after the *Dharmasūtras;* it shows clear advances in thinking on many fronts, especially in the sections relating to statecraft, royal functions, and judicial procedure. On the other hand, the *MDh* is older than any of the other metrical *Dharmaśāstras*, especially the four old ones ascribed to Yājñavalkya, Nārada, Bṛhaspati, and Kātyāyana. These show clear advances in technical vocabulary and judicial procedure, especially the widespread use of ordeals to ascertain the innocence or guilt of a defendant. The *MDh*, therefore, occupies the middle position at the point of transition from the prose and scholastic *Dharmasūtras* to the metrical *Dharmaśāstras* ascribed to authoritive divine beings.

Setting an absolute chronology is a more difficult task. The current scholarly consensus places the *MDh* sometime between the second century BCE and the second century CE. The issue is whether these upper and lower limits can be further refined and narrowed through internal and external evidence.

References in Manu to two ethnic groups, Śaka and Cīna (Chinese), suggest a lower limit of the first century BCE, which is supported by the relative chronology of other texts belonging roughly to the same period; and the references to the *MDh* in later literature (the play *Mṛcchakaṭika* by Śūdraka, for example, and the apparent fame of the *MDh* to the author of the third century CE *Kāmasūtra*) suggest an upper limit of the second century CE. So the best we can do on the available evidence is to date the *MDh* between the first century BCE and the second century CE. Another clue to its date is the mention of gold coins (see 8.213, 361). The earliest native gold coins discovered in India are from the Kushana dynasty in the second century CE. It is, of course, impossible to say from the archaeological absence that gold coins were not minted earlier. However, if we can use this criterion, the composition of the *MDh* may be placed closer to the second century CE.

Narrative Structure and Composition

Manu introduced two major innovations in comparison to the previous literature of the legal tradition, the *Dharmasūtras*. First, he composed his text entirely in verse, using the popular and simple *śloka* metre with four eight-syllabic feet. Second, he set his text within a narrative structure that consists of a dialogue between an exalted being in the role of teacher and others desiring to learn from him.

Late vedic texts, especially the early prose Upaniṣads, regularly cite verses in support of statements and viewpoints. It appears that these verses were somehow viewed as having greater authority and, therefore, able to lend greater support to the author's views, much like citations from scripture. The *Bṛhadāraṇyaka Upaniṣad*, for example, frequently cites supporting verses with the introduction 'In this connection there is this verse'.[8] We see this practice continued by the authors of the *Dharmasūtras*. They also present verses as providing support for or confirmation of views they have already presented in prose and introduce them with 'Now, they also quote', indicating that these verses were well-known sayings that experts would cite in support of a particular practice or viewpoint.[9] In the later *Dharmasūtras*, however, we find increasing use of verses not simply as citations but integrated into the composition.[10] This strategy is used with growing frequency by Vasiṣṭha, the author of the latest *Dharmasūtra*; chapters 25–7, for example, are completely in verse.

It appears that during the last few centuries prior to the common era *śloka* verses had assumed an aura of authority, and proverbial wisdom was transmitted as memorable verses. The logical outcome of this tendency was for texts themselves to be composed in verse, to give them authority.

In the legal literature, the earlier texts are in prose with verse citations and the later ones are composed entirely in verse. The first such text was that of Manu. His use of verse for the composition of his *Dharmaśāstra*, therefore, must have been part of a deliberate plan to lend the kind of authority to his text that would come only through this literary genre. We have, of course, the parallel examples of the epics *Mahābhārata* and *Rāmāyaṇa* composed in verse and claiming religious authority. The legal tradition followed the trail blazed by Manu; all later *Dharmaśāstras* are written in verse.

The second innovation in the composition of the *MDh* is its narrative structure. The *Dharmasūtras* are not only written in prose but are also presented as nothing more than scholarly works. There is no literary introduction; the author gets right down to business. He presents his material in a straightforward manner, and on points of

[8] See 2.2.3; 4.3.11; 4.4.6, 7, 8. See also *ChU* 3.11.2; 5.2.9; 5.10.9; 5.24.5; 7.26.2; 8.6.6.

[9] See *ĀpDh* 1.19.15; 1.25.9; 1.31.23; 1.32.23; 2.9.13; 2.13.6; 2.17.7; *BDh* 1.1.8; 1.2.11, 15, 17; 1.7.1; 1.8.23, 25, 53; 1.10.6, 23; 1.11.16, 14; 1.21.2; 2.1.6, 17, 21; 2.2.26; 2.3.14, 16, 19, 31, 45; 2.4.1, 10, 14, 18; 2.5.4, 7, 9; *VaDh* 1.22, 38; 2.6, 27, 30, 31, 41, 48; etc.

[10] For such verses, see *BDh* 1.10.26; 1.19.8; 2.6.32–42. Note also that the later additions to the *BDh*, such as the most of book 4, are in verse.

controversy and debate he presents opposing viewpoints. All this is eliminated by Manu. Here the real author is presented not as a scholar but as the primeval lawgiver, the Creator himself, and his intermediaries, his son Manu and the latter's disciple Bhṛgu. The law is promulgated authoritatively; there cannot be any debate, dissension, or scholarly give and take.

An anonymous group of seers approaches Manu and asks him to teach them the Law (*dharma*). Manu accedes to their wishes. He narrates the creation of the world up to the emergence of human society hierarchically arranged into the four social classes. Then he asks his pupil Bhṛgu to teach them the rest (1.59), reminding me of a busy professor letting his graduate assistant do the dirty work of teaching an undergraduate class. Bhṛgu takes up the task in earnest; the rest of the book is the oral teaching of Bhṛgu. The seers reappear only twice—once at the beginning of Chapter 5 when they ask how Brahmins can be subject to death, a question that leads to a discussion of food practices, purification, and the duties of women; and a second time at the beginning of Chapter 12 when they ask Bhṛgu to teach them the effects of actions (*karma*). The narrative structure given prominence at the opening of the text fizzles out; there is no conclusion to the narrative. A similar structure is found in the *Pañcatantra*, the famous book of animal tales, where the original setting—Viṣṇuśarman's instruction of princes in statecraft and policy under the guise of animal stories—is lost sight of in the conclusion.[11]

We have no way of knowing all the reasons for Manu's strategy of departing from the tradition of textual composition found in the *Dharmasūtras*. The tradition of dialogue where a teacher instructs a pupil, a son, or a king goes back to the Brāhmaṇas and the Upaniṣads. The literary structure of these dialogues, however, places these individuals within human history. The transition into divine instruction is found already in the *Chāndogya Upaniṣad*, where we have the instruction of Nārada by Sanatkumāra (7.1) and of Indra and Virocana by Prajāpati (8.7). Nevertheless, I think the example of the Buddhist texts was also a likely factor. For the first time in India, the words of a single charismatic individual were taken as the sole fountain of authority in a religious tradition. The doctrine of 'Buddha's word' (*buddhavacana*), that the sole form of textual authority is the

[11] See P. Olivelle, *The Pañcatantra: The Book of India's Folk Wisdom* (Oxford: Oxford University Press, 1997).

words of the Buddha, governed the production of texts both in the early forms of Buddhism and in the Mahāyāna. All texts begin with the preamble 'Thus have I heard', placing the text in the mouth of the Buddha and making the function of the 'author' merely that of a transcriber or re-teller of what he had heard. The narrator narrating what he had heard and placing his narrative in the distant past is also at the heart of the *Mahābhārata* structure.

Although its narrative structure is much simpler, the same is true of the *MDh* as well. We have here five layers of 'telling', 'hearing', and re-telling. At the most remote level, we have the Creator himself soon after his creative activity composing a treatise and reciting it to his son Manu (1.58). Manu is the first 'hearer'. He transmits it to Marīci and the other sages (1.58), who form the second tier of 'hearers'. At Manu's command, one of these sages, Bhṛgu, teaches the seers who had come to Manu with the mission of learning the Law. Bhṛgu's first word (1.60), significantly, is 'Listen'. This group of seers, still placed *in illo tempore*, constitutes the third tier of 'hearers'. The narrator of the entire text makes only a fleeting and implicit appearance in the very first verse of the text: 'As Manu was seated, absorbed in contemplation, the great seers came up to him, paid him homage in the proper manner, and said to him.' Here we have the voice of the narrator introducing the first group of characters; then he becomes silent except for two other fleeting appearances to introduce the seers' further request at 5.1–2 and to introduce Bhṛgu's final discourse at 12.2. Evidently the narrator himself, who at one level can be identified with the historical author of the text, heard the text presumably from the seers; or he has been eavesdropping on Bhṛgu's instruction of the seers. This narrator is the fourth 'hearer'. There is then the implied fifth 'hearer', that is, all those who listen to or read this text, including modern scholars. The last verse of the book, possibly part of an interpolated section, is directed at this audience: 'When a twice-born recites this Treatise of Manu proclaimed by Bhṛgu, he will always follow the proper conduct and obtain whatever state he desires.'

Although mediated by a series of tellers and hearers, the ultimate authority of the text lies in its original promulgator, the Creator himself. Paralleling the Buddhist doctrine of 'Buddha's words' and doing one better than that, the *MDh* grounds its authority on the words of the Self-existent One, the very ground of creation. This appeal to a single source of authority stands in sharp contrast to the traditional source of authority for and means of knowing the Law, namely the Veda supplemented by traditional texts and the conduct of the virtuous. Indeed, the *MDh* itself presents the latter doctrine when it discusses the sources of Law in Chapter 2. There is thus a disjuncture between the narrative structure of Chapter 1 and the body of the text. The author is a traditional pandit, and his habitual methods of reasoning, argumentation, and public presentation take over in the substantive parts of the text.

The Structure of the Treatise

The manuscript tradition of the *MDh* divides the text into twelve chapters. This appears to be an old division; it is followed by all the commentators. This division, however, is not original. It was probably imposed on the text when it was subjected to a revision that added several sections, most notably the Synopsis given at the conclusion of the first chapter. Although several of the chapters follow the natural sequence of topics, a close reading of the text shows that they are artificial divisions. The chapters also contain different topics that the author intended to be separate: Chapter 2 contains the sources of Law, rites of passage, and the duties of a student; the duties of a king are spread over Chapters 7, 8, and 9; the single topic of judicial procedure and the grounds for litigation is spread over Chapters 8 and 9; and Chapter 9 contains the final discussion of the king's duties and the duties of Vaiśyas and Śūdras. More importantly, however, the division into chapters obscures the latent and deeper structure of the text, a structure that spans the entire corpus and must go back to the author himself.

Manu uses the technique of 'transitional verse' to mark the conclusion of one subject and the beginning of another. Here is an example (2.25):

> I have described to you above succinctly the source of the Law, as also the origin of this whole world. Learn now the Laws of the social classes.

This verse marks the transition from the two introductory topics, the creation of the world and the sources of Law, to the main body of the text, the Law of the four social classes. Such a technique is unique to Manu; it is not used in the *Dharmasūtras* and sparingly, if at all, in the later *Dharmaśāstras*. Note also the use of the verb 'Learn' (*nibodhata*) in most transitional verses; this manner of expression becomes a signature of Manu. The device of transitional verses was an innovation conceived by Manu and provides an insight into the plan he had for his book. By following the trail of these transitional verses, we can uncover the overall plan and structure of the *MDh*. The chart below presents schematically the structure that emerges through this method together with the transitional verses at the beginning and/or end of topics, verses that provide the clues to uncovering that structure.

1. ORIGIN OF THE WORLD: 1.1–119

2. SOURCES OF THE LAW: 2.1–24

I have described to you above succinctly the source of the Law, as also the origin of this whole world. Learn now the Laws of the social classes. (2.25)

3. DHARMA OF THE FOUR SOCIAL CLASSES: 2.25–11.266

3.1. Rules Relating to Law: 2.25–10.131

3.1.1. Rules of Action in Normal Times: 2.26–9.336

3.1.1.1. Fourfold Dharma of a Brahmin: 2.26–6.97

I have explained to you above the fourfold Law of Brahmins, a Law that is holy and brings imperishable rewards after death. Listen now to the Law of kings. (6.97)

3.1.1.2. Rules of Action for a King: 7.1–9.325

I have described above in its entirety the eternal rules of action for the king. What follows, one should understand, are the rules of action for the Vaiśya and the Śūdra in their proper order. (9.325)

3.1.1.3. Rules of Action for Vaiśyas and Śūdras: 9.325–36

I have described above the splendid rules of action for the social classes outside times of adversity. Listen now to the rules for them in the proper order for times of adversity. (9.336)

3.1.2. Rules of Action in Times of Adversity: 10.1–129

I have described above the entire set of rules pertaining

to the Law of the four classes. Next, I will explain the splendid rules pertaining to penance. (10.131)

3.2. Rules Relating to Penance: 11.1–265

You have described this Law for the four classes in its entirety, O Sinless One! Teach us accurately the ultimate consummation of the fruits of actions. (12.1)

4. DETERMINATION REGARDING ENGAGEMENT IN ACTION (*karmayoga*): 12.3–116

Bhṛgu, the son of Manu and the very embodiment of the Law, said to those great seers: 'Listen to the determination with respect to engagement in action.' (12.2)

4.1. Fruits of Action: 12.3–81

I have declared to you above all the fruits arising from actions. Listen now to these rules of action for a Brahmin, rules that secure the supreme good. (12.82)

4.2. Rules of Action for Supreme Good: 12.83–115

I have explained to you above all the best means of securing the supreme good. A Brahmin who does not deviate from them obtains the highest state. (12.116)

The structure that emerges from tracing the transitional verses consists of four major divisions of uneven length and importance:

1. Creation of the world.
2. Sources of the Law.
3. The Law of the four social classes.
4. Law of action (*karma*), rebirth, and final liberation.

Obviously, the main section in terms of both length and importance is the third dealing with the four social classes. The other three are presented as a preamble, an introduction, and a concluding postscript. The preamble and the introduction are mentioned at the end of the second section (2.25) in the transitional verse that also introduces the central third section on the four social classes. The third section is mentioned also at its conclusion (12.1) in the transitional verse that introduces the final section on action.

The central third section has two major subdivisions, the first called 'rules relating to Law' and the second called 'rules relating to penance'. These two sections—3.1 and 3.2 in the chart—are mentioned only once, at the conclusion of the first of them (10.131). The first subsection (3.1) is the longest in the entire book and is further subdivided into two: rules of action in normal times and rules of action in times of adversity. These two subdivisions—3.1.1 and 3.1.2 in the chart—are also introduced just once in the transitional verse at the conclusions of the first of them (9.336).

There is a fourth level of division in section 3.1.1 on rules for normal times. This section has three further sub-sections. The first—3.1.1.1 in the chart—is called 'The Fourfold Dharma of a Brahmin', and its conclusion (6.97) also introduces the next subsection—3.1.1.2 in the chart—dealing with the king: 'I have explained to you above the fourfold Law of Brahmins. . . . Listen now to the Law of kings.' The third subdivision—3.1.1.3 in the chart—deals with the remaining two social classes, the Vaiśya and the Śūdra; it is introduced at the conclusion of the section on kings (9.325): 'I have described . . . the eternal rules of action for the king. What follows . . . are the rules of action for the Vaiśya and the Śūdra.'

The final postscript dealing with action (*karma*), rebirth, and liberation, which is introduced in 12.1, also has two subdivisions: the first (12.3–82) is on the fruits of actions and the second (12.83–115) is on achieving the highest bliss. These two are introduced in the transitional verse at the end of the first subsection (12.82): 'I have declared to you above all the fruits arising from actions. Listen now to these rules of action for a Brahmin, rules that secure the supreme good.'

We can then view the overall structure of the *MDh* schematically:

1. Origin of the World: 1.1–119
2. Sources of the Law: 2.1–24
3. Dharma of the Four Social Classes: 2.25–11.266
    - 3.1. Rules Relating to Law: 2.25–10.131
        - 3.1.1. Rules of Action in Normal Times: 2.26–9.336
            - 3.1.1.1. Fourfold Dharma of a Brahmin: 2.26–6.97
            - 3.1.1.2. Rules of Action for a King: 7.1–9.325
            - 3.1.1.3. Rules of Action for Vaiśyas & Śūdras: 9.325–36
        - 3.1.2. Rules of Action in Times of Adversity: 10.1–129
    - 3.2. Rules Relating to Penance: 11.1–265
4. Determination Regarding Engagement in Action (*karmayoga*): 12.3–116

4.1. Fruits of Action: 12.3–81

4.2. Rules of Action for Supreme Good: 12.83–115

The Content of the Treatise

The Law of a Brahmin

The largest portion of the central section (3.1.1) of the *MDh* is devoted to the fourfold Law of a Brahmin encompassing much of Chapter 2 and all of Chapters 3–6. This section is explicitly organized around the four orders of life (*āśramas*).[12] All the traditional material, however, could not be contained within the scheme of the four orders, especially the sections on the childhood rites of passage, rules of a bath-graduate (*snātaka*), and holy lifestyles falling outside the orders of forest hermit and wandering mendicant. Manu, however, attempts to squeeze these into the overall structure of the orders.

Chapter 4, on the bath-graduate, is sandwiched between Chapters 3 and 5, dealing with various aspects of a householder's life. We see the difficulty Manu had with blending the bath-graduate into the *āśrama* framework when we look at the beginnings of Chapters 3 and 4. Chapter 3 begins quite naturally with the return home of a student who has completed his vedic studies. The author deals with the selection of a bride and marriage, with a long disquisition on the various kinds of marriage. Then, at the beginning of Chapter 4, Manu has to repeat this within the context of the *āśrama* system: after dwelling at the teacher's house during the first part of his life, a man should return home, get married, and lead a householder's life during the second part. The fifth chapter is introduced with a question from the seers to Bhṛgu about how a Brahmin could be subject to death. This opens the way to a discussion of permitted and forbidden foods and means of bodily purification. The theme of the four *āśramas* is taken up again at the beginning of Chapter 6: after living as a householder a man may become a hermit and live in a forest; and again at 6.33: after living the third part of his life as a forest hermit, he should

[12] The four orders of life (*āśramas*) are: vedic student, householder, forest hermit, and wandering mendicant. For the history of this central institution of Hinduism, see Olivelle 1993.

become a wandering mendicant during the fourth and final period of his life.

Even though this section (3.1.1.1) is explicitly said to deal with the Law of Brahmins, a close examination shows that Manu is here following a practice common in ritual texts. They describe fully the ritual procedure only for the archetypal rite of a group of related rites; the description of the other rites (ectypes) consists of pointing out only those ritual elements unique to each and different from the archetype. For Manu, the Law of Brahmins constitutes the archetype, and he describes it fully. *Mutatis mutandis* these rules are applicable to all other social classes. Indeed, within this section itself Manu often points out how the Law is modified for other classes. For example, under initiation he points out the different times for the different classes, the different ways of manufacturing the girdle, different kinds of staff, and the like (2.41–7). Likewise, he enumerates the kinds of marriage and the number of wives permitted for the different classes (3.13). This principle of descriptive parsimony permits Manu to deal with the other classes, especially Vaiśyas and Śūdras, briefly. Only the rules specific to them are discussed.

The Rules for a King

As already noted, the section devoted to the king, statecraft, and law in the *MDh* is disproportionately large in comparison to Manu's predecessors within the expert tradition of Law. The disproportion becomes even more striking when we take into account the fact that this section deals with matters specific to the king and the Kṣatriya class, whereas the section on the Brahmin includes issues common to all social classes.

A close reading of the section on the king reveals that Manu organized his material around a simple structure in three parts. The first part, spanning 7.1–142, deals with the origin of the king; the organization of the state machinery, including the appointment of officials; the construction of the fort; the king's marriage; the conduct of foreign policy, including war; and finally taxation. It appears that Manu's narrative scheme here envisages a new king occupying a virgin territory. He is unmarried, he has to settle the land and build a capital, and he has to organize the state apparatus. This structure suited Manu's purpose well, because it enabled him to discuss all the points associated with statecraft. Real life, however, is quite another matter; most kings would gain a kingdom either through inheritance or through conquest. In either case there would be pre-existing cities, forts, and a state bureaucracy.

In the second part, Manu changes his narrative scheme to span a single day, from the morning when the king wakes up until nightfall when he goes to bed. Manu squeezes into a single day the description of all the duties of a king spread over 182 verses. The morning routine extends from 7.145 to 7.215; the afternoon routine from 7.216 to 7.222; and the evening routine from 7.223 to 7.226. This part concludes with the king going 'to bed at the proper time and [rising] up refreshed'.

The third part deals with the justice system and comprises the eighteen grounds for litigation. After dealing briefly with the organization of the court (8.1–46), Manu arranges his material on law and the dispensation of justice under the eighteen grounds for litigation, commonly called titles of law (8.47–9.251). The issues relating to evidence and the interrogation of witnesses are dealt with not separately but under the first ground for litigation, the non-payment of debts. This appears to have been a convention borrowed from the Arthaśāstric tradition, to which Manu is indebted for the material relating to the king.

Manu's organization of the eighteen grounds for litigation is based on a few clear principles. Manu's structure is significantly different from that of the extant *Arthaśāstra*, as well as from the other two major *Dharmaśāstras*, of Nārada and Yājñavalkya. The order of enumeration in the *MDh*, therefore, was probably the creation of Manu himself, and we get a glimpse into his systematic way of thinking also in his arrangement of these topics. His arrangement, I think, is far superior to and more systematic than any of the others and can be presented schematically:

A. Individual and group disputes (= 1–10)
B. Criminal law (= 11–15)
C. Personal law (= 16–17)
D. Public order and safety (= 18)

Manu begins with disputes between individuals and between groups. Such disputes must have been the most common reason for litigation and cover the first ten grounds. The first nine for the most part deal with individual disputes, with the possible exception of the fourth, on partnerships, where the dispute is between an individual and a partnership of which he is a member. Likewise, the seventh, on breach of contract, may happen between individuals and between an individual and a corporate body. The tenth, disputes over boundaries, can happen between individual landowners, but the typical dispute discussed by Manu concerns boundaries between villages.

The next category is criminal law, involving verbal and physical assault, theft, robbery/violence, and sexual crimes. Unlike in modern law, however, lawsuits for such crimes were not initiated by the state but by the injured parties.

The third category is personal or family law. The first ground for litigation under this rubric is disputes between a husband and a wife, although much of what is discussed is more general, relating to laws and conventions governing marital relationships. The second and clearly the more significant is the partition of inheritance. It is in these two topics that there is often an overlap with material covered under marriage, especially in Chapter 5. This was probably inevitable when the Dharmaśāstric tradition incorporated strictly legal matters and, therefore, had to deal with marriage and family in two places, under proper conduct (*ācāra*) and law (*vyavahāra*).

The final category is gambling and betting. One would have expected Manu to present rules for the orderly conduct of these practices, as is done in other texts.[13] Manu, however, was strictly opposed to gambling and betting. For him, these areas of social practice should be suppressed rather than regulated. It is, therefore, natural for him to follow his brief discussion of gambling with the important topic of the 'eradication of thorns' (*kaṇṭakaśodhana*), that is, the suppression of criminal activities, especially theft, in the kingdom. This is a topic found in all legal texts, but it falls outside the grounds for litigation. Litigation, according to ancient Indian jurisprudence, is initiated by private individuals; the king and his officials are explicitly barred from initiating lawsuits. The eradication of thorns, on the other hand, is one of the principal duties of a king; it is a police activity and falls outside the judicial process. Nevertheless, Manu sees the eradication of thorns and the suppression of gambling as part of the same administrative process.

The section on the duties of the king concludes with this pithy

[13] See e.g. *ĀpDh*, 2.25.12–14.

statement typical of Manu (9.324): 'Conducting himself in this manner and always devoted to the Laws pertaining to kings, the king should direct all his servants to work for the good of his people.'

The Rules for Vaiśyas and Śūdras

Manu's discussion of Vaiśyas and Śūdras, the last two of the social classes, is extraordinarily brief. Eight verses are devoted to the Vaiśya and just two to the Śūdra. Even granting that, according to the ritual principle of parsimony discussed earlier, much of the material for these two classes was included in the discussion of the Brahmin, one would have expected something more than just ten verses.

The reason for this brevity is unclear, but I think it must be understood within the context of the socio-political motives behind Manu's composition. Simply put, Manu's interest lay not in the lower classes of society, which he considered to be an ever-present threat to the dominance of the upper classes, but in the interaction between the political power and Brahmanical priestly interests, interests that were under constant threat ranging from the Aśokan imperial polity to the foreign invasions around the turn of the millennium.

On Sin and Penance

The methodical approach demonstrated in the sections on Brahmin and king is evident also in the chapter on sin and penance.[14] Manu begins the topic with a discussion on the efficacy of penance, on whether penance can actually remove sins. After justifying the efficacy of and the need for penance, he divides his inquiry into two sections: public sins (11.55–189), which occupy much of the discussion, and private or secret sins (11.227).

Manu first presents the major classifications of sins: (1) the five grievous sins that cause the loss of caste (*mahāpātaka:* 11.55–9); (2) a large group of secondary sins that also cause the loss of caste (*upapātaka;* 11.60–7); and (3) four further classes of sins (11.68–71) that cause a man (*a*) to be excluded from caste (*jātibhraṃśakara*), (*b*) to become mixed-caste (*saṃkīrṇakara*), (*c*) to be unworthy of receiving gifts (*apātrīkaraṇa*), and (*d*) to be impure (*malāvaha*). He concludes the classification of sins with this transitional verse: 'Listen

[14] There are, of course, some inconsistencies and extraneous material in this chapter. I will return to them later.

now attentively to the specific penances by which all these sins individually enumerated above may be removed' (11.72).

Manu then goes on to discuss the appropriate penances for each of the categories of sins: (1) the first four of the grievous sins (11.73–108), (2) secondary sins (11.109–24), and (3) the four further classes of sins (11.125–26). Finally, he turns from sins personally committed to association with sinners who have become outcastes as a result of their sins, a category that forms the fifth grievous sin (11.181–90). Manu introduces the last discussion with the transitional verse: 'I have described above the expiation for all four kinds of sinners. Listen now to the following expiations for those who associate with outcastes' (11.180). The mention of the four kinds of sinner has caused some confusion. Grievous and secondary sins make two. The third category consists of four sins, but the penances for the four are dealt with in two verses. I think Manu viewed the first (*jātibhraṃśakara*) as one class and presented the penances for it in a single verse (11.125). He appears to have viewed the other three as forming a single class, dealing with their penances in a single verse (11.126). So, we have four categories of penances relating to the sins listed previously. The attempt to come up with four sinners as indicated in verse 11.180 may have led a redactor to insert the four offences listed in 11.127–179.

The discussion of penance for publicly known sins ends with two crisp statements. First: 'No one should transact any business with uncleansed sinners; and under no circumstances should anyone abhor those who have been cleansed' (11.190). There follows an excursus containing miscellaneous items on sins and penances, which is clearly an interpolation. Manu concludes the section on penances for public sins with the transitional verse (227), which also gives the penances for private sins: 'By these observances should twice-born persons cleanse themselves of public sins; they may cleanse themselves of secret sins, however, through ritual formulas and burnt offerings.'

When we take out the accretions in this chapter, the clear and impressive structure of the original composition emerges. That this section on penance concludes the central portion of the treatise dealing with the Law of the four classes—number 3 in the structure I have outlined above—is evident in the opening verse of the last chapter: 'You have described this Law for the four classes in its entirety, O Sinless One! Teach us accurately the ultimate consummation of the fruits of actions' (12.1).

On *Karma*

Chapter 12, dealing with actions and their consequences, as well as with the attainment of ultimate happiness beyond the realm of rebirth, is quite different in style and substance from the rest of the book. There is insufficient evidence, however, to suggest that this chapter is a later addition. The entire chapter is taken up with the theme of action (*karma*), both the consequences of good and bad actions (*karmavipāka*) and the final triumph over action and the attainment of the supreme good beyond the process of rebirth. Broadly this discussion falls into two sections, the one dealing with the fruits of action (3–81) and the other dealing with actions leading to the supreme good (83–106). These two sections are divided by Manu's signature transitional verse:

> I have declared to you above all the fruits arising from actions.
> Listen now to these rules of action for a Brahmin, rules that
> secure the supreme good.

This chapter has also undergone redactorial interventions.

After it leaves the hands of the author, every text assumes an independent life. This is especially true in the case of texts published before the advent of printing. These pre-modern texts continue their life as they are copied by hand, read, studied, interpreted, and commented on by succeeding generations of scribes, readers, and scholars. It is this afterlife of a text that a critical edition uncovers through the collation of manuscripts and presents to the reader in its critical apparatus.

Both these aspects—the original text and the afterlife—presuppose that changes are introduced into the author's text by those responsible for its afterlife. Some of these changes are inadvertent, such as scribal errors and misreadings; others are deliberate, such as the different but equally cogent and intelligible readings found in different recensions and the additional verses found in numerous manuscripts. These changes introduced into the text and detectable through the examination of the extant manuscripts and commentaries can be readily identified. The manuscript and other evidence we possess, however, often do not cover the entire period from today to the time of the author. In the case of the *MDh*, we pick up the textual history midstream, at least several centuries after its composition.

If the later tradition of readers and copyists introduced changes, it is fair to assume that earlier generations did so too. In the translation, I have identified passages of possible interpolation as 'Excursus'; interpolation or not, they must at best be viewed as parenthetical statements. Readers can check for themselves how the text of Manu flows more smoothly when these 'Excursus' are ignored.

The Nature and Purpose of the Treatise

The year was 1794. The renowned orientalist William Jones published his English translation of the *MDh* and made the *Dharmaśāstra* tradition of India known to the rest of the world for the first time. This translation was not spurred simply by scholarly interest; it had also a practical purpose. In 1772 Warren Hastings, the British Governor-General, had proposed a plan for the administration of justice in which the Hindu law based on *Dharmaśāstra* was to play a key role. British judges needed access to the original legal texts of India to implement the British policy of 'administering native law to the natives' (Rocher 1969, 383). So was born what Lariviere (1989) has called a 'well-intentioned misunderstanding'. The British clearly misunderstood the nature of the ancient Indian *Dharmaśāstras* and their relation to actual practice and the adminstration of law in pre-colonial India.

What, then, is the relationship between the provisions of the *Dharmaśāstras*, such as the *MDh*, and real law administered by courts in India down the centuries? Do they record custom and relate to real law? Or are they merely pious wishes with no political sanction or purely panditic commentaries with no relation to custom (Lariviere 1997: 98). Beyond the administration of law, the issues also relate to the link between *Dharmaśāstra* and the social life in India through the centuries. Recent scholarship has moved closer to the first position: *Dharmaśāstras* are a record of customs and traditional standards of behaviour prevalent in particular places and times in India and are definitely related to the administration of justice (Lariviere 1997; Wezler 1999).

Dharmaśāstra, however, represents an expert tradition and, therefore, presents not a simple record of customs but a jurisprudential *reflection* on custom. Custom is taken here to a second order of discourse, a discourse that the native tradition calls *śāstra*. '*Dharmaśāstra*', thus, is a *śāstra* dealing with *dharma*. The relation between *Dharmaśāstra* and real life—whether it is law, social norms, or morality—can best be analysed, therefore, by taking the self-presentation of *Dharmaśāstra* as a *śāstra* seriously and asking the broader question: What is the connection between *śāstra* and practice? *Śāstras* were composed in a variety of fields: law, statecraft, grammar, medicine, astronomy, poetics, erotica, drama, and the like. These treatises represent a point of arrival within a tradition when the totality of knowledge created within it is presented authoritatively in a *śāstra*. It is also a point of departure for further reflection in the form of study and commentary.

The native reflections on *śāstra* presents '*śāstra*' as in some sense eternal and providing the pre-existing blueprint for a particular practice. Vātsyāyana in his *Kāmasūtra* (1.3.1–10) affirms the priority of *śāstra* over practice (*prayoga*). There are people who perform a practice without knowing the corresponding *śāstra*, but that practice would not have existed without the norms provided by the *śāśtra*. So courtesans practise the art of love without studying the *Kāmasūtra*, handlers of horses and elephants do so without knowing the *śāstras* dealing with these animals, and Brahmins speak Sanskrit without necessarily knowing the grammar of Pāṇini. Yet, Vātsyāyana insists, these rule-governed activities would not have existed but for their respective *śāśtras*: 'The *śāstra* alone, however removed it may be, is the cause of practice.' He concludes the discussion with an example: 'As people in the provinces do not transgress the bounds, knowing, "The king is there", so it is in this case.' As the absent king is the reason for people far away to observe the bounds of law and propriety, so the *śāstra*, though unlearned, is the reason why people engage in rule-bound activities. Irrespective of whether *śāstra* is logically or chronologically prior or posterior to practice, the native tradition draws a close connection between the two.

The important question for us, however, is how a *śāstra*, once it is produced, relates to ongoing practice. This relationship is not direct; the *śāstras* themselves do not provide blueprints for action. *Śāstras* exercised control over practice not directly but through the mediation of experts who were instructed in the *śāstras* in their youth and who, as adults, continued to read, reflect, and debate the *śāstras* among themselves. Turning to *Dharmaśāstra*, the experts were the Brahmins knowledgeable in these treatises, Brahmins whom the *MDh* calls 'scholar(s) of Law' (12.111). Although it is possible that passages from the *Dharmaśāstras* may have been cited in a court of law,[15] these texts did not have a function similar to civil and criminal codes of modern states within the administration of justice. The administration of justice is mediated by the expert judges, who are conversant both with the *Dharmaśāstras* and with the laws and customs of the particular region, caste, guild, or family involved in the dispute. The *Dharmaśāstras* never pretend to be comprehensive, to present all the laws and norms that govern the behaviour of people. Manu (8.41) clearly spells out the extra-śāstric knowledge required to judge lawsuits: 'A king who knows the Law should examine the Laws of castes, regions, guilds, and families, and only then settle the Law specific to each.' There certainly is more to law than what is given in the *śāstra*, and it was unwise of the British to equate *Dharmaśāstra* with Hindu law.

It is clear that the *MDh* seeks to present itself as an eternal document parallel to the Vedas and composed by the Creator himself. Its 'hegemonic' character is evident in its aim to present guidelines for a properly ordered society under the sovereignty of the king and the guidance of Brahmins. Although it presents the 'should' more often than the 'is' and may occasionally engage in pious wishes and wishful thinking, the amount of detail it presents with regard to diverse areas of human activity—ritual, food, marriage, inheritance, adoption, judicial procedure, taxation, punishment, penance—shows that it was not divorced from reality. The long literary tradition of *Dharmaśāstra*, the longest such tradition in India spanning over two millennia, shows that the *śāstras* were used continuously in the education of young Brahmins and perhaps even princes. It was this training in the *Dharmaśāstra* that the Brahmins selected as judges, lawyers, and arbiters brought to their judicial reasoning, deliberation, and judgments.

The purpose of a central document such as the *MDh* is

[15] Rocher (1993: 264) cites the *NSm* and the *Bṛhaspatismṛti* for early evidence of written forms of *Dharmaśāstras* being physically placed within a court during judicial proceedings.

multifaceted and hard to pin down. First, there are the aims of the author when he undertook the project. These are impossible to discern except when they are reflected in the composition itself. Second, there are the purposes to which the text was employed by succeeding generations of scholars, readers, and politicians. These are bound to be varied depending on time, place, and the varying goals of the individuals and institutions concerned. As a *śāstra*, however, and the premier *Dharmaśāstra* in Indian history, we can discern some of the roles it may have played both in learned discourse and in everyday life. The *MDh* was clearly not a 'how to' book; it was neither a *Handbook of Manners* nor a *Law Code*, although it contains aspects of both. Its connection with lived reality was not immediate but mediate. We can identify two significant aspects of this mediation. First, a central *śāstra* such as this would have been used in the instruction of budding scholars, principally young Brahmins; it must have been part of the standard curriculum for aspiring legal scholars in Brahmanical colleges such as the so-called *ghaṭikāsthānas* in southern India.[16] Secondly, it was a point of reference for the ongoing scholarly conversations, debates, and literary production in the field of *Dharmaśāstra*. Some of these debates and interpretations may indeed sound like panditic pedantry. But they also had serious and often practical purposes. After all, many of the medieval legal digests and commentaries were commissioned by kings and others were carried out under royal patronage.

The Socio-Political Background

If we assume that the *MDh* was composed around the turn of the millennium, give or take a century—and I think this is a plausible assumption—then we may be able at least to speculate about the social and political environment of the author and perhaps the motivations for its composition. Recently similar questions have been raised with reference to the epic *Mahābhārata*, especially by Hiltebeitel (2001) and Fitzgerald (forthcoming).

I think the socio-political environment that prompted the

[16] See C. Minakshi, *Administration and Social Life under the Pallavas* (Madras: University of Madras 1938), 186–212; K. A. Nilakantha Sastri, *The Colas* (Madras: University of Madras 1955), 629–33. Sastri shows that *Dharmaśāstra* was part of the curriculum in colleges such as Eṇṇāriyam and Tribhuvani.

composition of the great epic was not too different from that of the *MDh*. The time frame and the geography are more or less the same, and the authors of both works probably came from the class of educated and somewhat conservative Brahmins intent on protecting the rights and privileges of their class. They were probably composed after the collapse of the Maurya empire in the second century BCE. The Maurya empire, started by Candragupta about 320 BCE in the wake of Alexander the Great's incursion into north-western India, reached its zenith under his grandson Aśoka (268–233 BCE) but declined rapidly after his death. The last Maurya emperor, Bṛhadratha, was assassinated by Puṣyamitra, who inaugurated the Śuṅga dynasty. Historical memory considers Puṣyamitra to have been a Brahmin, and his dynasty was viewed as partial to Brahmin interests. The last Śuṅga was assassinated about 73 BCE. There followed the short-lived Kāṇva dynasty, also partial to Brahmin interests, that collapsed in 28 BCE. Roughly during this period, the north-western border regions of the subcontinent were ruled by Greek-Bactrian kings. Although the history is somewhat murky, around the turn of the millennium, possibly a bit earlier, a new political force, the Śakas of Central Asian origin, emerged in the north-western borders and swept across the north-western region of India proper. The Śakas were displaced by the Kuśānas, also from Central Asia, who extended their empire well into the Gangetic heartland.

We can isolate at least three socio-political elements that provide the background to the composition of the *MDh*. (1) The major element is certainly the historical reality and especially the historical memory of two or three centuries later of the Maurya state and especially of the Aśokan political, social, and religious reforms.[17] Aśoka was certainly a Buddhist; whether he was anti-Brahmanical is debatable. One thing that his reforms did was to displace the Brahmin from his privileged position within the social structure. The special relationship between the political power and the religious establishment represented by the Brahmin was broken. The Sanskrit compound *śramaṇa-brāhmaṇa* ('ascetic-brahmin'), used frequently

[17] That such a memory continued to exist long after the demise of Aśoka and the Maurya empire is demonstrated by the Buddhist literature devoted to Aśoka. See John Strong, *The Legend of King Asoka: A Study and Translation of the Asokavadana* (Princeton: Princeton University Press, 1983).

by Aśoka in his inscriptions, indicates that his social philosophy envisaged a dual class of religious people worthy of respect and support: the newly formed ascetic communities and the old Brahmin class. His prohibition of animal sacrifices, furthermore, undercut the very *raison d'être* of Brahmanical privilege: the Brahmin's ability to perform sacrifices for the well-being of society and for the furtherance of royal power symbolized principally in the royal horse sacrifice. The very creation of a Brahmanical genre of literature dedicated to Law (*dharma*) was possibly due to the elevation of this word to the level of imperial ideology by Aśoka (Olivelle forthcoming *a*).

(2) To add insult to injury, the Mauryas, as well as the Nandas who preceded them, were considered at least within Brahmanical historical memory as Śūdras. The usurpation of Kṣatriya royal privileges by Śūdras and the ensuing suppression of Brahmins are presented as the sure signals of the corrupt times of the Kali age. Such a political situation creates the mixture of social classes, the most serious social and moral corruption within Brahmanical ideology.

(3) Finally, there was the contemporary political reality. There were the foreign invasions first in the border regions of the northwest and then within the heartland that established foreign rule. Many of these rulers, especially the Bactrians and the Kuṣānas, were partial to Buddhism.

Reading the *MDh* one cannot fail to see and to feel the intensity and urgency with which the author defends Brahmanical privilege. A major aim of Manu was to re-establish the old alliance between priesthood and royalty, an alliance that in his view would benefit both the Brahmin and the king, thereby re-establishing the Brahmin in his unique and privileged position within society. We hear the repeated emphasis on the inviolability of the Brahmin in his person and in his property. He has immunity from the death penalty, from taxes, and from the confiscation of his property. The king is advised repeatedly that a Brahmin's property is poison. Stealing a Brahmin's gold is one of the five grievous sins, and the death penalty is imposed on the perpetrator. Devotion to Brahmins is a cardinal virtue of kings: 'Refusal to turn back in battle, protecting the subjects, and obedient service to Brahmins—for kings, these are the best means of securing happiness' (7.88). The reason why foreign ruling classes, such as the Greeks, Śakas, Persians, and Chinese, have fallen to the level of Śūdras, once again, is their lack of devotion to Brahmins: 'By neglecting rites and by failing to visit Brahmins, however, these men of Kṣatriya birth have gradually reached in the world the level of Śūdras' (10.43).

The Brahmanical privilege is threatened from two quarters: the Śūdra, within which class Manu often lumps all the lower classes of society, and the Mleccha (foreigner, barbarian). Now, it is true that even the *Dharmasūtras* contain passages that are anti-Śūdra. It is taken for granted that the sole duty of Śūdras is to serve the upper classes; penalties for killing a Śūdra are much less than for killing people of the upper classes; likewise, penalties are increased for guilty Śūdras; the list could go on. Yet we also see that Śūdras acted as cooks in Brahmin households. Āpastamba (2.28.11, 15) even says that one may learn aspects of the Law (*dharma*) from Śūdras. There is a virulence in Manu's rhetoric vis-à-vis Śūdras lacking in the *Dharmasūtras* that appears to indicate that there must be a subtext to it. How could the lowest class of society with little access to material resources pose such a threat to social order and to Brahmanical hegemony? The fear of the Śūdra contrasts sharply with Manu's view of Vaiśyas. These are dealt with in a dispassionate and straightforward way. Why were Vaiśyas, who are depicted as agriculturalists and traders, that is, people with resources, not a threat to the Brahmin–Kṣatriya alliance that Manu was attempting to forge and strengthen? At one level, I think, historical memory is at work here; Śūdras were once in power and posed a real threat to Brahmanical hegemony, and history can always repeat itself.

Beyond that, however, 'Śūdra' for Manu is often a code word; it identifies the enemy and it encompasses a wide cross-section of society, both past and present. It evoked the memories of bad old days; it heightened the anxiety that what happened under the Mauryas could be repeated. I also think that there was a contemporary threat to Brahmanical supremacy not so much from political power but from rival religious establishments, especially the Buddhist and the Jain monastic orders. I think Manu includes these within his code 'Śūdra'. The connection between Śūdra and the non-Brahmanical ascetic sects is drawn by Manu himself. In his advice regarding a Brahmin's residence, Manu (4.61) says: 'He should not live in a kingdom ruled by a Śūdra, teeming with unrighteous people, overrun by heretical ascetics, or swamped by lowest-born people.' Here we have a clear juxtaposition between a kingdom ruled by a Śūdra king and a region populated by heretical ascetics (principally, Buddhists and Jains), by lowest-born people, and by unrighteous men. Indeed, Manu's instruction (9.225) to the king about cleansing his kingdom of dangerous people includes men who belong to heretical sects. The strength of Buddhism in the north-western regions during this period and the patronage offered to them by what for Manu were Mleccha (foreign, barbarian) kings may also have influenced the connection between heretic and Śūdra/Mleccha.

Alongside Śūdras, we have the Mlecchas. Manu is cognizant of the regions occupied by the foreign barbarians, for at 2.23 he defines the areas outside the central Āryāvarta as the region of Mlecchas. Manu, however, does not have much to say about the Mlecchas in the rest of the book; his focus is on the Śūdras. Or, is the code 'Śūdra' meant also to encompass these other outsiders as well? Note that at 10.44 Manu presents the Mleccha groups such as Greeks, Śaka, and Chinese as sunk to the level of Śūdras, although they were Kṣatriyas by birth.

The ideology that drives Manu explains the plan of his book. He devotes 1,034 verses (38.6 per cent) to the discussion of the Brahmin and 971 verses (36 per cent) to matters relating to the king; these two take up three-quarters of the entire text. Manu's agenda is twofold: he wants to tell Brahmins how to behave as true Brahmins devoted to vedic learning and virtue, and he wants to tell kings how to behave as true kings, devoted to Brahmins and ruling the people justly. For this agenda he brings the authority of no less a person than the Creator himself, who is presented as the absent author of the text.

NOTE ON THE TRANSLATION

THE Italians say 'traduttori sono traditori'—translators are traitors—and with some justification. It is simply not possible to capture the full import and every nuance of a statement when rendering it into another language, especially a language between which exists a cultural and temporal chasm such as that between Sanskrit and English. Yet translation is not only possible; it is also a cultural imperative. One can become less of a traitor, however, by understanding the cultural, historical, and linguistic world of the source text and the target language, and this I have attempted to do.

Mine is not a 'literal' translation but seeks to be an accurate one. Literal translations, often requiring frequent parenthetical intrusions, may serve the function of a crib for those who know the original Sanskrit; they offer little to the reader without access to the original and are often unreadable. If this was simply a translation to accompany the critical edition, I could have presupposed a certain knowledge of Sanskrit in my readers and left tricky words untranslated. This translation, however, is intended for a general readership.

Several Sanskrit terms cause special difficulties in translation, some because of their wide semantic range and others because of difficulties in determining their precise meanings. The first and the most obvious is *dharma*. In general, I have translated the term as 'Law'. Although *dharma* means both more and less than law in modern usage, I think 'Law' can accurately capture a wide slice of its semantic spectrum, especially if we take into account the use of 'law' in such contexts as natural law, divine law, moral law, law of gravity, and Jewish law. In some contexts, however, 'Law' does not make sense. In 8.12 ff, for example, *dharma* is better translated as 'Justice'; in other contexts it means 'merit' (see 4.238; 7.79; 8.83; 11.23; 12.19); in 11.129–30 the negative *adharma* clearly means sin.

Guru is another difficult term. In a few cases it refers to the teacher (2.131, 231), but most frequently it does not. The general meaning is that of an elder, frequently the father, who deserves special respect. A good example of the multiple meanings of this term occurring in a single verse is 2.205. This term is context sensitive and I have translated it by a word that approximates its contextual meaning.

Sanskrit uses many terms for a Brāhmaṇa and a Kṣatriya. Attempting to duplicate these would have created confusion for the reader. I have used 'Brahmin' and 'Kṣatriya' uniformly, except when *dvija* ('twice-born') is used. This term in the *MDh* regularly refers to a Brahmin, but not always. In some contexts the meaning is ambiguous. I have, therefore, translated it as 'twice-born'.

Fines are often specified with just a number. When used in this manner (for example, 'he should be fined 100') the number refers to the common Indian copper coin Paṇa.

Consistency in translation is often achieved at the expense of accuracy. I have not tried to be consistent beyond reason in translating a particular word. I have already referred to the various nuances of *dharma*. A good example of different meanings of the same word is *dasyu*. In many contexts the word means a bandit, a low-life, or a low-born person (5.131; 7.143; 8.66). In other contexts, the term has a technical meaning, referring to a particular mixed caste (10.32, 45).

Some verses found in the vulgate version and given in Bühler's translation have been omitted in the critical edition. In order to preserve the numbering of the text scholars have become used to, however, I have maintained Bühler's numbering, thus eliminating the number of the omitted verses.

In the translation and notes unspecified references are to chapter and verse of the *MDh*.

GUIDE TO THE PRONUNCIATION OF SANSKRIT WORDS

SANSKRIT words, including proper names, are printed here with diacritical marks. Sanskrit diacritics are simple and, with a minimum of effort, should enable the reader to pronounce these words properly. A general rule is that an 'h' after a consonant is *not* a separate letter but merely represents the aspirated version of a consonant. Thus 'bh' is pronounced somewhat as in 'a*bh*or', and 'ph' not as in '*ph*ysics' but as in 'she*ph*erd'. The dental group of consonants (t, th, d, dh, n) are distinguished from the retroflex group indicated by a dot placed beneath (ṭ, ṭh, ḍ, ḍh, ṇ). The distinction in their pronunciation is somewhat difficult for the Western ear. The dentals are pronounced with the tip of the tongue placed behind the upper front teeth, and the sound is similar to the way these letters are pronounced in Romance languages such as French (for example, toi, de). The English pronunciation of these letters is closer to the Sanskrit retroflex, but the latter is pronounced with the tip of the tongue striking the roof of the mouth further back. Thus 'ṭ' is somewhat like *t* in '*t*ry', and 'ḍ' is like *d* in *d*ental. The difference between the dental 'n' and retroflex 'ṇ' is very difficult for untrained ears to distinguish and is better ignored. The same applies to the palatal sibilant 'ś' and the retroflex 'ṣ'; both may be pronounced as *sh* in '*sh*ame'. 'ṃ' nasalizes the preceding vowel sound, as in French *bon*. 'ḥ', with a dot underneath and most frequently at the end of a word, is a pure aspiration and is to be distinguished from the consonant 'h'. In practice, the vowel sound preceding it is pronounced faintly; thus 'ḥ' of *bhuvoḥ* is pronounced like the *ho* in Soho when it is pronounced with the accent on the first syllable and the second shortened. Finally, an apostrophe before a word indicates an elided 'a', which is not pronounced.

Pronounce Sanskrit	as in English
a	c*u*t
ā	f*a*r
i	s*i*t
ī	k*ee*p
u	p*u*t
ū	t*oo*
ṛ	*r*isk
e	pr*ay*
o	h*o*pe
ai	s*i*gh
au	s*ou*nd
c	*ch*urch
g	*g*ive
ṇ	a*n*ger
ñ	pu*n*ching

THE
LAW CODE OF MANU

EDITOR'S OUTLINE

CHAPTER ONE

CHAPTER TWO

CHAPTER THREE

CHAPTER FIVE

CHAPTER SIX

6.66–9	Conduct
6.70–1	Breath Control
6.72–5	Meditation
6.76–8	Meditation on the Body
6.79–85	Final Goal
6.87–96	Vedic Retiree
6.87–90	Superiority of the Householder
6.91–3	The Ten-Point Law
6.94–6	Retirement

CHAPTER SEVEN

7.1–226	The Law for the King
7.2–35	Origin of the King
7.14–31	Punishment
7.32–5	Proper Behavior
7.37–53	Cultivating Virtue and Learning
7.54–9	Appointment of Counsellors
7.60–2	Appointment of Officials
7.63–8	Appointment of an Envoy
7.69–76	Constructing the Royal Fort
7.77	Marriage
7.78–9	Appointment of Chaplain and Priests
7.80–1	Collectors and Supervisors
7.82–6	Devotion to Brahmins
7.87–97	War and Warrior Ethic
7.96–7	War Booty
7.99–113	Policies for Good Government
7.114–26	Organization of the State
7.114–19	Governance of Villages and Towns
7.120–4	Supervision of Officials
7.125–6	Wages
7.127–39	Taxes and Duties
7.140–1	Adjudicating Lawsuits
7.142–4	Protection of the Subjects
7.145–215	Morning Routine
7.147–55	Meeting with Counsellors
7.156–9	Constituents of the Circle
7.160–80	Political Strategy: I
7.181–200	War
7.201–5	Conduct in Victory
7.206–15	Political Strategy: II
7.216–22	Afternoon Routine

CHAPTER EIGHT

CHAPTER NINE

CHAPTER TEN

CHAPTER ONE

PROLOGUE

[1]Manu was seated, absorbed in contemplation, when the great seers
came up to him, paid homage to him in the appropriate manner, and
addressed him in these words: [2]'Please, Lord, tell us precisely and in
the proper order the Laws of all the social classes, as well as of those
born in between;* [3]for you alone, Master, know the true meaning of
the duties contained in this entire ordinance of the Self-existent
One, an ordinance* beyond the powers of thought or cognition.'
[4]So questioned in the proper manner by those noble ones, that
Being of boundless might paid honour to all those great seers and
replied: 'Listen!'

CREATION

[5]'There was this world—pitch-dark,* indiscernible, without distinguishing marks, unthinkable, incomprehensible, in a kind of deep
sleep all over. [6]Then the Self-existent Lord appeared—the Unmanifest manifesting this world beginning with the elements, projecting
his might, and dispelling the darkness. [7]That One—who is beyond
the range of senses; who cannot be grasped; who is subtle, unmanifest, and eternal; who contains all beings; and who transcends
thought—it is he who shone forth on his own.
[8]'As he focused his thought with the desire of bringing forth
diverse creatures from his own body, it was the waters that he first
brought forth; and into them he poured forth his semen. [9]That
became a golden egg, as bright as the sun; and in it he himself took
birth as Brahmā, the grandfather of all the worlds.
[10]'The waters are called "Nārā"; the waters, clearly, are the offspring of Nara. Because his first sojourn (*ayana*) was in them, tradition calls him "Nārāyaṇa". [11]That cause which is unmanifest and
eternal, which has the nature of both the existent and the non-existent—the Male produced from it is celebrated in the world as
Brahmā.*
[12]'After residing in that egg for a full year, that Lord on his own

split the egg in two by brooding on his own body. [13] From those two halves, he formed the sky and the earth, and between them the mid-space, the eight directions, and the eternal place of the waters.*

[14] 'From his body, moreover, he drew out the mind having the nature of both the existent and the non-existent; and from the mind, the ego—producer of self-awareness and ruler—[15] as also the great self (12.14), all things composed of the three attributes (12.24), and gradually the five sensory organs that grasp the sense objects. [16] By merging the subtle parts of these six* possessing boundless might into particles of his own body, moreover, he formed all beings. [17] Because the six parts of his physical frame become attached (*ā-śri*) to these beings, the wise call his physical frame "body" (*śarīra*). [18] The great elements enter it accompanied by their activities, as also the mind, the imperishable producer of all beings, accompanied by its subtle particles.

[19] 'From the subtle particles of the physical frames of these seven males* of great might, this world comes into being, the perishable from the imperishable. [20] Of these, each succeeding element acquires the quality specific to each preceding. Thus, each element, tradition tells us, possesses the same number of qualities as the number of its position in the series.* [21] In the beginning through the words of the Veda alone, he fashioned for all of them specific names and activities, as also specific stations.*

[22] 'The Lord brought forth the group of gods who are endowed with breath and whose nature is to act, the subtle group of Sādhyas, and the eternal sacrifice. [23] From fire, wind, and sun, he squeezed out the eternal triple Veda characterized by the Ṛg verses, the Yajus formulas, and the Sāman chants, for the purpose of carrying out the sacrifice. [24] Time, divisions of time, constellations, planets, rivers, oceans, mountains, flat and rough terrain, [25] austerity, speech, sexual pleasure, desire, and anger—he brought forth this creation in his wish to bring forth these creatures.*

[26] 'To establish distinctions among activities, moreover, he distinguished the Right (*dharma*) from the Wrong (*adharma*) and afflicted these creatures with the pairs of opposites such as pleasure and pain. [27] Together with the perishable atomic particles of the five elements given in tradition, this whole world comes into being in an orderly sequence. [28] As they are brought forth again and again, each creature follows on its own the very activity assigned to it in the

beginning by the Lord. [29] Violence or non-violence, gentleness or cruelty, righteousness (*dharma*) or unrighteousness (*adharma*), truthfulness or untruthfulness—whichever he assigned to each at the time of creation, it stuck automatically to that creature. [30] As at the change of seasons each season automatically adopts its own distinctive marks, so do embodied beings adopt their own distinctive acts.

[31] 'For the growth of these worlds, moreover, he produced from his mouth, arms, thighs, and feet, the Brahmin, the Kṣatriya, the Vaiśya, and the Śūdra.

Excursus: Second Account of Creation*

[32] 'Dividing his body into two, he became a man with one half and a woman with the other. By that woman the Lord brought forth Virāj. [33] By heating himself with ascetic toil, that man, Virāj, brought forth a being by himself—know, you best of the twice-born, that I am that being, the creator of this whole world.

[34] 'Desiring to bring forth creatures, I heated myself with the most arduous ascetic toil and brought forth in the beginning the ten great seers, the lords of creatures: [35] Marīci, Atri, Aṅgiras, Pulastya, Pulaha, Kratu, Pracetas, Vasiṣṭha, Bhṛgu, and Nārada. [36] They, in turn, brought forth seven other Manus of immense energy (1.61–2); the gods and the classes of gods; and the great sages of boundless might; [37] Yakṣas, Rākṣasas, Piśācas, Gandharvas, Apsarases, Asuras, Nāgas, Sarpas, and Suparṇas; the different groups of ancestors (3.192–201); [38] lightnings, thunderbolts, clouds, rainbow streaks, rainbows, meteors, storms, comets, and the manifold heavenly lights; [39] pseudo-humans,* monkeys, fish, birds of various kind, farm animals, wild animals, humans, predatory animals, and animals with incisors in both jaws (5.18n.); [40] worms, insects, moths, lice, flies, bugs, all creatures that sting and bite, and immobile creatures of various kind.

[41] 'In this manner through ascetic toil, those noble ones brought forth at my command this whole world, the mobile and the immobile, each creature in accordance with its activity.

Excursus: Classification of Fauna and Flora

[42] 'I will now explain to you exactly which type of activity is ascribed here to which type of creature, and also their relative order with

respect to birth. [43]Those born from placentas are farm animals, wild animals, predatory animals, animals with incisors in both jaws (5.18n.), Rākṣasas, Piśācas, and humans.

[44]'Those born from eggs are birds, snakes, crocodiles, fish, and turtles, as well as other similar land and aquatic animals.

[45]'Those born from warm moisture are creatures that sting and bite; lice, flies, and bugs; those born through heat; as well as other similar creatures.

[46]'Those born from sprouts are all flora propagated through seeds or cuttings. Those that bear copious flowers and fruits and die after their fruits mature are "plants" (*oṣadhi*); [47]those that bear fruits without flowers, tradition calls "forest lords" (*vanaspati*); and those that bear both flowers and fruits, tradition calls "trees" (*vṛkṣa*). [48]Various kinds of shrubs and thickets and different types of grasses, as also creepers and vines—all these also grow from either seeds or cuttings. [49]Wrapped in a manifold darkness caused by their past deeds (12.8–9), these come into being with inner awareness, able to feel pleasure and pain. [50]In this dreadful transmigratory cycle of beings, a cycle that rolls on inexorably for ever, these are said to represent the lowest condition, and Brahmā the highest.

Excursus: Cosmic Cycles

[51]'After bringing forth in this manner this whole world and me, that One of inconceivable prowess once again disappeared into his own body, striking down time with time.* [52]When that god is awake, then this creation is astir; but when he is asleep in deep repose, then the whole world lies dormant. [53]When he is soundly asleep, embodied beings, whose nature is to act, withdraw from their respective activities, and their minds become languid. [54]When they dissolve together into that One of immense body, then he, whose body contains all beings, sleeps tranquil and at ease. [55]Plunging himself into darkness, he lingers there for a long time together with his sense organs and ceases to perform his own activities. Then he emerges from that bodily frame. [56]When, after becoming a minute particle, he enters, conjoined, the seminal form of mobile and immobile beings, then he discharges the bodily frame.*

[57]'In this manner, by waking and sleeping, that Imperishable One

incessantly brings to life and tears down this whole world, both the mobile and the immobile.

Transmission of the Law

58 'After composing this treatise,* he himself in the beginning imparted it according to rule to me alone; and I, in turn, to Marīci* and the other sages. 59 Bhr̥gu here will relate that treatise to you completely, for this sage has learnt the whole treatise in its entirety from me.'

60 When Manu had spoken to him in this manner, the great sage Bhr̥gu was delighted. He then said to all those seers: 'Listen!'

Excursus: Time and Cosmology

61-2 There are six further Manus* in the lineage of this Manu, the son of the Self-existent One: Svārociṣa, Auttami, Tāmasa, Raivata, Cākṣuṣa of great energy, and the son of Vivasvat. Possessing great nobility and might, they each have brought forth their own progeny. 63 These seven Manus of immense energy, with the son of the Self-existent One at their head, gave rise to and secured this whole world, the mobile and the immobile, each in his own Epoch.

64 Eighteen Nimeṣas ('winks') make a Kāṣṭha ('second'), thirty Kāṣṭhas a Kalā ('minute'), thirty Kalās a Muhūrta* ('hour'), and thirty Muhūrtas a day-and-night. 65 The sun divides the day and the night, both the human and the divine. The night is meant for creatures to sleep, and the day to engage in activities.

66 For ancestors, a month constitutes a day and a night, divided into the two fortnights. The dark fortnight is the day for engaging in activities, and the bright fortnight is the night for sleeping.* 67 For gods, a year is a day and a night and their division is this: the day is the northward passage of the sun, and the night is its southward passage.

68 Listen now to a concise account of the duration of a day-and-night of Brahmā and of each Age in proper sequence. 69 The Kr̥ta Age is said to last 4,000 years. It is preceded by a twilight lasting 400 years and followed by a twilight of the same length. 70 For each of the three subsequent Ages, as also for the twilights that precede and follow them, the first number of the thousands and the

hundreds is progressively diminished by one.* [71] These four Ages, computed at the very beginning as lasting 12,000 years, are said to constitute a single Age of the gods. [72] The sum total of 1,000 divine Ages should be regarded as a single day of Brahmā, and his night as having the very same duration. [73] Those who know this propitious day of Brahmā lasting 1,000 Ages, as also his night with the same duration—they are people who truly know day and night.

[74] At the end of that day-and-night, he awakens from his sleep; and when he has woken up, he brings forth the mind, which is both existent and non-existent. [75] The mind, driven by the desire to create, transmutes the creation. From the mind is born ether, whose distinctive quality is said to be sound. [76] From ether, as it is being transmuted, is born wind—powerful, pure, and bearing all odours—whose distinctive quality is thought to be touch. [77] From the wind, as it is being transmuted, is produced light—shining, brilliant, and dispelling darkness—whose distinctive quality, tradition says, is visible appearance. [78] From light, as it is being transmuted, comes water, with taste as its distinctive quality; and from water, earth, with smell as its distinctive quality. That is how this creation was at the beginning.

[79] The divine Age mentioned previously as lasting 12,000 years—that multiplied 71 times is here referred to as an 'Epoch of a Manu'. [80] The countless Epochs of Manu, as also creation and dissolution—the Supreme Lord does this again and again as a kind of sport.

[81] In the Kṛta Age, the Law is whole, possessing all four feet;* and so is truth. People never acquire any property through unlawful means. [82] By acquiring such property, however, the Law is stripped of one foot in each of the subsequent Ages; through theft, falsehood, and fraud, the Law disappears a foot at a time.

[83] In the Kṛta Age, people are free from sickness, succeed in all their pursuits, and have a life span of 400 years. In the Tretā and each of the subsequent Ages, however, their life span is shortened by a quarter.* [84] The life span of mortals given in the Veda, the benefits of rites, and the power of embodied beings—they all come to fruition in the world in conformity with each Age.

[85] There is one set of Laws for men in the Kṛta Age, another in the Tretā, still another in the Dvāpara, and a different set in the Kali, in keeping with the progressive shortening taking place in each Age.*

[86] Ascetic toil, they say, is supreme in the Kṛta Age; knowledge in Tretā; sacrifice in Dvāpara; and gift-giving alone in Kali.

Excursus: Occupations of Social Classes

[87] For the protection of this whole creation, that One of dazzling brilliance assigned separate activities for those born from the mouth, arms, thighs, and feet. [88] To Brahmins, he assigned reciting and teaching the Veda, offering and officiating at sacrifices, and receiving and giving gifts. [89] To the Kṣatriya, he allotted protecting the subjects, giving gifts, offering sacrifices, reciting the Veda, and avoiding attachment to sensory objects; [90] and to the Vaiśya, looking after animals, giving gifts, offering sacrifices, reciting the Veda, trade, moneylending, and agriculture. [91] A single activity did the Lord allot to the Śudra, however: the ungrudging service of those very social classes (10.74–80).

Excursus: Excellence of the Brahmin

[92] A man is said to be purer above the navel. Therefore, the Self-existent One has declared, the mouth is his purest part.* [93] Because he arose from the loftiest part of the body, because he is the eldest, and because he retains the Veda,* the Brahmin is by Law the lord of this whole creation. [94] For, in the beginning, the Self-existent One heated himself with ascetic toil and brought him forth from his own mouth to convey divine oblations and ancestral offerings and to protect this whole world. [95] What creature can surpass him through whose mouth the denizens of the triple heaven always eat their oblations, and the forefathers their offerings (7.84)?

[96] Among creatures, living beings are the best; among living beings, those who subsist by intelligence;* among those who subsist by intelligence, human beings; and among human beings, Brahmins—so the tradition declares. [97] Among Brahmins, the learned are the best; among the learned, those who have made the resolve; among those who have made the resolve, the doers; and among doers, the Vedic savants.

[98] A Brahmin's birth alone represents the everlasting physical frame of the Law; for, born on account of the Law, he is fit for becoming Brahman. [99] For when a Brahmin is born, a pre-eminent

birth takes place on earth—a ruler of all creatures to guard the storehouse of Laws.* [100] This whole world—whatever there is on earth—is the property of the Brahmin. Because of his eminence and high birth, the Brahmin has a clear right to this whole world. [101] The Brahmin eats only what belongs to him, wears what belongs to him, and gives what belongs to him; it is by the kindness of the Brahmin that other people eat.*

Excursus: Treatise of Manu

[102] To determine which activities are proper to him and which to the remaining classes in their proper order, Manu, the wise son of the Self-existent, composed this treatise. [103] It should be studied diligently and taught to his pupils properly by a learned Brahmin, and by no one else.

[104] When a Brahmin who keeps to his vows studies this treatise, he is never sullied by faults arising from mental, oral, or physical activities; [105] he purifies those alongside whom he eats (3.183–6), as also seven generations of his lineage before him and seven after him; he alone, moreover, has a right to this entire earth.

[106] This treatise is the best good-luck incantation; it expands the intellect; it procures everlasting fame; and it is the ultimate bliss. [107] In this, the Law has been set forth in full—the good and the bad qualities of actions and the timeless norms of proper conduct—for all four social classes.

[108] Proper conduct is the highest Law, as well as what is declared in the Veda and given in traditional texts. Applying himself always to this treatise, therefore, let a twice-born man remain constantly self-possessed. [109] When a Brahmin has fallen away from proper conduct, he does not reap the fruit of the Veda; but when he holds fast to proper conduct, tradition says, he enjoys its full reward. [110] Seeing thus that the Law proceeds from proper conduct, the sages understood proper conduct to be the ultimate root of all ascetic toil.

EXCURSUS: SYNOPSIS

[111] Origin of the world [1.6–110].
Rules for consecratory rites [2.26–67].

Observance of the vow [2.69–139].
Service [2.140–244].
The most excellent rule regarding the final bath [2.245–6].
112 Marrying a wife [3.4–19].
Characteristics of the different types of marriage [3.20–44].
Rules regarding the great sacrifices [3.67–121, 285–6].
The timeless ordinance on ancestral rites [3.122–284].
113 Characteristics of the different occupations [4.2–12].
Observances of a bath-graduate [4.13–257].
Permitted and forbidden food [5.4–56].
Purification [5.58–109].
Cleansing of articles [5.111–45].
114 Law pertaining to women [5.147–68].
Hermit's life [6.1–32].
Renunciation [6.33–85].
Retirement* [6.87–96].
The entire Law pertaining to the king [7.1–226].
Adjudication of lawsuits [8.1–46].
115 Rules concerning the questioning of witnesses [8.62–123].
Law with respect to husbands and wives [9.1–102].
Law on partitioning of estates [9.104–219].
Gambling [9.221–8].
Eradication of thorns [9.252–93].
116 Conduct of Vaiśyas and Śūdras [9.326–35].
Origin of mixed classes [10.1–73].
Law in times of adversity for social classes [10.81–129].
Rules on penances [11.44–266].
117 The three passages into the transmigratory cycle resulting from action [12.1–81].
Final bliss [12.83–106].
Examination of the good and bad qualities of actions.

[118] The timeless Laws of regions, of hereditary groups, and of families.
Laws of heretical ascetic groups and guilds.*

All that Manu has set forth in this treatise.

[119] Just as, upon my request, Manu formerly taught me this treatise, so you too must learn it from me today.

CHAPTER TWO

THE LAW

[1] Learn the Law always adhered to by people who are erudite, virtuous, and free from love and hate, the Law assented to by the heart.

Excursus: Desire

[2] To be motivated by desire is not commended, but it is impossible here to be free from desire; for it is desire that prompts vedic study and the performance of vedic rites. [3] Intention is the root of desire; intention is the wellspring of sacrifices; and intention triggers every religious observance and every rule of restraint—so the tradition declares. [4] Nowhere in this world do we see any activity done by a man free from desire; for whatever at all that a man may do, it is the work of someone who desired it. [5] By engaging in them properly, a man attains the world of the immortals and, in this world, obtains all his desires just as he intended.

Sources of Law

[6] The root of the Law is the entire Veda; the tradition and practice of those who know the Veda; the conduct of good people; and what is pleasing to oneself. [7] Whatever Law Manu has proclaimed with respect to anyone, all that has been taught in the Veda, for it contains all knowledge. [8] After subjecting all this to close scrutiny with the eye of knowledge, a learned man should apply himself to the Law proper to him on the authority of the scriptures; [9] for by following the Law proclaimed in scripture and tradition, a man achieves fame in this world and unsurpassed happiness after death.

[10] 'Scripture' should be recognized as 'Veda', and 'tradition' as 'Law Treatise'. These two should never be called into question in any matter, for it is from them that the Law has shined forth. [11] If a twice-born disparages these two by relying on the science of logic, he ought to be ostracized by good people as an infidel and a denigrator of the Veda.

Knowledge of the Law

[12] Veda, tradition, the conduct of good people, and what is pleasing to oneself—these, they say, are the four visible marks of the Law. [13] The knowledge of the Law is prescribed for people who are unattached to wealth or pleasures; and for people who seek to know the Law, scripture is the highest authority.*

Contradictions in Law

[14] When there are two contradictory scriptural provisions on some issue, however, tradition takes them both to be the Law with respect to it; for wise men have correctly pronounced them both to be the Law. [15] After sunrise, before sunrise, and at daybreak—the sacrifice takes place at any of these times; so states a vedic scripture.*

Competence to Study the Law

[16] A man for whom it is prescribed that the rites beginning with the impregnation ceremony and ending with the funeral are to be performed with the recitation of vedic formulas—no one but he is to be recognized as entitled to study this treatise.*

The Sacred Land

[17] The land created by the gods and lying between the divine rivers Sarasvatī and Dr̥ṣadvatī is called 'Brahmāvarta'—the region of Brahman. [18] The conduct handed down from generation to generation among the social classes and the intermediate classes of that land is called the 'conduct of good people'.

[19] Kurukṣetra and the lands of the Matsyas, Pañcālas, and Śūrasenakas constitute the 'land of Brahmin seers', which borders on the Brahmāvarta. [20] All the people on earth should learn their respective practices from a Brahmin born in that land.

[21] The land between the Himalaya and Vindhya ranges, to the east of Vinaśana and west of Prayāga, is known as the 'Middle Region'.

[22] The land between the same mountain ranges extending from the eastern to the western sea is what the wise call 'Āryāvarta'—the region of the Āryas.

[23] The natural range of the black buck is to be recognized as the land fit for sacrifice; beyond that is the land of foreigners.*

[24] Twice-born people should diligently settle in these lands; but a Śūdra, when he is starved for livelihood, may live in any region at all.

> [25] I have described to you above succinctly the source
> of the Law, as also the origin of this whole world.
> Learn now the Laws of the social classes.

CONSECRATORY RITES

[26] The consecration of the body, beginning with the ceremony of impregnation, should be performed for twice-born men by means of the sacred vedic rites, a consecration that cleanses a man both here and in the hereafter. [27] The fire offerings for the benefit of the foetus, the birth rite, the first cutting of hair, and the tying of the Muñja-grass cord*—by these rites the taint of semen and womb is wiped from twice-born men. [28] Vedic recitation, religious observances, fire offerings, study of the triple Veda, ritual offerings, sons, the five great sacrifices, and sacrifices—by these a man's body is made 'brāhmic'.*

Childhood Rites

[29] The rule is that the birth rite of a male child* must be performed before his umbilical cord is cut; he is fed gold, honey, and ghee* to the accompaniment of vedic formulas.

[30] One should see to it that the child's naming ceremony is performed on the tenth or the twelfth day after birth, on a day or at a time* that is auspicious, or under a favourable constellation. [31] For a Brahmin, the name should connote auspiciousness; for a Kṣatriya, strength; for a Vaiśya, wealth; and for a Śūdra, disdain. [32] For a Brahmin, the name should connote happiness; for a Kṣatriya, protection; for a Vaiśya, prosperity; and for a Śūdra, service. [33] For girls, the name should be easy to pronounce and without fierce connotations, have a clear meaning, be charming and auspicious, end in a long final syllable, and contain a word for blessing.

[34] In the fourth month, one should perform the ceremony of taking the child out of the house; and in the sixth month, the feeding

with rice, as also any other auspicious ceremony cherished in the family.

[35] The first cutting of hair, according to the Law, should be performed for all twice-born children in the first or the third year, in accordance with the dictates of scripture.

Vedic Initiation

Time for Initiation [36] For a Brahmin, the vedic initiation should be carried out in the eighth year from conception; for a Kṣatriya, in the eleventh year from conception; and for a Vaiśya, in the twelfth year from conception. [37] For a Brahmin desiring eminence in vedic knowledge, it should be carried out in the fifth year; for a Kṣatriya aspiring to power, in the sixth year; and for a Vaiśya aspiring to a spirit of enterprise, in the seventh year.

Failure to be Initiated [38] For a Brahmin, the time for Sāvitrī* does not lapse until the sixteenth year;* for a Kṣatriya, until the twenty-second; and for a Vaiśya, until the twenty-fourth. [39] If, after those times, any of these three has not undergone consecration at the proper time, he becomes a Vrātya (10.20–23), fallen from Sāvitrī (2.38 n.) and spurned by Āryas. [40] Even in a time of adversity, a Brahmin should never establish vedic or matrimonial links* with such people, unless they have been cleansed according to rule.

Insignia: I [41] Students should wear the skin of a black antelope, a Ruru deer, or a male goat, and clothes of hemp, flax, or wool, according to the direct order of classes.

[42] For a Brahmin, the girdle should be made with a triple cord of Muñja grass, smooth and soft; for a Kṣatriya, with a bowstring of Mūrvā hemp; and for a Vaiśya, with a string of hemp. [43] When Muñja grass is unavailable, they should be made with Kuśa grass, the Aśmantaka plant, or Balvaja grass.* One should wrap the girdle around the waist three times and make one, three, or five knots.*

[44] For a Brahmin, the sacrificial cord is made with a triple strand of cotton thread twisted upward; for a Kṣatriya, with strands of hemp; and for a Vaiśya, with woollen strands.

[45] A Brahmin, according to the Law, is entitled to a wood-apple or Palāśa staff; a Kṣatriya, to a banyan or Khadira staff; and a Vaiśya, to a Pīlu or Udumbara staff. [46] In terms of length, a Brahmin's staff

should reach the hair; a Kṣatriya's the forehead; and a Vaiśya's the nose. [47] Every staff should be straight, without blemishes, pleasing to the eye, not liable to alarm people, with the bark intact, and undamaged by fire.

Food [48] Taking his chosen staff, he should worship the sun, walk around the fire clockwise, and go on his begging round according to rule. [49] An initiated Brahmin should beg placing the word 'Madam' at the beginning; a Kṣatriya, in the middle; and a Vaiśya, at the end.* [50] The very first time, he should beg from his mother, his sister, or his own mother's sister, or from some other woman who would not snub him.

[51] After collecting as much almsfood as he needs without guile, he should present it to his teacher, purify himself by sipping some water, and eat it facing the east. [52] Facing the east while eating procures long life; facing the south procures fame; facing the west procures prosperity; and facing the north procures truth. [53] A twice-born should always eat food after sipping some water and with a collected mind; after eating also he should sip water in the proper manner and rub water on the orifices.*

[54] He must always revere his food and eat it without disdain. When he sees the food, he should rejoice, look pleased, and receive it joyfully in every way. [55] For when food is revered, it always bestows strength and vigour; but when it is eaten without being revered, it destroys them both.

[56] He must not give his leftovers to anyone, eat between meals,* engage in overeating, or go anywhere while he is sullied with remnants.* [57] Eating too much harms his health, reduces his life expectancy, impedes heaven, hinders merit, and is despised by people; therefore, he should avoid it.

Sipping [58] A Brahmin should sip water at all times with the part of the palm linked to Brahmā, Prajāpati, or gods, but never with the part linked to ancestors.* [59] They call the flat surface at the base of the thumb the part linked to Brahmā; the base of the fingers, the part linked to Prajāpati; the finger tips, the part linked to gods; and the area beneath these two,* the part linked to ancestors.

[60] He should first sip water three times, then wipe his mouth twice, and finally rub water on his orifices, body, and head (2.53 n.). [61] A man who knows the Law and desires to become pure should always

do the sipping in a secluded place, using water that is not warm or frothy, employing the appropriate part of the palm, and facing east or north. 62 A Brahmin is purified by water reaching the heart; a Kṣatriya, by water reaching the throat; a Vaiśya, by water taken into the mouth; and a Śūdra, by water wetting the lips.

Insignia: II 63 When the right hand is raised, a twice-born man is called '*upavītin*'—wearing the cord in the sacrificial mode; when the left hand is raised, he is called '*prācīnāvītin*'—wearing the cord toward the east; and when it is worn around the neck, he is called '*nivītin*'—wearing the cord down.*

64 When the girdle, antelope skin, staff, sacrificial cord, or water pot is damaged, he should throw it in water and take a new one with the appropriate ritual formula.

Shaving Ceremony

65 The rule is that for a Brahmin the shaving ceremony* is to be performed in the sixteenth year; for a Kṣatriya, in the twenty-second; and for a Vaiśya, in the twenty-fourth (2.38 n.).*

Consecratory Rites for Women

66 For females, on the other hand, this entire series should be performed at the proper time and in the proper sequence, but without reciting any vedic formula, for the purpose of consecrating their bodies.

67 For females, tradition tells us, the marriage ceremony equals the rite of vedic consecration; serving the husband equals living with the teacher; and care of the house equals the tending of the sacred fires.

> 68 I have explained above the initiatory rite of twice-
> born men, a rite that signals a new birth and is sancti-
> fying. Learn now the activities connected with it.

THE STUDENT

Instruction

69 After initiating a pupil, the teacher should at the outset train him in purification, proper conduct, fire rituals, and twilight worship.

[70] When the pupil is ready for vedic recitation, he should sip water in the prescribed manner, dress in light clothing, bring his organs under control, face the north, and join his palms in '*brahmāñjali*'—then should he be taught. [71] At the beginning and at the end of a vedic lesson, he should always clasp his teacher's feet and recite the Veda with joined palms—tradition calls this '*brahmāñjali*', the vedic joining of palms. [72] He should clasp his teacher's feet by crossing his hands, touching the teacher's right foot with his right hand and the teacher's left with his left.

[73] When he is ready for vedic recitation, he should say to the teacher, 'Teach, Sir (*bho*)!', without being lazy at any time; and when commanded 'Stop!', he should cease. [74] At the beginning and at the end of vedic recitation, the student should always recite the syllable OṂ. If it is not recited at the beginning, the Veda slips away; if it is not recited at the end, the Veda wastes away. [75] When he is seated on sacred grass with the tips toward the east, cleansed by the purificatory blades of grass,* and purified by controlling his breath three times—then he becomes competent to recite OṂ.

The Syllable OṂ [76] The phonemes 'a', 'u', and 'm'—Prajāpati extracted these from the three Vedas, as also '*bhū*', earth; '*bhuvaḥ*', mid-space; and '*svar*', heaven. [77] Also from the three Vedas, Prajāpati, the Supreme Lord, squeezed out foot by foot the Sāvitrī verse:* 'That. . .'

[78] By softly reciting this syllable and this verse preceded by the Calls during the two twilights, a Brahmin who knows the Veda wins the merit of reciting the Veda itself. [79] By reciting these three one thousand times outside the village, a Brahmin is freed from even a grievous sin within a month, like a snake from its slough. [80] Someone who is a Brahmin, a Kṣatriya, or a Vaiśya by birth invites the censure of good people by cutting himself off from this verse and from the timely performance of his rite.

[81] The three inexhaustible Great Calls preceded by OṂ and the three-footed Sāvitrī verse should be recognized as the mouth of the Veda. [82] When a man recites this verse tirelessly for three years, becoming wind and assuming an ethereal form, he reaches the highest Brahman.* [83] The highest Brahman is the monosyllable OṂ; the highest ascetic toil is the control of breath; nothing is higher than the Sāvitrī; and truth is better than ascetic silence. [84] Offering ghee while

seated, offering oblations while standing*—all such vedic rites perish. The syllable (*akṣara*) OṂ should be recognized as imperishable* (*akṣara*); it is Brahman, it is Prajāpati.

Soft Recitation [85]The sacrifice consisting of soft recitation is ten times better than the sacrifice consisting of prescribed rites—a hundred times, if the recitation is done inaudibly; and a thousand times, if it is done mentally. [86]The four types of cooked oblations* along with the sacrifices consisting of prescribed rites—all these are not worth a sixteenth part of the sacrifice consisting of soft recitation. [87]Only by soft recitation does a Brahmin achieve success; on this there is no doubt. Whether he does anything else or not, a Maitra,* they say, is the true Brahmin.

Excursus: Control of the Organs

[88]As his organs meander amidst the alluring sense objects, a learned man should strive hard to control them, like a charioteer his horses.

[89]I will explain precisely and in their proper order the eleven organs described by wise men of old: [90]ear, skin, eyes, tongue, and the fifth, nostrils; anus, sexual organ, hands, feet, and speech, listed by tradition as the tenth. [91]Of these, the five in order beginning with the ear are called the organs of perception; and the five beginning with the anus, the organs of action. [92]Know that the eleventh is the mind, which, by virtue of its own distinctive quality, belongs to both groups. So, by mastering it, one masters both those quintets.

[93]By attachment to the organs, a man undoubtedly becomes corrupted; but by bringing them under control, he achieves success. [94]Desire is never quenched by enjoying desires; like a fire fed with ghee, it only waxes stronger. [95]Between a man who obtains all these and a man who gives them all up—giving up all desires is far better than obtaining them all. [96]Corrupted as these organs are by sensory objects, one cannot bring them under control as effectively by abstinence as by constant insight. [97]Vedas, gifts, sacrifices, constraints, and ascetic toils—none of these is ever successful for a man with a corrupt heart.

[98]When a man feels neither elation nor revulsion at hearing, touching, seeing, eating, or smelling anything, he should be recognized as a man who has mastered his organs. [99]Of all these organs, however, if a single one slips away, through that his wisdom slips

away, like water through the foot of a skin.* [100] By bringing the full range of his organs under control and by restraining his mind, a man will achieve all his goals without having to shrivel up his body through yoga.

Twilight Worship

[101] At the morning twilight, he should stand reciting softly the Sāvitrī verse until the sun comes into view; at the evening twilight, however, he should always remain seated until Ursa Major becomes clearly visible. [102] When he stands reciting softly at the morning twilight, he banishes any sin committed during the night; and when he sits at the evening twilight, he removes any taint contracted during the day. [103] A man who neither stands at the morning twilight nor sits at the evening twilight should be excluded like a Śūdra from all rites of the twice-born.

Vedic Recitation

[104] Intent on carrying out the ritual of daily recitation, he should go into the wilderness and, controlled and composed, recite at least the Sāvitrī verse near a place of water.

[105] Rules regarding the suspension of vedic recitation (4.101–27) have no bearing on Vedic Supplements,* on daily vedic recitation, and on ritual formulas used in fire offerings. [106] The daily vedic recitation is not subject to suspension, for tradition calls it a sacrificial session consisting of vedic recitation; it is a meritorious rite at which the vedic recitation takes the place of the burnt oblation and the factors causing a suspension act as the oblatory exclamation Vaṣaṭ.*

[107] When someone, after purifying and controlling himself, performs his vedic recitation for a year according to rule, that recitation will rain milk, curd, ghee, and honey on him every single day.

Persons Competent to Receive Vedic Instruction

[108] Kindling the sacred fire, begging almsfood, sleeping on the floor, and doing what is beneficial to his teacher—a twice-born who has undergone vedic initiation should do these until he has performed the rite of returning home.*

[109] The son of his teacher, a person who offers obedient service, a person who has given him knowledge, a virtuous person, an honest person,* someone close to him,* a capable man, someone who gives him money, a good man, and one who is his own*—these ten may be taught the Veda in accordance with the Law. [110] He must never impart instruction to anyone who has not requested it or who has requested it in an improper way; for in this world, a wise man, though learned, should conduct himself like an idiot. [111] A man who imparts in violation of the Law and a man who requests in violation of the Law—of these two, the one or the other will incur death or enmity.

[112] Do not sow knowledge where there is no merit or money, or at least proportionate service; you don't sow good seed on brackish soil. [113] Even in a time of dreadful adversity, a vedic savant should rather die with his knowledge; let him not sow it on barren soil.

[114] Vedic knowledge came up to the Brahmin and said, 'I am your treasure. Guard me! Do not hand me over to a malcontent. I shall thus become supremely strong. [115] A man you know to be honest, restrained, and chaste—only to such a Brahmin should you disclose me, as to a vigilant guardian of your treasure.'

[116] If, however, a man learns the Veda without permission by listening to someone who is reciting it, he is guilty of stealing the Veda and will go to hell.

Salutation

[117] He should greet first the person from whom he received knowledge—whether it is the knowledge of worldly matters, of the Veda, or of the inner self. [118] A well-disciplined Brahmin, although he knows just the Sāvitrī verse, is far better than an undisciplined one who eats all types of food and deals in all types of merchandise, though he may know all three Vedas.

[119] He should not sit on a bed or seat occupied by a superior, and he should rise from the bed or seat he is occupying before he greets such a person; [120] for when an older person comes near, the life-breaths of a younger person rise up, and as he rises up and greets him, he retrieves them. [121] When someone is conscientious about greeting and always renders assistance to the elderly, he obtains an increase in these four: life span, wisdom, fame, and power.

[122]When a Brahmin is greeting an older person, he must state his name after the greeting, saying, 'I am so-and-so'. [123]When greeting people who are ignorant of the greeting containing the proper name, as also any woman, a wise man should simply say 'I'.* [124]When he uses the greeting containing his own name, he should say '*bho*' at the end; the meaning of '*bho*'* contains the essential meanings of all proper names—that is the tradition handed down by the seers. [125]In greeting a Brahmin, he should say, 'May you live long, gentle Sir!'; and at the end of the name, he should pronounce 'a' and prolate the previous syllable.* [126]A learned man should not greet a Brahmin who does not know how to return a greeting; he is no better than a Śūdra.

[127]When he meets a Brahmin, he should ask him whether he is doing well (*kuśala*); a Kṣatriya, whether he is all right (*anāmaya*); a Vaiśya, whether his property is secure (*kṣema*); and a Śūdra, whether he is in good health (*ārogya*). [128]A person consecrated for sacrifice should not be addressed by name even if he is younger; a man conversant with the Law should address such a person using the words '*bho*' or 'Sir' (*bhavat*). [129]He should address a woman who is another man's wife and who is not a blood relative of his using the words 'Madam', 'Dear Lady', or 'Sister'. [130]He should rise up and say, 'I am so-and-so' to his maternal and paternal uncles, fathers-in-law, officiating priests, and elders who are younger than he. [131]He should honour a maternal aunt, a wife of a maternal uncle, a mother-in-law, and a paternal aunt as he would his teacher's wife; they are equal to his teacher's wife.

[132]The feet of his brother's wife of the same social class, he should clasp every day; but the feet of the wives of his paternal and maternal relatives,* only after returning from a journey. [133]Towards a sister of his father and mother and towards his own older sister, he should behave as towards his own mother; but the mother is more venerable than they.

Precedence

[134]Among fellow citizens, people with an age difference of ten years are regarded as friends; among fellow artisans, people with an age difference of five years; among vedic scholars, people with an age difference of three years; and among blood relatives, only people with a slight age difference.

[135]A 10-year-old Brahmin and a 100-year-old king, one should know, stand with respect to each other as a father to a son; but of the two, the Brahmin is the father. [136]Wealth, kin, age, ritual life, and the fifth, knowledge—these are the grounds for respect; and each subsequent one carries greater weight than each preceding. [137]Among persons of the three classes, one who possesses more of and to a higher degree these five grounds is more deserving of respect; and so is a Śūdra who is in his nineties.

[138]One should give way to people in vehicles or in their nineties, the sick, people carrying loads, women, bath-graduates, kings, and bridegrooms. [139]When such people encounter each other, however, a bath-graduate and a king are to receive greater honour; but when a king and a bath-graduate encounter each other, the king pays honour to the bath-graduate.

Teacher

[140]The twice-born man who initiates a pupil and teaches him the Veda together with the ritual books and the secret texts* is called 'Teacher'. [141]A man who teaches a section of the Veda or else the Vedic Supplements (2.105n.) for a living is called 'Tutor'. [142]The Brahmin who performs the rites beginning with the ceremony of impregnation according to rule and nourishes with food is called 'Elder'.* [143]The person who, after he has been chosen by someone, sets up the sacred fires and performs the cooked oblations and sacrifices such as the Agniṣṭoma offering on his behalf is called here his 'Officiating Priest'.

[144]He should consider the man who fills both his ears faithfully with the Veda as his father and mother and never show hostility towards him. [145]The teacher is ten times greater* than the tutor; the father is a hundred times greater than the teacher; but the mother is a thousand times greater than the father. [146]Between the man who gave life and the man who gave the Veda, the man who gave the Veda is the more venerable father; for a Brahmin's birth in the Veda is everlasting, both here and in the hereafter. [147]When, through lust for each other, his father and mother engender him and he is conceived in the womb, he should consider that as his mere coming into existence. [148]But the birth that a teacher who has fathomed the Veda brings about according to rule by means of the

Sāvitrī verse—that is his true birth, that is not subject to old age and death.

[149] A man who assists someone with vedic knowledge, be it a little or a lot, is also acknowledged here as his elder in recognition of that assistance with vedic knowledge.

[150] Even a younger Brahmin who brings about the vedic birth of an older individual and trains him in the Law proper to him becomes his father according to the Law. [151] The child sage, son of Aṅgiras, gave vedic instruction to his fathers; and having excelled them in knowledge, he called them 'Little Children'. [152] They became infuriated and raised the issue with the gods. The gods convened and told them: 'The child addressed you properly. [153] An ignorant man, surely, is the child, and the man who imparts the Veda is the father; for they address an ignorant man as "Child" and a man who imparts the Veda as "Father".'

[154] The seers have established this Law: 'In our eyes, only a vedic savant is an eminent man'; eminence does not come from age, grey hairs, wealth, or kin. [155] For Brahmins, seniority depends on knowledge, for Kṣatriyas on valour, and for Vaiśyas on grain and wealth; for Śūdras alone it depends on age. [156] A man does not become a 'senior' simply because his hair has turned grey. Gods call a man with vedic learning a 'senior', even though he may be young.

[157] Like an elephant made of wood, like a deer made of leather, is a Brahmin without vedic learning; these three only bear the name. [158] As fruitless as a eunuch with women, as fruitless as a cow with a cow, and as fruitless as a gift given to an ignorant man, is a Brahmin ignorant of the Veda.

[159] A man who wishes to promote the Law should instruct creatures about what is best without hurting them, employing pleasant and gentle words. [160] Only a man whose mind and speech have been purified and are always well-guarded acquires the entire fruit of reaching the end of the Veda. [161] Though deeply hurt, let him never use cutting words, show hostility to others in thought or deed, or use aberrant language that would alarm people.

[162] Let a Brahmin always shrink from praise, as he would from poison; let him ever yearn for scorn, as he would for ambrosia—[163] for, a man who is scorned sleeps at ease, wakes up at ease, goes about in this world at ease; but the man who scorned him perishes.

Vedic Study

[164] A twice-born whose body has been consecrated following this orderly sequence should gradually amass the riches of ascetic toil consisting of vedic study while he resides with his teacher. [165] A twice-born should study the entire Veda together with the secret texts (2.140 n.), as he carries out the various observances and special ascetic practices enjoined by vedic injunctions. [166] A Brahmin planning on undergoing ascetic toil should simply recite the Veda constantly; for vedic recitation is recognized here as the highest ascetic toil for a Brahmin. [167] When a twice-born, even while wearing a garland, performs his vedic recitation every day according to his ability, he is surely practising the fiercest ascetic toil down to the very tips of his nails. [168] When a Brahmin expends great effort in other matters without studying the Veda, while still alive he is quickly reduced to the status of a Śūdra, together with his children.

[169] According to a scriptural injunction, the first birth of a Brahmin is from his mother; the second takes place at the tying of the Muñja-grass girdle (2.27 n.), and the third at the consecration for a sacrifice. [170] Of these, the one signalled by the tying of the Muñja-grass girdle is his birth from the Veda. At this birth, the Sāvitrī verse is said to be his mother, and the teacher his father. [171] The teacher is called the father because he imparts the Veda, for a man does not become competent to perform any rite until the tying of the Muñja-grass girdle. [172] Such a man should not pronounce any vedic text, except when he offers a funerary oblation, for he is equal to a Śūdra until he is born from the Veda.

Observances

[173] After he has undergone vedic initiation, he is to be instructed in the observances and then taught the Veda in the proper order and according to rule. [174] The very same skin, cord, girdle, staff, and garment prescribed for him after his initiation are prescribed for him also during the observances.

[175] Bringing all his organs under control, a vedic student living with his teacher should observe these restrictions in order to increase his ascetic toil. [176] Every day, after purifying himself by bathing, he should offer quenching libations to gods, seers, and ancestors; wor-

ship the gods; and put firewood into the sacred fire. [177] He should avoid honey, meat, perfumes, garlands, savoury foods, women, all foods that have turned sour, causing injury to living beings, [178] rubbing oil on the body, putting collyrium on the eyes, using footwear or an umbrella, lust, hatred, greed, dancing, singing, playing musical instruments, [179] gambling, gossiping, slander, lies, looking at and touching women, and hurting others.

[180] He should always sleep alone and never ejaculate his semen; for when he voluntarily ejaculates his semen, he breaks his vow. [181] When a Brahmin student ejaculates his semen involuntarily in sleep, he should bathe, worship the sun, and softly recite three times the verse: 'May the virile strength return again to me. . . .'

Begging and Daily Duties [182] He should fetch a pot of water, flowers, cow dung, loose soil, and Kuśa grass—as much as required—and beg for food every day.

[183] Having made himself pure, a vedic student should gather almsfood every day from the houses of persons who do not neglect the Veda or sacrifices and who have distinguished themselves in the activities proper to them. [184] He should not beg from his teacher's family or from the families of his paternal or maternal relatives. When houses of other people are unavailable, however, he may beg from these, avoiding those listed earlier when those listed later are available. [185] When the kinds of person mentioned above are not available, he may beg from the entire village after purifying himself and curbing his speech; but he should avoid heinous sinners.*

[186] Having fetched firewood from afar, he should stack it above ground; and using that firewood, he should make offerings in the fire diligently morning and evening.

[187] If he fails to beg food or to put firewood into the sacred fire for seven nights without being sick, he should perform the penitential observance prescribed for a student who has broken his vow of chastity (11.119–24).

[188] Subsisting on almsfood every day, a votary should never eat a meal given by one person; tradition says that for a votary subsisting on almsfood is equal to a fast. [189] When he is invited, however, he may freely eat at an offering to the gods while keeping to his vow, and at an offering to ancestors, conducting himself like a seer; doing so does not violate his vow. [190] Wise men sanction this activity only for

Brahmins; this kind of activity is not commended at all for Kṣatriyas and Vaiśyas.

Conduct towards the Teacher

[191] When he is ordered by the teacher—or even when he is not—he should apply himself every day to vedic recitation and to activities beneficial to his teacher.

[192] Bringing his body, speech, organs of perception, and mind under control, he should stand with joined palms looking at his teacher's face. [193] He must always keep his right arm uncovered,* comport himself properly, cover himself well, and, when he is told 'Be seated', sit down facing the teacher.

[194] In his teacher's presence, his food, clothes, and apparel should always be of a lesser quality than his teacher's. He should wake up before his teacher and go to bed after him.

[195] He must never answer or converse with his teacher while lying down, seated, eating, standing,* or facing away; [196] he should do so standing up if the teacher is seated, approaching him if he is standing, going up to meet him if he is walking towards him, running after him if he is running, [197] going around to face him if he is turned away from him, coming close to him if he is far away, and bending down if he is lying down or standing at a lower level. [198] In his teacher's presence, he should always occupy a lower couch or seat; and, within his teacher's sight, he must not sit as he pleases.

[199] Even out of sight, he must not refer to his teacher by just his name or mimic his walk, speech, or mannerisms. [200] Wherever his teacher is slandered or reviled, he should either cover his ears or go somewhere else. [201] By slandering his teacher, he becomes an ass; by reviling him, a dog; by living off him, a worm; and by being jealous of him, an insect.

[202] When he is far away or angry, he must not pay his respects to his teacher; nor should he do so in the presence of a woman. When he is riding in a vehicle or seated on a chair, he should greet his teacher only after getting down. [203] He must not sit down with his teacher in such a way that the wind blows from the teacher towards him or from him towards the teacher; nor should he talk about anything out of his teacher's hearing. [204] He may sit by his teacher on

a cart drawn by an ox, horse, or camel; on a terrace or a spread of grass; or on a mat, rock, bench, or boat.

Teacher's Teacher and Other Instructors [205] In the presence of his teacher's teacher, he should behave towards him as towards his own teacher; and he must not greet his own elders unless he is permitted by his teacher.

[206] He should always behave in the very same manner towards his vedic instructors and his own blood relatives, as also towards those who keep him from what is unrighteous and who teach him what is beneficial.

Members of Teacher's Family [207] Towards distinguished persons, as well as towards the teacher's Ārya sons* and the teacher's own relatives, he should always behave just as he does towards his teacher.

[208] A teacher's son who teaches him—whether that son is younger than or of the same age as himself, or even if he is only a student of the ritual—is entitled to the same respect as his teacher. [209] He must not massage the limbs of his teacher's son, assist him at his bath, eat his leftovers, or wash his feet.

[210] The teacher's wives of equal class should receive the same honour as the teacher, but wives of unequal class should be honoured by rising up and greeting them. [211] He must not apply oil on his teacher's wife, assist her at her bath, massage her limbs, or do her hair. [212] Anyone who is over 20 and able to distinguish between the attractive and the unattractive should not greet here a young wife of his teacher by clasping her feet. [213] It is the very nature of women here to corrupt men. On that account, prudent men are never off guard in the presence of alluring young women. [214] For an alluring young woman is capable of leading astray not only the ignorant but even learned men under the sway of anger and lust. [215] He must not sit alone with his mother, sister, or daughter; the array of sensory organs is powerful and overpowers even a learned man. [216] A young man may freely pay his respects to the young wives of his teacher, however, by prostrating himself on the ground according to rule and saying: 'I am so-and-so.' [217] Recalling the Law followed by good people, he should clasp the feet of his teacher's wives upon his return from a journey and greet them every day.

[218] As a man discovers water by digging with a spade, so a student,

offering obedient service, discovers the knowledge contained in his teacher.

Rules of Conduct

[219] A student may shave his head or keep his hair matted; or else he may keep just his topknot matted.

He should never let the sun rise or set while he is asleep in a village. [220] If the sun should rise or set while he is asleep, whether deliberately or inadvertently, he should fast for one day while engaging in soft recitation. [221] If, after he had been asleep at sunrise or sunset, he does not perform the penance, he becomes saddled with a great sin. [222] After purifying himself by sipping water and becoming self-possessed, he should worship both twilights every day, softly reciting the prescribed formula in a clean spot and according to rule (2.103).

[223] If he sees a woman or a low-born man doing something conducive to welfare, he should do all of that diligently, or anything else that he is fond of. [224] Some say that Law and Wealth are conducive to welfare; others, Pleasure and Wealth; and still others, Law alone or Wealth alone. But the settled rule is this: the entire triple set* is conducive to welfare.

Mother, Father, Teacher [225] Teacher, father, mother, and older brother—these should never be treated with contempt especially by a Brahmin, even though he may be deeply hurt. [226] The teacher is the embodiment of Brahman; the father is the embodiment of Prajāpati; the mother is the embodiment of Earth; and one's brother is the embodiment of oneself. [227] The tribulations that a mother and a father undergo when humans are born cannot be repaid even in hundreds of years.

[228] He should do what is pleasing to these two every day, and always what is pleasing to his teacher. When these three are gratified, he obtains the fullness of ascetic toil. [229] Obedient service to these three is said to be the highest form of ascetic toil. Without their consent, he should not follow any other rule of conduct.* [230] For they alone are the three worlds; they alone are the three orders of life; they alone are the three Vedas; and they alone are called the three sacred fires. [231] The householder's fire is clearly the father; the south-

ern fire, tradition says, is the mother; and the offertorial fire* is the teacher—this is the most excellent triad of sacred fires.

[232] A householder who does not neglect these three will win the three worlds; and, shining with his own body, he will rejoice in heaven like a god. [233] He obtains this world by devotion to his mother, and the middle world by devotion to his father; but he obtains the world of Brahman only by obedient service to his teacher. [234] When someone has attended to these three, he has attended to all his duties; should someone not attend to them, all his rites bear him no fruit. [235] So long as these three are alive, he should not follow another rule of conduct; taking delight in what is pleasing and beneficial to them, he should always render them obedient service. [236] Whenever he undertakes any mental, verbal, or physical activity for the sake of the next world without inconveniencing them, he should inform them of it.

[237] When these three are gratified, a man has done all he has to do. This is the highest Law itself in person; all else is called subsidiary Law.

Non-Brahmin Teachers [238] A man with faith should accept fine learning even from a low-caste man; the highest Law even from a man of the lowest caste; and a splendid woman even from a bad family. [239] One should take ambrosia even from poison; words of wisdom even from a child; a good example even from an enemy; and gold even from filth. [240] Women, gems, learning, Law, purification, and words of wisdom, as well as crafts of various kinds, may be accepted from anyone.

[241] In a time of adversity, the rules allow a man to study the Veda under a person who is not a Brahmin; and, as long as he is studying, he should walk after that teacher and serve him obediently. [242] If he desires to attain the highest state, a pupil should not live all his life with a teacher who is not a Brahmin or who is a Brahmin but not a vedic scholar.

Life-long Student: I

[243] If he wishes to live with his teacher's family all his life, however, he should diligently serve the teacher until he is freed from his body. [244] When a Brahmin obediently serves his teacher until his body

comes to an end, he goes immediately to the eternal abode of Brahman.

Conclusion of Study

[245] Knowing the Law, he must not give any present to his teacher beforehand; but when, with his teacher's permission, he is ready to take his final bath, he should present the teacher with a gift according to his ability— [246] land, gold, a cow, or a horse; or at least an umbrella or footwear; or grain, vegetables, or clothes—and thus gladden his teacher.

Life-long Student: II

[247] If his teacher happens to die, he should maintain the same conduct towards his teacher's son possessing the right qualities—or towards his teacher's wife, or towards a person belonging to his teacher's ancestry (5.60 n.)—as he did towards his teacher. [248] If none of these is available, he should end his life by serving the sacred fire faithfully, standing during the day and seated at night (6.22 n.). [249] When a Brahmin lives the life of a vedic student in this manner without breaking his vow, he will go to the highest station and will not be reborn on earth again.

CHAPTER THREE

MARRIAGE

Conclusion of Study

[1]He should carry out the observance relating to the three Vedas at his teacher's house, an observance lasting thirty-six years, or one-half or one-quarter of that time, or else until he has learnt them.

[2]After he has learnt in the proper order the three Vedas or two of them, or at least one, without violating his chastity, he should undertake the householder's order of life. [3]When he has returned in accordance with the Law proper to him and received his vedic inheritance from his father, he should be honoured at the outset with the gift of a cow, as he sits on a couch wearing a garland.

Selection of a Bride

[4]After he has taken the concluding bath with his teacher's permission and performed the rite of returning home according to rule, the twice-born should marry a wife belonging to the same class and possessing the right bodily characteristics.

[5]A girl who belongs to an ancestry (5.60 n.) different from his mother's and to a lineage different from his father's, and who is unrelated to him by marriage, is recommended for marriage by a twice-born man.

[6]He should avoid these ten families when contracting a marriage alliance, even though they may be prominent and rich in cattle, goats, sheep, money, and grain: [7]families negligent about rites, deficient in male issue, without vedic learning, and with hairy bodies, as well as families prone to haemorrhoids, tuberculosis, dyspepsia, epilepsy, leukoderma, or leprosy.

[8]He must not marry a girl who has red hair or an extra limb; who is sickly; who is without or with too much bodily hair; who is a blabbermouth or jaundiced-looking; [9]who is named after a constellation, a tree, a river, a very low caste, a mountain, a bird, a snake, or a servant; or who has a frightening name. [10]He should marry a woman

who is not deficient in any limb; who has a pleasant name; who walks like a goose or an elephant; and who has fine body and head hair, small teeth, and delicate limbs.

[11] A wise man must not marry a girl who has no brother or whose father is unknown, for fear that the Law of 'female-son' may be in force.*

[12] At the first marriage, a woman of equal class is recommended for twice-born men; but for those who proceed further through lust, these are, in order, the preferable women. [13] A Śūdra may take only a Śūdra woman as wife; a Vaiśya, the latter and a woman of his own class; a Kṣatriya, the latter two and a woman of his own class; and a Brahmin, the latter three and a woman of his own class.

Prohibition of a Śūdra Wife [14] Not a single story* mentions a Brahmin or a Kṣatriya taking a Śūdra wife even when they were going through a time of adversity. [15] When twice-born men foolishly marry low-caste wives, they quickly reduce even their families and children to the rank of Śūdras.

[16] According to Atri and the son of Utathya, a man falls from his caste by marrying a Śūdra woman; according to Śaunaka, by fathering a son through her; and according to Bhṛgu, by producing all his offspring through her. [17] By taking a Śūdra woman to bed, a Brahmin will descend along the downward course; and by begetting a son through her, he falls from the very rank of a Brahmin. [18] When such a woman plays the leading role in his divine, ancestral, and hospitality rites, gods and ancestors do not partake of them, and he will not go to heaven. [19] No expiation is prescribed for a man who drinks the saliva from the lips of a Śūdra woman, who is tainted by her breath, and who begets himself* in her.

Types of Marriage

[20] Listen now in brief to these eight types of marriage for all four classes, some beneficial both here and in the hereafter, and some not. [21] They are the Brāhma, the Divine, the Seer's, the Prājāpatya, the Demonic, the Gāndharva, the Fiendish, and the Ghoulish, which is the eighth and the worst. [22] Which of these is lawful for which class, their respective merits and defects, the merits and demerits of each with respect to procreation—I will explain all this to you.

[23] The first six in the order enumerated should be considered lawful for Brahmins; the last four for Kṣatriyas; the same four, with the exception of the Fiendish, for Vaiśyas and Śūdras. [24] The first four, sages say, are recommended for Brahmins; the Fiendish alone for Kṣatriyas; and the Demonic for Vaiśyas and Śūdras. [25] The tradition recorded here, however, considers three of the last five as lawful and two as unlawful; one should never engage in the Demonic or the Ghoulish. [26] The two marriages proclaimed earlier, the Gāndharva and the Fiendish, whether undertaken separately or conjointly,* are viewed by tradition as lawful for Kṣatriyas.

[27] When a man dresses a girl up, honours her, invites on his own a man of learning and virtue, and gives her to him, it is said to be the 'Brāhma' Law. [28] When a man, while a sacrifice is being carried out properly, adorns his daughter and gives her to the officiating priest as he is performing the rite, it is called the 'Divine' Law. [29] When a man accepts a bull and a cow, or two pairs of them, from the bridegroom in accordance with the Law and gives a girl to him according to rule, it is called the 'Seer's' Law. [30] When a man honours the girl and gives her after exhorting them with the words: 'May you jointly fulfil the Law,' tradition calls it the 'Prājāpatya' procedure. [31] When a girl is given after the payment of money to the girl's relatives and to the girl herself according to the man's ability and out of his own free will, it is called the 'Demonic' Law. [32] When the girl and the groom have sex with each other voluntarily, that is the 'Gāndharva' marriage based on sexual union and originating from love. [33] When someone violently abducts a girl from her house as she is shrieking and weeping by causing death, mayhem, and destruction, it is called the 'Fiendish' procedure. [34] When someone secretly rapes a woman who is asleep, drunk, or mentally deranged, it is the eighth known as 'Ghoulish', the most evil of marriages.

[35] Giving a girl away by simply pouring water is recommended for Brahmins, while among the other classes it may be done through mutual love.

Sons from Different Types of Marriage [36] Brahmins, listen now as I describe accurately all that Manu has said regarding the merits of each of these marriages.

[37] A son who is born to a woman married according to the 'Brāhma' rite and who does good deeds rescues from evil ten

generations of forefathers before him and ten generations after him, with himself as the twenty-first; [38] a son born to a woman married according to the 'Divine' rite rescues seven generations before him and seven after him; a son born to a woman married according to the 'Seer's' rite, three before and three after; and a son born to a woman married according to 'Prājāpatya' marriage, six before and six after.

[39] From all four types of marriage beginning, in order, with 'Brāhma' are born sons who are eminent in vedic knowledge and respected by cultured people. [40] Endowed with beauty, spirit, and virtue, possessing wealth and fame, furnished with every delight, and righteous to the highest degree, they will live a hundred years. [41] But in the others—the remaining wicked types of marriage—are born sons whose speech is cruel and false and who hate the Veda and the Law.

[42] From irreproachable marriages are born children beyond reproach; from reproachable marriages are born children inviting people's reproach. Therefore, a man should avoid reproachable marriages.

Marriage Rite [43] The consecratory rite of taking the hand in marriage is prescribed only for brides of equal class. The following should be recognized as the procedure for the rite of marriage when brides are of unequal class. [44] When marrying an upper-class man, a Kṣatriya bride should take hold of an arrow, a Vaiśya bride a goad, and a Śūdra bride the hem of his garment.

Sexual Union

[45] Finding his gratification always in his wife, he should have sex with her during her season.* Devoted solely to her, he may go to her also when he wants sexual pleasure, except on the days of the moon's change.*

[46] The natural season of women, according to tradition, consists of sixteen nights, together with the other four days* proscribed by good people. [47] Of these nights, the first four as well as the eleventh and the thirteenth are disapproved; the remaining ten nights are recommended.*

[48] Sons are born when he has sex on even nights, and girls on odd nights. Desiring a son, therefore, he should have sex with his wife on

even nights during her season. [49] When the man's semen is dominant, it turns out to be a boy; when the woman's is dominant, a girl; and when both are equal, a hermaphrodite or a twin boy and girl. When both are weak or scanty, no conception takes place.*

[50] Regardless of the order of life in which a man lives, if he avoids women during the forbidden nights and during the other eight nights,* he becomes a true celibate.

Purchasing a Wife

[51] A learned father must never accept even the slightest bride-price for his daughter; for by greedily accepting a bride-price, a man becomes a trafficker in his offspring. [52] When relatives* foolishly live off a woman's wealth—slave women, vehicles, or clothes—those evil men will descend along the downward course.

[53] At a 'Seer's' marriage, some say, the bull and cow constitute the bride-price. That is totally false. Whether the amount is great or small, it is still a sale.* [54] When women's relatives do not take the bride-price for themselves, it does not constitute a sale. It is an act of respect to women, a simple token of benevolence.

Honouring Women

[55] If they desire an abundance of good fortune, fathers, brothers, husbands, and brothers-in-law should revere their women and provide them with adornments.

[56] Where women are revered, there the gods rejoice; but where they are not, no rite bears any fruit. [57] Where female relatives grieve, that family soon comes to ruin; but where they do not grieve, it always prospers. [58] When female relatives, not receiving due reverence, curse any house, it comes to total ruin, as if struck down by witchcraft.

[59] If men want to become prosperous, therefore, they should always honour the women on joyful occasions and festive days with gifts of adornments, clothes, and food.

Marital Harmony

[60] Good fortune smiles incessantly on a family where the husband always finds delight in his wife, and the wife in her husband.

[61] For, if the wife does not sparkle, she does not arouse her husband. And if the husband is not aroused, there will be no offspring. [62] When the wife sparkles, so does the entire household; but when she ceases to sparkle, so does the entire household.

Degradation of Families

[63] By contracting aberrant marriages, by neglecting rites, and by failing to study the Veda, respectable families quickly come to ruin; as also by disregarding Brahmins. [64] By practising crafts, by engaging in trade, by having children only from a Śūdra wife, by dealing in cattle, horses, and vehicles, by engaging in agriculture, by entering a king's service, [65] by officiating at sacrifices of people at whose sacrifices one is forbidden to officiate, and by denying the efficacy of rites, respectable families fall into disrepute; as also those families bereft of vedic knowledge.

[66] When they are rich in vedic knowledge, however, even poor families attain the status of 'respectable family' and achieve great fame.

THE HOUSEHOLDER

[67] A householder should perform the domestic rites in his nuptial fire according to rule, as also the five great sacrifices and the daily cooking.

Great Sacrifices

[68] A householder has five slaughter-houses: fireplace, grindstone, broom, mortar and pestle, and water pot. By his use of them, he is fettered. [69] To expiate successively for each of these, the great seers devised the five great sacrifices to be carried out daily by householders.

[70] The sacrifice to the Veda is teaching; the sacrifice to ancestors is the quenching libation; the sacrifice to gods is the burnt offering; the sacrifice to beings is the Bali offering; and the sacrifice to humans is the honouring of guests. [71] If a man never fails to offer these five great sacrifices to the best of his ability, he remains unsullied by the taints of his slaughter-houses in spite of living permanently at home.

[72] Gods, guests, dependants, ancestors, and oneself—when someone does not make offerings to these five, he has breath but no life at all.

[73] The five sacrifices are called Ahuta, Huta, Prahuta, Brāhmya-Huta, and Prāśita. [74] The Ahuta—'not offered in the fire'—is soft recitation. The Huta—'offered in the fire'—is a burnt offering. The Prahuta—'offered by scattering'—is the Bali offering to beings. The Brāhmya-Huta—'offered in Brahmins'—is the worship of Brahmins. The Prāśita—'consumed'—is the quenching libation to ancestors.

[75] He should apply himself here daily to his vedic recitation and to making offerings to gods; for by applying himself to making offerings to gods, he upholds this world, both the mobile and the immobile. [76] An oblation duly consigned to the fire reaches the sun; from the sun comes rain; from rain, food; and from food, offspring.*

[77] As all living beings exist dependent on air, so people in other orders of life exist dependent on the householder. [78] Because it is householders who sustain people in all three orders of life every day by giving them knowledge and food, the householder represents the most senior order of life.* [79] This is the order that must be shouldered assiduously by anyone who desires undecaying heaven and absolute happiness, an order that cannot be shouldered by people with feeble faculties.

[80] Seers, ancestors, gods, beings, and guests seek favours from the householder, which a wise man should grant them. [81] He should duly honour the seers by private vedic recitation, gods with burnt oblations, ancestors with an ancestral offering, humans with food, and beings with a Bali offering.

Ancestral Offerings [82] He should make an ancestral offering every day with food or water, or even with milk, roots, and fruits, gladdening his ancestors thereby. [83] He should feed at least a single Brahmin for the benefit of his ancestors as part of the five great sacrifices; at this,* he should never feed even a single Brahmin in connection with the offering to the All-gods.

Divine Offerings [84] From the oblation to All-gods that has been cooked, a Brahmin should offer portions in the domestic fire to the following deities every day and according to rule: [85] first to Fire and to Soma; then to both of them together; to the All-gods; to Dhanvantari; [86] to Kuhū—the goddess of the new moon; to

Anumati—the goddess of the full moon; to Prajāpati; to heaven and earth together; and finally to Sviṣṭakṛt—Fire who makes the offering flawless.

Bali Offerings [87] In this manner, having offered the burnt oblation properly, he should make the Bali offerings to Indra, Death, Lord of the waters (Varuṇa), and Moon, together with their attendants, making the offerings clockwise in the direction of each quarter. [88] He should make an offering by the door, saying: 'To the Maruts!'; by the water pot, saying: 'To the waters!'; and by the mortar and pestle, saying 'To trees!' [89] He should make a Bali offering to Śrī—the goddess of prosperity—by the head of the bed; to Bhadrakālī—the auspicious black goddess—by the foot of the bed; and to Brahman and the Lord of the house in the middle of the house.

[90] He should throw into the air a Bali offering to All-gods, as well as to beings that roam during the day and to those that roam at night. [91] In the back house,* he should make a Bali offering to Sarvānnabhūti—the power of all food. The remainder of the Bali oblation he should offer towards the south for the ancestors. [92] He should also gently place on the ground offerings for dogs, outcastes, dog-cookers, persons with evil diseases, crows, and worms.

[93] When a Brahmin honours all beings in this manner every day, he takes on a body of effulgence and goes by the direct route to the supreme abode.

Honouring Guests [94] After completing in this manner the Bali offering, he should feed a guest before anyone else and give almsfood to a mendicant student of the Veda according to rule. [95] By giving almsfood, a twice-born householder obtains as much merit as he does by giving a cow to a poor man according to rule.

[96] He should garnish some almsfood or a pot of water and present it in accordance with the rules to a Brahmin who knows the true meaning of the Veda. [97] Divine and ancestral oblations of ignorant men come to naught when the donors offer them foolishly to Brahmins who are the equivalent of ashes.* [98] Oblations offered in the fires that are the mouths of Brahmins, fires set ablaze by knowledge and ascetic toil, rescue a man from danger and from grievous sin.

[99] When a guest arrives, he should offer him a seat and water and give him food as well according to rule, after garnishing it according to his ability. [100] When a Brahmin resides without being treated with

respect, he takes away all the good works of even a man who lives by gleaning ears of grain (4.5 n.) or who makes daily offerings in the five sacred fires (3.185 n.). [101] Some straw, a place on the floor, water, and fourth, a pleasant word of welcome—at least these are never wanting in the houses of good people.

[102] Tradition defines a guest as a Brahmin who spends just one night. He is called 'guest' because his stay is brief.* [103] A Brahmin living in the same village or on a social visit cannot be considered a guest even when he comes to a house which has a wife or even sacred fires. [104] When foolish householders become attached to other people's cooking, the result is that after death they are born as the cattle of those who gave them food.

[105] A householder must never turn away a guest led there by the sun in the evening; and whether he arrives at the proper time or not, he should not let him remain in his house without food. [106] Nor should he eat anything that he does not serve his guest. Honouring a guest leads to wealth, fame, long life, and heaven.

[107] Guests of the highest status should receive the highest treatment with respect to seating, room, bed, accompanying them as they leave,* and paying honour to them; those of equal status should receive equal treatment; and those of inferior status should receive inferior treatment. [108] If another guest arrives after he has completed the offering to All-gods, however, he should provide him also with food according to his ability; but he need not make a fresh Bali offering.*

[109] A Brahmin must not advertise his family and lineage for the sake of a meal; for the wise call a man who flaunts these for a meal 'an eater of vomit'.

[110] A Kṣatriya is not called a 'guest' in the house of a Brahmin; nor is a Vaiśya, a Śūdra, a friend, a relative, or an elder. [111] If, however, a Kṣatriya comes to his house fulfilling the conditions of a guest,* he may freely feed him also after the Brahmins have finished their meal. [112] Even when a Vaiśya or a Śūdra arrives at his house fulfilling the conditions of a guest, he should show kindness and feed him along with his servants. [113] Even when others, such as his friends, visit his house out of mutual affection, he should make as special a preparation of food as he can and feed them along with his wife. [114] Newly married women, young girls, the sick, and pregnant women—these he may feed without hesitation right after the guests.

[115] When a fool eats before he gives food to these persons, as he eats he is unaware that he is being eaten by dogs and vultures. [116] Once the Brahmins, the dependants, and the servants have finished their meal, only then should the husband and wife eat what is left over. [117] After he has honoured the gods, seers, humans, ancestors, and the guardian deities of the house, the householder should eat what remains. [118] A man who cooks only for his own sake eats nothing but sin; for the food prescribed for good men is this—eating the leftovers of a sacrifice.

[119] He should honour a king, an officiating priest, a bath-graduate, an elder, a friend, a father-in-law, and a maternal uncle with a honey-mixture* when they visit him after the lapse of one year. [120] The rule is that a king and a vedic scholar should be honoured with a honey-mixture when a sacrifice is about to take place, but never outside the context of a sacrifice.

[121] When the evening meal is cooked, the wife should make a Bali offering without reciting vedic formulas. This is called 'offering to All-gods', and it is prescribed both in the evening and in the morning.

Ancestral Offerings

[122] After he has offered the sacrifice to ancestors,* a Brahmin who possesses a sacred fire should perform the monthly ancestral rite called the 'supplementary offering of rice balls'* on the new-moon day. [123] The wise call the monthly offering to ancestors the 'supplementary offering', and it should be performed diligently using the recommended kinds of meat (see 3.266–72).

[124] Who are the Brahmins to be fed at this rite and who are to be avoided? How many? And with what kinds of food?—I will explain all that completely.

Number of Invitees [125] Even if he is rich, he should feed two at an offering to gods, three at an offering to ancestors, or one at either offering; he should not indulge in feeding a large number. [126] A large number is detrimental to five things: offering proper hospitality, doing things at the right place and the right time, carrying out purifications, and finding Brahmins of quality. Therefore, he must not try to get a large number.

Quality of Invitees [127]This rite for the deceased performed at the new moon is well known by the name 'ancestral offering'. When a man is devoted to it, the same non-vedic rite for the deceased benefits him always.*

[128]Donors should present a divine or ancestral offering only to a vedic scholar; what is given to such an eminently worthy Brahmin yields abundant fruit. [129]He should feed even a single learned man at each rite to gods or ancestors rather than a lot of men ignorant of the Veda; he reaps thereby copious fruit. [130]He should search far and wide* for a Brahmin who has mastered the Veda; such a man is the proper recipient of divine and ancestral offerings, and tradition calls him a 'guest'. [131]For when one man who knows the Veda is gratified there, in terms of the Law he is worth all the men ignorant of the Veda who may eat there, be they in their millions. [132]Divine and ancestral offerings should be given to a man renowned for his knowledge, for hands smeared with blood cannot be cleansed with more blood. [133]A man will have to eat as many red-hot spikes, spears, and iron balls as the rice balls that someone ignorant of the Veda eats at his divine or ancestral offerings.

[134]Some Brahmins apply themselves to knowledge, some to ascetic toil, others to both ascetic toil and vedic recitation, and still others to ritual activities. [135]He should diligently present divine offerings only to those who apply themselves to knowledge, but he may present ancestral offerings to any of the four according to rule. [136]Between a man whose father is not a vedic savant but whose son has mastered the Veda and a man whose father has mastered the Veda but whose son is not vedic savant, [137]the man whose father is a vedic savant should be considered as superior.* The other deserves honour for the sake of venerating the Veda.

[138]A friend must not be fed at an ancestral offering; he is to be courted with presents. A twice-born who is deemed neither friend nor foe is the one who should be fed at an ancestral offering. [139]When a friend takes centre stage at his divine or ancestral offerings, he reaps no fruit from them after death. [140]When a man foolishly strikes up friendships by means of an ancestral offering, that lowest of twice-born, using ancestral offerings to make friends, will fall from heaven. [141]Such a sacrificial gift is ghoulish and twice-born people call it 'feeding-one-another'. It remains in this very world, like a blind cow in a single stall.*

[142] As a sower reaps no harvest when he sows his seeds on barren soil, so a giver earns no reward when he gives his oblation to a man ignorant of the Veda. [143] A sacrificial gift given to a learned man according to rule makes both the givers and the receivers partake of its rewards both here and in the hereafter.

[144] He may, if he so wishes, honour a friend at an ancestral offering but never a foe even if he is quite handsome; for an oblation is fruitless in the hereafter when it is eaten by an enemy. [145] He should make every effort to feed at his ancestral offering either a scholar of the Ṛgveda who has mastered that Veda, or an Adhvaryu priest who has mastered that vedic branch, or a scholar of the Sāmaveda who has learnt it completely. [146] When any one of these is received with honour and eats the ancestral offering of someone, his ancestors up to the seventh generation derive unending satisfaction.

[147] This, clearly, is the primary method in presenting divine and ancestral offerings. What follows, on the other hand, should be considered a secondary method that has always been followed by good people. [148] One may feed the following: maternal grandfather, maternal uncle, sister's son, father-in-law, teacher, daughter's son, son-in-law, and relative, as also one's officiating priest and a person for whom one officiates as a priest.

[149] A man who knows the Law must never probe into the qualifications of a Brahmin at a rite to the gods; when he undertakes an ancestral rite, however, he should diligently probe into his qualifications.

Unfit Invitees [150] Brahmins who are thieves, fallen from their caste, or impotent,* or who follow the livelihood of infidels—Manu has declared these unfit to participate at divine or ancestral offerings. [151] Men who have matted hair, who do not recite the Veda, who are bald-headed,* who are gamblers, and who officiate at sacrifices offered by groups of people—these also must not be fed at an ancestral offering. [152] Physicians, temple priests, meat sellers, and those who live by trade—these should be avoided at divine and ancestral offerings.

[153] A servant of a village or a king; someone with bad nails or black teeth; someone who opposes his teacher or has abandoned the sacred fire; a usurer; [154] someone suffering from consumption; a cattle herder; a man who sets up a household before his older brother (see

3.171); someone who neglects his ritual duties or hates the Veda; a man who sets up a household after his younger brother; someone linked to an association;* [155] a performer; a vedic student who has broken his vow of chastity; a husband of a Śūdra woman; a son of a remarried woman (9.175); a one-eyed man; someone who lets his wife's paramour live in his house; [156] someone who teaches for a fee, as also the person taught by such a teacher; a pupil or teacher of a Śūdra; a man of uncouth speech; a son of an adulteress (3.174); a son of a widow (3.174); [157] someone who repudiates his father, mother, or teacher without good reason; someone who has established vedic or matrimonial links with people fallen from their caste; [158] an arsonist; a poisoner; someone who eats from the son of an adulteress; a seller of Soma; a seafarer; a panegyrist; an oil-miller; a suborner of perjury; [159] someone who wrangles with his father; a gambler; a man who drinks liquor; someone with an evil disease;* a heinous sinner (2.185 n.); a hypocrite; a poison vendor;* [160] someone who manufactures bows and arrows; a lover of one's sister-in-law (3.173); a treacherous friend; a man who lives by gambling; someone whose teacher is his son; [161] an epileptic; someone with scrofula or leukoderma; a slanderer; an insane person; a blind man; and someone who scoffs at the Vedas—these persons should be avoided.

[162] A trainer of elephants, oxen, horses, or camels; an astrologer by profession; a bird breeder; a combat trainer; [163] someone who breaches canals or takes delight in obstructing them;* an architect; a messenger; a tree planter; [164] someone who uses dogs for sport; a professional falconer; a man who rapes virgins; a cruel man; someone who adopts a Śūdra occupation; a man who officiates at sacrifices of corporate bodies; [165] someone lacking in proper conduct; an impotent man (3.150 n.); someone who is always asking for things; a farmer by profession; a club-footed man; someone condemned by good people; [166] a man who keeps sheep or buffaloes; a husband of a woman who has had a man before (5.163); someone who carries corpses—these persons should be diligently avoided.

[167] At both divine and ancestral offerings, a man who is wise and the highest of the twice-born should avoid these lowest of the twice-born, men of despicable conduct alongside whom it is unfit to eat. [168] For a Brahmin who does not recite the Veda becomes extinguished like a grass-fire, and he should not be given a divine offering; no one pours an offering in the ashes (3.97 n.).

[169] I will explain in full detail the fruit a donor reaps in the hereafter when he feeds at a divine or ancestral offering a man alongside whom it is unfit to eat. [170] What is eaten by Brahmins who do not keep to their vows, by people such as those who set up a household before their older brothers, and by other individuals alongside whom it is unfit to eat—all that is undoubtedly eaten by fiends.

[171] When someone gets married or begins to perform the daily fire sacrifice before his older brother, he is to be considered a Parivettṛ—'a man who sets up a household before his older brother'; and that older brother is a Parivitti—'a man who sets up a household after his younger brother'. [172] A man who sets up a household before his older brother, a man who sets up a household after his younger brother, the woman who marries such a man, the man who gives her away, and, fifth, the priest who performs the wedding—they all go to hell. [173] When a man has a lustful affair with the wife of his deceased brother, even if she has been legally appointed for leviratic union (9.57–70), he should be considered a Didhiṣūpati—'lover of his sister-in-law'. [174] Two types of sons, Kuṇḍa and Golaka, are born from someone else's wife. If her husband is alive, he is a Kuṇḍa—'son of an adulteress'; and if her husband is dead, he is a Golaka—'son of a widow'. [175] These two creatures, born in someone else's field (9.33), make the divine or ancestral offering given to them futile to the donor both here and in the hereafter.*

[176] When a man alongside whom it is unfit to eat looks at persons alongside whom it is fit to eat as they are taking their meal, the foolish donor fails to reap the reward of feeding as many of them as have been looked at by that man. [177] When a blind man looks at them, he destroys the fruit of feeding ninety of them; a one-eyed man, sixty; a man suffering from leukoderma, one hundred; and a man with an evil disease, one thousand. [178] When a man who officiates at sacrifices of Śūdras touches the Brahmins with a limb of his, the donor fails to reap the fruit of giving non-sacrificial offerings to as many Brahmins as have been touched by that man. [179] When even a Brahmin learned in the Veda greedily accepts anything from such a man, he quickly comes to ruin, like an unbaked clay pot in water.

[180] What is given to a seller of Soma turns into excrement; what is given to a physician turns into pus and blood; what is given to a temple priest perishes; what is given to a usurer lacks stability; [181] what is given to a trader has no effect either in this world or the

next; and what is given to a twice-born man born to a remarried woman is like an oblation offered in ashes (3.97 n.). [182] The wise declare that the food given to other evil men enumerated above (3.150–66), men alongside whom it is unfit to eat, turns into fat, blood, flesh, marrow, and bone.

Persons Who Purify Those Alongside Whom They Eat [183] Brahmins who purify a row of eaters defiled by someone alongside whom it is unfit to eat—listen to a complete enumeration of such Brahmins, who purify those alongside whom they eat. [184] Men of pre-eminence in all the Vedas and in all the expository texts,* as also descendants in a line of vedic scholars, should be regarded as persons who purify those alongside whom they eat. [185] An expert in the three Nāciketa* fire altars; a man who maintains the five sacred fires;* a man who knows the Trisuparṇa verse; a man who knows the six Vedic Supplements (2.105 n.); a son of a woman married according to the 'Brāhma' procedure (3.27); a man who sings the Jyeṣṭha Sāmans; [186] a man who knows the meaning of the Veda, as also one who teaches it; a vedic student; a man who has given a thousand;* a 100-year-old man—these should be regarded as Brahmins who purify those alongside whom they eat.

Invitations [187] When an ancestral offering is about to take place, he should duly invite the kind of Brahmins mentioned above, a minimum of three, either on the preceding day or on the very day of the offering.

[188] When a twice-born has been invited to an ancestral rite, both he and the person performing the rite should constantly keep themselves controlled and refrain from vedic recitation; [189] for the ancestors stand by those twice-born who have been invited, follow them like the wind, and sit by them as they sit.

[190] If a Brahmin who has been invited to a divine or ancestral offering according to rule becomes delinquent in any way, that evil man will become a pig. [191] If someone invited to an ancestral offering has a sexual encounter with a Śūdra woman, he will assume all the sins committed by the donor of that offering.

Classes of Ancestors [192] The ancestors are the primeval deities*—they are free from anger, devoted to purification, and always chaste; they have laid down their arms; and they are highly exalted.

193 From whom do they all originate; who should be worshipped and according to what specific rules—listen to an account of all that.

194 Tradition holds that the various groups of ancestors are the sons of all the seers headed by Marīci, seers who are the children of Manu, the son of Hiraṇyagarbha (1.34–5). 195 Somasads, the sons of Virāj, are known in tradition as the ancestors of the Sādhyas. Agniṣvāttas, the sons of Marīci, are widely known in the world as the ancestors of the gods. 196 Barhiṣads, the sons of Atri, are known in tradition as the ancestors of Daityas, Dānavas, Yakṣas, Gandharvas, Serpents, Rākṣasas, Suparṇas, and Kinnaras. 197 The ancestors of Brahmins are called Somapas; of Kṣatriyas, Havirbhujs; of Vaiśyas, Ājyapas; and of Śūdras, Sukālins. 198 Somapas are the sons of Kavi; Haviṣmats, the sons of Aṅgiras; Ājyapas, the sons of Pulastya; and Sukālins, the sons of Vasiṣṭha. 199 Anagnidagdhas, Agnidagdhas, Kāvyas, Barhiṣads, Agniṣvāttas, and Saumyas—these should be regarded as the ancestors only of Brahmins. 200 It should be understood, however, that these principal classes of ancestors we have enumerated have also here countless sons and grandsons.

201 From the seers were born the ancestors; from the ancestors, the gods and demons; and from the gods, the whole world, the mobile and the immobile, in due order.

202 Even some water offered to them with a generous spirit* using vessels made of silver or inlaid with silver leads to an imperishable reward.

Preparatory Rites 203 Ancestral offerings are far more significant for twice-born persons than divine offerings; for, according to tradition, a divine offering is a preliminary rite confering vigour upon the ancestral offering. 204 He should perform at the outset an offering to gods, which provides protection to ancestral rites; for fiends plunder an ancestral offering lacking such protection. 205 He should seek to begin and end an ancestral offering with offerings to gods; it should never begin or end with offerings to ancestors. Should he, instead, seek to begin or end with offerings to ancestors, he will quickly come to ruin together with his offspring.

206 He should daub a clean and secluded area with cow dung and carefully make that area slope towards the south; 207 ancestors are always gratified by offerings made in places that are clean, secluded, in the open, and by the water's edge.

[208]On separate seats properly arranged and spread with sacred grass, he should seat the Brahmins after they have sipped water. [209]After seating those irreproachable Brahmins on their seats, he should honour them with fragrant perfumes and garlands, beginning with the ones associated with the divine offering.

[210]Having brought water and sesame seeds along with purificatory Kuśa blades for them, the Brahmin should make an offering in the sacred fire with the collective consent of those Brahmins. [211]At the outset he should offer to Agni, Soma, and Yama oblations that confer vigour, and then satisfy the ancestors by offering them sacrificial food according to rule. [212]If a sacred fire is not available, however, he should offer the oblation simply in the hand of a Brahmin; for Brahmins who have seen the vedic formulas declare that the sacred fire is a twice-born.

[213]They call these highest of twice-born men the ancient gods of the ancestral offering, free from anger, totally serene, and devoted to invigorating the world.

Principal Offerings [214]He should perform in the fire the entire series of rites so that they end in the south;* pour water on the ground with his right hand; [215]make three balls from the remainder of the sacrificial food with a collected mind; face the south and lay them down following the same procedure as at the pouring of water; [216]offer those balls in accordance with the rules, while keeping himself ritually pure; wipe his hand on those blades of sacred grass as the share of those who partake of leavings;* [217]sip some water; turn around towards the north; control his breath slowly three times; worship the six seasons and the ancestors while reciting ritual formulas; [218]once again pour the remaining water gently near the balls; smell those balls with a collected mind in the order they were laid down; [219]remove a small portion from each ball in the proper order; and get those seated Brahmins to eat them first according to rule.

[220]If his father is alive, however, he should lay down the balls only for the preceding ancestors; or he may get his own father to eat the ancestral offering like one of the Brahmins.* [221]If his father is dead but his grandfather is alive, on the other hand, he should first recite his father's name and then his great-grandfather's. [222]Manu has declared that either his grandfather may eat that ancestral offering or he may freely perform it on his own with his grandfather's permission.

[223] After pouring water mixed with sesame seeds along with purificatory Kuśa blades into their hands, he should offer a piece of those balls to each, saying, 'Svadhā be to them!'

Feeding the Brahmins [224] Carrying with both his hands and by himself the vessel heaped with food, he should set it down gently in front of the Brahmins while thinking of his ancestors. [225] When food is brought without being held with both hands, evil-minded demons forcibly snatch it away. [226] Keeping himself ritually pure and with a collected mind, he should set down on the ground properly the side dishes, such as sauces and vegetables; milk, curd, ghee, and honey; [227] various kinds of foods and delicacies; roots and fruits; and delicious meats and fragrant drinks.

[228] After bringing all these, he should dish them out gradually with a collected mind and keeping himself ritually pure, pressing all the side dishes on them. [229] He must never shed a tear, become angry, tell a lie, touch the food with his foot, or flip it around. [230] A tear makes the food go to ghosts;* anger, to enemies; a lie, to dogs; touching with the foot, to fiends; and flipping around, to evil-doers.

[231] He should give ungrudgingly anything that the Brahmins may wish. He should narrate vedic disputations; it is pleasing to the ancestors. [232] At a rite for ancestors, he should make them listen to recitations of the Veda, legal treatises, stories, epic narratives, Purāṇas, and ancillary texts.* [233] He should cheerfully gratify the Brahmins and feed them at a leisurely pace, pressing on them repeatedly the main and the side dishes.

[234] He should diligently feed a son of his daughter at an ancestral offering, even if he is only a vedic student; place a goat's wool blanket on each seat; and scatter sesame seeds on the ground. [235] At an ancestral offering, three things confer purity: daughter's son, goat-wool blanket, and sesame seeds; and three things are commended: purification, absence of anger, and doing things unhurriedly. [236] All the food should be very warm, and they should eat it in silence; and even when the donor enquires about it, the Brahmins should not comment on the quality of the sacrificial food. [237] As long as the food is warm, as long as they eat it in silence, and as long as they do not comment on the quality of the sacrificial food, the ancestors partake of it. [238] What is eaten wearing a turban on the head, what is eaten facing the south, or what is eaten wearing sandals, is undoubtedly eaten by fiends.

[239] A Cāṇḍāla, a pig, a cock, a dog, a menstruating woman, or a eunuch must not look at the Brahmins while they are eating. [240] What is seen by any of these during a fire offering, the giving of a gift, a ritual feeding, or a divine or ancestral oblation, becomes inefficacious. [241] A pig spoils with its breath, a cock with the waft from its wings, a dog with its gaze, and a low-caste man with his touch. [242] If someone is lame or one-eyed, lacks a limb, or has an excess limb, he should also be removed from that place, even if he is a servant of the donor.

[243] Should a Brahmin or a mendicant come there for food, he should honour him according to his ability with the permission of those Brahmins.

[244] Mixing all the varieties of food together, he should drench it with water and deposit it in front of the diners after they have finished their meal, scattering it on the ground. [245] The remnants of food and what has been scattered on the sacred grass are the share of those who have died before their initiation or committed suicide, and of young women of the family. [246] The fragments fallen on the ground at an ancestral offering are declared to be the share of all the deceased servants who have not been dishonest or crooked.

Rite for the Newly Deceased [247] For a deceased twice-born, he should perform the rite without the Sapiṇḍa* offerings; omitting the offering to gods, he should feed the ancestral offering to one person and lay down one rice ball. [248] Once the rite of Sapiṇḍa has been performed for him in accordance with the Law, his sons should offer the balls exactly in the above manner.*

Conclusion of the Meal [249] After eating an ancestral offering, if someone gives his leftovers to a Śūdra, that foolish man will fall down head first into the Kālasūtra hell. [250] If a man who has eaten an ancestral offering gets into bed with a Śūdra woman that day, his ancestors will lie in her faeces during that month.

[251] He should ask them 'Have you eaten well?'; when they are sated, he should give them water for sipping; and when they have sipped water, he should give them leave to go, saying 'Please, stay around!'* [252] Immediately thereafter, the Brahmins should simply say to him: 'May there be Svadhā!', for the exclamation 'Svadhā' is the highest benediction in all ancestral offerings.

[253] Then, after they have finished eating, he should inform those

Brahmins of the leftover food and, with their permission, do exactly as they instruct.

[254] At an offering to ancestors, one should say, 'Have you eaten well?'; at a cow-pen offering,* 'Was it well cooked?'; at an offering for prosperity,* 'Was it delicious?'; and at a divine offering, 'Was it tasty?'

[255] The afternoon, Darbha grass, proper preparation of the location, sesame seeds, liberal outlay, proper preparation of food, and excellent twice-born men—these are what ensures success at ancestral rites. [256] Darbha grass, purifier, forenoon, sacrificial foods of every kind, purifier, and what was stated above—these should be regarded as what ensures success at divine rites. [257] Food of sages,* milk, Soma, meat, food without elaborate preparation, and natural salt are, by their very nature, called 'sacrificial food'.

Concluding Rites [258] After he has dismissed those Brahmins, he should make himself pure and collected, control his speech, turn towards the south, and implore his ancestors for these favours: [259] 'May donors amidst us thrive, may the Vedas and progeny! May the generous spirit never abandon us! And may we have a lot to give!'

[260] Immediately after he has laid down the balls in this manner, he should feed them to a cow, a Brahmin, a goat, or the fire, or else throw them in water. [261] Some perform the laying down of the balls towards the east; others feed them to birds or throw them in fire or water.

[262] The wife who is wedded according to the Law, devoted to her husband, and intent on worshipping the ancestors may eat the middlemost of those balls in the proper manner, if she wants to have a son. [263] She will give birth to a son endowed with long life, fame, intelligence, wealth, progeny, righteousness, and goodness.

[264] After he has washed his hands and sipped some water, he should prepare food for his paternal relatives; give that well-garnished food to his paternal relatives; honour also his maternal relatives; [265] let the scattered fragments remain until the Brahmins have been dismissed; and then perform the domestic Bali offering—that is the settled Law.

Food at Ancestral Rites [266] I will explain exhaustively the types of sacrificial food that are efficacious for a long time and those that are efficacious in perpetuity, when they are offered to the ancestors according to rule.

[267] By offering sesame seeds, rice, barley, beans, water, roots, and fruits according to rule, ancestors of men rejoice for one month; [268] by offering fish, for two months; by offering the meat of the common deer, for three months; by offering sheep meat, for four months; by offering here the meat of birds, for five months; [269] by offering goat meat, for six months; by offering the meat of the spotted deer, for seven months; by offering the meat of the Eṇa antelope, for eight months; by offering the meat of the Ruru deer, for nine months; [270] by offering boar or buffalo meat, they are satisfied for ten months; by offering rabbit or turtle meat, for eleven months; [271] and by offering beef, milk, or milk-rice, for one year. The satisfaction from the meat of a Vārdhrīṇasa horn-bill lasts for twelve years. [272] The Kālaśāka herb, the Mahāśalka crustacean, the meat of the rhinoceros and the red goat, and honey, as well as every type of sage's food (3.257 n.) are efficacious in perpetuity.

Times for Ancestral Rites [273] When someone mixes any kind of food with honey and offers it on the thirteenth day of a fortnight during the rainy season and under the Magha* constellation, that also is clearly inexhaustible. [274] 'Would that a man be born in our family who would offer us milk-rice with honey and ghee on the thirteenth day during the elephant's eastern shadow.'* [275] Whatever a man gives properly, with a generous spirit, and according to rule, in the other world it becomes eternal and inexhaustible for his ancestors.

[276] The lunar days in the dark fortnight beginning with the tenth but excluding the fourteenth are commended for ancestral offerings; the other days are unlike these. [277] As the later fortnight is better for an ancestral offering than the earlier fortnight,* so the afternoon is better than the forenoon. [278] When a man performs them on even days and constellations, he obtains all his wishes; whereas when he worships the ancestors on uneven days and constellations, he obtains distinguished children.

[279] He should carry out the ancestral offering tirelessly, correctly, and according to rule until its completion, wearing the sacrificial cord over the right shoulder and under the left arm, carrying blades of Darbha grass in his hand, and performing each rite so as to end in the south (3.214 n.). [280] He must not perform an ancestral offering at night—for the night belongs to fiends—or during the two twilights, or soon after sunrise.

[281] Following this procedure, he should perform here an ancestral offering three times a year—in the winter, in the summer, and in the rainy season—but the five sacrifices, every day.

[282] The rule is that the fire oblation at an ancestral rite must not be offered in the ordinary fire. A twice-born man who maintains the three sacred fires shall not perform an ancestral offering except on a new-moon day. [283] Even if a Brahmin simply satiates his ancestors with water after he has bathed, he obtains thereby the full reward of performing an ancestral rite.

[284] The fathers, they say, are the Vasus; the grandfathers are the Rudras; and the great-grandfathers are the Ādityas—this is an ancient scriptural statement.

Conclusion

[285] He should become a man who always eats 'residue' and who always partakes of 'ambrosia'. 'Residue' is what remains after people have eaten, and 'ambrosia' is the leftovers of a sacrifice.

> [286] I have explained to you all the rules relating to the five sacrifices. Listen now to the rules relating to the livelihood of Brahmins.

CHAPTER FOUR

THE BATH-GRADUATE

[1] After spending the first quarter of his life at his teacher's, a twice-born man should marry a wife and spend the second quarter of his life at home.*

Right Livelihood

[2] Except during a time of adversity, a Brahmin ought to sustain himself by following a livelihood that causes little or no harm to creatures. [3] He should gather wealth just sufficient for his subsistence through irreproachable activities that are specific to him, without fatiguing his body.

[4] Let him sustain himself by means of 'true' and 'immortal', or by means of 'mortal' and 'fatal', or even by means of 'truth-cum-falsehood'; but under no circumstances by means of the 'dog's life'. [5] Gleaning and picking* should be considered the 'true'; what is received unasked is the 'immortal'; almsfood that is begged is the 'mortal'; and agriculture, tradition says, is the 'fatal'. [6] Trade is the 'truth-cum-falsehood', and he may sustain himself even by that. Service is called the 'dog's life'; therefore, he should avoid it altogether.

[7] Let him be a man who stores grain sufficient to fill a granary, a man who stores grain sufficient to fill a jar,* a man who has sufficient grain to last three days, or a man who keeps nothing for the next day. [8] Among all these four types of twice-born householders, each should be recognized as superior to the ones preceding it and better at winning the heavenly world, according to the Law. [9] One of these may engage in the six activities; another may live by three; yet another by two; and a fourth may subsist through the sacrificial session of the Veda.* [10] A man who lives by gleaning and picking should be totally dedicated to the daily fire sacrifice and always offer only the sacrifices at the new- and full-moon days and at the solstices. [11] He must never follow a worldly occupation for the sake of livelihood, but subsist by means of a pure, upright, and honest livelihood proper to a Brahmin.

[12] One who seeks happiness should become supremely content and self-controlled, for happiness is rooted in contentment and its opposite is the root of unhappiness.

Observances

[13] Subsisting by one of these means of livelihood, a twice-born who is a bath-graduate should follow these observances, which procure heaven, long life, and fame.

[14] He should perform diligently the daily rituals specific to him prescribed in the Veda; for, by performing them according to his ability, he attains the highest state. [15] He must never seek to obtain wealth (*artha*) with excessive passion, through forbidden activities, when he already has sufficient wealth, or from just anyone even in a time of adversity; [16] nor shall he be passionately attached to any of the sensory objects (*artha*) out of lust, but using his mind he should stamp out any excessive attachment to them. [17] He should forsake all pursuits (*artha*) that interfere with his vedic recitation, eking out a living some way or other, for that recitation constitutes the fulfilment of all his obligations. [18] He should comport himself here in such a way that his attire, speech, and mind are in harmony with his age, occupation, wealth (*artha*), learning, and family background.

Study

[19] Every day, he should explore the treatises*—those that aid in the quick development of one's mind, those that facilitate the acquisition of wealth, and those that promote well-being—as well as ancillary texts* of the Veda; [20] for, the more a man studies treatises, the more he comes to understand and the more brightly shines his understanding.

Ritual Duties

[21] He must never fail to offer every day and according to his ability the sacrifices to seers, gods, beings, humans, and ancestors.

[22] Some individuals who are experts in the sacrificial science and free from striving offer these great sacrifices incessantly in just their organs. [23] Others offer breath in speech and speech in breath every

day, recognizing that the sacrifice reaches its inexhaustible consummation in speech and breath. [24] Still other Brahmins offer these sacrifices daily through knowledge alone, recognizing by the eye of knowledge that the execution of those sacrifices is rooted in knowledge.*

[25] A twice-born man, moreover, should always offer the fire sacrifice at the beginning and end of each day and night; the new-moon and the full-moon sacrifice at the end of each fortnight; [26] the new-harvest sacrifice at the end of each harvest; the seasonal sacrifices at the end of each season; an animal sacrifice at the end of each half-year; and Soma sacrifices at the end of each year. [27] A twice-born who has established the sacred fires, if he wants to live a long life, must never eat a new crop without offering the new-harvest sacrifice, or meat without offering an animal sacrifice; [28] for his sacred fires crave for the new crop and meat and, if they have not been honoured with an offering of the new crop and an animal oblation, yearn to eat his very lifebreaths.

Reception of Guests

[29] No guest should stay at his house without being honoured with a seat, food, and a bed, or with water, roots, and fruits, according to his ability. [30] He must never honour the following even with a word of welcome: ascetics of heretical sects; individuals engaging in improper activities, observing the 'cat vow', or following the way of herons (4.195–6); hypocrites; and sophists. [31] At rites for gods and ancestors, he should honour individuals who have bathed after completing the Vedas, vedic learning, or vedic vows,* who are vedic scholars, or who are householders, but avoid individuals different from these. [32] As far as he is able, a householder should give to those who do not cook* and share with all beings without causing hardship to himself.

Rules of Conduct: I

[33] If a bath-graduate is tormented by hunger, he may request money from the king, from a client at whose sacrifices he officiates, or from a resident pupil, but from no one else—that is the settled rule. [34] If he has the capacity, a Brahmin bath-graduate should never torment

himself with hunger or, if he has the means, wear dirty or worn-out clothes.

[35] He shall keep his nails clipped, his hair and beard trimmed, and himself restrained; wear white clothes; remain pure; and apply himself every day to his vedic recitation and to activities conducive to his own welfare. [36] He shall carry a bamboo staff, a waterpot filled with water, and a broom of sacred grass, and wear a sacrificial cord and a pair of bright gold earrings.

[37] He must never look at the sun as it rises or sets, when it is eclipsed or reflected in water, or when it is in the middle of the sky. [38] He must not step over a rope to which a calf is tied, run in the rain, or look at his reflection in water—that is the fixed rule. [39] A mound of earth,* a cow, a god, a Brahmin, ghee, honey, and a crossroads—he should circumambulate these clockwise, as also notable trees.

Relationship with Women

[40] Though aroused, he must never have sex with his wife after the onset of her menstrual period, or even lie on the same bed with her; [41] for when a man has sex with a woman besmirched with menstrual blood, his wisdom, energy, strength, sight, and life-force waste away. [42] When he avoids a woman besmirched with menstrual blood, his wisdom, energy, strength, sight, and life-force will wax stronger.

[43] He must never eat with his wife or look at her while she is eating, sneezing, yawning, or seated at ease; [44] nor should the Brahmin, if he wants energy, look at her while she is applying collyrium to her eyes or oil on her body, or when she is undressed or giving birth.

Voiding Urine and Excrement

[45] He must never eat food wearing just a single garment; bathe naked; or urinate on a road, on ashes, in a cow pen, [46] on ploughed land, into water, onto a mound or a hill, in a dilapidated temple, onto an anthill, [47] into occupied animal holes, while walking or standing, by a river bank, or at the top of a hill. [48] He must never void urine or excrement facing the wind, a fire, a Brahmin, the sun, water, or cows.

[49] Restraining his voice, remaining steadfastly attentive, covering his body, and wrapping his head, he should ease himself after strewing the ground with sticks, clods, leaves, or grass. [50] During the day,

he should void urine and excrement facing the north, at night facing the south, and at the two twilights in the same way as during the day. [51] Under a shadow or in a place that is pitch-dark, a Brahmin may do so during the day or at night facing any direction he pleases, as also when he fears for his life.

[52] When someone urinates towards a fire, the sun, the moon, water, a twice-born man, a cow, or the wind, his wisdom perishes.

Rules of Conduct: II

[53] He must never blow on a fire with his mouth; look at a woman when she is naked; throw anything filthy into a fire; warm his feet over it; [54] place it under his bed; step over it; place it by his feet; hurt living creatures; [55] eat, travel, or sleep during the time of twilight; scribble on the ground; take off his own garland;* [56] deposit urine, excrement, sputum, blood, poison, or anything smeared with filth in water; [57] sleep alone in an abandoned house; awaken a sleeping superior;* speak with a menstruating woman; or go to a sacrifice uninvited.

[58] Within an enclosure for the sacred fire, in a cow pen, in the presence of Brahmins, during his vedic recitation, and while eating, he shall keep his right arm uncovered (2.193 n.). [59] He must never prevent a cow from suckling her calf or report it to anyone. When he sees a rainbow in the sky, he should wisely refrain from pointing it out to anyone.

[60] He must never reside in a village full of unrighteous people or where diseases run rampant; go on a journey alone; stay long on a mountain; [61] or live in a kingdom ruled by a Śūdra, teeming with unrighteous people, overrun by people belonging to heretical ascetic sects, or swamped by lowest-born people.

[62] He must never eat anything from which the oil has been extracted; eat beyond capacity; eat very early in the morning or very late in the evening; eat again in the evening after taking his meal in the morning; [63] undertake useless activities; drink water from his cupped hands; eat food placed on his lap; be in any way inquisitive; [64] dance; sing; play a musical instrument; clap; whistle; make noises when sexually excited; [65] wash his feet in a brass vessel at any time; eat from a broken plate or from one that looks repulsive to him; [66] or use footwear, a garment, a sacrificial cord, an ornament, a garland, or a waterpot previously used by others.

[67] He must never travel with draught animals that are untrained, hungry, or sick, or that have broken horns, bad eyes, damaged hoofs, or deformed tails. [68] He should always travel with ones that are well trained and swift and possess good marks, colour, and appearance, without driving them too hard with the whip.

[69] He should avoid the morning sun, the smoke from a funeral pyre, and broken seats. He must never cut his nails or hair;* bite off his nails with his teeth; [70] crush clods of earth; tear off grass with his fingernails; or engage in activities that are fruitless or have unpleasant future consequences. [71] A man who crushes clods, tears off grass, or bites his nails will quickly come to ruin, as also an informant and one who neglects purifications.

[72] He must never engage in a combative discussion or wear a garland outdoors.* Riding on the back of cattle is altogether reprehensible. [73] He must not enter an enclosed village or house by any passage other than the door; and at night, he should keep far away from the foot of any tree.

[74] He must never play with dice; fetch his sandals by himself; eat while lying in bed; eat anything placed in his hand or on a seat; [75] eat anything containing sesame after sunset; sleep here naked; or go anywhere while he is sullied with remnants (2.56 n.). [76] He should eat with his feet wet, but never go to sleep with wet feet; by eating with wet feet, he obtains a long life.

[77] He must never enter a place difficult of access and hidden from sight; look at urine or excrement; cross a river swimming; [78] or, if he wishes to live long, step on hair, ash, bones, shards, cotton seeds, or chaff.

[79] He must never live in the company of outcastes, Cāṇḍālas, Pulkasas, fools, arrogant men, lowest-born people, or Antyāvasāyins. [80] He must never give a Śūdra advice, leftovers, or anything offered to the gods; teach him the Law; or prescribe an observance to him. [81] Whoever teaches him the Law or whoever prescribes an observance to him will plunge along with him into that darkness called Asaṃvṛta.

[82] He must never scratch his head with both hands together; touch his head while he is sullied with remnants (2.56 n.); or take a bath excluding the head. [83] He should refrain from pulling the hair or striking the head;* and after taking a bath including the head, he should not apply oil to any part of his body.

People from Whom Gifts May Not Be Accepted

84 He must never accept gifts from a king who is not from a royal lineage; from people who operate abattoirs, oil-presses, or taverns; or from people who gain their living by keeping brothels. 85 One oil-press equals ten abattoirs; one tavern equals ten oil-presses; one brothel equals ten taverns; and one king equals ten brothels. 86 A king, tradition tells us, is equal to a butcher who operates ten thousand abattoirs; to accept a gift from him is a horrendous deed.

87 When someone accepts a gift from a king who is greedy and who deviates from the provisions of the authoritative texts, he will go in turn to these twenty hells: 88 Tāmisra, Andha-Tāmisra, Mahā-Raurava, Raurava, Kālasūtra-Naraka, Mahā-Naraka, 89 Saṃjīvana, Mahā-Vīci, Tapana, Saṃpratāpana, Saṃghāta, Sakākola, Kuḍmala, Pūtimṛttika, 90 Lohaśaṅku, Ṛjīṣa, Pathin, Sālmalī, Nadī, Asipatravana, and Lohacāraka.

91 Knowing this and yearning for well-being after death, Brahmins who are learned and vedic savants do not accept gifts from a king.

Morning Duties

92 He should wake up at the time sacred to Brahman* and reflect on matters relating to Law and Wealth, on the bodily discomforts they cause, and on the true meaning of the Veda.

93 After getting up and answering the call of nature, he should perform the purifications and, with a collected mind, stand for a long time engaged in soft recitation during the morning twilight and, at its proper time, also during the evening twilight (2.101–3). 94 Because they performed their twilight devotions for a long time, the seers obtained long life, wisdom, fame, renown, and eminence in vedic knowledge.

Vedic Study

95 On the full-moon day of Śrāvaṇa (July–August) or Prauṣṭhapada (August–September), a Brahmin should commence his annual course of study according to rule and intently study the Vedas for four and a half months. 96 In the forenoon of the first day of the bright fortnight of either Puṣya (December–January) or Māgha

(January–February), a twice-born should perform the rite of terminating his vedic study outside the village.

[97] After performing in this manner the rite of terminating his vedic study outside the village in accordance with the authoritative texts, he should suspend recitation for two days and the intervening night, or just during that single day and night. [98] After that time, however, he should recite the Vedas intently during the bright fortnights and all the Vedic Supplements (2.105 n.) during the dark fortnights.

[99] He must never recite indistinctly or in the presence of Śūdras. After reciting the Veda during the last part of the night, he must not go back to sleep even if he is worn out. [100] In accordance with the aforementioned rule, he must recite the metrical sections of the Veda every day; outside a time of adversity, a twice-born must intently recite both the metrical sections of the Veda and the Brāhmaṇas.

Suspension of Vedic Recitation

[101] Anyone engaged in vedic recitation should always abstain on the following occasions when vedic recitation is to be suspended, as also should anyone engaged in teaching vedic recitation to students in the prescribed manner.

[102] When the wind becomes audible at night or kicks up the dust during the day—experts in recitation regard these as two occasions for suspending vedic recitation during the rainy season. [103] When there is lightning, thunder, and rain,* and when there is a shower of large meteors, Manu has enjoined the suspension of vedic recitation until the same time the following day. [104] It should be noted that vedic recitation is to be suspended only when these occur after the fires have been kindled, and also when clouds appear out of season. [105] When a noise erupts in the sky, when there is an earthquake, or when halos surround the heavenly lights—even if these happen in season—one should know that vedic recitation is to be suspended until the same time the following day. [106] When lightning and the rumbling of thunder occur after the fires have been kindled, however, the suspension of recitation lasts as long as the heavenly lights are visible; if the other event also occurs, then the recitation is suspended at night as during the day.*

[107] Those who want to adhere strictly to the Law should suspend vedic recitation permanently in villages and towns and wherever

there is a foul smell. [108] Vedic recitation is to be suspended in a village where there is a corpse, in the presence of a Śūdra, at the sound of weeping, and near a gathering of people.

[109] In water, in the middle of the night, after voiding urine or excrement, when he is sullied with remnants (2.56 n.), or after he has eaten an ancestral offering, a man should not even review it in his mind. [110] After accepting an invitation to an offering on behalf of a newly deceased person, a learned twice-born should not recite the Veda for three days, as also during the period of birth-impurity (5.58 f.) affecting the king and during an eclipse. [111] As long as the smell and stain of an offering on behalf of a newly deceased person lingers on the body of a learned Brahmin, he should not recite the Veda.

[112] He must not recite the Veda lying down, putting his feet up, or squatting with a band tied around his waist and knees;* after eating meat; after eating any food given by someone in a period of birth-impurity (5.58 ff.); [113] when there is fog; at the sound of arrows; during both twilights; on the new-moon day; on the fourteenth day of a fortnight; on the full-moon day; and on the eighth day of a fortnight. [114] The new-moon day destroys the teacher; the fourteenth day destroys the pupil; and the eighth and full-moon days destroy the Veda. Therefore, he should avoid them altogether.

[115] A twice-born must not recite during a dust storm, when the horizons have turned crimson, at the howling of jackals or the cry of dogs, donkeys, and camels, and when he is seated in a row.

[116] He must never recite the Veda near a cemetery, in the outskirts of a village, in a cow pen, wearing the same clothes he had on during sexual intercourse, or after accepting something at an ancestral offering. [117] After accepting anything at all, whether animate or inanimate, given at an ancestral offering, he should suspend vedic recitation; for the hand of a twice-born, tradition tells us, is his mouth.

[118] After robbers have raided the village, after a turmoil caused by fire, and after anything out of the ordinary has happened, he should know that vedic recitation is to be suspended until the same time the following day.

[119] The suspension, tradition tells us, lasts for three nights both after commencing and after concluding the annual course of study; for a day and a night, however, on the eighth day of a fortnight and on the final night of every season.

[120] He must never recite the Veda while he is on a horse, tree, elephant, donkey, or camel; in a ship or vehicle; on arid land; [121] during an altercation or a brawl; in the midst of a military unit or a battle; soon after eating; when he has indigestion; after vomiting or having an acidic belch; [122] without obtaining the consent of any guest of his; when there is a strong wind; when blood is flowing from his body; or when he has been wounded by a weapon.

[123] He must never recite Ṛc-verses or Yajus-formulas within earshot of Sāman chanting, after reciting the conclusion of a Veda,* and after reciting an Āraṇyaka. [124] The Ṛgveda is connected with the gods and the Yajurveda with humans; but the Sāmaveda, tradition tells us, is connected with ancestors. Its sound, therefore, is impure. [125] Knowing this, learned men recite first the extract of the triple Veda daily and in the proper order and then the Veda.*

[126] When a farm animal, frog, cat, dog, snake, mongoose, or rat passes in between,* he should know that vedic recitation is to be suspended for a day and a night.

[127] These alone are the two occasions for suspending vedic recitation which a twice-born should diligently avoid every day: when his place of recitation has not been cleansed and when his body has not been purified.*

Rules of Conduct: III

[128] The new-moon day, the eighth day of a fortnight, the full-moon day, and the fourteenth day of a fortnight—on these days, a twice-born who is a bath-graduate should always remain chaste, even if his wife is in her season (3.46–50).

[129] He must never take a bath after eating, when he is sick, in the dead of the night, regularly with his clothes on,* or in an unknown body of water.

[130] He must never tread deliberately on the shadow of these: god,* elder, king, bath-graduate, teacher, reddish-brown cow, and a man consecrated for a sacrifice. [131] At midday and midnight, after eating an ancestral offering containing meat, and during both twilights, he should not tarry at a crossroads. [132] He must not step deliberately on used bath-powders, water from a bath, urine, excrement, blood, phlegm, spittle, or vomit.

[133] He must not consort with an enemy, a friend of an enemy, an

unrighteous person, or a thief—as also with another man's wife; [134] for there is nothing in this world as sure to shorten a man's life as consorting with someone else's wife. [135] A Kṣatriya, a snake, and a learned Brahmin—however feeble these may be, he must never treat them with contempt, if he wants to prosper; [136] for when a man treats these three persons with contempt, they will reduce him to ashes. A wise man, therefore, should not treat these three with contempt. [137] He must not hold himself in contempt for his past failures; he should pursue prosperity until death, never deeming it too difficult to achieve.

[138] He should say what is true, and he should say what is pleasant; he should not say what is true but unpleasant, and he should not say what is pleasant but untrue—that is the eternal Law. [139] He should call a lucky thing 'Lucky'; or rather he should call everything 'Lucky'.* He should never start a senseless feud or an argument with anyone.

[140] He must never travel very early in the morning, very late in the evening, at high noon, with an unknown person, alone, or with Śūdras.

[141] He must not ridicule people who have too few or too many limbs, who are uneducated, who are very old, who lack beauty or wealth, or who are of low birth.

[142] When a Brahmin is sullied with remnants (2.56n.), he must never touch with his hand a cow, a Brahmin, or a fire; nor, if he is healthy, should he look at the heavenly lights in the sky while he is impure. [143] If he touches any of these while he is impure, he should always touch his organs and all his limbs with water, and his navel with his palm. [144] Unless he is sick, he must not touch his orifices without a good reason, and he should refrain from touching the hair on any of his private parts.

[145] He should apply himself to auspicious rites and good conduct, control himself, subdue his senses, and tirelessly perform soft recitations and fire offerings every day. [146] No misfortune befalls those who apply themselves to auspicious rites and good conduct, control themselves every day, and perform soft recitations and fire offerings. [147] It is the soft recitation of the Veda that he should tirelessly perform every day at the proper time—for this is his highest Law, they say; others are called secondary Laws. [148] By reciting the Veda constantly, by performing purifications, by engaging in ascetic toil, and by

showing no hostility to any creature, he gets to remember his former birth. [149] When, while recalling his former birth, a twice-born recites the Veda, by that constant recitation of the Veda, he obtains unending bliss. [150] He should always make Sāvitra and pacificatory offerings on the days of the moon's change (3.45 n.) and always worship the ancestors on the eighth and the day following the eighth of each fortnight.

[151] Urine, water from washing the feet, remnants of food, and dirty water—he should dispose of all these far away from his house. [152] Voiding excrement, adorning oneself, bathing, brushing the teeth, applying collyrium, and the worship of gods—all these should be done only in the morning.

[153] He should visit gods and righteous Brahmins; the ruler, for the sake of protection; and elders on the days of the moon's change (3.45 n.). [154] He should greet elderly persons, offer them his seat, pay them obeisance with joined palms, and follow behind them as they leave (3.107 n.).

[155] He should tirelessly follow the root of the Law, namely, the conduct of good people, which is well set forth in scripture and tradition and is closely tied to the activities proper to him— [156] for by good conduct he obtains long life; by good conduct he obtains the kind of offspring he desires; by good conduct he obtains inexhaustible wealth; and good conduct neutralizes unlucky marks.* [157] A man of evil conduct becomes an object of reproach in the world, is always miserable, is afflicted with disease, and lives a very short life. [158] Even if he has no lucky marks at all, a man who follows the conduct of good people, who has a generous spirit (3.202 n.), and who is free from resentment, lives a hundred years.

[159] He should carefully avoid all activities that are under someone else's control, and diligently pursue those that are under his own control. [160] Whatever is under someone else's control—that is suffering; whatever is under one's own control—that is happiness. He should know that this, in a nutshell, is the definition of suffering and happiness. [161] He should diligently engage in those activities that give him inner joy and avoid those that do not.

Avoiding Violence

[162] He must never cause harm to his teacher, instructor, father, mother, elder, Brahmins, cows, and all who are given to austerities.

[163] He should eschew infidelity, denigrating the Vedas, disparaging the gods, hatred, arrogance, pride, anger, and harshness.

[164] He must not raise a stick against another person or bring it down on anyone in anger, except a son or a pupil; these he may beat in order to discipline them (8.299). [165] If a twice-born merely threatens a Brahmin with murderous intent, he will meander in the Tāmisra hell for one hundred years. [166] If he strikes him deliberately in anger with even a blade of grass, he will be reborn in evil wombs for twenty-one births. [167] If a man foolishly draws blood from the body of a Brahmin who is not attacking him, he will experience intense suffering after death. [168] A man who draws blood will be eaten by others in the next world for as many years as the number of dust particles from the earth that the spilled blood lumps together.

[169] A wise man, therefore, must never threaten a twice-born person, strike him even with a blade of grass, or draw blood from his body.

Following the Path of Righteousness

[170] A man who is unrighteous, who has gained his wealth dishonestly, and who always takes delight in causing injury will never achieve happiness in this world. [171] Even when he has been brought low as a result of his righteous conduct, let him never turn to unrighteous ways, seeing how quickly the fortunes of unrighteous and evil men are reversed.

[172] Like the earth,* practising unrighteousness does not produce instant results in this world; but turning around gradually, it cuts off its perpetrator by his roots. [173] If not himself, then his sons; if not his sons, then his grandsons—an unrighteous act once committed never fails to repay its perpetrator. [174] Through unrighteous ways a man first prospers; then he experiences good fortune; next he vanquishes his opponents; but in the end he is destroyed root* and all.

[175] He should always take delight in speaking the truth, in following the Law, in conforming to the Ārya ways, and in purifying himself. With his speech, hands, and stomach controlled, he should discipline his disciples according to the Law. [176] He should abandon any activity relating to Wealth or Pleasure that is in violation of Law, and even activities sanctioned by Law when they will result in future unhappiness or are repugnant to the world (2.224n.).

[177]He must never conduct himself in a fickle manner with his hands, feet, eyes, or speech; follow crooked ways; or show hostility to others in thought or deed. [178]The path trodden by his fathers, the path trodden by his grandfathers—let him tread along that path of good people; no harm will befall him when he travels by that path.

Family and Social Relations

[179]Officiating priests; family priests; teachers; maternal uncles; guests; dependants; children; the aged; the sick; doctors; paternal, affinal, and maternal relatives; [180]father; mother; sisters; brother; son; wife; daughter; and slaves—he should not get into arguments with any of these. [181]By forswearing arguments with them, he is freed from all sins; and when he is conquered by them, the householder conquers all these worlds.

[182]The teacher is the ruler of Brahman's world; the father, of Prajāpati's world; the guest, of Indra's world; the officiating priests, of the world of gods; [183]the sisters, of the world of Apsarases; maternal relatives, of the world of the Viśvedevas; affinal relatives, of the world of the waters; and the mother and maternal uncles, of the earth. [184]The children, the aged, the feeble, and the sick are to be regarded as the rulers of space. His older brother is equal to his father, and his wife and son are his own body. [185]His slaves are his own shadow, and his daughter is the object of supreme compassion. When he is assailed by any of these, therefore, he should always bear it without losing his temper.

Accepting and Giving Gifts

[186]Even if he is qualified to accept gifts, he should avoid becoming addicted to that practice, for by accepting gifts his vedic energy is quickly extinguished. [187]Without knowing the procedure prescribed by Law for accepting things, a wise man should never accept a gift even if he is racked by hunger.

[188]When an ignorant man accepts gold, land, a horse, a cow, food, clothes, sesame seeds, or ghee, he is reduced to ashes like a piece of wood. [189]Gold and food burn up his life-force; a cow and land, his body; a horse, his sight; clothes, his skin; ghee, his energy; and sesame seeds, his offspring. [190]When a twice-born neither engages in

ascetic toil nor recites the Veda and yet loves to receive gifts, he will sink along with the donor, as a man would sink in water along with his stone float.* 191 An ignorant man, therefore, should fear any kind of gift; for by accepting even a trifling gift, an ignorant man sinks like a cow in the mud.

192 A man who knows the Law should not give even water to a twice-born observing the 'cat-vow', to an evil man observing the 'heron-vow', or to one who does not know the Veda; 193 for an object of value given to any of these three, even if it has been acquired in accordance with the rules, affects both the giver and the receiver adversely after death. 194 As a man making a crossing with a stone float sinks in the water, so will the ignorant beseecher and the ignorant donor sink to the bottom.

Hypocrisy

195 A man who always displays the banner of righteousness and yet is greedy and deceitful, who deludes the world, who is given to violence, and who beguiles everybody should be viewed as one who observes the 'cat-vow'. 196 A twice-born who goes around with downcast eyes but is cruel, given to furthering his own ends, crooked, and being falsely sanctimonious, is a man who is observing the 'heron-vow'. 197 Brahmins who observe the 'heron-vow' and those who display the marks of a cat fall into the Andha-Tāmisra hell as a result of that evil act.

198 After committing a sin, he must never perform a penitential observance under the pretext that he is doing it as a meritorious act, thus covering up his sin with his observance and deceiving women and Śūdras. 199 Such Brahmins are denounced by vedic savants both here and in the hereafter, and that observance, carried out covertly, goes to the fiends.

200 When someone earns his livelihood by wearing the insignia of a religious profession* to which he does not belong, he takes upon himself the sins of those belonging to that religious profession and is reborn in the womb of an animal.

Using What Belongs to Others

201 He must never bathe in a reservoir that belongs to someone else. By doing so, he will be tainted with a portion of the evils committed

by the man who constructed that reservoir. [202]When a man uses someone's vehicle, bed, seat, well, garden, or house without permission, he gets a quarter of the owner's sins. [203]He should always bathe in rivers, natural ponds,* lakes, pools, and springs.

[204]A wise man should always practise the central virtues and not busy himself constantly with the secondary observances.* A man falls when he devotes himself to the secondary observances while neglecting the central virtues.

Unfit Food

[205]A Brahmin must never partake of food* at a sacrifice offered by someone who is not a vedic scholar or who officiates as a priest for a large number of people, or at one offered by a woman or an effeminate man (3.150n.). [206]When such persons offer an oblation, it is unpropitious for virtuous people and disagreeable to gods; therefore, he should avoid it.

[207]He must also never eat the following: food given by someone who is drunk, angry, or sick; food contaminated with hair or insects or touched deliberately with the foot; [208]food looked at by a murderer of a Brahmin,* touched by a menstruating woman, pecked by a bird, or touched by a dog; [209]food smelled by a cow; in a special way, food given after a public announcement; food given by a group or by a prostitute; food that is despised by learned men; [210]food given by a thief, a musician, a carpenter, a usurer, a man consecrated for a sacrifice, a miser, a prisoner, a shackled man, [211]a heinous sinner (2.185n.), a eunuch, a promiscuous woman, or a hypocrite; food that has turned sour or is stale; food of a Śūdra; leftovers (2.56n.); [212]food given by a physician, a hunter, a cruel man, someone who eats leftovers, or an Ugra; food of a woman impure by reason of childbirth; food served at a meal where someone sips water during the meal; food given during the ten days of impurity resulting from a birth; [213]food given without respect; meat procured capriciously (5.27); food given by a woman without a husband; food of an enemy, the chief of a town, or an outcaste; food someone has sneezed upon; [214]food given by a slanderer, a liar, a trafficker in rituals, an actor, a tailor, an ingrate, [215]a blacksmith, a Niṣāda, a theatrical performer, a goldsmith, a basket-weaver, an arms merchant, [216]those who raise dogs, liquor merchants, a washerman, a dyer, a heartless man, some-

one who lets his wife's paramour live in his house [217] or who condones a paramour, or someone who is bossed by his wife in every way; food of persons during the first ten days after a death in their family; food offered to a newly deceased person, and unappetizing food.

[218] The food of a king robs his energy; the food of a Śūdra, his eminence in vedic knowledge; the food of a goldsmith, his life-force; and the food of a leather-worker, his fame. [219] The food of an artisan destroys his offspring, and the food of a dyer, his strength. The food of a group or of a prostitute cuts him off from the worlds. [220] The food of a physician is pus; the food of a promiscuous woman is semen; the food of a usurer is excrement; and the food of an arms merchant is filth. [221] The food of those others who have been listed in order as people whose food is unfit to be eaten—the wise declare that to be skin, bones, and hair.

[222] If someone eats the food of any one of them unintentionally, he should fast for three days; if he eats intentionally—as also when he consumes semen, urine, or excrement—he should perform an arduous penance (11.212).

[223] A learned twice-born must never eat cooked food given by a Śūdra who lacks a spirit of generosity (3.202 n.). If he is without sustenance, he may accept from such a man only raw provisions sufficient for a single day.

[224] The gods once evaluated the food of a miserly vedic scholar and that of a generous usurer and pronounced the two to be equal. [225] Prajāpati came up to them and said, 'Don't make equal what is unequal. The food of the generous man is cleansed by the spirit of generosity, whereas the other food is defiled by the lack of generosity.'

Gifts and their Rewards

[226] He should tirelessly make sacrificial offerings and give gifts every day in a spirit of generosity; for, when done with a generous spirit and using justly earned wealth, they become inexhaustible. [227] Finding a suitable recipient, he should practise daily the Law of giving comprising sacrificial offerings and gifts, according to his ability and with a cheerful heart. [228] When he is asked, he should give ungrudgingly at least something, for one day he may encounter that special recipient who will rescue him from all.*

229 One who gives water obtains satiety; one who gives food, inexhaustible happiness; one who gives sesame seeds, the kind of offspring one desires; one who gives a lamp, the finest eyesight. 230 One who gives land, obtains land; one who gives gold, long life; one who gives a house, superb dwellings; one who gives silver (*rūpya*), peerless beauty (*rūpa*); 231 one who gives clothes, residence in the same world as the Moon; one who gives a horse (*aśva*), residence in the same world as the Aśvins; one who gives an ox, bounteous prosperity; one who gives a cow, the summit of the sun; 232 one who gives a vehicle or bed, a wife; one who gives security, lordship; one who gives grain, eternal happiness; and one who gives the Veda (*brahman*), equality with Brahman. 233 The gift of the Veda far exceeds every other gift, whether it is the gift of water, food, cows, land, clothes, sesame seeds, gold, or ghee.

234 With whatever disposition a man makes a particular gift, he will be received with honour and obtain that very thing with the very same disposition. 235 When due respect is shown in accepting and in giving a gift, both the receiver and the giver go to heaven; but when the opposite happens, both go to hell.

236 He must not flaunt his austerities, lie about a sacrifice* he has performed, revile Brahmins even though aggrieved, or brag about a gift he has given. 237 A sacrifice is lost by telling a lie about it, austerity by flaunting it, longevity by reviling Brahmins, and a gift by bragging about it.

Accumulating Merit

238 Gradually and without hurting any creature, he should pile up merit (*dharma*) like termites an anthill, so as to secure an escort in the next world; 239 for in the next world, neither father nor mother stands by him as his escort; nor does son, wife, or relative. Only merit stands by him. 240 Alone a creature is born, and alone it dies. Alone it enjoys the fruits of its good deeds, alone also the fruits of its evil deeds. 241 While his relatives discard the dead body on earth as if it were a piece of wood or a clod of earth and depart with averted faces, his merit accompanies him. 242 To secure an escort, therefore, let him gradually pile up merit every day; for with merit as his escort, he will cross over the darkness that is difficult to cross. 243 The escort quickly leads that man, who is devoted to the Law (*dharma*)

and whose sins have been erased by ascetic toil, to the next world, glittering with an ethereal body.

244 He should always build relationships with people of the highest possible rank and avoid anyone of a lower rank, if he wants to raise his family to a higher rank. 245 By going to people of the highest possible rank and by avoiding those who are lower, a Brahmin achieves distinction; by doing the opposite, he is reduced to the level of a Śūdra.

246 A man who adheres to these observances—a man who is resolute in his undertakings, who is gentle and controlled, and who does not associate with people of cruel conduct or cause harm to anyone—wins heaven by controlling himself and giving gifts.

Acceptance of Gifts and Food

247 Firewood, water, roots, fruits, food spontaneously given, honey, and the gift of freedom from fear (6.39 n.)—he may accept these from anyone. 248 Prajāpati has determined that almsfood that is brought and presented without being requested beforehand may be accepted even from a man of evil conduct. 249 If a man spurns such almsfood, his ancestors will not eat from him for fifteen years, and the sacred fire will not convey his offerings.

250 Bed, house, Kuśa grass, perfumes, water, flowers, gems, curd, grain, fish, milk, meat, or vegetables—these he should never reject. 251 He may accept a gift from anyone for the purpose of supporting his elders and dependants and honouring gods and guests; but he may not use it to gratify himself.

252 At a time when his elders have passed away or he is living at home without them and he is seeking a means of sustenance, he may always accept gifts from good people.

253 A sharecropper, a friend of the family, and one's cowherd, slave, and barber—among Śūdras, these are the ones whose food is fit to be eaten, as also a person who has presented himself.*

254 He should present himself accurately in all this: what sort of a person he is, what sort of work he wants to perform, and in what manner he will serve that person. 255 A man who misrepresents himself to good people is the worst sinner in the world; he is a thief, a man who steals his very self. 256 All things are founded on speech;

speech is their root; and from speech they proceed. A man who steals speech is guilty of stealing everything.

Old Age and Retirement

257 After he has freed himself according to rule from his debts* to the great seers, ancestors, and gods, he should hand over everything to his son and live in complete equanimity. 258 Living alone in a secluded place, he should always reflect on what is beneficial to himself; for, by reflecting alone, he attains supreme bliss.

> 259 I have explained above the invariable means of livelihood for a Brahmin householder, as also the splendid set of observances for a bath-graduate which enhances his spirit. 260 When a Brahmin, knowing the vedic teachings, follows this mode of life, he frees himself always from sins and is exalted in heaven.

CHAPTER FIVE

PROLOGUE

[1] After they had heard the Laws of a bath-graduate described in this manner, the seers said this to the noble-minded Bhṛgu born from the fire:* [2] 'How, O Lord, does Death prevail over Brahmins, who know the vedic teachings and follow the Law specific to them described in this manner?'

[3] Bhṛgu, the embodiment of the Law and the son of Manu, said to those great seers: 'Listen to the fault because of which Death seeks to kill Brahmins.'

FORBIDDEN FOOD

[4] Death seeks to kill Brahmins because of the failure to recite the Vedas, the dereliction of the rules of proper conduct, laziness, and faults with respect to food.

[5] Garlic, leeks, onions, and mushrooms are foods forbidden* to twice-born persons; and so is anything growing in an impure medium. [6] He should scrupulously eschew the following: the red sap of trees; juices flowing from incisions on trees; Śelu fruit; cow's colostrum; [7] Kṛsara porridge, Saṃyāva cake,* milk-rice, or cake prepared for no good reason; meat of an unconsecrated animal (5.27–57); food offered to deities; and sacrificial oblations.

[8] The milk of a cow within ten days after giving birth; milk of camels, single-hoofed animals, and sheep; milk of a cow that is in heat or has lost its calf; [9] milk of all wild animals except buffaloes; and milk of women—these he should eschew, as also anything that has turned sour. [10] Among foods turned sour, he may eat curd and all curd products, as well as the extracts of wholesome flowers, roots, and fruits.

[11] He should eschew all carnivorous birds, as also those that live in villages; single-hoofed animals, except those explicitly permitted;* plovers; [12] Kalaviṅka sparrows; Plava herons; Haṃsa geese; Cakra sheldrakes; village fowl; Sārasa cranes; Rajjuvāla fowl; Dātyūha waterfowl; parrots; mynahs; [13] birds that feed by pecking; web-footed

birds; Koyaṣṭhi cranes; birds that feed by scratching with their feet; birds that catch fish by diving; meat from a slaughter-house; dried meat; [14]Baka egrets; Balāka ibis; Kākola ravens; Khañjarīṭaka wagtails; fish eaters; village hogs; and every kind of fish.

[15]A man who eats the meat of some animal is called 'eater of that animal's meat', whereas a fish-eater is an 'eater of every animal's meat'. Therefore, he should eschew fish. [16]The Pāṭhīna and the Rohita fish may be eaten when they are used in an offering to gods or ancestors; Rājīva, Siṃhatuṇḍa, and Saśalka fish may be eaten at any time.

[17]He must never eat those that wander alone; unknown animals or birds, even if they are listed among those that are permitted; as also all animals with five nails.* [18]Among animals with five nails, they say, the porcupine, the hedgehog, the monitor lizard, the rhinoceros, the tortoise, and the rabbit may be eaten; as also animals with incisors in only one jaw,* with the exception of the camel.

[19]By eating mushrooms, a village hog, garlic, a village fowl, onion, or leek intentionally, a twice-born falls from his caste. [20]If he eats one of these six unwittingly, he shall perform the Sāntapana or the ascetics' lunar penance (11.213, 219). If he eats any of the others, he shall fast for one day. [21]To cleanse himself of what he may have eaten unwittingly, a Brahmin should perform at least one arduous penance (11.212) each year; but he is cleansed of what he has eaten intentionally through the specified penance.

[22]To perform sacrifices Brahmins may kill sanctioned animals and birds, as also to feed their dependants; Agastya did that long ago. [23]For, at the ancient sacrifices of seers and at the Soma offerings of Brahmins and Kṣatriyas, the sacrificial cakes were prepared with the meat of permitted animals and birds.

[24]Any non-forbidden food or delicacy infused with oil* may be eaten even if it is stale, as also any leftovers from a sacrificial oblation. [25]Though they have not been infused with oil, however, dishes made with barley or wheat, as well as milk preparations, may be eaten by the twice-born, even if they have stood for a long time.

> [26]I have described above completely what foods are forbidden and what permitted to the twice-born. I will now explain the rule on eating and on avoiding meat.

EATING MEAT

[27] He may eat meat when it is sacrificially consecrated, at the behest of Brahmins, when he is ritually commissioned according to rule, and when his life is at risk.*

[28] Prajāpati created this whole world as food for lifebreath; all beings, the mobile and the immobile, are nourishment for lifebreath. [29] The immobile are food for the mobile; the fangless for the fanged; the handless for the handed; and the timid for the brave. [30] The eater is not defiled by eating living beings suitable for eating, even if he eats them day after day; for the creator himself fashioned both the eaters and the living beings suitable for eating.

[31] 'The sacrifice is the reason for eating meat'—this, the tradition says, is the rule of gods. Doing it for any other purpose is called the rule of fiends.* [32] When a man eats meat—whether it was purchased, procured by himself, or offered by someone else—after making an offering to gods and ancestors, he does not become defiled. [33] Except in a time of adversity, a twice-born man who knows the rules must never eat meat in contravention of the rules; if he eats meat in contravention of the rules, after death he will be eaten forcibly by those very animals. [34] In the afterlife, the sin of someone who hunts animals for profit is not as great as that of a man who eats meat procured capriciously. [35] If a man refuses to eat meat after he has been ritually commissioned according to rule (5.27 n.), after death he will become an animal for twenty-one lifetimes. [36] A Brahmin must never eat animals that have not been consecrated with ritual formulas. Abiding by the eternal rule, however, he must eat those that have been consecrated with ritual formulas.

[37] If he gets the urge, let him make an animal out of butter or flour; but he must never entertain the desire to kill an animal for a futile reason. [38] When a man kills an animal for a futile reason, after death he will be subject in birth after birth to being slain as many times as the number of hairs on that animal.

[39] The Self-existent One himself created domestic animals for sacrifice,* and the sacrifice is for the prosperity of this whole world. Within the sacrifice, therefore, killing is not killing. [40] When plants, domestic animals, trees, beasts, and birds die for the sake of a sacrifice, they will in turn earn superior births. [41] The honey-mixture (3.119 n.), a sacrifice, an offering to gods or ancestors—at no other

occasion than these, Manu has declared, may animals be killed. [42] When a twice-born man who knows the true meaning of the Veda kills animals for these purposes, he leads himself and those animals to the highest state. [43] Whether he lives at home, at his teacher's, or in the wilderness, a twice-born man who is self-possessed must never, even in a time of adversity, carry out a killing that is not sanctioned by the Veda. [44] When a killing is sanctioned by the Veda and well-established in this mobile and immobile creation, it should be regarded definitely as a non-killing; for it is from the Veda that the Law has shined forth.

[45] If someone, craving his own pleasure, harms harmless creatures, he will not find happiness anywhere while he is still alive or after death. [46] When someone has no desire to tie up, kill, or cause pain to living creatures and seeks the welfare of all beings, he obtains endless bliss. [47] Whatever a man contemplates, whatever a man undertakes, whatever a man takes a liking to—all that he obtains without effort, when he does no harm to any creature.

[48] One can never obtain meat without causing injury to living beings, and killing living beings is an impediment to heaven; he should, therefore, abstain from meat. [49] Reflecting on how meat is obtained and on how embodied creatures are tied up and killed, he should quit eating any kind of meat. [50] When a man refrains from eating meat like a goblin, except when the rules prescribe it, he is loved by the world and is not tormented by diseases.

[51] The man who authorizes, the man who butchers, the man who slaughters, the man who buys or sells, the man who cooks, the man who serves, and the man who eats—these are all killers. [52] There is no greater sinner than a man who, outside of an offering to gods or ancestors, wants to make his own flesh thrive at the expense of someone else's.

[53] A man who abstains from meat and a man who offers the horse sacrifice every year for a hundred years—the reward for their meritorious acts is the same. [54] Even by living on pure fruits and roots and by eating the food of sages, a man fails to obtain as great a reward as he would by abstaining completely from meat.

[55] 'Me he (*mām sa*) will eat in the next world, whose meat (*māṃsa*) I eat in this world'—this, the wise declare, is what gave the name to and discloses the true nature of 'meat'* (*māṃsa*).

[56] There is no fault in eating meat, in drinking liquor, or in having

sex; that is the natural activity of creatures. Abstaining from such activity, however, brings great rewards.

> [57] I will now explain the purification after a death, as well as the purification of things, precisely and in their proper order for all four classes.

BODILY PURIFICATION

Death or Birth of a Person Belonging to the Same Ancestry

[58] Someone who has teethed, someone younger, or someone who has had his first cutting of hair* (2.35)—when any of these dies, all his relatives become impure; the same is prescribed after the birth of a child. [59] A ten-day period of impurity following a death is prescribed for those who belong to the same ancestry; alternatively, that period may last until the collection of bones,* or for three days, or for a single day.

[60] The relationship based on common ancestry* stops with the seventh generation; the relationship based on offering libations,* on the other hand, stops only when someone's birth and name are no longer remembered.

[61] The same holds true at a birth. The birth-impurity, however, affects only the mother and the father. The mother alone is subject to the period of birth-impurity; the father becomes pure by bathing.* [Number 62 is omitted] [63] On the contrary, it is after spilling his seed that a man is purified by simply bathing; the impurity resulting from a seminal relationship adheres to him for three days.*

[64] Those who touch the corpse are purified in ten days, but those who offer libations in three.* [65] A pupil who performs the funerary rites of his deceased teacher, on the other hand, is on a par with those who carry a corpse and is purified in ten days.

[66] After a miscarriage, a woman is purified after the same number of days as the months of her pregnancy. A menstruating woman becomes wholesome by taking a bath after her menstrual flow has ceased.

[67] When males die before the first cutting of their hair (2.35), tradition tells us, the impurity lasts a single night; but when they die after the cutting of their hair, purity is considered to be restored after three nights. [68] When a child under two dies, its relatives should

decorate its corpse and lay it down* in a clean spot outside the village; the ceremony of collecting its bones is omitted.* [69] Neither the consecration with fire nor the offering of water is done for such a child; after leaving it behind in the wilderness like a piece of wood, one should keep the observances for just three days. [70] Relatives should not offer libations of water for a child under three; they may do so optionally if it has teethed or if its naming ceremony has been performed.

[71] When someone who had been a fellow student dies, tradition prescribes the observances for one day. In the event of a birth, the purity of those related through offering libations (5.60 n.) is considered to be restored after three days. [72] The relations of unmarried women are purified in three days, but her siblings* are purified exactly according to the prescribed rule.*

[73] For three days they are to eat food without artificial salt, bathe by immersion, abstain from eating meat, and sleep separately on the floor.

Death in a Distant Region [74] The above set of rules concerning impurity after death is prescribed only when a death has occurred close by; when it has happened far away, kinsmen and relatives* should know that the procedure is as follows.

[75] When someone living in a far-away place dies and one hears of it within ten days of his death, one becomes impure only for the remainder of that ten-day period. [76] If one hears of it after the lapse of ten days, one becomes impure for three days; but if it is after a year, one is purified simply by bathing. [77] When a man hears about the death of a paternal relative or the birth of a son after the lapse of ten days, he becomes pure by immersing himself in water with his clothes on. [78] When a child or someone belonging to a different ancestry dies in a far-away place, one is purified instantly by immersing oneself in water with one's clothes on.

Overlapping Periods of Impurity [79] If during one ten-day period of impurity another death or birth occurs, a Brahmin remains impure only until the end of the initial ten-day period.

Death of Significant Others [80] At the death of one's teacher, they prescribe a three-day period of impurity; and at the death of the teacher's son or wife, the settled rule is a day and a night. [81] One becomes impure for three days at the death of a vedic scholar living near by, and for two days plus the intervening night at the death of one's maternal uncle, pupil, officiating priest, or maternal relative. [82] At the death of a king, anyone residing within his realm remains impure that day from dawn to dusk or that night from dusk to dawn (4.106 n.). At the death of someone who is not a vedic scholar, a vedic savant, or an elder,* one remains impure for a full day.

Periods of Impurity for Different Classes [83] A Brahmin is purified in ten days, a Kṣatriya in twelve, a Vaiśya in fifteen, and a Śūdra in a month. [84] One should not prolong the days of impurity or postpone one's fire rituals; while performing that rite, even a uterine brother (5.72 n.) becomes immune to impurity.*

Impurity from Touch [85] When someone touches a Divākīrti,* a menstruating woman, an outcaste, a woman who has given birth, or a corpse—as also a person who has touched any of these—he is purified by bathing. [86] At the sight of an impure person, he should make himself ritually pure by sipping water and then softly recite the Solar formulas according to his capacity, and the Pāvamānī verses to the best of his ability. [87] After touching a human bone, a Brahmin is purified by bathing if the bone was greasy, but simply by sipping water, touching a cow, or gazing at the sun, if the bone was dry.

Libations for the Dead [88] A votary* shall not offer a libation until he has completed his vow; but once he has completed his vow and offered the libation, he is purified in just three days. [89] Libations are omitted in the case of people born through capricious caste mingling;* those living in ascetic orders; suicides; [90] and women who have joined heretical sects, roam about at will, harm their foetus or husband, or drink liquor. [91] By carrying his own deceased teacher, tutor (2.141), father, mother, or elder, a votary (5.88 n.) does not break his vow.

Funeral Path [92] A dead Śūdra should be carried out through the southern gate of the city, and a twice-born person through the western, the northern, or the eastern gate, as appropriate.*

Instant Purification of Kings [93] The taint of impurity does not affect kings, votaries, and those engaged in a sacrificial session; for they are seated on the seat of Indra and are ever one with *brahman*.*

[94]Instant purification is prescribed for a king on the seat of majesty—the reason for this is that he is seated for the protection of his subjects—[95]as also for people killed in a riot or battle, by lightning or the king, or in defence of cows or Brahmins, and for anyone the king wants.*

[96]Soma, Fire, Sun, Wind, Indra, the Lords of wealth and water, and Yama—the king is the embodiment of these eight guardians of the world (see 7.4). [97]The lords of the world abide within the king, and no period of impurity is prescribed for him; for it is the lords of the world who both bring about and erase purity and impurity in mortal beings.

[98]When a man is killed in battle with upraised weapons according to the Kṣatriya law, the settled rule is that for him both sacrifice and purification are accomplished instantly.

[99]After completing the required rite, a Brahmin is purified by touching water, a Kṣatriya his conveyance (7.75 n.) or weapon, a Vaiśya his goad or reins, and a Śūdra his staff (see 8.113).

> [100]I have explained to you above, O Brahmins, the purification in the case of people belonging to the same ancestry (5.60 n.). Listen now to the purification after death in the case of all those belonging to different ancestries.

Death of a Person Belonging to a Different Ancestry

[101]If a Brahmin carries the corpse of a twice-born person unrelated to him by ancestry as if he were a relative, or if he carries a close (2.109 n.) relative of his mother, he is purified in three days. [102]If he eats their food, on the other hand, his purification takes ten full days; but if he neither eats their food nor stays at their house, it takes just one day. [103]If someone willingly follows a corpse, whether it is that of a paternal relative or of someone else, he is purified after he has bathed with his clothes on, touched the fire, and eaten some ghee.

[104]When one's own people are present, one should never let a Śūdra carry a Brahmin's corpse, for a sacrificial offering defiled by a Śūdra's touch does not lead a person to heaven.

Means of Purification

[105] Knowledge, austerity, fire, food, earth, mind, water, smearing with cow dung, wind, rites, sun, time*—these are the agents of purification for embodied beings.

[106] Purifying oneself with respect to wealth, tradition tells us, is the highest of all purifications; for the truly pure man is the one who is pure with respect to wealth, not the one who becomes pure by using earth and water.

[107] Learned men are purified by forbearance; those who do forbidden things, by giving gifts; those who commit secret sins, by soft recitation; and pre-eminent experts in the Veda, by ascetic toil. [108] What needs cleaning is cleansed by using earth and water, a river by its current, a woman defiled in thought by her menstrual flow, and Brahmins by renunciation.* [109] The body is cleansed with water, the mind by truth, the elemental self (12.12) by learning and austerity, and the intellect by knowledge.

> [110] I have explained to you above the determination
> with regard to bodily purification. Listen now to the
> determination with regard to the purification of dif-
> ferent kinds of articles.

PURIFICATION OF ARTICLES

[111] The wise have determined that metal objects, jewels, and anything lapidary are cleaned with ash, water, and earth. [112] When they are unstained, gold vessels are cleaned with water alone, as also the aquatic, the lapidary, or any silver article that is unembellished.* [113] Gold and silver issued from the union of fire and water; they are best cleaned, therefore, using their very sources. [114] The cleaning of copper, iron, brass, pewter, tin, and lead is done using as appropriate alkali, acid, and water.

[115] All liquids, tradition tells us, are cleaned by straining; solids, by sprinkling water; and wooden articles, by planing.

[116] During a sacrificial rite, sacrificial vessels are rubbed with the hand; the Camasa-cups and Graha-ladles, on the other hand, are cleaned by washing; [117] the Caru-pots, Sruk-spoons, and Sruva-spoons are cleaned with warm water, as are Sphya-swords, Śūrpa-winnows, Śakaṭa-carts, pestles, and mortars.

[118]The rule is that large quantities of grain or clothes are cleaned by sprinkling them with water, whereas small quantities are cleaned by washing them with water. [119]Skin and wicker are to be cleaned the same way as cloth; and vegetables, roots, and fruits, the same way as grain. [120]Silk and wool are cleaned with saline earth, goat's wool blankets with ground Ariṣṭa fruit, fine fabric with Bel fruit, and linen with yellow mustard. [121]A discerning man should clean conch and horn, as well as articles made of bone and ivory, the same way as linen, or else with cow's urine or water. [122]Grass, wood, and straw are cleaned by sprinkling water on them, a house by scrubbing it or by smearing it with cow dung, and earthenware by firing it again.* [Number 123 is omitted] [124]Scrubbing, smearing with cow dung, sprinkling, scraping, and letting cows stay in it—by these five means a plot of land is purified.

[125]Anything that birds have pecked, cows have sniffed, or hair or insects have fouled, or over which someone has shaken or sneezed, is cleaned by spreading some earth over it. [126]Whenever anything is being cleaned, one should keep applying earth and water until the smell and stain are gone from the article smeared with a foul substance.

[127]Gods invented three means of purification for Brahmins: being unaware that something is impure, sprinkling it with water, and getting it verbally declared as suitable.

Statutory Purity of Things

[128]Water collected on the ground is pure if it is sufficient to slake the thirst of a cow, is uncontaminated with foul substances, and has the right odour, colour, and taste. [129]The hand of an artisan is always pure, as are goods displayed for sale; the almsfood received by a student is always ritually clean—that is the settled rule. [130]A woman's mouth is always pure; so is a bird when it makes a fruit to fall, a calf when it makes the milk to flow, and a dog when it catches a deer. [131]The meat of an animal that has been killed by a dog or some other predator, or by a Cāṇḍāla or some other lowlife, is pure—that is the judgement of Manu.

[132]All orifices above the navel are ritually clean; those below are ritually unclean, as are the foul substances that shed from the body.

[133] Flies, droplets of water,* shadows, cows, horses, rays of the sun, dust, earth, wind, and fire—these should be regarded as ritually clean to the touch.

PURIFICATION OF THE BODY

[134] To purify oneself after voiding urine or excrement and to clean any of the twelve bodily impurities, one should use a sufficient amount of earth and water. [135] Body oil, semen, blood, marrow,* urine, faeces, ear-wax, nails, phlegm, tears, discharge of the eyes, and sweat—these are the twelve impurities of man.

[136] A man intent on purifying himself should apply one lump of earth on the penis, three on the anus, ten on one hand,* and seven on both. [137] This is the purification for householders. It is twice that much for students, three times for forest hermits, and four times for ascetics. [138] After he voids urine or excrement, he must sip water and touch the orifices with water (2.53 n.); he must do so every time he prepares to recite the Veda or to eat his food.

[139] A man who desires bodily purification should first sip water three times and then wipe the mouth with water twice; but a woman or a Śūdra sips and wipes just once. [140] Śūdras who abide by the proper mode of conduct should shave their heads once a month, follow the rules of purification laid down for Vaiśyas, and eat the leftover food of twice-born persons.

[141] Drool spattering from the mouth does not make someone sullied if it does not fall on his body; nor does hair from the beard getting into the mouth or anything stuck between the teeth. [142] Drops falling on a man's feet while he is pouring water for someone else to sip are to be considered similar to water on the ground and do not make him ritually impure. [143] If a sullied person touches a man carrying something in his hand, he becomes pure by sipping some water without laying that thing down.*

[144] After vomiting or purging, one should bathe and consume some ghee; after eating food, one should simply sip some water; and after sexual intercourse tradition requires one to take a bath. [145] After sleeping, sneezing, eating, spitting, telling a lie, and drinking water, as also when one is about to recite the Veda, one should sip some water even though one is already ritually pure.

[146] I have explained to you above all the rules of purification, as well as the cleaning of articles, applicable to all the social classes. Listen now to the Law with respect to women.

LAW WITH RESPECT TO WOMEN

Lack of Independence

[147] Even in her own home, a female—whether she is a child, a young woman, or an old lady—should never carry out any task independently.* [148] As a child, she must remain under her father's control; as a young woman, under her husband's; and when her husband is dead, under her sons'. She must never seek to live independently. [149] She must never want to separate herself from her father, husband, or sons; for by separating herself from them, a woman brings disgrace on both families.*

[150] She should be always cheerful, clever at housework, careful in keeping the utensils clean, and frugal in her expenditure.

Duties towards Husband

[151] The man to whom her father or, with her father's consent, her brother gives her away—she should obey him when he is alive and not be unfaithful to him when he is dead. [152] The invocation of blessings and the sacrifice to Prajāpati are performed during marriage to procure her good fortune; the act of giving away* is the reason for his lordship over her. [153] In season and out of season, in this world and in the next, the husband who performed the marriage consecration with ritual formulas always gives happiness to his woman.

[154] Though he may be bereft of virtue, given to lust, and totally devoid of good qualities, a good woman should always worship her husband like a god. [155] For women, there is no independent sacrifice, vow, or fast; a woman will be exalted in heaven by the mere fact that she has obediently served her husband. [156] A good woman, desiring to go to the same world as her husband, should never do anything displeasing to the man who took her hand, whether he is alive or dead.

[157] After her husband is dead, she may voluntarily emaciate her body by eating pure flowers, roots, and fruits; but she must never

mention even the name of another man. [158] Aspiring to that unsurpassed Law of women devoted to a single husband, she should remain patient, controlled, and celibate until her death. [159] Untold thousands of Brahmins who have remained celibate from their youth have gone to heaven without producing offspring to continue their family line. [160] Just like these celibates, a good woman, though she be sonless, will go to heaven when she steadfastly adheres to the celibate life after her husband's death.* [161] When a woman is unfaithful to her husband because of her strong desire for children, she is disgraced in this world and excluded from the husband's world. [162] No recognition is given here to offspring fathered by another man or begotten on another's wife; nor is it taught anywhere that a good woman should take a second husband.

[163] When a woman abandons her own husband of lower rank and unites with a man of higher rank, she only brings disgrace upon herself in the world and is called 'a woman who has had a man before'. [164] By being unfaithful to her husband, a woman becomes disgraced in the world, takes birth in a jackal's womb, and is afflicted with evil diseases (3.159 n.).

[165] A woman who controls her mind, speech, and body and is never unfaithful to her husband attains the worlds of her husband, and virtuous people call her a 'good woman'. [166] By following this conduct, a woman who controls her mind, speech, and body obtains the highest fame in this world and the world of her husband in the next.

Funeral

[167] When a wife who has conducted herself in this manner and who belongs to the same class as her husband dies before him, a twice-born man who knows the Law should cremate her with his sacred fire and sacrificial implements. [168] After he has given his sacred fires to his predeceased wife at her funeral, he should marry a wife again and establish anew his sacred fires.

CONCLUDING STATEMENT ON THE HOUSEHOLDER

[169] In accordance with these rules, he should never neglect the five sacrifices; and, marrying a wife, he should live at home during the second quarter of his life.*

CHAPTER SIX

FOREST HERMIT

[1] After living this way in the householder's order according to rule, a twice-born bath-graduate should duly live in the forest, controlling himself and mastering his organs.*

Time and Procedure

[2] When a householder sees his skin wrinkled, his hair turned grey, and his children's children, he should take to the wilderness. [3] Giving up village food and all his belongings, he should go to the forest, entrusting his wife to his sons or accompanied by her.

[4] Taking with him his sacrificial fires and the implements required for his domestic fire rituals, he should depart from the village to the wilderness and live there with his organs controlled.

Mode of Life

[5] Using various kinds of ritually clean sage's food (3.257 n.), or vegetables, roots, and fruits, he should continue to offer the same great sacrifices (3.68–70) according to rule. [6] He should wear a garment of skin or tree bark; bathe in the morning and evening; always wear matted hair; and keep his beard, body hair, and nails uncut.

Great Sacrifices [7] He should give Bali offerings and almsfood to the best of his ability with whatever food he eats and honour those who visit his hermitage with water, roots, fruits, and almsfood. [8] He should be always diligent in his vedic recitation; remain controlled, friendly, and collected; be always a giver and never a receiver of gifts; be compassionate towards all creatures; [9] offer the daily fire sacrifice in his three sacred fires according to rule, without neglecting the new-moon and full-moon sacrifices at their proper time; [10] and offer the constellation-sacrifice,* the sacrifice of first fruits (4.26), the seasonal sacrifices, the Turāyaṇa* sacrifice and the Dākṣāyaṇa* sacrifice, in their proper sequence. [11] With ritually clean sage's foods that grow in spring and autumn and that he has gathered himself, he should offer separately the sacrificial cakes and oblations of milk-rice according to rule.

Food [12] After he has offered that most ritually clean oblation of forest produce to the gods, he may avail himself of what remains, as also of salt that he has manufactured himself.

[13] He may eat vegetables growing on land or in water; flowers, roots, and fruits coming from ritually clean trees; and oils extracted from fruits. [14] He must avoid honey, meat, the Bhauma plant,* mushrooms, the Bhūstṛṇa plant, the Śigruka horseradish, and the Śleṣmātaka fruit.

[15] In the month of Āśvayuja (September–October), he must throw away the sage's food that he had previously collected, as also vegetables, roots, fruits, and old garments.

[16] He must never eat anything grown on ploughed land, even if it has been thrown away by someone; or flowers and fruits grown in a village, even if he is in dire straits.

[17] He may eat food that has been cooked with fire or ripened by time; he may use a grindstone or use his teeth as a mortar; [18] he may clean up immediately* after eating or maintain a supply of food sufficient for a month, six months, or a year.

[19] Having gathered food to the best of his ability, he may eat it at night, during the day, at every fourth mealtime, or at every eighth mealtime;* [20] or he may maintain himself during the bright and dark halves of the month according to the lunar rule (11.217), or eat boiled barley-gruel once at the end of each half-month; [21] or he may subsist permanently on just flowers, roots, and fruits that have ripened by time and wilted on their own—abiding by the Vaikhānasa doctrine.*

Austerities [22] He should roll on the ground or stand on tiptoes all day; spend the day standing and the night seated,* bathing at dawn, midday, and dusk; [23] surround himself with the five fires* in the summer; live in the open air during the rainy season; and wear wet clothes in the winter—gradually intensifying his ascetic toil. [24] Bathing at dawn, noon, and dusk, he should offer quenching libations to ancestors and gods, and engaging in ever harsher ascetic toil, he should inflict punishment on his body.

Homeless Ascetic [25] After depositing his sacred fires in his body* according to rule, he should become a sage without house or fire, subsisting on roots and fruits, [26] making no effort to obtain pleasurable things, remaining celibate, sleeping on the ground, showing no attachment to any place of shelter, and making his home at the foot of a tree.

[27] He should beg for almsfood just sufficient to sustain life only from Brahmin ascetics and from other twice-born householders living in the forest. [28] Or, while continuing to live in the forest, he may collect almsfood from a village and eat eight mouthfuls, receiving the almsfood in a leaf-cone, in a potsherd, or in the hand.

Conclusion

[29] To attain the full perfection of his self, a Brahmin living in the forest must pursue these and other observances, as also the various Upaniṣadic scriptures, [30] and, to enhance his knowledge and ascetic toil and to purify his body, also those pursued by seers, Brahmins, and householders.

[31] Or he may set out in a north-easterly direction and, subsisting on water and air, walk straight on steadfastly until his body drops dead. [32] When a Brahmin has discarded his body through any one of these means employed by the great seers, freed from sorrow and fear, he will be exalted in the world of Brahman.

WANDERING ASCETIC

[33] After spending the third quarter of his life this way in the forest, he should cast off his attachments and wander about as an ascetic during the fourth.* [34] When a man goes forth as an ascetic after he has moved from order to order, offered sacrifices, subdued his senses, and become worn out by giving alms and oblations, he will prosper after death.

Qualification

[35] Only after he has paid his three debts (4.257 n.), should a man set his mind on renunciation (1.114 n.); if he devotes himself to renunciation without paying them, he will proceed downward.* [36] Only after he has studied the Vedas according to rule, fathered sons in keeping with the Law, and offered sacrifices according to his ability, should a

man set his mind on renunciation; [37]if a twice-born seeks renunciation without studying the Vedas, without fathering sons, and without offering sacrifices, he will proceed downward (6.35 n.).

Initiation

[38]Only after he has offered a sacrifice to Prajāpati at which all his possessions are given as the sacrificial gift and after he has deposited the sacred fires within himself (6.25 n.), should a Brahmin go forth from his home as an ascetic.

[39]Worlds of resplendent energy await a vedic savant who goes forth from his home as an ascetic after bestowing freedom from fear* on all creatures. [40]Because that twice-born has not been the cause of even the slightest fear to creatures, he has nothing to fear from anyone after he is freed from his body.

[41]After departing from home with a cloth for straining water, the sage should wander about, ignoring the sensual delights presented to him.

Mode of Life

[42]To achieve success, he must always wander alone, without any companions; recognizing that success comes to the solitary man, he will forsake no one and no one will forsake him. [43]He should live without fire or house, enter a village to obtain food, be dispassionate, keep no store, and remain a silent sage and mentally composed. [44]A bowl, the foot of a tree, a ragged piece of cloth, a solitary life, and equanimity towards all—these are the marks of a renouncer.*

[45]He should long neither for death nor for life, but simply await his appointed time, as a servant his wages. [46]He should place his foot on a spot purified by his sight,* drink water purified by a cloth, speak words purified by truth, and follow conduct purified by the mind.

[47]He must bear harsh words with patience; never treat anyone with contempt; never start a feud with anyone merely for the sake of this body; [48]never show ire towards anyone who is irate with him; bless those who curse him; and never utter an untrue word scattered across the seven gates.*

[49] Taking delight in what pertains to the self, he should remain seated without longings or sensual attachments. With himself as his only companion, he should walk about here, seeking felicity.*

Begging and Food

[50] He must never try to obtain almsfood by interpreting portents or omens, by his knowledge of astrology or palmistry,* by giving counsel, or by engaging in debates.

[51] He should never visit a house crowded with ascetics, Brahmins, birds, dogs, or other beggars; [52] and always go about with his head and beard shaved, with his nails clipped, carrying a bowl, a staff, and a water-pot, and without causing harm to any creature.

[53] His bowls must be non-metallic and undamaged; and tradition says that they are to be cleaned with just water, like Camasa-cups at a sacrifice (5.116). [54] A gourd, a wooden bowl, a clay bowl, and a wicker bowl—Manu, the son of the Self-existent One, has proclaimed these as the bowls of ascetics.

[55] He may go on his begging round only once a day. He must not be overly attached to getting a lot; for when an ascetic is overly attached to almsfood, he becomes attached also to sensual objects. [56] An ascetic should go on his daily begging round only when the smoke has cleared, the pestles are at rest, the embers are extinguished, the people have finished their meal, and the dishes have been put away.

[57] When he receives nothing, he must not become dejected; when he receives something, it must not make him elated. He should gather food just sufficient to sustain his life and become free from attachment to his belongings. [58] He should hold anything received with a show of reverence in total disdain; even an ascetic who has freed himself is shackled by what is received with a show of reverence.* [59] By eating little and by spending the day standing and the night seated (6.22 n.) in solitude, he should pull his organs back as they are being drawn away by sensory objects. [60] By restraining his organs, by stamping out love and hatred, and by ceasing to harm any creature, he becomes fit for immortality.

Yogic Meditation

[61] He should reflect on the diverse paths humans take as a result of their evil deeds; on how they fall into hell; on the tortures they endure in the abode of Yama; [62] on how they are separated from the ones they love and united with the ones they hate; on how they are overcome by old age and tormented by diseases; [63] on how the inner self departs from this body, takes birth again in a womb, and migrates through tens of billions of wombs; [64] and on how embodied beings become linked with pain as a result of pursuing what is against the Law and with imperishable happiness as a result of pursuing the Law as one's goal.

[65] By yogic meditation, he should also reflect on the subtle nature of the highest self and on its appearance in the highest and the lowest of bodies (6.73).

Conduct [66] Though decked in finery, he should pursue the Law in whichever order he may live, treating all creatures alike; an emblem does not accomplish the Law.* [67] Although the fruit of the Kataka tree makes water clear, yet the water does not become clear by mere mention of its name.

[68] To protect living creatures, he should walk always—whether at night or during the day—only after inspecting the ground even at the cost of bodily discomfort. [69] To purify himself of killing living creatures unintentionally during the day or at night, an ascetic should bathe and control his breath six times.

Breath Control [70] Controlling the breath even three times according to rule while reciting the Calls and the syllable OṂ is to be considered the highest type of ascetic toil for a Brahmin. [71] As the impurities of metallic ores are burnt away when they are blasted in a furnace, so the faults of the organs are burnt away by suppressing the breath.

Meditation [72] He should burn away his faults by suppressing his breath, his taints by concentration, his attachments by the withdrawal of senses, and his base qualities by meditation. [73] Through the practice of meditation, he should discern the course of this inner self through the highest and the lowest of creatures (6.65), a difficult course to grasp for persons with uncultivated minds.

[74] When a man possesses right understanding, he is not fettered by actions; but when he lacks understanding, he enters the transmigratory cycle. [75] By ceasing to harm living creatures, by withdrawing the organs from their attachments, by performing vedic rites, and by practising fierce austerities, individuals do attain that state* here on earth.

Meditation on the Body [76] Constructed with beams of bones, fastened with tendons, plastered with flesh and blood, covered with skin, foul-smelling, filled with urine and excrement, [77] infested with old age and sorrow, the abode of sickness, full of pain, covered with dust, and impermanent—he must abandon this dwelling place of ghosts.* [78] When a tree falls from a river bank, the bird leaves the tree; when he abandons this body in like manner, he escapes the alligator's painful grasp.*

Final Goal [79] Consigning his good deeds to people he likes and his evil deeds to people he dislikes, he attains the eternal Brahman through the practice of meditation. [80] When by the passion of his spirit he frees himself from attachment to every object of passion,* then he wins eternal happiness both here and in the hereafter. [81] When he gives up all attachments gradually in this manner, freed from all the pairs of opposites, he comes to rest in Brahman alone.

[82] Everything prescribed here is contingent on meditation; for no one ignorant of the highest self can reap the fruits of his rites. [83] He should practise the soft recitation of vedic texts relating to sacrifice, gods, and self, as also those named 'Vedānta'—[84] this is the refuge of the ignorant, as indeed of the learned; this is the refuge of those who seek heaven, as of those who yearn for the infinite.

[85] If a twice-born lives as a wandering ascetic following the above sequence of practices, he will cast off his sins in this world and attain the highest Brahman.

> [86] I have explained to you above the Law pertaining to self-controlled ascetics. Listen now to the ritual discipline of vedic retirees (1.114n.).

VEDIC RETIREE

Superiority of the Householder

[87] Student, householder, forest hermit, and ascetic: these four distinct orders have their origin in the householder. [88] All of these, when they are undertaken in their proper sequence as spelled out in the sacred texts, lead a Brahmin who acts in the prescribed manner to the highest state. [89] Among all of them, however, according to the dictates of vedic scripture, the householder is said to be the best, for he supports the other three. [90] As all rivers and rivulets ultimately end up* in the ocean, so people of all the orders ultimately end up in the householder.

The Ten-Point Law

[91] Twice-born men belonging to all these four orders must always observe the ten-point Law diligently. [92] Resolve, forbearance, self-control, refraining from theft, performing purifications, mastering the organs, understanding, learning, truthfulness, and suppressing anger: these are the ten points of the Law. [93] Those Brahmins who learn the ten points of the Law and, after learning, follow them, attain the highest state.

Retirement

[94] When a twice-born man has followed the ten-point Law with a collected mind, learned the Vedānta according to rule, and freed himself from debt (4.257n.), he may retire (1.114n.). [95] Casting off the inherent evil of rites by retiring from all ritual activities, being self-controlled, and reciting the Veda, he should live at ease under the care of his son.

[96] When a man retires from ritual activities in this manner and, free from attachments, devotes himself completely to his duties, he erases his sins by this retirement and attains the highest state.

> [97] I have explained to you above the fourfold Law of
> Brahmins, a Law that is holy and brings imperishable
> rewards after death. Listen now to the Law of kings.

CHAPTER SEVEN

THE LAW FOR THE KING

[1] I will explain the Laws pertaining to kings—how a king should conduct himself, how he came into being, and how he can attain the highest success.

Origin of the King

[2] A Kṣatriya who has received the vedic consecration* according to rule has the obligation to protect this whole world in accordance with the norms; [3] for when people here were without a king and fleeing in all directions out of fear, to protect this whole world the Lord created the king [4] by extracting eternal particles from Indra, Wind, Yama, Sun, Fire, Varuṇa, Moon, and the Lord of wealth.*

[5] Because the king was fashioned out of particles from these chiefs of the gods, he overpowers all beings by reason of his energy. [6] Like the sun, indeed, he burns eyes and minds; no one on earth can bear to gaze upon him. [7] He is Fire, he is Wind, he is the Sun, he is the Moon, he is the King of the Law [Yama], he is Kubera, he is Varuṇa, and he is the Great Indra—by reason of his power.

[8] A king, though a mere child, must never be treated with disrespect, thinking he is just a human being; for it is a great deity who stands here in human form. [9] When approached recklessly, a fire burns only that single man, but the fire that is the king burns his family, together with all his livestock and wealth.

[10] After examining truthfully the task to be accomplished, his own strength, the time, and the place, he assumes in turn every aspect* in order to fully implement the Law; [11] he, in whose benevolence lies Padmā, the goddess of prosperity, in whose valour lies victory, and in whose anger lies death—for he is made from the energies of them all.*

[12] The man who in his folly hates him perishes without doubt; for the king makes up his mind to destroy him quickly. [13] When the king issues a Law favourable to those he favours or unfavourable to those out of favour, therefore, no one should transgress that Law.*

Punishment [14]For the king's sake, the Lord formerly created Punishment,* his son—the Law and protector of all beings—made from the energy of Brahman. [15]It is the fear of him that makes all beings, both the mobile and the immobile, accede to being used* and not deviate from the Law proper to them.

[16]The king should administer appropriate Punishment on men who behave improperly, after examining truthfully the place and the time,* as well as their strength and learning. [17]Punishment is the king; he is the male; he is the leader; he is the ruler; and, tradition tells us, he stands as the surety for the Law with respect to the four orders of life. [18]Punishment disciplines all the subjects, Punishment alone protects them, and Punishment watches over them as they sleep—Punishment is the Law, the wise declare. [19]When he is wielded properly after careful examination,* he gives delight to all the subjects; but when he is administered without careful examination, he wreaks total havoc.

[20]If the king fails to administer Punishment tirelessly on those who ought to be punished, the stronger would grill the weak like fish on a spit; [21]crows would devour the sacrificial cakes; dogs would lap up the sacrificial offerings; no one would have any right of ownership; and everything would turn topsy-turvy. [22]The whole world is subdued through Punishment, for an honest man is hard to find; clearly, it is the fear of Punishment that makes the whole creation accede to being used (7.15 n.). [23]Gods, demons, Gandharvas, fiends, birds, and snakes—even these accede to being used only when coerced by Punishment. [24]All the social classes would become corrupted, all boundaries would be breached, and all the people would revolt, as a result of blunders committed with respect to Punishment. [25]Wherever Punishment, dark-hued and red-eyed, prowls about as the slayer of evil-doers, there the subjects do not go astray—so long as its administrator ascertains correctly.

[26]The proper administrator of Punishment, they say, is a king who speaks the truth, acts after careful examination (7.19 n.), is wise, and has a masterly grasp of Law, Wealth, and Pleasure. [27]When a king administers Punishment properly, he flourishes with respect to the triple set (2.224 n.); but the king who is lustful, partial, and vile is slain by that very Punishment. [28]For Punishment is immense energy, and it cannot be wielded by those with uncultivated selves. It assuredly slays a king who deviates from the Law, along with his

relatives; [29] then he oppresses the fort, the realm, and the mobile and the immobile world, as well as sages and gods dwelling in mid-space. [30] Punishment cannot be justly administered by someone who is without assistants, who is foolish or greedy, who is irresolute, or who is attached to sensual objects. [31] Punishment can only be administered by someone who is honest and true to his word, who acts in conformity with the Treatises, who has good assistants, and who is wise.

Proper Behaviour [32] Within his realm, he should act in accordance with the rules; upon his enemies, he should impose harsh punishments; towards his friends and loved ones, he should behave without guile; and to Brahmins, he should show compassion. [33] When a king behaves in this manner, though he may eke out a living by gleaning, his fame spreads in the world like a drop of oil on water. [34] When a king, with no control over himself, behaves in the opposite way, his fame contracts in the world like a drop of ghee on water.

[35] The king was created as the protector of people belonging to all social classes and orders of life who, according to their rank, are devoted to the Law specific to them.*

> [36] I will explain to you precisely and in their proper
> order all that he, along with his deputies, should do as
> he protects his subjects.

Cultivating Virtue and Learning

[37] After getting up in the morning,* the king should pay his respects to learned Brahmins who are experts in the triple Veda and follow their admonitions; [38] and every day he should render assistance to old and upright Brahmins who know the Veda, for even fiends always honour a man who renders assistance to the elderly. [39] Even if he is a disciplined man, he should always learn the rules of discipline from them; for a disciplined king never comes to ruin.

[40] Because they lacked discipline, numerous kings came to ruin along with their possessions; and because of discipline, even those residing in the forest* gained kingdoms. [41] Because he lacked discipline, Vena came to ruin; and so did King Nahuṣa, Sudas Paijavana, Sumukha, and Nimi. [42] Because of discipline, on the other hand, Pṛthu, as well as Manu, obtained a kingdom; Kubera, lordship over wealth; and the son of Gādhi,* the rank of a Brahmin.

[43] From experts in the three Vedas, he should learn the triple Veda, the timeless science of government, logical reasoning, and the philosophy of self; and from the common people, commercial enterprises.

[44] Day and night he should strive vigorously to subdue his organs; for when he has subdued his own organs, he is able to bring his subjects under his control.

[45] He must strenuously steer clear of the vices that result in grief: the ten stemming from pleasure and the eight arising from wrath; [46] for when a king is addicted to vices stemming from pleasure, he is cut off from Law and Wealth, but when he is addicted to those arising from wrath, he is cut off from his very life.

[47] Hunting, gambling, sleeping during the day, disparaging others, women, liquor, music, song, dance, and useless travel—this is the set of ten stemming from pleasure. [48] Slander, violence, hostility, envy, resentment, plunder, verbal abuse, and physical assault—this is the set of eight arising from wrath.

[49] Wise men identify the root of both these sets, and it is greed. He should diligently overcome it; for both these sets originate from it. [50] Drinking, gambling, women, and hunting—one should recognize these four in the order enumerated as the most harmful of the set stemming from pleasure. [51] Physical assault, verbal abuse, and plunder—one should recognize these three as always the most harmful of the set stemming from wrath. [52] Within the latter group of seven, which run rampant everywhere, a self-composed man should recognize that each preceding vice is more perilous than each subsequent.

[53] Between vice and death, they say, vice is far worse; a man given to vice sinks to the very bottom (6.35 n.), whereas a man free of vice goes to heaven after death.

Appointment of Counsellors

[54] The king should appoint seven or eight counsellors.* They must be individuals who are natives of the land,* well-versed in the Treatises, brave, well-accomplished, and coming from illustrious families, individuals who have been thoroughly investigated. [55] Even an easy task becomes difficult when undertaken by a single individual, especially if he has no associates; how much harder a kingdom yielding great revenue?

[56] He should confer with them daily on general matters relating to alliance and war, and about the state, revenue, and security, as also the pacification of acquisitions. [57] After ascertaining their views about his affairs, first from each individually and then from all of them as a group, he should do what is in his best interest. [58] From the most distinguished and sagacious Brahmin among them, however, the king should seek the most important counsel, the one relating to the sixfold strategy (7.160). [59] Trusting him completely, he should always entrust all his affairs to him and proceed with any task only after reaching a decision jointly with him.

Appointment of Officials

[60] He should also appoint other officials.* They must be individuals who are honest, intelligent, steadfast, and able to collect revenues properly, individuals who have been thoroughly investigated. [61] He should appoint as many tireless, clever, and wise men as are required to carry out his obligations, [62] employing the brave and the clever amongst them, individuals coming from illustrious families, in financial affairs; the honest in mines and factories; and the timid in the interior of his residence.

Appointment of an Envoy

[63] He should also appoint an envoy. He must be an expert in all the Treatises; able to grasp a hint, bearing, or gesture;* be honest and clever; and come from an illustrious family. [64] A man who is loyal, honest, and clever; who has a sharp memory and knows the right time and place; and who is handsome, fearless, and eloquent—such a man is recommended as a king's envoy.

[65] The army depends on the official; the enforcement of order, on the army; the treasury and the realm, on the king; and alliance and its reverse on the envoy. [66] For an envoy is the one who forges an alliance; and he is the one who splits allies apart. An envoy does the kind of work that splits people apart.

[67] By means of concealed hints and gestures, he should decode the bearing, hints, and gestures of the rival king with the help of seducible men in his service and uncover his plans with the help of his servants.

[68] After finding out all the plans of the rival king accurately, he should take* the kinds of measures that would prevent damage to himself.

Constructing the Royal Fort

[69] He should settle in a region that is dry, abounding in grain, populated mainly by Āryas, healthy, beautiful, with submissive neighbours, and providing a comfortable living.

[70] A fortress secured by a desert, a fortress with an earthen rampart, a fortress surrounded by water, a fortress protected by a forest, a fortress guarded by soldiers, and a fortress protected by a hill—finding safety in such a fortress, he should settle in a fort. [71] He should try his very best to find safety in a hill fortress;* for the hill fortress, because of its numerous superior features, is the most excellent of them. [72] Animals, creatures living in holes, and fish find safety in the first three of them; and monkeys, humans, and gods in the last three, respectively. [73] As their enemies do not harm these when they have found safety in a fortress, so his foes do not harm a king who has found safety in a fortress.

[74] One archer positioned on a rampart can fight off a hundred, and one hundred can fight off ten thousand. On account of this, a fortress is most excellent. [75] It should be well supplied with weapons, money, grain, conveyances,* Brahmins, artisans, machines, fodder, and water.

[76] At its centre, he should have a house built for himself, a house that is spacious, secure, and bright, suitable for all seasons, and provided with pools and groves.

Marriage

[77] After establishing his residence there, he should marry a wife who belongs to the same class, has the right bodily characteristics (3.8–10), comes from a prominent family, is charming, and possesses beauty and fine qualities.

Appointment of Chaplain and Priests

[78] He should also appoint a chaplain and choose his officiating priests. They are to perform on his behalf the domestic rites, as well as those requiring three sacred fires.*

[79] The king should perform various sacrifices accompanied by generous sacrificial gifts; and to acquire merit, he should distribute luxuries and money to Brahmins.

Collectors and Supervisors

[80] He should employ trusted officials to collect annual taxes from his realm, strictly follow tradition in his dealings with the population, and behave like a father towards his people.

[81] He should appoint perspicacious supervisors of various kinds to oversee different areas, and they should inspect all the activities of the men responsible for his affairs.

Devotion to Brahmins

[82] He should pay honour to Brahmins who have returned from their teacher's house; for this is the inexhaustible treasure deposited with Brahmins decreed for kings. [83] Neither thief nor enemy can steal it, and it never perishes. Therefore, the king should deposit this inexhaustible treasure with Brahmins.

[84] It never spills, it never falls, it never perishes at all—an offering made in the mouth of a Brahmin is far superior to oblations made in the fire. [85] A gift to a non-Brahmin brings an equal reward; to a Brahmin by name, a double reward; to one who is advanced in vedic study, a thousandfold reward; and to a man who has completely mastered the Veda, an infinite reward. [86] For, whether the reward a man receives after death is large or small is contingent on his spirit of generosity (3.202 n.) and on the excellence of the recipient.

War and Warrior Ethic

[87] When challenged by rivals—whether they are stronger, weaker, or of equal strength—as he protects his subjects, a king must never back away from battle, recalling the Law of Kṣatriyas. [88] Refusal to turn back in battle, protecting the subjects, and obedient service to

Brahmins—for kings, these are the best means of securing happiness. [89] When kings fight each other in battles with all their strength, seeking to kill each other and refusing to turn back, they go to heaven.

[90] When he is engaged in battle, he must never slay his enemies with weapons that are treacherous,* barbed, or laced with poison, or whose tips are ablaze with fire. [91] He must never slay a man standing on the ground,* an effeminate man (3.150 n.), a man with joined palms, a man with loose hair, a seated man, a man declaring 'I am yours', [92] a sleeping man, a man without his armour, a naked man, a man without his weapons, a non-fighting spectator, a man engaging someone else, [93] a man with damaged weapons, a man in distress, a badly wounded man, a frightened man, or a man who has turned tail—recalling the Law followed by good people.

[94] When a man is killed in battle by the enemy as he turns tail frightened, he takes upon himself all the evil deeds committed by his master; [95] while any good deeds that a man killed as he turns tail has stored up for the hereafter, all of that his master takes from him.

War Booty [96] Whatever a man wins—chariot, horse, elephant, parasol, money, grain, livestock, women, all goods, and base metal—all that belongs to him. [97] A pre-emptive share,* however, should be given to the king—so states the vedic scripture; and the king should distribute among the soldiers anything that has not been won in single combat.

> [98] I have set forth above the eternal Law of warriors
> without elaboration. A Kṣatriya must never deviate
> from this Law, as he kills his enemies in battle.

Policies for Good Government

[99] The king should seek to acquire what he has not acquired, preserve diligently what he has acquired, augment what he has preserved, and distribute what he has augmented on worthy recipients.* [100] These he should recognize as the four means of securing the goals of man;* and he should execute them properly and tirelessly every day. [101] What he has not acquired, he should seek to acquire with military force; what he has acquired, he should preserve with vigilance; what he has preserved, he should augment through profitable investments; and what he has augmented, he should distribute through gifts.

[102] He should keep his military force in constant readiness, constantly display his might, constantly guard his secrets, and constantly probe his enemy's weaknesses. [103] The whole world stands in awe of the man who keeps his military force in constant readiness; it is with military force, therefore, that he should subdue all creatures. [104] He should always act without guile and never with guile; and, guarding himself well at all times, he should detect the guile employed by his enemies. [105] He must not let the enemy discover any weakness of his, but discover any weakness of the enemy; he should hide his limbs like a tortoise* and conceal his own weak points.

[106] He should ponder over his affairs like a heron, dart off like a rabbit, snatch like a wolf, and attack like a lion.

[107] As he thus engages in conquest, he should bring under his control all the adversaries he encounters by the use of the strategies beginning with conciliation.* [108] If, after the employment of the first three strategies, they still do not submit, then he should undoubtedly subdue them by military force and in due course bring them under his control. [109] Among all four strategies beginning with conciliation, experts always recommend conciliation and military force for the enhancement of his realm.

[110] As a weeder plucks the weeds and protects the corn, so the king should protect his realm and kill his adversaries. [111] When a king in his folly oppresses his own realm indiscriminately, he is soon deprived of his kingdom and his life, along with his relatives. [112] As living beings destroy their lives by oppressing their bodies, so kings too destroy their lives by oppressing their realms.

[113] He should observe this rule always in managing his realm, for when his realm is well managed, the king prospers with ease.

Organization of the State

Governance of Villages and Towns [114] He should station well-supervised constabularies in the middle of two, three, and five villages, as also in the middle of one hundred villages for the protection of his realm. [115] He should appoint superintendents responsible for one village, for ten villages, for twenty villages, for one hundred villages, and for one thousand villages.

[116] When troubles arise in a village, the superintendent of that village should, in due course, report them personally to the

superintendent of ten villages, and he in turn, to the superintendent of twenty village. [117]The superintendent of twenty villages should report all that to the superintendent of a hundred villages, and he in turn should report them personally to the superintendent of a thousand villages.

[118]The superintendent of a village shall avail himself of the food, drink, firewood, and the like that the villagers are required to supply daily to the king. [119]The superintendent of ten villages shall enjoy benefits from one 'family';* the superintendent of twenty villages, from five 'families'; the superintendent of a hundred villages, from one village; the superintendent of a thousand villages, from one town.

Supervision of Officials [120]Their activities pertaining to the villages, as well as those undertaken by each individually, should be overseen vigilantly by another loyal officer of the king.

[121]In each city he should appoint a general manager of all affairs, a man of high stature* and fierce appearance, like a planet among the stars.

[122]He should always make the circuit of all those officials personally and investigate their conduct within their jurisdictions thoroughly through resident spies; [123]for the king's officials, appointed to protect the people, often become swindlers seizing the property of others—he must protect his subjects from them. [124]When these evil-minded men extort money from people who have business* with them, the king should confiscate all their property and send them into exile.*

Wages [125]He should fix a daily allowance for women in the royal service and for menial servants in accordance with their rank and duties. [126]One Paṇa should be given as maintenance for those at the bottom and six Paṇas for those at the top, as also a set of clothes every six months and one Droṇa of grain every month.

Taxes and Duties

[127]The king should levy taxes on traders after taking into consideration the price of purchase and sale, the distance of transport, maintenance and other expenses, and the cost of security.

[128]The king should always assess taxes in his realm after careful

consideration so that both he and those who do the work get their fair reward. [129] As leeches, calves, and bees eat their food a little at a time, so a king should gather annual taxes from his realm a little at a time. [130] Of livestock and gold, the king shall take a one-fiftieth share; and of grains, an eighth share, or a sixth or twelfth. [131] He shall also take a sixth share of trees, meat, honey, ghee, perfumes, herbs, condiments, flowers, roots, fruits, [132] leaves, vegetables, grass, skins, cane, earthen vessels, and everything made of stone.

[133] Even at the point of death, he shall never extract a tax from a vedic scholar, nor shall a vedic scholar living within his realm languish from hunger. [134] When a vedic scholar languishes from hunger within the domain of a king, before long his own realm will also languish from hunger. [135] After ascertaining the man's learning and conduct, he should provide him with a means of subsistence consistent with the Law and protect him in every way, as a father his own natural son (9.166). [136] When such a person practises the Law every day under the protection of the king, it augments the king's life span, wealth, and realm.

[137] He should make the common people in his realm who live by trade pay at least something annually under the rubric of a tax. [138] The king should make artisans and craftsmen, as also self-employed Śūdras, contribute one day's work each month.

[139] He must not cut off his own root and that of others through excessive greed; for by cutting off his own root, he does harm both to himself and to them.

Adjudicating Lawsuits

[140] After he has tried a lawsuit, the king should be both harsh and gentle; a king who is both harsh and gentle earns high esteem.

[141] When he becomes tired of trying lawsuits filed by people, he should install on that seat a leading minister who knows the Law, is wise and self-disciplined, and comes from an illustrious family.

Protection of the Subjects

[142] Arranging in this manner for the discharge of all his obligations, he should protect these subjects with care and vigilance. [143] When bandits abduct from his realm subjects screaming for help, while he

and men in his service stand by—he is surely dead, he is not alive. [144] For a Kṣatriya, the protection of his subjects is the highest Law; the enjoyment of the specified rewards* binds the king to this Law.

Morning Routine

[145] He should rise in the last watch of the night (4.92 n.), perform his personal purifications with a collected mind, make the fire offering, pay his respects to Brahmins, and enter his splendid assembly hall.

[146] Standing there, he should greet all his subjects cheerfully and then dismiss them. After dismissing all his subjects, he should confer with his counsellors.

Meeting with Counsellors [147] Climbing up to a hilltop or a terrace, retiring to a solitary spot, or withdrawing to a wild area or a bare tract, he should confer with them unobserved. [148] When common people, as they conspire, do not discover a king's plans, he will enjoy the entire earth, even though his treasury is empty.

[149] Idiots, the dumb, the blind, the deaf, animals, old people, women, foreigners (2.23 n.), the sick, and the crippled—he should have these removed when he confers with his counsellors. [150] He should pay special attention to this, because these wretched people and animals, but women in particular, betray secret plans.

[151] At midday or midnight, when he is not tired or worn out, he should reflect on these matters either in consultation with his counsellors or alone—on Law, Wealth, and Pleasure (7.100 n.), [152] and on how they may be acquired all together when they are in mutual opposition; on giving his young girls in marriage; on protecting his young boys; [153] on dispatching ambassadors; on tying up the remaining loose ends of his undertakings;* on the activities within the women's quarters; on the conduct of his spies; [154] on the entire eightfold agenda,* as also the set of five,* meticulously; on the affection and disaffection towards him; on the activities in the circle of neighbouring kingdoms;* [155] on the activities of the buffer king;* on the conduct of the power-hungry king; and on the activities of the neutral king and, with great diligence, of the enemy king.

Constituents of the Circle [156] The above constituents, in brief, form the root of the circle of neighbouring kings; eight others also have been enumerated, bringing the total, according to the tradition, to twelve.* [157] There are also five others and they are called official, realm, fort, treasury, and army. These are enumerated with reference to each of the above, the total coming to seventy-two.*

[158] He should recognize that his immediate neighbour is his enemy, as also anyone rendering assistance to the enemy; that his enemy's immediate neighbour is an ally; and that the one beyond these two is neutral. [159] He should prevail over them by conciliation and the other strategies (7.107 n.), employed both separately and collectively, and by valour and policy.

Political Strategy: I [160] He should constantly think about the sixfold strategy: forging alliances, waging war, marching into battle, remaining stationary, pursuing a double stratagem,* and seeking asylum. [161] After forging an alliance or waging war, he should carefully examine the state of affairs and adopt the tactic of remaining stationary, marching into battle, pursuing a double stratagem, or seeking asylum.

[162] The king should realize that there are two ways to forge an alliance, to wage war, to march into battle, to remain stationary, to pursue a double strategem, and to seek asylum. [163] He should know that there are two kinds of alliance: the one is when both parties march together into battle with the same objective—it is of immediate significance; the other is its opposite—and it looks to the future. [164] Tradition records two types of war: the one is waged on one's own and for one's own ends, whether it is at a proper time or not; the other is occasioned when an ally has initiated the offensive. [165] Marching into battle is said to be of two types: the one is undertaken alone when an urgent situation has suddenly arisen; the other is undertaken in coalition with an ally. [166] Tradition records two types of remaining stationary: the one is undertaken when he is gradually weakened either by fate or due to his past deeds; and the other is undertaken as a favour to an ally. [167] Experts in the relative merits of the sixfold strategy present two types of the double stratagem: the one is when the army remains stationary and the other is when the ruler remains stationary, for the success of his undertakings (7.160 n.). [168] Tradition records two types of seeking asylum: the one is intended to attain his objective when he is harassed by enemies; the other is to gain renown among good people.

[169] When he is convinced that his future dominance is certain and that any immediate disadvantage is slight, then he should resort to an

alliance. [170] When he believes that all his subjects are in exceedingly high spirit and that he himself is overwhelmingly powerful, then he should consider waging war. [171] When he believes in his heart that his own army is in high spirit and prosperous and that the opposite is true of his adversary, then he should march into battle against his enemy. [172] When he is weak in terms of mounted units and infantry, then he should diligently remain stationary, while gradually appeasing the enemy. [173] When the king believes that the enemy is stronger in every respect, then he should divide his army in two and accomplish his objective (7.160n.). [174] When he has become extremely vulnerable to his enemy's forces, then he should quickly seek asylum with a strong and righteous king. [175] Should that king keep both his own subjects and the forces of his enemy in check, he should always serve him like a teacher with all his strength. [176] Even in that case, however, if he notices a liability resulting from his asylum, he should, even in that condition, resort to the good war without hesitation. [177] A politically astute king should employ all the strategies in such a way that his allies, neutrals, or enemies do not prevail over him.

[178] He should probe closely into the current status and the future shape of all his undertakings, as well as the positives and the negatives of all his past undertakings. [179] When a man knows the positives and the negatives with respect to the future, takes quick decisions with respect to the present, and knows the remaining loose ends of his past undertakings, he will not be overpowered by his enemies.

[180] He should arrange everything in such a way that his allies, neutrals, or enemies never prevail over him—that is political strategy in a nutshell.

War [181] When the king launches a military expedition against the realm of an enemy, he should advance at a measured pace towards the enemy's fort according to the following plan.

[182] The king should start a military expedition during the auspicious month of Mārgaśīrṣa (November–December), or towards the months of Phālguna (February–March) or Caitra (March–April), depending on the shape of his armed forces. [183] Even at other times when he foresees certain victory, he should undoubtedly declare war and launch the expedition, as also when a calamity has struck the enemy.

[184] He should first make the necessary arrangements for his home territory, gather provisions for the expedition according to rule, secure a base for military operations, deploy spies suitably, [185] secure the three types of road,* and inspect the six divisions* of his army—and only then march in battle formation at a measured pace against the enemy's fort.*

[186] He should be extremely vigilant about an ally who is secretly in league with the enemy, as well as about someone who has returned after going over to the enemy's side; for such a man is a very dangerous foe.

[187] He should march along his road arrayed in one of the following battle formations: staff, wagon, boar, crocodile, needle, and eagle.* [188] He should deploy his troops in the direction from which he expects danger; always set up his own camp arrayed in the lotus formation;* [189] post the commander-in-chief and the general of the army in every direction;* designate the direction from which he expects danger as the frontal direction; [190] deploy on all sides platoons of reliable soldiers with whom signals have been arranged, who are adept both at holding their ground and at pressing an attack, and who are fearless and unwavering; [191] deploy a small group to fight in close quarters and freely spread out a large group; send them into battle arrayed in the needle (7.187n.) and the thunderbolt* formations; [192] fight with chariots and horses on level ground, with boats and elephants in marshy lands, with bows in areas covered with trees and shrubs, and with swords and shields on flat land; [193] and deploy men from the lands of the Kurus, Matsyas, Pañcālas, and Śūrasenas, as well as tall and agile men, on the front lines. [194] After arraying the troops in battle formation, he should rouse them and inspect them closely; and he should monitor their behaviour even when they are engaged in combat with enemy troops.

[195] After laying siege to the enemy, he shall remain stationary—he should plunder his realm; constantly ruin his supplies of fodder, food, water, and fuel; [196] demolish reservoirs, ramparts, and moats; launch surprise assaults* against him; frighten him at night; [197] foment sedition among the seditious; keep close watch over enemy activity; and when omens are propitious, fearlessly launch the attack with the determination to win.

[198] He should strive to triumph over his enemies through conciliation, gifts, and fomenting dissension, employed collectively or sep-

arately, but never through war. [199] Victory and defeat in battle are uncertain for the two combatants; he should, therefore, avoid war. [200] When the aforementioned three strategies fail, then let him, always on guard, pursue war in such a manner that he will triumph over his enemies.

Conduct in Victory [201] After the victory, he should pay homage to gods and righteous Brahmins; grant exemptions; and issue proclamations of amnesty.*

[202] After ascertaining the collective wishes of them all, he should install there a relation of the enemy king and draw up a treaty; [203] make the Laws commonly held among them authoritative; and honour the new ruler, together with his chief officials, with precious gifts. [204] When carried out at the appropriate time, the unwelcome seizure of desirable property and their welcome distribution are both commendable.

[205] All activities here depend on divine and human dispensations. Of these, however, the divine is inscrutable; action is possible only with respect to the human.*

Political Strategy: II [206] Alternatively, he may leave after diligently working out an alliance with him,* recognizing that ally, gold, and land are the three rewards. [207] After taking into consideration the foe at his heel and his rescuer from the rear* within the circle of kings, he should secure the rewards of his campaign from his opponent either as ally or as foe.

[208] A king does not prosper as much by getting gold and land as by securing a firm ally who, although currently weak, has future potential. [209] A man who knows the Law and is mindful of favours received, whose subjects are content, and who is loyal, steadfast in his undertakings, and agile, is commended as an ally.

[210] The wise consider a man who is intelligent, brave, clever, generous, mindful of favours received, and steadfast, and who comes from an illustrious family, to be a very dangerous foe. [211] Conduct worthy of an Ārya, sound judgement with regard to men, valour, compassion, and constant generosity—these represent the qualities of a neutral.

[212] For his own well-being, a king may abandon without hesitation even a land that is safe and always yields abundant crops and on which livestock thrive. [213] A man should save his wealth for a time of adversity, save his wife even at the cost of his wealth, and always save

himself even at the cost of his wife and wealth. [214] When he sees every kind of adversity rising up fiercely in unison, a wise man should employ all the strategies collectively and individually. [215] The one who employs the strategies, the goal to be achieved through the strategies, and all the strategies in their entirety—relying on these three, he should strive for his own success.

Afternoon Routine

[216] After conferring about all this with his counsellors in this manner,* he should do his exercises and take his bath at midday, and go to his private quarters to take his meal.

[217] There he should eat food that has been thoroughly examined by servants who are completely loyal, knowledgeable about time, and incorruptible, while reciting ritual formulas that remove poison. [218] He should cleanse everything with antidotes that neutralize poison and always carefully wear on his body gems that counteract poison. [219] Women who have been thoroughly examined and whose clothing and jewellery have been searched shall wait on him attentively with fans, water, and perfumes.

[220] He should take similar care of his vehicles (7.75 n.), beds, seats, and food, as well as of his bath, grooming, and all his ornaments.

[221] After his meal, he should relax in his private quarters with his women, and after relaxing, once again turn his attention at the proper time to his affairs. [222] Dressed in his regalia, he should again inspect his armed forces, all his conveyances, and his weapons and trappings.

Evening Routine

[223] After performing the evening twilight worship, he should arm himself and receive reports in his inner chambers from secret informants and spies about their activities.

[224] After withdrawing to another secure chamber and dismissing those people, he should again enter his private quarters to take his meal escorted by women.* [225] After eating something there once again while he is being entertained with music, he should go to bed at the proper time and rise up refreshed.

[226] A king should follow this schedule when he is healthy; but when he is unwell, he may delegate all this to his officials.

CHAPTER EIGHT

THE JUSTICE SYSTEM

Court

1 When the king is going to try a case, he should enter the court modestly accompanied by Brahmins and counsellors who are experts in policy. 2 Seated or standing there, dressed in modest clothes and ornaments, and raising his right hand, he should look into the cases of the plaintiffs 3 every day in accordance with the standards of the region and those specified in the legal texts, lawsuits that fall individually under the eighteen avenues of litigation.

Grounds for Litigation

4 Of these, (i) the first is non-payment of debts; (ii) deposits; (iii) sale without ownership; (iv) partnerships; (v) non-delivery of gifts; 5 (vi) non-payment of wages; (vii) breach of contract; (viii) cancellation of a sale or purchase; (ix) disputes between owners and herdsmen; 6 (x) the Law on boundary disputes; (xi) verbal assault; (xii) physical assault; (xiii) theft; (xiv) violence; (xv) sexual crimes against women;* 7 (xvi) Law concerning husband and wife; (xvii) partition of inheritance; and (xviii) gambling and betting. These are the eighteen grounds on which litigation may be instituted in this world.

8 These are the areas in which, for the most part, disputes among people arise; and the king should decide their cases based on the eternal Law.

Legal Proceedings

Judges 9 When the king does not try a case personally, however, he should appoint a learned Brahmin to do so. 10 Entering the main court itself accompanied by three assessors, he should try the cases brought before the king, either seated or standing. 11 The place where three Brahmins versed in the Vedas and a learned officer of the king sit, they call the court of Brahman.

Pursuit of Justice [12] When Justice (*dharma*), pierced by Injustice* (*adharma*), comes to the court for redress and the court officials do not pluck out that dart from him, then they are themselves pierced by it. [13] A man must either not enter the court or speak candidly; by refusing to speak or by speaking deceitfully, he commits a sin. [14] When Justice is struck by Injustice, and Truth by Untruth, while the court officials remain idle onlookers, then they are themselves struck down. [15] Stricken, Justice surely strikes back; defended, Justice defends. Therefore, never strike at Justice, lest Justice, stricken, wipes us out. [16] Lord Justice is truly the bull (*vṛṣa*), and a man who impedes (*alam*) him the gods call a low-born (*vṛṣa-la*). Therefore, one should never trample Justice. [17] Justice is the only friend who follows a man even in death; for all else perishes along with the body.*

[18] One-quarter of an Injustice goes to the perpetrator, one-quarter to the witness, one-quarter to all the court officials, and one-quarter to the king. [19] The king, on the other hand, becomes sinless, the court officials are freed, and the sin falls squarely on the perpetrator, when a man deserving condemnation is condemned.

Excursus: **Śūdras as Legal Interpreters** [20] Let a king, if he so wishes, get someone who is a Brahmin only by name to interpret the Law, or even someone who simply uses his birth to make a living, but under no circumstances a Śūdra. [21] When a Śūdra interprets the Law for a king, his realm sinks like a cow in mud, as he looks on helplessly. [22] The entire realm, stricken with famine and pestilence, quickly perishes, when it is teeming with Śūdras, overrun by infidels, and devoid of twice-born people.

Judicial Conduct and Reasoning [23] Ascending the throne of justice with his body covered and his mind composed, he should pay homage to the guardian deities of the world and open the trial. [24] Paying attention only to these two—what is and what is not in accord with the provisions of polity (*artha*), and what is and what is not in accord with the Law (*dharma*)—he should try all the cases brought by litigants in the order of their social class.

[25] He should discover the internal disposition of men by external signs—voice, colour, expression, bearing, eyes, and gestures. [26] Inner thoughts are discerned by the bearing, expressions, gait, gestures, and manner of speaking, and by changes in the eyes and face.

Excursus: **Property of Minors and Women** [27]The king should protect the estate inherited by a child until he has returned home after his studentship or until he is no longer a minor.*

[28]The same protection must be extended to barren women, women without sons or bereft of family, women devoted to their husbands, widows, and women in distress. [29]If their in-laws (2.132 n.) usurp their property while they are alive, a righteous king should discipline them with the punishment laid down for thieves.

Excursus: **Lost and Stolen Property** [30]Any property that is lost and without an owner should be kept in deposit by the king for three years. Before the lapse of three years, the owner can claim it; after that the king may take it. [31]A man who claims 'This is mine' and, when questioned according to rule, identifies its physical appearance, number, and the like correctly, is the owner and deserves to have that property; [32]but if he is ignorant of the exact place and time when it was lost and its colour, physical appearance, and size, he deserves a fine equal in value to that property.

[33]The king may take one-sixth of any lost property that is recovered, or else one-tenth or one-twelfth, calling to mind the Law practised by good people. [34]Lost property that is recovered shall remain in the care of competent officials, and the king should have any thieves caught in connection with its disappearance executed by an elephant.

[35]When a man states truthfully in regard to a treasure-trove 'This is mine', the king may take one-sixth or one-twelfth of it. [36]If he lies, however, he should be fined one-eighth of his wealth or, after reckoning the value of the treasure, a smaller portion.

[37]When a learned Brahmin finds a treasure-trove that had been buried by his ancestors, however, he may take the whole of it; for a Brahmin is the supreme lord of all. [38]When the king discovers an ancient treasure-trove buried in the ground, he should give one-half of it to Brahmins and deposit one-half in the treasury; [39]the king, by proving protection, is entitled to one-half of all ancient treasure-troves and of minerals in the ground, for he is the supreme lord of the earth.

[40]The king must restore to individuals of all classes any property of theirs stolen by thieves; if the king retains it for himself, he incurs the sin of its thief.

Judicial Conduct and Reasoning [41] He who knows the Law should examine the Laws of castes, regions, guilds, and families, and only then settle the Law specific to each. [42] Even men living far away endear themselves to the world when they stick to the activity specific to each and carry out their specific activities.

[43] Neither the king nor any official of his shall initiate a lawsuit independently; nor shall he in any way suppress an action brought before him by someone else.

[44] As a hunter traces the location of an animal by the trail of blood, so a king should trace the location of justice by deductive reasoning. [45] When he is conducting a judicial proceeding, he should pay close attention to the truth, the object of the suit, himself, the witnesses, the place, the time, and the appearance.*

[46] He should ratify the acknowledged practices of virtuous men and righteous twice-born individuals, if such practices do not conflict with those of a particular region, family, or caste.

Grounds for Litigation: I Non-payment of Debts

[47] When a creditor petitions for the recovery of his money from a debtor and the facts are established, the king should compel the debtor to return the money to the creditor.

[48] He should constrain the debtor and force him to pay, using any means by which the creditor may recover his money. [49] Money loaned may be recovered by invoking the Law, by litigation, by cunning, by traditional strategies,* and fifth, by force. [50] Should a creditor recover his money from the debtor on his own, he must not be prosecuted by the king simply for recovering his own money.

[51] If a man denies that he took a loan when it has been established by evidence, he should compel that man to return the money to the creditor and in addition impose a small fine proportionate to his means. [52] When the debtor, told in court to pay up, denies the charge, the plaintiff should produce a document or offer some other evidence.

[53] When the plaintiff produces something that is not documentary evidence; produces and then disavows it; does not realize that his earlier points contradict the ones he makes subsequently; [54] states his case and then backs away from it; does not acknowledge under questioning a point that has been clearly established; [55] secretly discusses

with witnesses a document which is prohibited from being discussed; objects to a question clearly articulated; retreats; [56] does not speak when he is ordered 'Speak!'; does not prove what he asserts; and does not understand what goes before and what after—such a plaintiff loses his suit. [57] When a plaintiff says 'I have people who know', but when told 'Produce them' does not produce them, the judge should declare him also the loser for these very reasons.*

[58] If the plaintiff fails to present his case, he is subject to corporal punishment and a fine in accordance with the Law; and if the defendant fails to respond within three fortnights, he loses the case in the eyes of the Law. [59] The amount that one man falsely denies and the amount that the other falsely claims—the king should impose a fine equal to double those amounts on those two men ignorant of the Law.

[60] When a man is summoned to court by a creditor and denies the charge under questioning, he may be convicted through the testimony of at least three witnesses given in the presence of the king and Brahmins.

> [61] I will now explain what sorts of individual creditors
> may call as witnesses in lawsuits and how they should
> be made to speak the truth.

Qualifications of Witnesses [62] Householders, men with sons, natives of the region (7.54 n.), Kṣatriyas, Vaiśyas, and Śūdras, when they are called by the plaintiff, are competent to give testimony, and not just anybody, except in an emergency. [63] Trustworthy men of all social classes may be called as witnesses in lawsuits, men who know the Law in its entirety and are free from greed; individuals different from these should be excluded.

[64] Individuals who have a stake in the suit; individuals close to the litigants; their associates and enemies; individuals with a criminal record; the very sick; and men of ill repute—these must not be called as witnesses. [65] The king may not be called as a witness, nor should the following: an artisan; a performer; a vedic scholar; an individual bearing the insignia of a religious profession (4.200 n.); one who has severed all attachments; [66] a totally subservient individual; a reprehensible person; a bandit; a criminal; an old person; a child; a single person;* an individual of the lowest birth or with impaired organs; [67] someone in distress; an intoxicated or insane person; someone

tormented by hunger or thirst, or suffering from fatigue; a lovesick or angry person; and a thief.

68 For women, women shall give testimony; for the twice-born, twice-born individuals of equal rank; for Śūdras, upright Śūdras; and for the lowest-born, those of the lowest birth. 69 Anyone who has personal knowledge may give testimony for litigants when the event has taken place inside a house or in the wilderness, or in a case involving bodily harm. 70 When there is no one else, even a woman, a child, an old man, a pupil, a relative, a slave, or a servant may give testimony.

71 He should recognize the trembling in the voices of children, old men, and sick persons, as also of individuals with deranged minds, when they give false testimony.

72 He must not investigate* the witnesses in all cases of violence, theft, sexual crimes, and verbal and physical assault.

Assessing Testimony 73 When witnesses are in disagreement, the king should accept the testimony of the majority; when they are equally divided, the testimony of those distinguished by superior qualities; and when men with superior qualities are in disagreement, the testimony of Brahmins.

74 Testimony is valid when it is based on what the witness himself has seen or heard. When a witness speaks truthfully with respect to that, he does not suffer any loss of merit or wealth. 75 If, in a court of Āryas, a witness says something deceitfully contrary to what he has seen or heard, after death he will plunge headlong into hell and suffer the loss of heaven.

76 When a person, even though he is not listed as a witness* in the plaint, has seen or heard anything pertaining to the trial and he is questioned during the trial, he also should testify in accordance with what he saw or heard.

77 Even one man free from greed may be appointed as a witness, but never women, even if they are many and honest, because the female mind is unsteady; nor even other men tainted with defects.

78 Only what witnesses testify to in a forthright manner should be accepted as valid in a trial; anything different that they may testify to deceitfully for the sake of the Law has no validity.*

Questioning of Witnesses* 79 When the witnesses have gathered in the court, the judge should examine them in the presence of the plaintiff and the defendant, exhorting the witnesses in the following manner:

> [80] What you know about any mutual transaction between these two individuals pertaining to this lawsuit—state all that truthfully; for you are the witnesses in this matter. [81] If a witness speaks the truth when he testifies, he will obtain magnificent worlds, as well as unsurpassing fame here below; such speech is honoured by Brahman. [82] If he speaks an untruth when he testifies, he will be bound tightly by the fetters of Varuṇa and lie helplessly for one hundred lifetimes; therefore, he should speak the truth when he testifies. [83] By truth, the witness is purified; by truth, merit is increased. Witnesses of all social classes, therefore, should speak only the truth. [84] For the self alone is the witness of the self; the self, likewise, is the refuge of the self. Do not disdain your own self, the supreme witness of men. [85] Evil doers undoubtedly think, 'No one sees us'; yet gods see them clearly, and so does their own inner self. [86] Heaven, earth, waters, heart, moon, sun, fire, Yama, wind, night, the two twilights, and the Law—these know the conduct of all embodied beings.

[87] In the presence of gods and Brahmins* and in the forenoon, the judge, after purifying himself, should ask the twice-born individuals, who have purified themselves and are facing the north or the east, to give truthful testimony. [88] He should question a Brahmin, saying 'Speak'; a Kṣatriya, saying 'Speak the truth'; a Vaiśya, with a reference to cows, seeds, and gold;* but a Śūdra, with a reference to these sins that cause loss of caste.

> [89] The worlds to which tradition consigns a murderer of a Brahmin, a killer of a woman or child, a betrayer of a friend, and an ingrate—those worlds will be yours, if you testify falsely. [90] Whatever good deeds you have done since birth, dear man, all that will go to the dogs, if you testify dishonestly. [91] 'I am all alone'—should you think like that about yourself, good man; there dwells always in your heart this sage, who observes your good and evil deeds! [92] This god, Yama the son of Vivasvat, dwells in your heart. If you have no quarrel with him, then you do not have to go to the Ganges or the Kuru land.* [93] Naked,

blind, shaven-headed, and racked with hunger and thirst, a man who gives false testimony will have to go to his enemy's house carrying a skull-bowl to beg for almsfood. [94] If anyone gives a false answer when questioned at a judicial investigation, in blind darkness that sinner will fall headlong into hell. [95] A person who goes to a court and testifies to what is contrary to the facts or to what he has not seen is like a blind man, eating fish along with the bones. [96] When his discerning Kṣetrajña, 'the knower of the field' (12.12–13n.), remains unperturbed as a man is giving testimony—gods know of no man superior to him in this world. [97] Listen, my friend, to an orderly enumeration of how many relatives of his a man kills* when he gives false testimony in a particular case. [98] He kills five by false testimony concerning livestock; ten, by false testimony concerning cows; one hundred, by false testimony concerning horses; and one thousand, by false testimony concerning a human being. [99] He kills the born and yet to be born by giving false testimony concerning gold; and he kills all by false testimony concerning land—never give false testimony concerning land. [100] False testimony concerning water,* they say, is similar to that concerning land; the same is true of false testimony concerning the sexual enjoyment of women and concerning all gems, whether they are aquatic or lapidary (5.111–12n.). [101] After taking careful note of all these evils resulting from false testimony, tell the truth forthrightly just as you saw or heard.

[102] He should treat Brahmins who are cattle herders, traders, artisans, performers, servants, or money lenders, just like Śūdras.

Excusable False Testimony [103] When a man, even though he knows the truth, gives evidence in lawsuits contrary to the facts for a reason relating to the Law, he does not fall from the heavenly world; that, they say, is divine speech. [104] When telling the truth will result in the execution of a Śūdra, Vaiśya, Kṣatriya, or a Brahmin, a man may tell a lie; for that is far better than the truth.

[105] Such persons, performing the highest expiation for the sin of false testimony, should offer to the goddess Sarasvatī oblations of milk-rice dedicated to the goddess Speech. [106] Alternatively, such a person may offer an oblation of ghee in the fire according to

rule, reciting the Kūṣmāṇḍa formulas, the verse to Varuṇa: 'Untie, Varuṇa . . .' or the three formulas addressed to water.*

Failure to Give Evidence [107] When a man who is not sick fails to testify for three fortnights in cases pertaining to debts and the like, he becomes liable for the entire debt and is fined one-tenth of the total.*

Signs of False Testimony [108] When an illness, a fire, or the death of a relative is seen to afflict a witness within seven days of his testimony, he should be compelled to pay the debt and a fine.

Oaths and Ordeals [109] When two persons are litigating matters for which there are no witnesses and the judge is unable to discern the truth, he should discover it even by means of an oath.* [110] Great sages, as well as gods, have taken oaths to settle a case. Vasiṣṭha* also made an oath before King Paijavana.

[111] A wise man must not take an oath falsely even with regard to a trifling matter; for by taking an oath falsely, he comes to ruin here and in the hereafter. [112] Taking an oath is not a sin causing loss of caste when it is made in connection with lovers, marriages, fodder for cows, or firewood, or to protect a Brahmin.

[113] He should make a Brahmin swear by the truth; a Kṣatriya by his conveyance (7.75 n.) and weapons; a Vaiśya by his cattle, seeds, and gold; and a Śūdra by all the sins causing loss of caste.*

[114] Alternatively, he may make the person carry fire, stay submerged in water, or touch separately the heads of his sons and wife. [115] When the blazing fire does not burn a man, the water does not push him up to the surface, and no misfortune quickly strikes him,* he should be judged innocent by reason of his oath. [116] Long ago when Vatsa was accused by his younger brother, Fire, the world's spy, did not burn a single hair of his because he told the truth.*

False Testimony [117] Every case where perjured testimony has been given should be declared a mistrial, and any judgement rendered there should be annulled.

[118] Testimony given through greed, delusion, fear, friendship, lust, anger, ignorance, or immaturity is considered false.

> [119] I will explain in order the specific punishments for
> a person who gives false testimony for any one of
> these reasons.

Punishment for Perjury [120]For giving false testimony through greed, he should be fined 1,000;* through delusion, the lowest fine (8.138); through fear, double the middle fine; through friendship, four times the lowest fine; [121]through lust, ten times the lowest fine; through anger, three times the highest fine; through ignorance, a full 200; and through immaturity, just 100. [122]These are said to be the punishments for false testimony prescribed by the wise in order to prevent the miscarriage of justice and to arrest injustice.

[123]When individuals of the three classes give false testimony, a righteous king should first fine them and then execute* them; a Brahmin, on the other hand, should be sent into exile.

Varieties of Punishment [124]Manu, the son of the Self-existent One, has proclaimed ten places upon which punishment may be inflicted. They are applicable to the three classes; a Brahmin shall depart unscathed. [125]They are: genitals, stomach, tongue, and hands; feet are the fifth; and then, eyes, nose, ears, wealth, and body.

[126]He should inflict punishment on those deserving punishment only after he has fully ascertained the motive, as also the time and place, accurately, and considered carefully the ability of the criminal and the severity of the crime. [127]Unjust punishment shatters his fame and destroys his reputation in this world, and it is also an obstacle to heaven in the next; therefore, he should avoid it completely. [128]When a king punishes those who do not deserve to be punished and neglects to punish those who deserve it, he brings great infamy upon himself and he will also go to hell.

[129]He should employ first the punishment of verbal reprimand; next a public denunciation; third, a fine; and finally, corporal punishment. [130]If he is unable to restrain them even with corporal punishment, then he should impose on them all these four.

> [131]I will explain fully the terms spread across the world relating to copper, silver, and gold for use in commercial transactions among people.

Weights [132]The fleck of dust seen when the sun shines through a lattice is called Trasareṇu,* the primary weight. [133]One should know that eight Trasareṇus make one Likṣā in weight; three Likṣās, one Rājasarṣapa; three Rājasarṣapas, one Gaurasarṣapa; [134]six Gaurasarṣapas, one middling Yava; three Yavas, one Kṛṣṇala; five Kṛṣṇalas, one Māṣa; sixteen Māṣas, one Suvarṇa; [135] four Suvarṇas, one Pala; and ten Palas, one Dharaṇa.

One should know that two Kṛṣṇalas weighed together make one silver Māṣaka, [136] and sixteen Māṣakas, one silver Dharaṇa, as also a Purāṇa. A copper Kārṣika, however, should be known as a Kārṣāpaṇa, or simply Paṇa; [137] ten Dharaṇas, as one silver Śatamāna; and four Suvarṇas, as one Niṣka in weight.

Fines [138] Tradition has determined 250 Paṇas as the lowest fine; 500 Paṇas should be considered the middle fine; and 1,000 Paṇas, the highest. [139] If the debtor admits that he owes the debt, he ought to be fined 500; but if he denies, twice as much—that is Manu's decree.

Rates of Interest: I [140] A money-lender may assess the rate of interest decreed by Vasiṣṭha (*VaDh* 2.50) for the increase of capital and charge 1.25 per cent per month. [141] Alternatively, he may charge 2 per cent, keeping in mind the Law followed by good men; for by charging 2 per cent he does not become guilty of a sin involving money. [142] He may charge exactly 2 per cent, 3 per cent, 4 per cent, or 5 per cent interest per month, according to the descending order of the classes.

[143] If a pledge together with any profits it may yield has been furnished, however, the creditor shall not receive any interest on the loan; nor shall the pledge be alienated or sold because the time has lapsed.* [144] He must not make use of a pledge by force; if he makes use of it, he forfeits the interest and must reimburse the owner the original value of the pledge. Otherwise, the creditor becomes guilty of stealing the pledge.

Pledges [145] Neither a pledge nor a deposit is liable to forfeiture due to the passage of time; they may be recovered even after they have been held for a long time. [146] The owner never loses his title to anything enjoyed through his benevolence, or to cows, camels, draught animals, horses, and animals delivered for breaking in.

[147] When an owner looks on silently as something is being enjoyed by others in his presence for ten years, he is not entitled to recover it. [148] If something is enjoyed within his own locality* and he is neither mentally incapacitated nor a minor, he loses any legal right to it; the user is entitled to that property.

[149] Pledges, boundaries, assets of minors, open deposits, sealed

deposits, women, and the possessions of the king and of vedic scholars are never lost on account of enjoyment.

Rates of Interest: II [150] When a foolhardy man makes use of a pledge without the consent of its owner, he shall refund half the interest as compensation for that use.

[151] Interest on a loan shall never exceed twice the principal when fixed at one time; and on grain, fruits, wool, and draught animals, it shall not exceed five times.* [152] An interest rate set above the legal limit is exorbitant and cannot be enforced; that is called the path of usury—he is entitled to only 5 per cent.

[153] He must not charge interest beyond one year or an unauthorized rate. [Authorized forms of interest are] cyclical interest, periodic interest, contractual interest, and interest paid by manual labour.*

[154] When someone is unable to repay a debt and wants to redo the contract, he should first pay the accrued interest and then renew the evidentiary instrument. [155] If he cannot come up with the money at that time, he should renew the instrument; he is obliged to pay as much interest as is due.*

[156] When someone has entered into a contract accruing cyclical interest with a specified place and time, he shall not obtain its reward if he disregards that place and time.

[157] When experts in sea voyages capable of forecasting profits with respect to particular places and times fix an interest rate, that is exactly the rate for repayment.

Surety [158] When a man stands here* as a surety to produce someone and fails to produce him, he must pay the man's debt from his own funds.

[159] A son is not obliged to pay a debt related to being a surety, vain gifts,* gambling debts, what is owed for liquor, or any remaining portions of fines and duties. [160] The above rule applies only to someone who stands as surety for appearance; when a man who has stood as surety for repayment dies, even his heirs can be compelled to pay it.*

[161] When someone who was a surety other than for repayment dies and the circumstances under which he became a surety are fully known, on what grounds can the creditor later demand payment of the debt? [162] If the money had been consigned to the surety and he

has sufficient money, the rule is that the consignee should pay the debt from his own funds.*

Validity of Transactions [163] Transactions carried out by persons who are intoxicated, insane, distressed, or totally subservient, by children or the aged, or by unauthorized persons, are invalid. [164] Agreements, even if they are well substantiated, are void if their provisions are contrary to settled Law based on established usage.

[165] A fraudulent mortgage or sale, a fraudulent gift or receipt, and wherever deceit is detected—all that must be annulled.

[166] If the person who took the loan is lost and the loan was used for the family, it should be paid by the relatives from their own funds even if they are living separately after the partitioning of the estate. [167] A transaction carried out for the benefit of the family even by someone totally subservient, whether it is in one's own or in a distant region, must not be rescinded by his superior.

[168] What is given under the threat of force, what is enjoyed under the threat of force, and any document prepared under the threat of force—all transactions executed under the threat of force Manu has declared to be null and void.

[169] Three suffer for the sake of others: witnesses, surety, and family; but four prosper: Brahmin, moneylender, merchant, and king.

Impartiality of the King [170] A king must never take what he ought not to take, even if he is impoverished; nor must he forgo what he ought to take—be it an amount ever so little—even if he is rich. [171] By taking what he ought not to take and by eschewing what he ought to take, the king's weakness is broadcast; and he comes to ruin here and in the hereafter. [172] By taking what is due to him, by bringing together the social classes,* and by protecting the weak, the king enhances his power; and he prospers here and in the hereafter.

[173] Like Yama, therefore, the ruler should lay aside his own likes and dislikes and follow Yama's pattern of behaviour (9.307), suppressing his anger and mastering his organs.

[174] When a king foolishly judges cases in a manner contrary to the Law, his enemies will soon bring that evil man under their dominion. [175] When he controls love and hatred and looks into cases in accordance with the Law, his subjects follow him, like rivers the ocean.

Recovery of Debt [176] When a debtor reports a creditor seeking to recover a debt on his own initiative, the king should compel him to pay the money to the creditor and in addition a fine equal to a quarter of the debt.

[177] A debtor belonging to the same or a lower caste should settle with his creditor even through manual labour (8.153); but a debtor who is superior should repay it in instalments.

Conclusion [178] In this manner, the king should adjudicate equitably lawsuits filed by litigants, lawsuits whose outcome is based on witnesses and evidence.

Grounds for Litigation: II Deposits

[179] A wise man should entrust a deposit to a man who is born in an illustrious family, has an impeccable character, knows the Law, speaks the truth, has a large following, is wealthy, and is an Ārya.

[180] A man should recover an article in exactly the same condition as when he deposited it in the hand of another person—as the delivery, so the recovery.

[181-2] When a man refuses to hand over a deposit to the depositor upon request and no witnesses are available, the judge should do the following out of the presence of the depositor. He should have spies of proper age and appearance actually deposit gold with that man under some pretext and then get them to request it.* [183] If he returns it in the same manner and condition as deposited, then there is nothing to the charges that the adversaries have brought against him. [184] If, however, he does not duly return that gold to them, he should be arrested and compelled to return both*—that is the fixed rule of the Law.

[185] An open or a sealed deposit should never be returned to a next-of-kin. In the event of a mishap, they both perish; although if there is no mishap, they do not perish.* [186] When he gives them of his own accord to the next-of-kin of a deceased depositor, neither the king nor the depositor's relatives should press charges against him.

[187] One should seek to obtain that article by friendly means, without resorting in any way to subterfuge; or, after probing closely into the character of the depositary, he should settle the matter peacefully.

[188] That is the rule for the settlement of all open deposits; in the case of a sealed deposit, he is in the clear, unless he has removed something from it.* [189] He is not obliged to return a deposit that is stolen by thieves, washed away in a flood, or burnt up in a fire, unless he had removed something from it.

[190] Using all the investigative methods as well as vedic oaths, the judge should examine anyone accused of appropriating a deposit or of demanding a deposit that has not been made. [191] A man who does not hand over a deposit and a man who requests the return of a deposit he has not made—both these should be punished like thieves and fined an amount equal to the deposit. [192] A man who has appropriated an open deposit, as well as a man who has appropriated a sealed deposit—the king should compel both without distinction to pay a fine equal to its value. [193] If a man appropriates the property of others by fraudulent means, however, he and his accomplices should be put to death publicly using diverse modes of execution.

[194] When a man makes an open deposit having a specific quality and quantity in the presence of the community, it should be acknowledged to have that very quality and quantity; if someone testifies falsely with regard to it, he ought to be punished. [195] If a deposit is given or received privately, then it should be returned privately—as the delivery, so the recovery.*

> [196] Thus shall the king make judgements regarding
> property that has been handed over as an open deposit
> or entrusted out of affection as a sealed deposit, without maltreating the person holding the deposit.

Grounds for Litigation: III Sale without Ownership

[197] When a man who is neither the owner nor authorized by the owner sells someone else's property, the king should not let that man, a thief pretending not to be a thief, offer testimony;* [198] and the man should also be fined—if he did it in the owner's presence, he should be made to pay a fine of 600; if he did it outside his presence and has no excuse, his liability is the same as for theft (see 8.332 n.).

[199] When a gift or sale is made by someone other than the owner, it should be considered null and void in accordance with the firm principle of legal process.

[200] In a case where a man is seen to enjoy something without any

evidence of legal title to it, title is the proof of ownership and not enjoyment—that is the settled rule. [201] When a man acquires some property through a sale in the presence of the community, he obtains that property with a clear title through legal purchase. [202] If, however, the initial seller cannot be produced but the property is cleared by the public purchase, he must not be punished; he is released by the king and the man who lost the property gets it back.

Fraudulent Sales [203] It is improper to sell one commodity mixed with another, a flawed product, or something that measures less than claimed, located far away, or is concealed.

[204] If a man shows one girl to the bridegroom and gives another, the groom may marry both for the same price—so has Manu decreed (3.53 n.). [205] When a man gives a girl who is insane, suffers from leprosy, or has lost her virginity, he should not be punished if he has disclosed the defects beforehand.

Grounds for Litigation: IV Partnerships

[206] If one officiating priest chosen for a sacrifice quits his work, his partners should give him a share proportionate to the work he has performed. [207] If a priest quits his work after the sacrificial fees have been distributed, he should receive the full share but get someone else to complete the work.

[208] At a ritual where sacrificial fees are specified for each component, the priest performing a given component should receive the specified fee or all should share the entire fee. [209] At the establishment of the sacred fires, the Adhvaryu priest should take the chariot, the Brahman priest the steed, the Hotr̥ priest the horse, and the Udgātr̥ priest the cart used for the purchase of Soma. [210] Among all the priests, half of the fee goes to the principals; one-half of that to those in the next rank; one-third of that to those entitled to a third; and one-quarter of that to those entitled to a quarter.*

[211] Men who carry out their activities in this world by forming partnerships should allocate shares by applying these principles.

Grounds for Litigation: V Non-delivery of Gifts

[212] When someone has pledged a monetary gift to a man who begs in order to fulfil the Law but who later does not follow through, he is

not obliged to deliver that gift. [213]If that man proceeds to enforce payment out of pride or greed, however, the king should fine him one Suvarṇa to atone for that theft.

> [214]I have described above accurately the non-delivery of a gift that accords with the Law. Next, I will explain the non-payment of wages.

Grounds for Litigation: VI Non-payment of Wages

[215]When a servant who is not sick fails to perform his stipulated work out of pride, he should be fined eight Kṛṣṇalas, and he should not be paid his wages. [216]If he was sick, however, he should perform the work stipulated at the outset after he has recovered his health; and he should receive his wages even if a very long time has elapsed. [217]Whether he is sick or well, if he does not have the stipulated work carried out, he should not be paid his wages, even if only a small portion of the work remains undone.

> [218]I have described above completely the Law relating to the non-payment of wages. Next, I will explain the Law relating to persons who breach a contract.

Grounds for Litigation: VII Breach of Contract

[219]When a man belonging to a village, region, or corporate entity enters into a contract truthfully and then breaks it out of greed, the king should banish that man from his realm.* [220]He should arrest that man who has violated the compact and fine him 6 Niṣkas, each weighing 4 Suvarṇas, and a silver Śatamāna.

[221]In this manner, a righteous king should apply the rules of punishment to individuals who violate compacts within a village, caste, or association.

Grounds for Litigation: VIII Cancellation of Sale or Purchase

[222]After buying or selling anything, if someone here regrets his decision, he may return or take back that article within ten days. [223]After ten days, however, he may neither return nor make someone return;

if someone does take back or return, the king shall fine him 600 (see 8.120n.).

224 When a man gives away a defective girl without disclosing her defects (8.205), the king shall personally impose on him a fine of 96 Paṇas. 225 When a man maliciously asserts that a girl is not a virgin, he should be fined 100 (see 8.120n.) if he cannot demonstrate her defect. 226 The ritual formulas of marriage are applicable only to virgin girls and nowhere among any people to non-virgins, for they are excluded from the rituals prescribed by Law. 227 The ritual formulas of marriage are a sure sign that she is the wife, and learned men should recognize that they reach their completion at the seventh step.*

228 After a given transaction has been completed, if someone here regrets his decision, the king should place him on the path of the Law in accordance with the above rules.

Grounds for Litigation: IX Disputes between Owners and Herdsmen

> 229 I will explain accurately and in strict accordance with the Law the disputes between owners and herdsmen over transgressions with respect to farm animals.

Safety of the Herd 230 During the day the liability for their safety lies with the herdsman, and during the night with the owner, provided they are at his house; otherwise, the herdsman becomes liable.

231 When a herdsman is paid in milk, he may milk the best cow out of ten with the consent of the owner; that is the payment for an uncompensated herdsman.

232 If an animal is lost, is ravaged by worms, is killed by dogs, or perishes in a dangerous place because of inadequate effort, it is the herdsman who must pay compensation. 233 If an animal is seized by robbers, the herdsman is not required to pay compensation, provided he raised the alarm and informs his master at the proper time and place.

234 When animals die, the herdsman should give their owners both ears, skin, tails, bladders, tendons, and yellow bile, and point out their distinguishing marks.

235 If goats or sheep are cornered by wolves, however, and the

herdsman fails to come to their assistance, the herdsman shall be culpable for any that a wolf may attack and kill. [236] As they are roaming the woods while being kept under check in a single group, if a wolf pounces upon and kills one, the herdsman is not culpable for that.

Damage to Crops [237] An open field extending one hundred 'bows' or three rod's throws* shall be left around a village; three times as large around a town. [238] If farm animals damage unfenced crops within that area, the king must not punish the herdsman for that.

[239] One should erect there a fence over which a camel cannot look and cover every hole through which a dog or pig could poke its head.

[240] When damage is done to a fenced field alongside a road or at the edge of a village, a fine of 100 (see 8.120n.) should be imposed if a herdsman was present; if the animals are without a herdsman, they should be impounded. [241] When damage is done in other fields, one and a half Paṇas should be assessed for each animal; and in every case, the owner of the field ought to be compensated for the crop—that is the fixed rule.

[242] Manu has declared that a cow within ten days after giving birth, bulls, and animals dedicated to gods are not subject to punishment, whether they are attended by a herdsman or not.*

[243] For an offence committed by the owner of a field, the fine shall be ten times his share; half that amount, if the offence was committed by the servants without the knowledge of the owner.*

> [244] A righteous king should follow these rules with regard to transgressions committed by owners, by animals, and by herdsmen.

Grounds for Litigation: X Boundary Disputes

[245] When a dispute arises between two villages with respect to a boundary, the king should ascertain the boundary in the month of Jyeṣṭha (May–June) when landmarks are most clearly visible.*

Boundary Markers [246] He should establish boundary trees: banyan, pipal, Kiṃśuka, cotton-tree, Sāla, palm, and trees with milky sap; [247] as also thickets, different kinds of bamboo, Śamī, creepers, mounds, reeds, and thickets of Kubjaka. In this way, the boundary will not disappear. [248] Reservoirs, wells, ponds, and waterways should be constructed at the intersection of boundaries, as also temples of gods.

[249] Seeing that in the world controversies constantly arise due to people's ignorance of boundaries, he should also have other concealed boundary markers ensconced—[250] stones, bones, cow's hair, chaff, ashes, potsherds, dried cow dung, bricks, coal, pebbles, and sand. [251] He should also have other similar substances that the soil would not decay over time ensconced as hidden markers at the intersection of boundaries.

Settling Boundary Disputes [252] By means of these markers, the king should ascertain the boundary between two litigants, as also by continuous prior possession and by a watercourse. [253] If doubt persists even after seeing the markers, the resolution of a boundary dispute will have to rely solely on witnesses.

[254] Witnesses to a boundary should be questioned about the boundary markers in the presence of the village communities and the two litigants. [255] In accordance with the unanimous decision regarding the boundary they render upon questioning, he should make a record of the boundary, as well as of all their names. [256] Putting earth on their heads, wearing garlands and red clothes, and being made to swear each by his good deeds (8.90), they shall render a truthful decision. [257] When they render a decision in the above manner, they remain untainted as truthful witnesses; but when they render a contrary decision, they should be fined 200 (see 8.120).

[258] When witnesses are unavailable, however, four villagers resident in the vicinity, after making themselves ritually pure, should determine the boundary in the presence of the king. [259] When native inhabitants (7.54 n.) of neighbouring villages are unavailable as witnesses to a boundary, however, he may even question the following men who roam the forest: [260] hunters, fowlers, herdsmen, fishermen, root-diggers, snake-catchers, gleaners, and others who inhabit the forest. [261] When, upon questioning, they identify a particular landmark at the intersection of the boundaries, he should establish it as the landmark between the two villages according to the Law.

[262] It should be recognized that the determination of boundary markers between fields, wells, reservoirs, gardens, and houses depends on the evidence of neighbours. [263] If neighbours give false

evidence when people are litigating boundary markers, the king should impose the middle fine (8.138) on each of them individually.

[264] If someone appropriates a house, reservoir, garden, or field through intimidation, he should be fined 500; the fine is 200 if it was done inadvertently (8.120 n.).

[265] When it is impossible to ascertain the boundary, a king who knows the Law should apportion land between them on his own on the basis of utility*—that is the settled rule.

> [266] I have described above the entire Law relating to
> decisions regarding boundaries. Next, I will explain
> how cases of verbal assault are to be decided.

Grounds for Litigation: XI Verbal Assault

[267] For assailing a Brahmin, a Kṣatriya ought to be fined 100, and a Vaiśya 150 or 200; but a Śūdra ought to suffer corporal punishment (8.120 n.). [268] A Brahmin should be fined 50 for abusing a Kṣatriya, 25 for abusing a Vaiśya, and 12 for abusing a Śūdra. [269] For a violation by a twice-born against a person of the same social class, the fine is 12; the fine is doubled when extremely foul language is used.

[270] If a once-born man hurls grossly abusive words at twice-born men, his tongue shall be cut off, for he originated from the lowest part.* [271] If he invokes their names and castes with disdain, a red-hot iron nail ten fingers long should be driven into his mouth. [272] If he arrogantly gives instruction on the Law to Brahmins, the king should pour hot oil into his mouth and ears.

[273] If a man arrogantly makes false statements about someone's learning, country, caste, occupation, or physical features, he should be fined 200. [274] If a man calls someone 'one-eyed', 'lame', or some other similar name, he should be fined at least 1 Kārṣāpaṇa, even if what he says is true.

[275] If a man hurls accusations at his mother, father, wife, brother, child, or elder, he should be fined 100, as also a man who fails to give way to an elder.

[276] In cases involving a Brahmin and a Kṣatriya, a discerning king should impose the following punishment: the lowest fine on the Brahmin and the middle fine on the Kṣatriya (8.138). [277] On a Vaiśya and a Śūdra also, exactly the same punishment,* except the cutting

of the tongue, should be imposed according to their respective class—that is the firm conclusion.

> [278] I have described above accurately the rules concerning the punishment for verbal assault. Next, I will explain how cases of physical assault are to be decided.

Grounds for Litigation: XII Physical Assault

Personal Injury [279] When a lowest-born man uses a particular limb to injure a superior person, that very limb of his should be cut off—that is Manu's decree. [280] If he charges with his hand or with a stick, his hand ought to be cut off; if he strikes with his foot in anger, his foot ought to be cut off. [281] If a low-born man attempts to occupy the same seat as a man of a high rank, the king should brand him on the hip and send him into exile or have his buttocks slashed. [282] If he arrogantly spits at such a person, the king should cut off both his lips; if he urinates at him, his penis; and if he breaks wind at him, his anus. [283] If he grabs him by the hair, the king should cut off both his hands without a second thought, as also if he grabs him by the feet, the beard, the neck, or the testicles.

[284] One who bruises the skin, as also one who draws blood, is to be fined 100; and one who wounds the flesh, 6 Niṣkas. One who breaks a bone, however, should be sent into exile.* [285] For injuring any kind of tree, a fine should be imposed proportionate to its utility—that is the fixed rule. [286] If someone strikes humans or animals in order to inflict pain, the king should impose a punishment proportionate to the severity of the pain.

[287] For doing severe harm to a limb, and likewise to vigour and blood, a man should be compelled to defray the expenses of the recovery or to pay a total fine.*

Damage to Property [288] When someone damages the property of another, whether it is deliberate or inadvertent, he should pay reparation to the other and give an equal amount to the king.

[289] In the case of leather, leather utensils, or wooden or clay products, the fine is five times their value; so also in the case of flowers, roots, and fruits.

Injuries Caused by Vehicles [290] With respect to a vehicle, its driver, and its owner, they posit ten exemptions; in other cases punishment is decreed. [291] When the nose-rope snaps; when the yoke breaks; when the vehicle skids to one side; when it slides backwards; when the axle of the vehicle breaks; when a wheel breaks; [292] when bindings, halters, or reins snap; and when the driver cries out, 'Get out of the way!'—in these cases Manu has declared that there should be no punishment.

[293] When the vehicle veers off due to the driver's incompetence, however, and it results in injury, the owner should be fined 200; [294] but if the driver is skilled, then it is the driver who ought to be fined; and if he is unskilled, all the riders should be fined 100 each.

[295] In a case where the driver kills living creatures when his path is obstructed by farm animals or a vehicle, the punishment shall be enforced without hesitation. [296] If a human being is killed, he becomes immediately subject to the same liability as a thief; half that much for a large animal, such as a cow, elephant, camel, or horse. [297] For injuring a small farm animal, the fine is 200; for a beautiful animal or bird, 50; [298] for a donkey, goat, or sheep, 5 Māṣas; and for killing a dog or a pig, 1 Māṣa.

Corporal Punishment [299] When they misbehave, a wife, son, slave, pupil, or uterine brother may be beaten with a rope or a bamboo strip [300] on the back of their bodies and never on the head. If he beats them in any other way, his liability is the same as for theft.

> [301] I have described above completely how to decide
> cases of physical assault. Next, I will explain the rules
> for deciding the punishment for theft.

Grounds for Litigation: XIII Theft

Suppression of Thieves [302] The king should exert the utmost effort in suppressing thieves. Suppressing thieves will expand both his fame and his realm; [303] for the king who gives security is always worthy of worship, and his sacrificial session* will continuously expand with the granting of safety (6.39 n.) as its sacrificial fee.

Obligation to Offer Protection [304] A sixth portion of everyone's merits goes to the king who protects; a sixth portion of their demerits likewise goes to him when he fails to protect. [305] When one studies, sacrifices, gives gifts, and performs worship, the king takes a sixth portion of it as his share by providing proper protection.

306 By protecting creatures according to the Law and by putting to death those who merit execution, the king offers day after day sacrifices with sacrificial fees of one hundred thousand.

307 When a king gathers levies, taxes, duties, gifts, and fines without providing protection, he will immediately go to hell. 308 They call a king who gathers a sixth portion as levy without providing protection 'one who gathers all the filth of the entire population'. 309 When a king disregards proper bounds, is an infidel, is rapacious, fails to provide protection, and is predatory, one should know that he is headed along the downward course.

310 He should strenuously suppress the wicked by three means: imprisonment, shackling, and diverse forms of corporal punishment (8.320 n.); 311 for by suppressing the wicked and by gratifying the virtuous kings are always purified, just as twice-born men by sacrifices.

312 The king should always forgive litigants, children, the aged, and the sick who may insult him, if he wants to do what is beneficial to himself. 313 He who bears patiently when those in anguish insult him will be exalted in heaven for it, but he who does not forgive because of his royal status will go to hell for it.

Punishment of Thieves 314 A wise thief, with his hair loose, should go to the king confessing his theft: 'I have done this. Punish me,' 315 and carrying on his shoulder a pestle, a club of Khadira wood, a spear with both ends sharpened, or an iron rod.

316 Whether he is punished or released, the thief is released from the theft; but if the king fails to punish him, he takes upon himself the thief's guilt. 317 The murderer of a learned Brahmin (4.208 n.) rubs his sin off on the man who eats his food, an adulterous wife on her husband, a pupil and a patron of a sacrifice on the teacher, and a thief on the king. 318 When men who have committed sins are punished by kings, they go to heaven immaculate, like virtuous men who have done good deeds.

319 A man who steals a rope or a bucket from a well or tears down a place for distributing water should pay a fine of 1 Māṣa and restore that article. 320 A man who steals more than 10 Kumbha-measures of grain is subject to corporal punishment;* even in lesser cases he

should be fined eleven times the amount and made to restore that property to the owner. [321] The same goes for articles sold by weight. When it is more than 100 of gold, silver, and the like, and of the most excellent clothes, he is subject to capital punishment; [322] but when it is more than 50, his hand ought to be cut off. In lesser cases, on the other hand, the king should set a fine of eleven times the value of the property.

[323] For abducting men from illustrious families and especially women, and for stealing gems of great value, a man merits the death penalty.

[324] For stealing large farm animals, as also weapons and medicine, the king should set a punishment after taking into account its time and purpose;* [325] in the case of cows belonging to Brahmins, the cleaving of the heel;* and for stealing farm animals, half his foot should be cut off immediately.

[326] For stealing thread, cotton, liquor-yeast, cow dung, molasses, curd, milk, buttermilk, water, grass, [327] vessels made of bamboo or cane, any kind of salt, clay vessels, earth, ash, [328] fish, birds, oil, ghee, meat, honey, other animal products, [329] other similar kinds of food, boiled rice, and all kinds of cooked food—the fine is twice the value of the stolen property. [330] For flowers, green grain, shrubs, creepers, trees, and small quantities of unhusked grain, the fine is 5 Kṛṣṇalas. [331] For husked grain, vegetables, roots, and fruits, the fine is 100 if it is committed outside the owner's presence, and 50 if it is committed in his presence (8.332 n.).

[332] When an act is committed with force and in the presence of the victim, it is 'violence'; when it is committed outside his presence,* it is 'theft', and so is an act that someone commits and then denies.

[333] When a man steals these articles after they have been prepared for use, the king should fine him 100, as also a man who steals fire from a house.

[334] The king should deprive a thief of the very limb with which he commits a crime against men, to serve as a deterrent.

[335] A king should never fail to punish even his father, teacher, friend, mother, wife, son, or personal priest when they deviate from the Law proper to them. [336] In a case where an ordinary person is fined 1 Kārṣāpaṇa, the king should be fined 1,000—that is the fixed rule.* [337] With respect to theft, the liability for a Śūdra is eight times; for a Vaiśya, sixteen times; for a Kṣatriya, thirty-two times; [338] and for

a Brahmin, sixty-four times, or fully 100 times, or twice sixty-four times; for he knows whether it is good or bad.*

[339] Roots and fruits from trees, wood for a fire, and grass to feed cows—Manu has declared that these do not constitute theft.

[340] If a Brahmin desires to obtain money from the hands of a man who takes what is not given—even if he does so by means of officiating at that man's sacrifices or teaching him—that Brahmin is equal to a thief. [341] When a twice-born is on the road and his provisions are exhausted, he ought not to be punished for taking two roots or two stalks of sugar-cane from the field of another man.

[342] When someone ties up those that are not tied, releases those that are tied, or takes away a slave, horse, or carriage, his liability is the same as for theft.*

> [343] A king who undertakes the suppression of thieves
> in this manner obtains fame in this world and unsur-
> passing happiness after death.

Grounds for Litigation: XIV Violence

[344] If a king desires to obtain the seat of Indra and inexhaustible and imperishable fame, he should never ignore even for a moment a man who perpetrates violence.* [345] A man who perpetrates violence should be considered far more evil than someone who is offensive in speech, who steals, or who assaults with a rod.* [346] A king who condones a man who engages in violence is quickly brought to ruin and becomes the object of hatred.

[347] The king must never release violent men who strike terror in all creatures eyeing either friendship or a large monetary gain.

Permissible Violence [348] Twice-born men may take up arms when the Law is thwarted or when the vicissitudes of time bring calamity upon twice-born classes. [349] When a man kills in accordance with the Law to protect his life, in a conflict over sacrificial fees, or in defence of women or Brahmins, he remains untainted.

[350] When an assailant attacks with the intent to kill—whether he is an elder, a child, an old person, or a learned Brahmin—one may surely kill him without hesitation. [351] In killing an assailant, the killer incurs no fault; whether it is done openly or in secret, wrath there recoils on wrath.

Grounds for Litigation: XV Sexual Crimes against Women

Sexual Crimes against Married Women [352] When men violate the wives of others, the king should disfigure their bodies with punishments that inspire terror and then execute them (8.6n.; 8.284n.); [353] for such violations give rise to the mixing of social classes among the people, creating deviation from the Law that tears out the very root and leads to the destruction of everything.

[354] When a man carries on a conversation secretly with another man's wife, he is subject to the lowest fine (8.138) if he has been previously accused of similar offences. [355] If someone who has not been previously accused engages in such conversation for a good reason, however, no guilt attaches to him, for he has committed no transgression.

[356] If a man converses with the wife of another at a sacred ford, in a wild tract, in a forest, or at the confluence of rivers, he is guilty of adultery. [357] Doing favours, dallying, touching the ornaments or clothes, and sitting together on a bed—all this, tradition tells us, constitutes adultery. [358] When a man touches a woman at an inappropriate place or permits her to touch him—all such acts done with mutual consent, tradition tells us, constitute adultery.

[359] In the case of adultery, everyone other than a Brahmin merits the death penalty; women of all four classes are to be guarded always with the utmost care.

[360] Mendicants, bards, men consecrated for sacrifice, and artisans may converse with women, unless they have been explicitly banned. [361] A man should never converse with women when he has been forbidden to do so; when someone speaks after being forbidden, he ought to be fined 1 Suvarṇa.

[362] The above rule does not apply to wives of travelling performers or to wives who earn a living on their own, for such men get their women to attach themselves to men and, concealing themselves, get them to have sexual liaisons. [363] When someone engages in secret conversations with such women, as also with female slaves serving a single master and with female wandering ascetics, he shall be compelled to pay a small fine.

Male Sexual Assault [364] A man who defiles a virgin against her will merits immediate execution. When a man of equal status defiles a willing virgin, however, he is not subject to execution. [365] No fine should be imposed on a virgin who falls in love with a man superior to herself; but if she makes love to a man inferior to herself, she should be put under restraint and confined to her house. [366] When a man of inferior status makes love to a superior woman, however, he merits execution; if he makes love to a woman of equal status, he should pay a bride-price* if her father so desires.

[367] If a man arrogantly violates a virgin by force, two of his fingers* should be cut off immediately, and he should also be fined 600. [368] A man of equal status who defiles a willing girl shall not be subject to the cutting of his fingers, but he should be compelled to pay a fine of 200 to deter repetition.

Female Sexual Assault [369] If a virgin violates another virgin, she should be fined 200, pay three times the bride-price, and receive ten lashes. [370] When a woman violates a virgin, however, her head ought to be shaved immediately—alternatively, two of her fingers should be cut off—and she should be paraded on a donkey.

Adultery [371] When a woman, arrogant because of the eminence of her relatives and her own feminine qualities, becomes unfaithful to her husband, the king should have her devoured by dogs in a public square frequented by many. [372] He should have the male offender burnt upon a heated iron bed; they should stack logs and burn up that villain there.

[373] When a convict is accused again within a year, the fine is doubled; likewise when a man has sex with a Vrātya or a Caṇḍāla woman. [374] When a Śūdra has sex with a guarded or unguarded woman of a twice-born class—he loses a limb and all his possessions, if she was unguarded. If she was guarded, a Śūdra loses everything;* [375] a Vaiśya is imprisoned for a year and all his property is confiscated; and a Kṣatriya is fined 1000 and his head is shaved using urine. [376] If a Vaiśya or a Kṣatriya has sex with an unguarded Brahmin woman, the Vaiśya is fined 500 and the Kṣatriya 1,000 (see 8.120n.). [377] If any of these two has sex with a guarded Brahmin woman, he should be punished in the same way as a Śūdra or he should be burnt with a straw-fire. [378] A Brahmin who has forcible sex with a guarded Brahmin woman should be fined 1000; for sex with a willing partner, he should be fined 500.

[379] Shaving the head is prescribed as the death penalty for Brah-

mins; but the other social classes are actually subject to the death penalty. [380] The king should never put a Brahmin to death, even if he has committed every sort of crime; he should banish such a Brahmin from his kingdom along with all his property, without causing him hurt. [381] There is no greater violation of the Law on earth than killing a Brahmin; therefore, a king should not even think of killing a Brahmin.

[382] If a Vaiśya has sex with a guarded Kṣatriya woman or a Kṣatriya with a guarded Vaiśya woman, both ought to receive the same punishment as a man who has sex with an unguarded Brahmin woman. [383] When a Brahmin has sex with those two types of guarded women, however, he should be compelled to pay a fine of 1,000; likewise, when a Kṣatriya or a Vaiśya has sex with a Śūdra woman, the fine is 1,000. [384] For sex with an unguarded Kṣatriya woman, a Vaiśya is fined 500, but a Kṣatriya has his head shaved using urine or is levied the same fine. [385] When a Brahmin has sex with an unguarded Kṣatriya or Vaiśya woman or with a Śūdra woman, he shall be fined 500, but 1,000 for sex with a lowest-born woman.

[*Excursus*]

Miscellanea [386] The king in whose capital there is no thief, no adulterer, no person who uses offensive speech, no person who uses violence, and no person who commits physical assault, will attain the world of Indra.* [387] The suppression of these five within his territory secures for the king paramountcy among his peers and fame among his people.

[388] If the patron of a sacrifice gets rid of an officiating priest or an officiating priest the patron when both are capable of performing the rite and are untainted by any fault, each is fined 100.

[389] A mother, father, wife, or son ought never to be abandoned. Anyone who abandons these when they have not fallen from their caste shall be fined 600 by the king.

[390] When twice-born men living in hermitages are arguing with each other about any duty, the king should never pronounce on the Law, if he cares for his own welfare. [391] Accompanied by Brahmins, the king should first pay them due reverence, pacify them initially with soothing words, and then teach them the Law specific to them.

[392] When a Brahmin fails to feed his two worthy neighbours—the

one living in front of his house and the one behind—at a festival attended by twenty Brahmins, he ought to be fined 1 Māṣaka. [393] When a vedic scholar fails to feed another virtuous vedic scholar at auspicious rites, he should be compelled to give twice that amount of food and a gold Māṣaka.

[394] A blind man, an idiot, a cripple, a man over 70, and someone who takes care of vedic scholars—no one should compel these to pay any tax.

[395] The king should always honour vedic scholars, the sick and the afflicted, children, the aged, the poor, men from illustrious families, and Āryas.

[396] A washerman shall wash clothes thoroughly and gently on a smooth cotton-wood board. He must not use some clothes to carry the other clothes or let others wear those clothes.*

[397] A weaver receiving thread weighing 10 Palas must return cloth weighing 1 Pala more; if he does otherwise, he should be compelled to pay a fine of 12.*

Control of Trade [398] When men who have experience in offices for levying duties and expertise in all types of merchandise have fixed the value of each commodity, the king should take one-twentieth of that. [399] When someone exports goods that are designated a royal monopoly or that are forbidden out of greed, the king should confiscate all his property. [400] When a man bypasses an office for levying duties, buys or sells at forbidden times, or falsifies the enumeration of goods, he should be fined eight times what he tried to hide.

[401] After investigating the provenance of every commodity, its destination, and how long it is held by the vendor, as well as gain and loss, he should fix the sale and purchase prices. [402] Every five days or every fortnight the king should publicly fix the prices of commodities. [403] All balances, measures, and weights should be stamped with the proper mark and should be re-inspected every six months.

Ferries and Tolls [404] A vehicle should be assessed 1 Paṇa at a ferry; a porter's load, half a Paṇa; an animal or woman, a quarter Paṇa; and a porter without a load, one-eighth of a Paṇa. [405] Vehicles loaded with goods should be assessed a toll according to the value of the goods; empty vehicles and porters without loads should be assessed some small amount.

[406] For long voyages the toll should correspond to the place and the

time. It should be understood that this applies to voyages along rivers; for sea voyages, there is no set rate (8.157).

[407] Women over two months pregnant, wandering ascetics, sages, Brahmins, and those wearing the insignia of a religious profession (4.200 n.) should not be forced to pay tolls on a ferry.

[408] Whenever anything within a boat is damaged due to the negligence of the boatmen, it is the boatmen who should pay reparation collectively, each according to his share.

> [409] I have described above how to decide a lawsuit
> brought by passengers in a boat relating to the neg-
> ligence of boatmen on the water; when it is an act of
> god, there shall be no punishment.

Occupations of Social Classes [410] The king should make Vaiśyas pursue trade, moneylending, agriculture, and cattle herding, and make Śūdras engage in the service of twice-born people.

[411] A Brahmin should support a Kṣatriya or a Vaiśya who is starved for a livelihood out of compassion and employ them in activities proper to them. [412] If a Brahmin makes twice-born men who have undergone vedic initiation do slave labour against their will through greed and to show off his power, the king should fine him 600. [413] He may, however, make a Śūdra, whether he is bought or not, do slave labour; for the Śūdra was created by the Self-existent One solely to do slave labour for the Brahmin.

[414] Even when he is released by his master, a Śūdra is not freed from his slave status; for that is innate in him and who can remove it from him? [415] There are seven kinds of slaves: a man captured in war, a man who makes himself a slave to receive food, a slave born in the house, a purchased slave, a gifted slave, a hereditary slave, and a man enslaved for punishment.

[416] Wife, son, and slave—all these three, tradition tells us, are without property. Whatever they may earn becomes the property of the man to whom they belong.

[417] A Brahmin may confidently seize property from a Śūdra, because there is nothing that he owns; for he is a man whose property may be taken by his master.

[418] The king should strenuously make Vaiśyas and Śūdras perform the activities specific to them; for when they deviate from their specific activities, they throw this world into confusion.

[419] Every day the king should pay attention to his administrative centres, conveyances (7.75 n.), daily income and expenditure, mines, and treasury. [420] When the king thus brings to a satisfactory conclusion all these legal matters, he gets rid of all sins and attains the highest state.

CHAPTER NINE

Grounds for Litigation: XVI Law Concerning Husband and Wife

[1] For a husband and wife who stay on the path pointed out by the Law, I shall declare the eternal Laws for both when they are together and when they are apart.*

Guarding the Wife [2] Day and night men should keep their women from acting independently; for, attached as they are to sensual pleasures, men should keep them under their control. [3] Her father guards her in her childhood, her husband guards her in her youth, and her sons guard her in her old age; a woman is not qualified to act independently (5.147–9).

[4] A father is reprehensible, if he does not give her away at the proper time; a husband, if he does not have sex with her at the right time (3.45 n.); and a son, if he fails to guard his mother when her husband is dead. [5] Women in particular should be guarded against even the slightest evil inclination, for when they are left unguarded, they bring grief to both families (5.149 n.). [6] Seeing that this is clearly the highest Law of all social classes, even weak husbands strive to guard their wives; [7] for by carefully guarding his wife, a man guards his offspring, his character, his family, himself, and the Law specific to him.

[8] The husband enters the wife, becomes a foetus, and is born in this world. This, indeed, is what gives the name to and discloses the true nature of 'wife' (*jāyā*)—that he is born (*jāyate*) again in her.* [9] For, a wife bears a son resembling the man she loves; to ensure the purity of his offspring, therefore, he should carefully guard his wife.

[10] No man is able to thoroughly guard women by force; but by using the following strategies, he will be able to guard them thoroughly. [11] He should employ her in the collection and the disbursement of his wealth, in cleaning, in meritorious activity, in cooking food, and in looking after household goods. [12] When they are kept confined within the house by trusted men, they are not truly

guarded; only when they guard themselves by themselves are they truly well guarded.

[13] Drinking, associating with bad people, living away from the husband, travel, sleep, and staying in the houses of others—these are the six things that corrupt women. [14] They pay no attention to beauty, they pay no heed to age; whether he is handsome or ugly, they make love to him with the single thought, 'He's a man!' [15] Lechery, fickleness of mind, and hard-heartedness are innate in them; even when they are carefully guarded in this world, therefore, they become hostile towards their husbands. [16] Recognizing thus the nature produced in them at creation by Prajāpati, a man should make the utmost effort at guarding them. [17] Bed, seat, ornaments, lust, hatred, behaviour unworthy of an Ārya, malice, and bad conduct—Manu assigned these to women.*

[18] No rite is performed for women with the recitation of ritual formulas—that is well-established Law. 'Without strength or ritual formula, women are the untruth'*—that is the fixed rule. [19] There are, likewise, numerous scriptural passages recited in the sacred books. Listen to a sample of these intended to expose the true character of women. [20] Here is an illustration of it:* 'May my father keep from me the seed that my mother, roaming about unfaithful to her husband, craved!' [21] When a woman contemplates anything harmful to her husband in her mind, this is said to be a thorough expiation of that infidelity.

Elevation of Wife to Husband's Status [22] When a wife unites with her husband according to rule, she takes on the qualities he has, like a river uniting with the ocean. [23] Akṣamālā, a woman of the lowest birth, when she united with Vasiṣṭha—as also Śārṅgī with Mandapāla—became worthy of great respect.* [24] These and other women of low birth attained high status in this world by reason of the eminent qualities of their respective husbands.

> [25] I have described above the splendid conduct of a
> husband and wife commonly practised in the world.
> Next, listen to the Laws that pertain to progeny, Laws
> that bring happiness here and in the hereafter.

Importance of Wife [26] On account of offspring, a wife is the bearer of many blessings, worthy of honour, and the light within a home;

indeed, in a home no distinction at all exists between a wife (*strī*) and Śrī, the Goddess of Fortune. [27] She begets children; and when they are born, she brings them up—day in, day out, the wife, evidently, is the linchpin of domestic affairs. [28] Offspring, rites prescribed by Law, obedient service,* the highest sensuous delights, and procuring heaven for oneself and one's forefathers—all this depends on the wife.

[29] A woman who controls her mind, speech, and body and is never unfaithful to her husband attains the worlds of her husband, and virtuous people call her a 'good woman' (= 5.165). [30] By being unfaithful to her husband, on the other hand, a woman becomes disgraced in the world, takes birth in a jackal's womb, and is afflicted with evil diseases (= 5.164).

> [31] Listen now to this holy disquisition, profitable to all, carried out by virtuous people and by great ancient sages with regard to a son.

To Whom Belongs a Son? [32] It is acknowledged that a son belongs to the husband; but scripture is divided with respect to the sire—some argue for the man who fathered the child, others for the 'owner of the field'.*

[33] Tradition holds that the woman represents the field and the man the seed; all embodied beings spring from the union of field and seed. [34] Sometimes the seed is pre-eminent, at other times the female womb; but when both are equal, that offspring is greatly esteemed.

[First Opinion] [35] Between the seed and the womb, the seed is considered dominant; for the offspring of all creatures is marked by the characteristics of the seed (10.70–2). [36] When someone sows a particular kind of seed in a field prepared at the proper time, the very same kind sprouts in that field displaying its own qualities. [37] This earth, indeed, is called the eternal womb of creatures; yet the seed, as it develops, does not manifest any of the qualities associated with the womb. [38] Even when different kinds of seed are sown by farmers in the very same plot at the right time, they are seen in the world to sprout differently, each according to its nature. [39] Vrīhi-rice, Śāla-rice, mung beans, sesame seeds, beans, barley, garlic, and sugar-cane—all these sprout according to their seed. [40] For one kind to be sown and quite another to be produced—that is simply impossible. Whatever kind of seed is sown, that same kind sprouts forth.*

[Second Opinion] [41] A wise and well-trained man, therefore, possessing knowledge and discrimination and desiring a long life, should never sow his seed in the wife of another man. [42] In this connection, those who know the past relate verses sung by Wind showing that a man must never sow his seed in someone else's wife. [43] 'When someone shoots an arrow at the vitals of an animal that has already been pierced, his arrow is wasted; in like manner a seed is wasted when discharged in someone else's wife.' [44] Even as those who know the past regard this earth as the wife of Pṛthu, so they say that a field belongs to the man who cleared the stumps and the deer to the man who owns the arrow.*

[45] Wife, self, and offspring—that is the full extent of 'man'. Brahmins, likewise, proclaim this: 'The husband, tradition says, is the wife.' [46] Neither sale nor dismissal cuts the wife loose from her husband; this we consider the Law established formerly by Prajāpati. [47] Once is a partition made; once is a virgin given away; once is it said 'I give'—these three are done only once each.

[48] As in the case of cows, mares, female camels, slave women, female buffaloes, female goats, and ewes, the sire does not own the offspring, so is it also in the case of women. [49] When men who have seeds but no fields sow them in someone else's field, once the crop has grown they do not receive any of the harvest. [50] Even if a bull fathers a hundred calves on someone else's cows, the calves belong to the owner of the cows; the bull has spilled his semen in vain. [51] Likewise, when men without fields sow their seed in someone else's field, they create profits for the owner of the field; the owner of the seed reaps no fruit.

[52] If an agreement* has not been reached between the owner of the field and the owner of the seed with respect to the fruit, the owner of the field clearly reaps the profit; the womb is mightier than the seed. [53] When a field is handed over by contractual agreement to someone for sowing the seed, however, we see in the world that both the owner of the seed and the owner of the field receive shares from it. [54] When a seed, carried by flood or wind, sprouts in someone's field, it belongs solely to the owner of the field; the sower does not reap its fruit.*

[55] This is the Law with regard to the offspring of cows, mares, slave women, female camels, female goats, ewes, female birds, and female buffaloes.*

> [56] I have described to you above the relative importance of the seed and the womb. Next, I shall explain the Law pertaining to women during a time of adversity.

Levirate [57] Tradition holds that for a younger brother, the wife of his older brother is the same as the wife of an elder;* and for an older brother, the wife of his younger brother is the same as a daughter-in-law. [58] Except in a time of adversity, if an older brother has sex with his younger brother's wife or a younger brother with his older brother's wife, they become outcastes, even if they have been duly appointed.

[59] If the line is about to die out, a wife who is duly appointed may obtain the desired progeny through a brother-in-law or a relative belonging to the same ancestry (5.60 n.). [60] The appointed man should smear himself with ghee, approach the widow at night in silence, and beget a single son, never a second. [61] Some who are knowledgeable in these matters, seeing that this leaves the purpose of the couple's appointment unfulfilled in terms of the Law, endorse begetting a second son in such women.* [62] When the purpose of his appointment to the widow has been fulfilled according to rule, however, they should behave towards each other as an elder and a daughter-in-law. [63] If, on the contrary, the appointed couple disregard the rules and behave lustfully with one another, both become outcastes, he as a molester of a daughter-in-law, and she as a violator of an elder's bed.

[64] Twice-born men should never appoint a widowed woman to another man, for in appointing her to another man, they assail the eternal Law.* [65] The nuptial formulas nowhere mention appointment, nor do injunctions relating to marriage sanction the remarriage of widows. [66] This Law of beasts, despised by learned twice-born men, was extended to humans also during the reign of Vena (7.41–2 n.). [67] He was a pre-eminent royal sage, who once ruled the entire earth and, his mind overcome by lust, created the intermixing of classes. [68] Since that time, good people denounce anyone who is senseless enough to appoint a woman to have children after her husband dies.

[69] If the husband of a virgin dies after their betrothal, her brother-in-law should take her in the following manner. [70] Obtaining her

according to rule, as she is dressed in white* and devoted to pure observances, he should have sex with her once every time she is in season (3.45 n.) until she bears a child.

Contract of Betrothal [71] After giving away a virgin to someone, a prudent man must never give her away again, for in giving what has already been given, he becomes guilty of a lie with respect to a human being (8.98). [72] Even after he has accepted a virgin according to rule, he may reject her if she is found to be dishonourable, diseased, or defiled, or if she had been given deceptively. [73] If a man gives a virgin with defects without revealing them, one may break the contract with that evil man who gave the virgin (8.205, 224–7).

Absence of Husband [74] A man should provide for his wife before he goes away on business, for even a steadfast woman will go astray when starved for a livelihood. [75] If he provides for her before going away, she should live a life of restraint; but if he leaves without providing for her, she may maintain herself by engaging in respectable crafts.

[76] A wife should wait for eight years when her husband has gone away for a purpose specified by Law, for six years when he has gone for learning or fame, and for three years when he has gone for pleasure.

Repudiation of a Wife [77] For one year let a husband tolerate a wife who loathes him; after one year, he should confiscate her inheritance and stop cohabiting with her. [78] If a wife commits a transgression against her husband who is deranged, drunk, or sick, deprived of her ornaments and belongings, she should be cast out for three months. [79] If a wife loathes a husband who has become insane, fallen from caste, or impotent (3.150 n.), who is without semen, or who has contracted an evil disease (3.159 n.), she must neither be abandoned nor deprived of her inheritance.

[80] When a wife drinks liquor or is dishonest, cantankerous, sick, vicious, or wasteful, she may be superseded at any time by marriage to another wife. [81] A barren wife may be superseded in the eighth year; a wife whose children die, in the tenth; a wife who bears girls, in the eleventh; but a foul-mouthed wife, at once. [82] If a wife is sickly but affectionate and rich in virtue, he may marry a wife to supersede her with her consent; she should never be treated with disrespect.

[83] If a wife who has been superseded storms out of the house

incensed, however, she should be locked up immediately or repudiated in the presence of the family.

[84] If, after she is forbidden, a wife drinks liquor, albeit at festivals, or visits shows and fairs, she should be fined 6 Kṛṣṇalas.

Seniority among Wives [85] If twice-born men marry women of their own class as well as others, the order of their class determines their seniority, as also how they are honoured and where they reside. [86] Among all these, only the wife of equal class may care for her husband's physical needs or participate in his daily rites prescribed by Law, never a wife belonging to a different class. [87] If he foolishly gets another wife to carry these out while a wife of equal class is available, he becomes exactly like a Brahmin-Cāṇḍāla described by the ancients.

Marriage of Daughters [88] When there is a suitor who is eminent, handsome, and of equal status, one should give the girl to him according to rule, even if she has not attained the proper age.* [89] Even if she has reached puberty, a girl should rather remain at home until death; one should never give her to a man bereft of good qualities.

[90] For three years shall a girl wait after the onset of her puberty; after that time, she may find for herself a husband of equal status. [91] If a woman who has not been given in marriage finds a husband on her own, she does not incur any sin, and neither does the man she finds. [92] A girl who chooses a husband on her own must not take with her any ornament coming from her father or mother or given by her brothers; if she takes, it is theft.

[93] A man who takes a girl after she has reached puberty shall not pay a bride-price, for the father has lost his ownership of her by frustrating her menses.

[94] A 30-year-old man should marry a charming girl of 12 years, or an 18-year-old, a girl of 8 years—sooner, if his fulfilling the Law would suffer. [95] A husband marries a wife given to him by gods, not from his own desire. He should always support that good woman, thereby doing what is pleasing to the gods.

[96] Women were created to bear children, and men to extend the line; therefore, scriptures have prescribed that the Law is to be carried out in common with the wife.

[97] If, after the bride-price has been paid for the girl, the man who

paid the price dies, she should be given to the brother-in-law, if she consents to it. [98] Even a Śūdra should not take a bride-price when he gives his daughter; for by accepting a bride-price, he is engaging in a covert sale of his daughter. [99] That after promising her to one man, she is then given to another—such a deed was never done by good people of ancient or recent times. [100] The covert sale of a daughter for a payment under the name 'bride-price'—we have never heard of such a thing even in former generations.

[101] 'Fidelity to each other should be observed until death'—this should be recognized as the highest Law between husband and wife put in a nutshell. [102] A husband and wife, after they have completed the marriage rite, should always work hard so as to prevent them from being unfaithful to each other and thus being split apart.

> [103] I have described above the Law concerning husband and wife based on love, as well as the way to obtain offspring in times of adversity. Listen now to the Law of inheritance.

Grounds for Litigation: XVII Partition of Inheritance

[104] After the father and mother have passed on,* the brothers should gather together and partition the paternal inheritance evenly; for they are incompetent while those two are alive.

Primogeniture [105] The eldest alone, on the contrary, ought to take the entire paternal estate, and the others should live as his dependants just as they did under their father.

[106] As soon as the eldest is born, a person becomes a 'man with a son' and is released from his debt to the ancestors (4.257n.); that son, therefore, is entitled to the entire amount. [107] Only that son to whom he passes on his debt and through whom he obtains immortality is born through the Law; others, they say, are born through lust.

[108] The eldest should look after the younger ones as a father his sons; and they should behave towards their eldest brother as towards their father, in accordance with the Law. [109] It is the eldest who makes the family prosper, the eldest who brings it to ruin; the eldest receives the highest honour in the world, and the eldest is never treated with disrespect by good people. [110] When the eldest behaves the way the eldest should, he is like a mother, he is like a father; but

when he fails to behave the way the eldest should, he should receive the same honour as a relative.

Partition and Seniority [111] They should either live together in this manner, or rather, separately with a desire for merit. Living separately increases merit; therefore, the act of separation is meritorious.

[112] The pre-emptive share of the eldest is one-eightieth, as well as the best item in the entire estate; the middle son gets one-half of that; and the youngest, one-quarter. [113] The eldest and the youngest shall take what has been prescribed; the shares of the sons other than the eldest and the youngest are the same as that of the middle son. [114] Within each category of property, the first-born shall take the finest item, as well as anything exceedingly special and the best out of each ten. [115] When the brothers are equally accomplished in what they do, there is no pre-emptive share out of each ten; a little something should be given to the eldest, however, as a token of respect.

[116] Once the pre-emptive share has been subtracted in the above manner, the rest should be apportioned in equal shares. If, on the other hand, the pre-emptive share has not been subtracted, the apportioning of shares should be carried out as follows: [117] the eldest son gets a double share; the son born next gets one and a half; and the younger ones gets a single share each—that is the settled Law.

[118] From their shares, however, the brothers shall give individually to the unmarried girls—one-quarter from the share of each. Those unwilling to give will become outcastes.

[119] A single goat, sheep, or one-hoofed animal left over after the distribution should never be divided; the rule is that a single goat or sheep left over goes to the eldest.

Seniority of Leviratic Sons [120] If a younger brother begets a son on the wife of the eldest, then the division is equal—that is the settled Law. [121] That the principal should become the subordinate is impossible according to the Law; in procreation, the father is the principal. Therefore, one should allocate a share to that son in accordance with the Law.*

Seniority among Sons of Different Wives [122] How is the partition done when the youngest son is born to the senior-most wife and the first-born son to the junior-most wife? If such a doubt arises, [123] the first-born should take one bull as his pre-emptive share;

thereafter, the other inferior bulls are taken by those junior to him according to the seniority of their mothers. [124] The eldest son born to the senior-most wife, on the other hand, shall take fifteen cows together with a bull; thereafter, the others receive shares according to the seniority of their mothers—that is the fixed rule.

[125] Among sons born uniformly to wives of equal status, seniority is not based on their mothers; they declare seniority to be based on birth. [126] In the Subrahmaṇyā* texts also, tradition tells us, it is the eldest by birth who makes the invocation. Tradition also tells us that even between twins in the same womb seniority is based on birth.

'Female-Son' and her Sons [127] A man without a son should make his daughter a 'female-son'* in the following manner: 'The child this girl bears will be the one who performs my ancestral rites.'

[128] In ancient times, Dakṣa himself, the lord of creatures, made 'female-sons' in the above manner for the multiplication of his lineage. [129] After adorning them and with a joyful heart, he gave ten of them to Dharma, thirteen to Kaśyapa, and twenty-seven to King Soma.*

[130] A son is the same as one's self, and a daughter is equal to a son; while she stands there as his very self, how can someone else take his property?

[131] Anything that is part of a mother's separate property becomes the share of her unmarried daughters; and the daughter's son shall take the entire property of a man without a son. [132] The daughter's son shall indeed take the entire estate of the father who is without a son, and he shall offer two rice-balls, one to his father and one to his maternal grandfather. [133] The world does not recognize any difference between a son's son and a daughter's son with respect to the Law, for both the father of the one and the mother of the other sprang from his own body (9.139). [134] If, however, a son is born after a 'female-son' has been appointed, the division in that case is equal; for a woman has no claim to primogeniture (9.120–1 n.).

[135] If a 'female-son' somehow dies sonless, the husband of that 'female-son' shall indeed take the property without hesitation. [136] When a daughter, whether she is appointed or not, bears a son by a man of equal status—by that son his maternal grandfather becomes a man who has a son's son, and the latter shall offer him the rice-ball and inherit his property.

[137]Through a son a man gains the worlds; through a son's son he obtains eternal life; but through the son's grandson he attains the crest of the sun. [138]The Self-existent One himself has called him 'son' (*putra*) because he rescues (*trā*) his father from the hell named Put. [139]The world does not acknowledge any difference between a son's son and a daughter's son, for a daughter's son also rescues him in the hereafter, just like a son's son (9.133).

[140]The son of a 'female-son' shall offer the first rice-ball to his mother, the second to her father, and the third to her father's father.

Adopted Son [141]When a man's adopted son is endowed with all the fine qualities, he may indeed inherit his estate, even if that son has been obtained from a different lineage. [142]Under no circumstances shall an adopted son inherit his biological father's lineage or estate. The offering of the rice-ball is consequent upon inheriting the lineage and estate; so when a man gives a son for adoption, the son's obligation to perform his funerary rites comes to an end.

Leviratic Sons [143]The son of an unappointed woman and a son fathered by a brother-in-law on a woman who already has a son—neither of these is entitled to a share; the former is born to a prostitute and the latter is born of lust. [144]If the rules have not been followed, a male born even to an appointed woman is not entitled to inherit the paternal estate; for he was begotten by an outcaste (9.58, 63).

[145]A son born to an appointed woman shall inherit it, just as a natural son; that seed and its issue belong by Law to the owner of the field (9.48–51). [146]The man who keeps his deceased brother's property and wife should produce an offspring for his brother and hand over the brother's property to him.

[147]When an unappointed woman obtains a son either through her brother-in-law or someone else, that son, born through lust, is not entitled to the estate; he is said to have been wrongly begotten.

> [148]These should be recognized as the rules for partition when the wives belong to the same caste. Listen now to the rules regarding sons of the same man born to several wives belonging to different castes.

Sons by Wives of Different Castes [149]If a Brahmin has four wives in the proper order, tradition lays down the following rule regarding partition among sons born to those wives. [150]The ploughman, the stud bull, the vehicle, the ornament,* and the house is to be given to the Brahmin as his pre-emptive share, as well as one share from the best property.* [151]The Brahmin shall take three shares of the inheritance; the son by a Kṣatriya wife, two shares; the son by a Vaiśya wife, one and a half shares; and the son by a Śūdra wife, one share.

[152]Alternatively, a man who knows the Law may divide his entire estate into ten shares and carry out a partition consistent with the Law according to the following rule: [153]the Brahmin shall take four shares; the son by a Kṣatriya wife, three; the son by a Vaiśya wife, two; and the son by a Śūdra wife, one. [154]Whether he has a proper son or no son at all,* the Law requires that he give no more than one-tenth to a son by a Śūdra wife.

[155]The son of a Brahmin, Kṣatriya, or Vaiśya by a Śūdra wife does not share in the inheritance; his only property is whatever his father may give him.

[156]Alternatively when all the sons of a twice-born man are born from wives of equal class, after giving a pre-emptive share to the eldest, the rest should take equal shares.*

[157]A Śūdra, however, has only a wife of his own class; no other wife is prescribed for him (3.13). All the sons born to such a wife, even if there are a hundred of them, shall receive equal shares.

Twelve Types of Son [158]Of the twelve types of son that Manu, the son of the Self-existent, has decreed for men, six are both relatives and heirs and six are relatives but not heirs. [159]A natural son, a son begotten on the wife, a son given in adoption, a constituted son, a son born in secret, and a son adopted after being abandoned—these are the six who are both relatives and heirs. [160]A son born to an unmarried woman, a son received with marriage, a purchased son, a son born to a remarried woman, a son given in adoption by himself, and a son by a Śūdra wife—these are the six who are relatives but not heirs.

[161]A man gains the same distinction by crossing the darkness with the aid of bad sons as he does by crossing the water with the aid of bad boats.

[162]If a natural son and a son begotten on the wife are heirs to the estate of the same man, the one whose paternal estate it is shall take

it, and not the other.* [163] The natural son is the sole master of his father's wealth; nevertheless, so as not to be unkind, he should provide maintenance for the others. [164] When the natural son divides the paternal inheritance, he should give a one-sixth or one-fifth share of the paternal property to the son begotten on the wife. [165] The natural son and the son begotten on the wife receive shares of the paternal estate; but the other ten according to their order share in the lineage and the estate.*

[166] When a man fathers a son by himself through his own duly wedded wife, he should be recognized as a *natural son*—the principal son.* [167] When a wife of someone who is dead, impotent, or sick bears a son after she has been appointed in accordance with the Law specific to her, tradition calls him a *son begotten on the wife*. [168] When during a time of adversity a mother or a father joyfully gives their son in adoption with the ceremonial pouring of water, a son belonging to the same class as the recipient, he should be known as a *son given in adoption*. [169] When someone installs a boy of equal class as his son, a boy who knows right from wrong and is endowed with filial qualities, he should be recognized as a *constituted son*. [170] When in someone's house is born a son whose father is unknown, he is a *son born in secret* within the house; and he belongs to the man whose wife gave birth to him. [171] When a boy has been abandoned by his mother and father or by one of them and he is taken by someone as his son, he is called a *son adopted after being abandoned*. [172] When an unmarried girl gives birth to a son secretly in her father's house, one should call him by the name *son born to an unmarried woman*; the offspring of an unmarried girl belongs to the man who marries her. [173] When a pregnant woman is married off, whether her condition is disclosed or not, the child in the womb belongs to the man who marries her and is called *son received with marriage*. [174] When someone purchases a boy directly from his mother and father so he may have a child, whether that child is of the same class or not, he is his *purchased son*. [175] When a woman who has been abandoned by her husband or is a widow marries again and begets a son of her own will, he is called *son of a remarried woman*. [176] Such a woman or one who has gone away and returned, so long as she has not been deflowered, is fit to perform the marriage ceremony once again with her husband according to the rite of remarriage. [177] When someone who has no mother or

father or who has been abandoned without cause offers himself up to a man, tradition calls him a *son given in adoption by himself.* [178]When a Brahmin fathers a son by a Śūdra woman out of lust, tradition calls him a *Pāraśava* (10.8), because while still able (*pārayan*) he is a corpse (*śava*).

[179]The son a Śūdra begets by a slave woman or by a slave woman married to a slave may take a share with his father's permission—that is the settled Law.*

[180]The eleven sons enumerated above beginning with the *son begotten on the wife*—wise men call these the surrogates of a son necessitated by the possible interruption of rites (9.166 n.). [181]Those who are designated here as sons because of congruity but who are born from another man's seed belong only to the one from whose seed they were born and to no one else (9.35–40).

[182]If among several brothers born to the same father one gets a son, Manu has declared that through that son they all become men who have sons. [183]If among all the wives of the same husband one gets a son, Manu has declared that through that son they all become women who have sons.*

[184]In the absence of each superior son each son inferior to him is entitled to the estate; but if several of them are of equal rank, all of them share the estate. [185]The sons inherit the father's estate—not the brothers, not the fathers. The estate of a man who has no son, however, is inherited by his father or by his brothers.

Alternative Heirs [186]To three water is offered; to three rice-balls are given; and the fourth offers them—there is no room for a fifth.* [187]The closest relative of a person belonging to the same ancestry shall take his property; beyond such a relative, a man belonging to the same family, the teacher, or a pupil. [188]When none of these is available, pure and disciplined Brahmins learned in the triple Veda share the estate; in this way, the Law is not hurt. [189]The king must never take the property of a Brahmin—that is the rule; but, in the absence of any heir, the king may take the property of persons belonging to the other classes.

[190]When a man has died childless, a son should be procured for him through a man of the same lineage, and any estate the deceased may have should be handed over to that son. [191]When two individuals fathered by two men litigate over the property held by the

wife, each shall take the estate of his own biological father to the exclusion of the other.*

Women's Property [192] When their mother dies, all the uterine brothers and sisters should divide the maternal estate equally among themselves. [193] If those sisters have any daughters, one should joyfully give them also, as is proper, something from their maternal grandmother's property.

[194] Tradition presents six types of women's property: what a woman receives at the nuptial fire, what she receives when she is taken away, what she is given as a token of love, and what she receives from her brothers, mother, and father. [195] What she receives subsequent to the marriage and what her husband gives her out of affection—upon her death that property goes to her children even if her husband is alive.

[196] In a 'Brāhma', 'Divine', 'Seer's', 'Gāndharva', or 'Prājāpatya' marriage, the property of a woman is awarded to her husband alone, if she dies childless. [197] In a 'Demonic' or a subsequent form of marriage, on the other hand, any property given to a woman is awarded to her mother and father, if she dies childless (3.20–34).

[198] Any property given somehow to a woman by her father goes to the unmarried Brahmin daughter, or to that daughter's offspring.

[199] Women must never alienate the common property of the family or even her own private property without the consent of her husband.

[200] Any ornaments worn by a woman while her husband was alive shall not be partitioned by his heirs; if they do, they fall from their caste.

Disqualification from Inheritance [201] The following receive no shares: the impotent (3.150 n.), outcastes, those born blind or deaf, the insane, the mentally retarded, mutes, and anyone lacking manly strength. [202] It is right, however, that a wise man should provide all of them with food and clothing according to his ability until the end; if he does not, he will become an outcaste. [203] If, on the other hand, any of these, the impotent and so forth, somehow want to have wives and do have issue, their offspring are entitled to a share.

Partition of Non-ancestral Property [204] If the eldest acquires any assets after his father's death, a share of it goes to his younger brothers, provided they are pursuing their studies. [205] If all of them are uneducated, however, and they acquire assets by their own labour, then the division is equal, given that it is not part of the paternal estate—that is the fixed rule. [206] Assets that someone acquires through learning, on the other hand, belong to him alone, as do presents from friends, wedding gifts, and anything given with the honey-mixture (3.119n.).

[207] If one of the brothers, quite able to live by his own activity, does not want any property, he may be stripped of his share after giving something for his maintenance. [208] If one of them earns anything by his own labour without utilizing the paternal property, he need not share it against his will, as it was acquired by his own effort.

[209] If the father recovers any missing ancestral property, he need not share it with his sons against his will, as it was acquired by himself.

Miscellaneous Rules of Partition [210] If parties to a partition again live together and subsequently undertake a new partition, then the division is equal; primogeniture is inoperative there.

[211] If the oldest or the youngest among them is debarred from the distribution of shares or if either of them dies, his share is not lost.* [212] Having assembled together, the uterine brothers, as well as reunited brothers and uterine sisters, should jointly divide it equally among themselves.

[213] When the eldest defrauds his younger brothers through greed, he shall no longer be the eldest. Stripped of his share, he should be punished by the king. [214] All brothers who pursue improper activities are unfit to inherit the property. The eldest, moreover, must not establish his own separate property without first giving to his younger brothers.

[215] If prior to partition the brothers undertake a joint enterprise, on no account shall the father give unequal shares to his sons.

[216] A son born after partition shall inherit the entire paternal property; or, if he has brothers who have reunited, he shall share it with them.*

[217] The mother shall receive the inheritance of a childless son; and if the mother is also dead, the father's mother shall inherit that property.

[218] If something is uncovered after all debts and assets have been divided according to rule, it shall be divided equally. [219] A garment, a

vehicle, an ornament, prepared food, water, women, and security measures are declared to be exempt from partition.

> [220] I have described above the division of property and the ritual procedure for sons* beginning in due order with the son begotten on the wife. Listen now to the Law pertaining to gambling.

Grounds for Litigation: XVIII Gambling and Betting

[221] The king shall suppress gambling and betting from his realm; they are the two vices of rulers that devastate a kingdom. [222] Gambling and betting amount to open theft; the king should make constant effort at eradicating them both.

[223] When it is done with inanimate things, people call it 'gambling'; when it is done with living beings, on the other hand, it is known as 'betting'.

[224] The king should have anyone who engages in or facilitates gambling or betting executed, as also Śūdras wearing marks of twice-born men. [225] He should quickly banish from his capital gamblers, performers, entertainers, men belonging to heretical sects, individuals engaging in illicit activities, and liquor vendors. [226] When these clandestine thieves remain in a king's realm, they constantly harass his decent subjects with their illicit activities.

[227] In a former age* gambling was seen to create great enmity; therefore, an intelligent man should never engage in gambling even for fun. [228] When a man engages in it openly or in secret, the kind of punishment to be imposed on him is left to the discretion of the king.

Excursus: Types of Punishment

[229] When a Kṣatriya, a Vaiśya, or a Śūdra is unable to pay a fine, he should acquit himself of the debt through work; a Brahmin, on the other hand, should pay it off in instalments.

[230] The king should punish women, children, the insane, the elderly, the poor, those without guardians, and the sick with a lash, a cane, a rope, and the like.

[231] When those appointed to adjudicate lawsuits, inflamed by the

heat of money,* undermine cases brought by litigants, the king should confiscate all their property. [232] He should put to death those who forge royal edicts, corrupt the constituents of the realm,* or kill women, children or Brahmins, as also those who give aid to his enemies.

[233] Whenever something has been adjudicated and a judgement issued, he should recognize it as executed according to the Law and not bring it back again.* [234] If an official or a judge settles a case wrongly, the king himself should settle it and fine him 1,000 (8.120 n.).

Grievous Sins Causing Loss of Caste [235] A murderer of a Brahmin, a man who drinks liquor, a thief, and a man who has sex with an elder's wife—all these men should be considered individually as guilty of a grievous sin causing loss of caste (11.55 n.).

[236] If any of these four fails to perform the penance, the king should determine for them a punishment, both corporal and pecuniary, that accords with the Law. [237] For sex with an elder's wife, the man should be branded with the mark of a vagina; for drinking liquor, with the sign of a tavern; for stealing, with the figure of a dog's foot; and for killing a Brahmin, with the figure of a headless man. [238] These wretched men—with whom one is not permitted to eat, to participate at a sacrifice, to recite the Veda, or to contract marriages—shall roam the earth, excluded from all activities relating to the Law. [239] Branded with marks, they shall be forsaken by their paternal and maternal relations; they should be shown no compassion and paid no reverence—that is Manu's decree.

[240] If they do perform the prescribed penance, on the other hand, the king should not brand the higher classes on the forehead, but make them pay the highest fine (8.138). [241] For these offences, the middle fine should be imposed on a Brahmin, or he should be exiled from the realm along with his property and belongings. [242] When others commit these sins, however, they deserve to have all their property confiscated, if they did them thoughtlessly, or to be executed,* if they did them wilfully.

[243] A good king must never take the property of someone guilty of a grievous sin causing loss of caste; if he takes it out of greed, he becomes tainted with the same sin. [244] He should offer that fine to Varuṇa by casting it into water, or present it to a Brahmin endowed

with learning and virtue. [245] Varuṇa is the lord of punishment, for he holds the rod of punishment over kings; and a Brahmin who has mastered the Veda is the lord of the entire world. [246] When a king refrains from taking the fines of evil-doers, in that land are born in due course men with long lives; [247] the farmers' crops ripen, each as it was sown; children do not die; and no deformed child is born.

[248] If a man of a lower class deliberately torments Brahmins, the king should kill him using graphic modes of execution (9.279 n.) that strike terror into men. [249] A king incurs as great a sin by releasing someone who ought to be executed as by executing someone who ought not to be executed; but he gains merit by its proper exercise.

Conclusion of Grounds for Litigation

[250] I have described above in great detail how lawsuits brought by litigants and falling within the eighteen avenues of litigation are to be decided (see 8.3).

[251] Carrying out properly in this manner his duties flowing from the Law, the king should both seek to acquire territories not yet acquired and protect well those that have been acquired.*

Eradication of Thorns

[252] After properly settling the country and building a fort according to textual norms, he should direct his maximum effort constantly at the eradication of thorns.* [253] By protecting those who follow the Ārya way of life and by clearing the thorns, kings devoted to the protection of their subjects reach the highest heaven. [254] When a king collects taxes without suppressing thieves, on the other hand, it will cause an upheaval in his realm and he will be cut off from heaven. [255] When his realm, sheltered by the power of his arm, is made secure, it will always thrive, like a regularly watered tree.

[256] The king, using spies as his eyes, should identify the two kinds of thieves who steal the property of others: those who operate overtly and those who operate covertly. [257] Of these, the overt cheats are those who live by trading in various merchandise, and the covert cheats are people such as thieves and bandits of the wild.

[258] Bribe-takers, frauds, cheats, gamblers, those who live by adjuring good luck, fortune-tellers, [259] high officials and physicians who act crookedly, those engaged in exhibiting their artistic skills, skilled prostitutes—[260] people such as these should be recognized as open thorns on his people's side, and others, the non-Āryas wearing Ārya marks, as operating in secret. [261] After identifying these through honest undercover agents practising those same occupations and instigating them through mobile agents posted in various spy establishments, he should lure them into his power. [262] After publicizing accurately the crimes they have committed in their respective activities, the king should duly punish them, each in proportion to his capacity and his crime. [263] For without punishment, it is impossible to suppress the crimes of evil-minded thieves who prowl the land in secret.

[264] Assembly halls, water-booths, sweetmeat-shops, brothels, taverns, restaurants, crossroads, memorial trees, fairs, theatres, [265] dilapidated parks, wild tracts, artisans' workshops, abandoned houses, groves, and parks—[266] the king should have these types of place patrolled by mobile and stationary squads and by mobile agents* in order to interdict thieves.

[267] By means of clever former thieves who had been their associates and companions and who are adept at their various activities, he should identify and instigate them. [268] Under the pretext of attending a banquet, seeing Brahmins, or watching feats of valour, they should assemble these people in one place. [269] Those who do not gather there and those who have become suspicious of the source, the king should forcibly attack and kill, along with their friends and paternal and maternal relatives (2.132 n.).

[270] A righteous king must never execute a thief unless he is caught with the stolen goods; if he is caught with the stolen goods and the tools of his trade, the king should execute him without hesitation. [271] He should also execute every individual within any village who gives food, implements, or shelter to thieves.

[272] When individuals appointed to guard the provinces and rulers of border districts who have been summoned remain uninvolved during raids, he should promptly punish them like thieves. [273] When a man who gains his livelihood by the Law deviates from the conventions of the Law, the king should make him also suffer a punishment, for he has deviated from the Law specific to him. [274] When a village is

being raided, a dyke is being breached, or a highway robbery is taking place, whoever fails to hasten there with help according to his ability should be banished along with his belongings.

[275] Those who rob the king's treasury, those who act contrary to his interests, and those who conspire with his enemies—he should inflict diverse kinds of capital punishment on them.

[276] When robbers cut through walls and commit theft at night, the king should cut off their hands and impale them on sharp stakes. [277] After the first offence, he should have two fingers of a pickpocket cut off; after the second, the hands and the feet; and after the third, he ought to be executed. [278] Those who provide fire, food, weapons, or shelter, and those who receive stolen goods—the king should punish these like thieves.

[279] Someone who breaks a reservoir should be killed by drowning or clean execution;* or else, he should repair it and be made to pay the highest fine (8.138). [280] He should kill without hesitation those who break into the treasury, the armoury, or a temple, and those who steal elephants, horses, or chariots.*

[281] Someone who steals water from a reservoir constructed long ago or cuts off its water intake should be made to pay the lowest fine (8.138). [282] Anyone who drops filth on a royal highway, except in an emergency, should pay a fine of 2 Kārṣapaṇas and promptly clean up that filth; [283] but if it was an individual with an emergency, an old man, a pregnant woman, or a child, that person merits a reprimand and should be made to clean it up—that is the settled rule.

[284] Any physician guilty of malpractice is subject to a fine, the lowest in the case of non-humans and the middle in the case of humans (8.138). [285] Anyone who destroys a bridge, a flag, a pole, or a statue should repair the entire damage and pay a fine of 500 (see 8.120 n.).

[286] For adulterating unadulterated substances, and for breaking or improperly boring gems, the punishment is the lowest fine. [287] If a man deals with equivalent commodities as if they were unequal, even if he does so in terms of value, he shall receive the lowest or the middle fine.*

[288] He should locate all prisons along the royal highway where people will see the criminals, grieving and mutilated.

[289] He should promptly execute (8.123 n.) anyone who breaches the rampart, fills the moat, or breaks the gates.

[290] For all types of black magic, a fine of 200 should be imposed, as also for root-witchcraft (11.64 n.) when done by an unrelated person, and for various types of sorcery. [291] Anyone who sells infertile seed corn or jacks up the price of seed corn,* or who destroys boundary marks, shall be executed with mutilation.*

[292] A goldsmith who operates dishonestly, however, is the most wicked of all thorns, and the king should have him cut to pieces with razor knives.

[293] For stealing agricultural implements, weapons, and medicine, the king should impose a punishment taking into account the time and the purpose.*

***Excursus*: Constituents of a Kingdom** [294] Lord, official, capital, realm, treasury, army, and ally—these seven basic constituents are said to form a complete kingdom.

[295] Among these seven basic constituents of a kingdom in the order enumerated, a grave evil affecting each preceding one must be considered the more serious. [296] In this world, a kingdom is propped up by the seven limbs like a tripod and no single one of them is superfluous, because of their mutual dependence on the special quality of each. [297] For each limb is specially suited to carry out specific tasks; the one that accomplishes a particular task is said to be the most important with respect to it.

***Excursus*: Activities of the King** [298–9] By means of spies, by a display of strength, and by engaging in enterprises, he should identify his own and his enemy's relative strength and ascertain the relative gravity of all the adversities and evils affecting his enemy and himself; and only then should he embark on any operation. [300] Indeed, he must embark on his operations repeatedly, though repeatedly exhausted; for Fortune devotes herself only to a man who embarks on his operations.

[301] Kṛta-age, Tretā-age, Dvāpara-age, and Kali-age—the king's activities constitute all these; for the king is said to be the age. [302] When he is asleep, he is Kali; when he is awake, he is Dvāpara; when he is ready to undertake operations, he is Tretā; and when he is on the march, he is Kṛta.

[303] The king should follow the energetic activity of Indra, Sun, Wind, Yama, Varuṇa, Moon, Fire, and Earth.* [304] As Indra showers rain during the four months of the rainy season, so the king,

following the Indra-vow, should shower delights upon his realm. [305] As Sun extracts water through its rays during the eight months,* so the king should constantly extract taxes from his realm; for this is the Sun-vow. [306] As Wind moves about infiltrating all creatures, so the king should infiltrate with his mobile spies; for that is the Wind-vow. [307] As Yama, when the time has come, holds friend and foe alike in his grip, so the king should hold his subjects in his grip; for that is the Yama-vow. [308] As we see people bound with fetters by Varuṇa, so the king should capture criminals; for that is the Varuṇa-vow. [309] When his subjects are as delighted in him as are people when they see the full moon, that king is observing the Moon-vow. [310] When the king is always inflamed and ablaze against evil-doers and crushes evil rulers of border districts, tradition calls it the Fire-vow. [311] The Earth supports all creatures equally; when a king supports all creatures in the same manner, he is observing the Earth-vow.

> [312] In this and other ways should the king, always alert and tireless, suppress thieves within his own realm and even in others.*

***Excursus* on Brahmins** [313] Even in the face of the deepest adversity, he must never anger Brahmins; for when they are angered, they will destroy him instantly along with his army and conveyances (7.75 n.). [314] They made the fire a consumer of everything, the ocean undrinkable, and the moon to wane and wax*—who would not be destroyed when he angers these? [315] When angered, they could create other worlds and other guardians of the world, they could convert gods into non-gods—who would prosper when he injures these? [316] The worlds and the gods always exist by taking refuge in them, and their wealth is the Veda—who would injure them if he wishes to live?

[317] Whether he is learned or not, a Brahmin is a great deity, just as Fire is a great deity, whether it is consecrated or not. [318] Even in cemeteries, the Fire, full of energy, is never tainted; and when it is offered with oblations at sacrifices, it flares up again. [319] Similarly, even if they engage in every undesirable act, Brahmins should be honoured in every way; for they are the highest deity.

[320] When a Kṣatriya becomes haughty in any way in his behaviour towards Brahmins, the Brahmin himself must become their controller, for the Kṣatriya sprang from the Brahmin. [321] Fire sprang from water, Kṣatriya from Brahmin,* and metal from stone; their

all-pervasive energy is quenched when confronting their own source. [322]The Kṣatriya does not flourish without the Brahmin, and the Brahmin does not prosper without the Kṣatriya; but when Brahmin and Kṣatriya are united, they prosper here and in the hereafter.

[323]After giving to Brahmins the money collected from all the fines and handing over the kingdom to his son, the king should meet his death in battle.

Conclusion of the Rules for Kings

[324]Conducting himself in this manner and always devoted to the Laws pertaining to kings, the king should direct all his servants to work for the good of his people.

> [325]I have described above in its entirety the eternal rules of action for the king. What follows, one should understand, are the rules of action for the Vaiśya and the Śūdra in their proper order.

RULES OF ACTION FOR VAIŚYAS AND ŚŪDRAS

Rules for Vaiśyas

[326]After undergoing initiatory consecration and getting married, a Vaiśya should devote himself constantly to trade and to looking after farm animals; [327]for, after creating them, Prajāpati handed over to the Vaiśya the farm animals, and to the Brahmin and the king, all creatures.

[328]'I don't want to look after farm animals'—a Vaiśya should never entertain such a wish, and when there is a willing Vaiśya, under no circumstances shall anyone else look after them. [329]He shall acquaint himself with the relative values of gems, pearls, coral, metals, threads, perfumes, and condiments. [330]He should be knowledgeable about sowing seeds, the good and bad qualities of farmland, all the various ways of weighing and measuring, [331]the desirable and undesirable properties of goods, the good and bad aspects of regions, the probable profit and loss of merchandise, and how best to raise farm animals. [332]He should be well-informed about the wages to be

paid to servants, the different languages of people, the manner of storing goods, and the procedures of buying and selling.

333 He should make the utmost effort at making his assets grow in accordance with the Law and diligently distribute food to all creatures.

Rules for Śūdras

334 For the Śūdra, on the other hand, the highest Law leading to bliss is simply to render obedient service to distinguished Brahmin householders who are learned in the Veda. 335 When he keeps himself pure, obediently serves the highest class, is soft-spoken and humble, and always takes refuge in Brahmins, he obtains a higher birth.

CONCLUSION OF THE LAW OUTSIDE TIMES OF ADVERSITY

336 I have described above the splendid rules of action for the social classes outside times of adversity. Listen now to the rules for them in the proper order for times of adversity.

CHAPTER TEN

RULES FOR TIMES OF ADVERSITY

Mixed Classes

The Four Classes [1]Devoted to their respective activities, the three twice-born classes should study the Veda; but it is the Brahmin who should teach them, not the other two—that is the firm principle. [2]The Brahmin must know the means of livelihood of all according to rule, and he should both teach them to the others and follow them himself.

[3]Because of his distinctive qualities, the eminence of his origin, his observance of restrictive practices, and the distinctive nature of his consecration, the Brahmin is the lord of all the classes.

[4]Three classes—Brahmin, Kṣatriya, and Vaiśya—are twice-born; the fourth, Śūdra, has a single birth. There is no fifth.

[5]In all the classes, children born in the direct order of class* to wives who are of equal class and married as virgins should be recognized as belonging to the same class by birth. [6]Sons fathered by twice-born men on wives of the class immediately below theirs are considered only 'similar', disdained as they are due to their mother's defect.

[7]That is the eternal rule with respect to those born from women of the class immediately below. The following should be recognized as the righteous rule with respect to those born from women two or three classes below.

Mixed Classes: First Discourse [8]From a Brahmin man by a Vaiśya girl is born a son called Ambaṣṭha; and by a Śūdra girl, a Niṣāda, also called Pāraśava. [9]From a Kṣatriya man by a Śūdra girl is born a son called Ugra, who is cruel in his behaviour and in his dealings, a being with the physical characteristics of both a Kṣatriya and a Śūdra.

[10]A Brahmin's children by the three lower classes, a Kṣatriya's by the two lower classes, and a Vaiśya's by the one lower class—tradition calls these six 'low-born' (10.46n.).

[11]From a Kṣatriya man by a Brahmin girl is born a Sūta by caste;

sons of a Vaiśya by Kṣatriya and Brahmin women are a Māgadha and a Vaideha, respectively; [12] and from a Śūdra by Vaiśya, Kṣatriya, and Brahmin women are born respectively an Āyogava, a Kṣattr̥, and a Cāṇḍāla, the worst of all men—so originates the intermixture of classes.

[13] As when there is a difference of two classes in a birth, tradition calls them Ambaṣṭha and Ugra if the difference is in the direct order; in like manner they are Kṣatr̥ and Vaideha, if it is in the inverse order. [14] The sons of twice-born men by women of the class immediately below theirs that have been enumerated in their proper order—they are given the name 'Promixate', because of their mother's defect.

Mixed Classes: Second Discourse [15] From a Brahmin man by an Ugra girl is born a son called Āvr̥ta; by an Ambaṣṭha girl, an Ābhīra; and by an Āyogava girl, a Dhigvaṇa.

[16] From a Śūdra man are born in the inverse order three 'low-borns': Āyogava, Kṣattr̥, and Cāṇḍāla, the worst of all men. [17] Three further 'low-borns' (10.46 n.) are born in the inverse order: from a Vaiśya man, a Māgadha and a Vaideha; and from a Kṣatriya man, a Sūta.*

[18] From a Niṣāda man by a Śūdra woman is born a Pulkasa by caste; a son born from a Śūdra man by a Niṣāda woman, tradition tells us, is a Kukkuṭa. [19] A child born from a Kṣattr̥ man by an Ugra woman is said to be a Śvapāka; and from a Vaidehaka man by an Ambaṣṭha woman, a Veṇa.

[20] When children fathered by twice-born men on women of equal class do not keep the observances and have fallen from the Sāvitrī (2.38 n.), they should be called by the name Vrātya (2.39). [21] From a Vrātya of the Brahmin class are born the evil-natured Bhr̥jjakaṇṭaka, the Āvantya, the Vāṭadhāna, the Puṣpadha, and the Śaikha. [22] From a Vrātya of the Kṣatriya class are born the Jhalla, the Malla, the Licchivi, the Naṭa, the Karaṇa, the Khasa, and the Draviḍa. [23] From a Vrātya of the Vaiśya class are born the Sudhanvan, the Ācārya, the Kāruṣa, the Vijanman, the Maitra, and the Sātvata.*

Mixed Classes: Third Discourse [24] By adultery among the classes, by marrying forbidden women, and by abandoning the activities proper to them, originate the intermixture of classes.* [25] I will enumerate completely those who are of mixed origin, born in the direct and in the inverse order and mutually connected.

[26] Sūta, Vaidehaka, Cāṇḍāla, the worst of men, Māgadha, Kṣatṛ, and Āyogava—[27] these six beget children similar in class to themselves by women of their own class, by women of their mother's caste, and by women of higher castes. [28] As from two of the three classes is born a child that is one's own self—being born from a woman of his own class because of the contiguity—so the same process applies to excluded men.* [29] These same men beget on each other's wives large numbers of excluded children even more vile than they and despicable. [30] Just as a Śūdra man begets an excluded child from a Brahmin woman, so also an excluded man begets from women of the four classes a child subject to even greater exclusion.

[31] Having sex in the inverse order, excluded men beget children subject to even greater exclusion, the low-born beget low-born children, generating as many as fifteen classes. [32] On an Āyogava woman—a Dasyu man begets a Sairandra, who, although not a slave, gains his livelihood as a slave, is skilled at adorning and personal attendance, and lives by trapping animals; [33] a Vaideha man begets a Maitreyaka, who has a sweet voice, eulogizes men constantly, and rings the bell at dawn; [34] and a Niṣāda man begets a Mārgava, that is, a Dāśa, who lives by working on ships and whom people living in Āryāvarta (2.22) call a Kaivarta. [35] By Āyogava women, who are non-Āryas, wear the clothes of the dead, and eat despicable food, are born severally these three low-borns.

[36] From a Niṣāda man is born a Kārāvara, who works on leather; from a Vaidehaka, an Andhra and a Meda,* both of whom dwell outside the village. [37] On a Vaideha woman—a Cāṇḍāla man begets a Pāṇḍusopāka, who deals in bamboo; and a Niṣāda man begets an Āhiṇḍika. [38] On a Pulkasa woman, a Cāṇḍāla man begets a Sopāka,* a wicked man who gains his living as an executioner and is despised by good people. [39] A son born to a Niṣāda woman by a Cāṇḍāla man is an Antyāvasāyin, who operates in cemeteries and is despised even by excluded people.

[40] These castes arising from intermixture and described above according to their fathers and mothers—whether they conceal their caste or are open about it—should be recognized by their respective activities (10.57).

[41] The six types of son born to women belonging to one's own or the class immediately below have characteristics of a twice-born; but tradition regards all the 'delinquent-born' (10.46n.) as having the

same characteristics as Śūdras. 42 By the power of austerity and semen, in each succeeding generation they attain here among men a higher or a lower status by birth.

43 By neglecting rites and by failing to visit Brahmins, however, these men of Kṣatriya birth have gradually reached in the world the level of Śūdras—44 Puṇḍrakas, Coḍas, Draviḍas, Kāmbojas, Yavanas, Śakas, Pāradas, Pahlavas, Cīnas, Kirātas, and Daradas.* 45 All the castes in the world that are outside those born from the mouth, arms, thighs, and feet—whether they speak foreign or Ārya languages—tradition calls Dasyus.

Occupations, Residence, and Dress 46 The 'low-born' among the twice-born, as well as those that tradition calls 'delinquent-born',* should live by occupations despised by the twice-born—47 to Sūtas, management of horses and chariots; to Ambaṣṭhas, medicine; to Vaidehakas, taking care of women; to Māgadhas, trade; 48 to Niṣādas, fishing; to Āyogavas, carpentry; to Medas, Andras, Cuñcus, and Madgus, hunting wild animals; 49 to Kṣattṛs, Ugras, and Pulkasas, trapping and killing animals living in burrows; to Dhigvaṇas, working in leather; and to Veṇas, playing drums.

50 These should live by memorial trees and in cemeteries, hills, and groves, well-recognizable* and living by the occupations specific to them.

Cāṇḍālas and Śvapacas 51 Cāṇḍālas and Śvapacas, however, must live outside the village and they should be made Apapātras.* Their property consists of dogs and donkeys, 52 their garments are the clothes of the dead; they eat in broken vessels; their ornaments are of iron; and they constantly roam about.

53 A man who follows the Law should never seek any dealings with them. All their transactions shall be among themselves, and they must marry their own kind. 54 They depend on others for their food, and it should be given in a broken vessel. They must not go about in villages and towns at night; 55 they may go around during the day to perform some task at the command of the king, wearing distinguishing marks. They should carry away the corpses of those without relatives—that is the settled rule. 56 They should always execute those condemned to death in the manner prescribed by authoritative texts and at the command of the king; and they may take the clothes, beds, and ornaments of those condemned to death.

Further Discourse on Mixed Classes [57] An unknown man without the proper complexion,* born from a squalid womb, a non-Ārya with some measure of Ārya features—one should detect such a man by his activities (10.40). [58] Un-Ārya conduct, harshness, cruelty, and the neglect of rites reveal in this world a man who is born from a squalid womb. [59] He will possess the character of either his father or his mother, or of both; a man born from an evil womb is never able to conceal his nature. [60] If he is the result of a mixed union, even a man born in a prominent family will undoubtedly partake of his parents' character to a greater or a lesser extent.

[61] Wherever these 'delinquent-born' (10.46 n.) individuals, who corrupt the social classes, are born, that realm quickly comes to ruin together with its inhabitants.

Advance to Higher Classes [62] For excluded individuals, giving up their life without artifice* for the sake of a Brahmin or a cow, or in the defence of women or children is the means for achieving success.

[63] Abstention from injuring, truthfulness, refraining from anger, purification, and mastering the organs—this, Manu has declared, is the gist of the Law for the four classes.

[64] If an offspring of a Brahmin man from a Śūdra woman were to bear children from a superior partner, within seven generations the inferior attains the superior caste; [65] a Śūdra thus attains the rank of a Brahmin, and so does a Brahmin the rank of a Śūdra*—one should understand that this rule holds good also for offspring born from a Kṣatriya or a Vaiśya man.

[66] If it be asked: who is superior? A child born accidentally to a Brahmin man by a non-Ārya woman or a child of a non-Ārya man by a Brahmin woman? [67] This is the resolution: a child born to an Ārya man by a non-Ārya woman becomes an Ārya by reason of his attributes, while a child born to a non-Ārya man by an Ārya woman is a non-Ārya. [68] Neither of these should be permitted to receive vedic initiation—that is the settled Law; the former because of the inferiority of his birth and the latter because he was born in the inverse order of class. [69] As a good seed sprouting in a good field grows vigorously, so a child born to an Ārya man by an Ārya woman is worthy of receiving all the consecratory rites.

[70] Some wise men extol the seed, others the field, and yet others both the seed and the field. In this regard, the settled rule is as

follows. [71] A seed planted in a bad field dies midstream; a field without seed also is just bare land. [72] By the power of the seed, children born from animals became seers, receiving honour and acclaim; therefore, they extol the seed (9.32–56).

[73] The creator evaluated a non-Ārya who acts like an Ārya and an Ārya who acts like a non-Ārya and declared: 'They are neither equal nor unequal.'

Occupations of the Four Classes

[74] Brahmins who are established in that whose source is the Veda* and are devoted to the activities specific to them should duly live by the six occupations in their proper order: [75] teaching and studying, offering sacrifices and officiating at sacrifices, and giving and accepting gifts are the six occupations of a highest-born person.

[76] Of these six activities, however, three provide him with a livelihood: officiating at sacrifices, teaching, and accepting gifts from a completely pure person.

[77] From the Brahmin, three Laws are suspended with respect to the Kṣatriya: teaching and officiating at sacrifices, and the third, accepting gifts; [78] the same are suspended also with respect to the Vaiśya—that is the settled rule; for Manu, the Prajāpati, has not prescribed these Laws with respect to these two.

[79] Use of arms and weapons has been prescribed as the livelihood for the Kṣatriya; and trade, animal husbandry, and agriculture for the Vaiśya. Their Law, however, is giving gifts, studying, and offering sacrifices. [80] Among the activities specific to each, the most admirable are: studying the Veda for the Brahmin, protecting the people for a Kṣatriya, and trade alone for the Vaiśya.

Occupations in Times of Adversity

Brahmins [81] When a Brahmin is unable to earn a living by means of the activities specific to him given above, he may live by means of the Kṣatriya Law, for the latter is the one right below him. [82] If it be asked: what happens if he is unable to earn a living by either of these two means? Taking up agriculture or cattle-herding, he should earn a living by the occupation of a Vaiśya.

[83] A Brahmin, or even a Kṣatriya, who earns a living by the Vaiśya

occupation, should try his best to avoid agriculture, which involves injury to living beings and dependence on others.* [84] People think that agriculture is something wholesome. Yet it is an occupation condemned by good people; the plough with an iron tip lacerates the ground as well as creatures living in it.

[85] When someone, deprived of livelihood, is forced to abandon this strict adherence to the Law, he may sell goods traded by Vaiśyas to increase his wealth, with the following exceptions. [86] He should avoid condiments of every kind; cooked food; sesame seeds; stones; salt; farm animals; human beings; [87] every type of dyed cloth; cloth made of hemp, flax, or wool even if they are undyed; fruits; roots; medicines; [88] water; weapons; poison; meat; Soma; all types of perfume; milk; honey; curd; ghee; oil; beeswax; molasses; Kuśa grass; [89] all wild animals; fanged animals; birds; liquor; indigo; lac; and all one-hoofed animals.

[90] An individual engaged in agriculture may freely sell pure sesame seeds that he has cultivated himself, provided they are to be used for purposes relating to the Law and have not been stored for long. [91] If someone uses sesame seeds for purposes other than eating, anointing the body, and giving as a gift, he will become a worm and plunge into the excrement of dogs together with his ancestors.

[92] By selling meat, lac, or salt, a Brahmin falls immediately from his caste; by selling milk, he becomes a Śūdra in three days; [93] but by selling here the other commodities deliberately, a Brahmin is reduced in seven days to the rank of a Vaiśya.

[94] Condiments may be bartered for condiments—but never salt for condiments—cooked food for uncooked food, and sesame seeds for an equal amount of grain.

Kṣatriyas [95] A Kṣatriya who has fallen on hard times may earn his living by all the above means; but under no circumstances should he even think of living by a superior occupation. [96] If a man of inferior birth out of greed lives by activities specific to his superiors, the king shall confiscate all his property and promptly send him into exile (8.123 n.). [97] Far better to carry out one's own Law imperfectly than that of someone else perfectly; for a man who lives according to someone else's Law falls immediately from his caste.

Vaiśyas [98] When a Vaiśya is unable to sustain himself through the Law proper to him, he may live by the occupation of even a Śūdra, refraining, however, from forbidden acts; and he should discontinue it when he is able.

Śūdras [99] When a Śūdra is unable to enter into the service of twice-born men and is faced with the loss of his sons and wife, he may earn a living by the activities of artisans—[100] that is, the activities of artisans and various kinds of crafts the practice of which best serves the twice-born.

Further Occupations for Brahmins [101] A Brahmin firmly committed to his way of life and unwilling to follow the Vaiśya occupations may pursue the following Law when he is languishing through lack of a livelihood. [102] A Brahmin who has fallen on hard times may accept gifts from anybody; that something pure can be sullied is impossible according to the Law. [103] By teaching, officiating at the sacrifices of, and accepting gifts from, despicable individuals, Brahmins do not incur any sin, for they are like fire and water.*

[104] When someone facing death eats food given by anyone at all, he remains unsullied by sin, as the sky by mud. [105] Ajīgarta, tormented by hunger, went up to his son to kill him; and he was not tainted with sin, as he was seeking to allay his hunger. [106] Vāmadeva, a man with a clear vision of what accords with and what is against the Law, finding himself in dire straits and trying to save his life, wanted to eat dog's meat, and yet remained unsullied. [107] Bharadvāja, a man of great austerities, when he and his sons were tormented by hunger in a desolate forest, accepted many cows from the carpenter Bṛbu. [108] Viśvāmitra, a man with a clear vision of what accords with and what is against the Law, when he was tormented by hunger, came to eat the rump of a dog, taking it from the hand of a Cāṇḍāla.*

[109] Accepting gifts, officiating at sacrifices, and teaching—among these, accepting gifts is the worst and the most reprehensible for a Brahmin with respect to the hereafter. [110] Officiating at sacrifices and teaching always pertain to those who have undergone consecratory rites, whereas accepting pertains even to a lowest-born Śūdra. [111] A sin committed by teaching or officiating at a sacrifice is removed by soft recitation and oblations, but a sin incurred by accepting a gift is removed only by discarding it and performing ascetic toil. [112] A Brahmin without a livelihood may even glean or pick single grains (4.5 n.) from anywhere; gleaning is superior to accepting gifts, and picking single grains is superior to even that.

[113] When Brahmin bath-graduates are in dire straits and want wares or money, they should petition the king; if he refuses to give, they ought to abandon him.

[114] Unploughed land is less tainted than ploughed land; and among a cow, a goat, a sheep, gold, grain, and cooked food, each preceding one is less tainted than each subsequent.

Acquisition of Property [115] Seven means of acquiring wealth are in accordance with the Law: inheritance, finding, purchase, conquest, investment, work, and acceptance of gifts from good people. [116] The ten means of livelihood are: learning, craft, employment, service, cattle-herding, trade, agriculture, fortitude, begging, and lending on interest.

[117] A Brahmin or a Kṣatriya must never lend money on interest; to pursue activities dictated by the Law, however, he may lend to an evil man at a small interest.

[118] Even if a Kṣatriya collects 25 per cent as his share during a time of adversity, he is freed from that taint by protecting his subject to the best of his ability. [119] The Law specific to him is conquest, and he must not turn back in the face of danger; when he protects Vaiśyas with his weapons, he may collect a levy in accordance with the Law: [120] from Vaiśyas, a one-sixth share of the grain crop and a duty of one-twentieth on other commodities, with a minimum of 1 Kārṣāpaṇa; and from Śūdras, artisans, and craftsmen, the contribution of their services (7.128–32).

Livelihood of Śūdras [121] If a Śūdra desires to earn a living, he may serve a Kṣatriya, or he may seek to earn a living by serving even a wealthy Vaiśya. [122] He should serve Brahmins for the sake of heaven or for the sake of both, for when he has the name 'Brahmin' attached to him,* he has done all there is to do. [123] The service of a Brahmin alone is declared to be the pre-eminent activity of a Śūdra, for whatever other work he may do brings him no reward.

[124] They* must allocate a suitable livelihood for him from their own family resources, taking into account his ability and skill, and the number of his dependants. [125] They should give him leftover food, old clothes, grain that has been cast aside, and the old household items.

[126] A Śūdra is not affected by any sin causing loss of caste, nor is he entitled to any consecratory rite. He has no qualification with regard

to the Law, but he is not prohibited from following the Law.* [127] Those who know the Law and yearn to follow it, however, incur no sin and receive praise when they imitate the practices of good men, without reciting any ritual formulas; [128] for a Śūdra obtains this world and the next without enduring disdain to the extent that he imitates the practices of good men without giving way to envy.

[129] Even a capable Śūdra must not accumulate wealth; for when a Śūdra becomes wealthy, he harasses Brahmins.

CONCLUSION OF THE LAWS OF THE FOUR CLASSES

[130] I have described above the Laws for the four classes
during times of adversity; when they are properly followed, people attain the highest state.

[131] I have described above the entire set of rules pertaining to the Law of the four classes. Next, I will
explain the splendid rules pertaining to penance.

CHAPTER ELEVEN

PENANCES

Excursus: Occasions for Giving and Begging

[1] A man seeking to extend his line; a man preparing to perform a sacrifice; a traveller; a man who has performed the sacrifice at which all his possessions are given away; a man who begs for the sake of his teacher, father, or mother; a student of the Veda; and a sick man— [2] these nine should be known as 'bath-graduates', Brahmins who are beggars pursuant to the Law. Gifts must be given to these destitutes in proportion to their eminence in vedic learning.*

[3] To these Brahmins food should be given along with the sacrificial fees; to others, it is said, cooked food should be given outside the sacrificial arena.* [4] The king should bestow all sorts of precious gifts on Brahmins learned in the Veda according to their merits, as well as fees for the purpose of sacrifices.

[5] When a married man marries another wife after begging for the expenses, his reward is only sensual pleasure; the resultant offspring belongs to the man who defrayed the expenses.*

[7] A man who has sufficient resources to maintain his dependants for three years, or someone who has more than that, is entitled to drink Soma. [8] If a twice-born man who possesses fewer resources than that drinks Soma, he will not reap its reward, even though he may never have drunk Soma before. [9] When a man of means gives to outsiders while his own people live in misery, that is counterfeit Law, dripping with honey but poisonous to taste. [10] If a man does anything for his welfare after death to the detriment of his dependants, it will make him unhappy both when he is alive and after he is dead.

[11] While a righteous king is ruling, if a man offering a sacrifice finds that his sacrifice is interrupted for want of a single item, he may, especially if he is a Brahmin, [12] take that article from the house of a Vaiśya who has a large herd of animals but has failed to perform rites or to drink Soma, in order to complete the sacrifice.* [13] He may freely take two or three items from the house of a Śūdra; for a Śūdra has nothing to do with sacrifices. [14] He may also take it without a

second thought even from the house of a man who has a hundred cows but has not established his sacred fires or from that of a man who has a thousand cows but has not offered a sacrifice. [15] He may also take it from a man who is always a taker and never a giver, if he refuses to give it; thus his fame will spread and his merits will increase.

[16] Likewise, when a man has not eaten during six mealtimes (6.19n.), at the seventh mealtime he may take from someone who performs no rites, keeping to the rule of leaving no provisions for the next day,* [17] and taking it from his threshing floor, field, or house, or from any place where he can find something. If the man questions him, however, he should confess it to him.

[18] A Kṣatriya must never take anything belonging to a Brahmin; if he has no sustenance, however, he may take what belongs to a Dasyu or a man who neglects his rites. [19] When a man takes money from evil persons and gives them to the virtuous, he makes himself a raft and carries them both* to the other side. [20] The wise call the wealth of those devoted to sacrifice the property of gods; the possessions of those who do not offer sacrifice, on the contrary, is called the property of demons.

[21] A righteous king should never punish such a man,* for it is because of the Kṣatriya's foolishness that the Brahmin is languishing with hunger. [22] After finding out who his dependants are and enquiring into his learning and virtue, the king should provide him with provisions for a righteous livelihood from his own house. [23] After providing him with a livelihood, he should protect him in every way, for by protecting him the king receives from him one-sixth of his merits.

[24] A man who knows the Law should never beg money from a Śūdra to perform a sacrifice; for when the patron of a sacrifice begs in this way, after death he is reborn a Cāṇḍāla. [25] If a Brahmin begs money for a sacrifice and does not devote all of it to that purpose, he will become a Bhāsa vulture or a crow for one hundred years.

[26] If a man seizes what belongs to a god or a Brahmin out of greed, in the next world that evil man will live on the leftovers of vultures.

Excursus: Miscellaneous Topics

Times of Adversity [27]If he is unable to perform the prescribed animal and Soma sacrifices, he should offer as an expiation the Vaiśvānara oblation at the turn of the year.*

[28]When during a normal time a twice-born follows the Law according to the mode for a time of adversity, he will not receive its reward after death—that is indisputable. [29]All the gods, the Sādhyas, and the great Brahmin sages, afraid of death during times of adversity, created a substitute for the rule. [30]When someone, though able to follow the principal mode, yet lives according to the secondary mode, that fool will obtain no reward for it after death.

Power of Brahmins [31]A Brahmin who knows the Law shall not inform the king about any matter; solely with his own power should he chastise men who do him harm. [32]Between the king's power and his own, his own power is far more potent. A twice-born, therefore, should punish enemies solely with his own power, [33]and make use of vedic texts of Atharva-Āṅgīrasa—that is indisputable. Clearly, speech is the Brahmin's weapon; with that a twice-born should strike down his enemies.

[34]A Kṣatriya overcomes his adversities by the power of his arms; a Vaiśya and a Śūdra, by means of wealth; and a Brahmin, through soft recitation and sacrifices. [35]A Brahmin is called the creator, the chastiser, the teacher, and the benefactor; one should never say anything unpleasant to him or use harsh words against him.

Sacrifices [36]A girl, a young woman, an uneducated man, or a fool should never act as the officiant at the daily fire sacrifice, nor should a man who is in great anguish or who has not undergone initiatory consecration; [37]for, when these perform the offering, both they and the person to whom the fire sacrifice belongs fall into hell. Therefore, only a man who has mastered the Veda and is an expert in the vedic rituals should be an officiant.

[38]When a Brahmin fails to give a horse dedicated to Prajāpati as a sacrificial fee at the rite for establishing the sacred fires in spite of having the resources to do so, he is reduced to the level of one who has not established his sacred fires. [39]A man who has mastered his organs and has a spirit of generosity (3.202n.) may perform other meritorious acts; but under no circumstances should he offer sacri-

fices here with inadequate sacrificial fees. [40] Organs, honour, heaven, life span, fame, offspring and livestock—a sacrifice with inadequate sacrificial fees destroys all these; a man with inadequate resources, therefore, should not offer a sacrifice (11.7–8).

[41] If a Brahmin who has established his sacred fires abandons his fires deliberately, he should perform the lunar penance (11.217) for one month; for it is equal to killing a hero.*

[42] Those who perform their daily fire sacrifice by obtaining money from a Śūdra are considered reprehensible among vedic savants, for they are the officiating priests of Śūdras. [43] Stepping with his foot on the heads of these ignorant men who serve the fires of Śūdras, the giver crosses over difficulties.

Justification of Penance

[44] When a man fails to carry out prescribed acts, performs disapproved acts, and is attached to the sensory objects, he is subject to a penance.

[45] The wise acknowledge a penance for a sin committed unintentionally; some, on the basis of vedic evidence, admit it even for a deliberately committed sin. [46] A sin committed unintentionally is cleansed by vedic recitation, whereas a sin committed deliberately through folly is cleansed with various types of penance. [47] When a twice-born, either by fate or by what he did in a previous life, finds himself in a condition requiring the performance of a penance, he should not associate with good people before performing that penance.*

[48] Some evil men become disfigured because of the bad deeds committed in this world, and some because of deeds done in a previous life. [49] A man who steals gold gets rotten nails; a man who drinks liquor, black teeth; the murderer of a Brahmin, consumption; a man who has sex with his elder's wife, skin disease; [50] a slanderer, a smelly nose; an informant, a smelly mouth; a man who steals grain, the loss of a limb; a man who adulterates grain, an excess limb; [51] a man who steals food, dyspepsia; a man who steals speech,* smelly breath; a man who steals clothes, leukoderma; and a man who steals horses, lame legs.* [53] In this way, as a result of the remnants of their past deeds, are born individuals despised by good people: the mentally retarded, the mute, the blind, and the deaf, as well as those who are deformed.

[54]Therefore, one should always do penances to purify oneself; for individuals whose sins have not been expiated are born with detestable characteristics.

Categories of Sin

Grievous Sins Causing Loss of Caste [55]Killing a Brahmin, drinking liquor, stealing,* and having sex with an elder's wife—they call these 'grievous sins causing loss of caste'; and so is establishing any links with such individuals (11.181–2).

[56]A lie concerning one's superiority,* a slander that reaches the king's ear, and false accusations against an elder are equal to killing a Brahmin. [57]Abandoning the Veda, reviling the Veda, giving false testimony, killing a friend,* eating unfit food or forbidden food—these six are equal to drinking liquor. [58]Stealing deposits, men, horses, silver, land, diamonds, or gems, tradition tells us, is equal to stealing gold. [59]Sexual intercourse with uterine sisters, unmarried girls, lowest-born women, and the wives of a friend or son, they say, is equal to sex with an elder's wife.

Secondary Sins Causing Loss of Caste [60]Killing a cow; officiating at the sacrifice of an individual at whose sacrifice one is forbidden to officiate; adultery; selling oneself; forsaking one's teacher, mother, father, vedic recitation, sacred fire, or son; [61]an elder brother permitting a younger brother to marry before him; a younger brother marrying before his older brother (3.171); giving a girl in marriage to or officiating at a sacrifice of either of these; [62]deflowering a virgin; usury; breaking the vow;* selling a reservoir, park, wife, or son; [63]remaining as a Vrātya (2.39); abandoning a relative; giving instruction as a paid teacher; receiving instruction from a paid teacher; selling proscribed commodities; [64]supervising any kind of mine; constructing large equipment; injuring plants; living off one's wife; sorcery; root-witchcraft;* [65]cutting down live trees for firewood; undertaking activities solely for one's own sake; eating reprehensible food; [66]remaining without establishing the sacred fires; acting like a woman; non-payment of debts; studying fallacious treatises; living a corrupt life; engaging in vices; [67]stealing grain, base metals, and livestock; sex with women who drink; killing a woman, a Śūdra, a Vaiśya, or a Kṣatriya; and being an infidel—these are secondary sins causing loss of caste.

Further Categories of Sin [68]Making a Brahmin cry, smelling liquor or substances that should not be smelt, cheating, and sexual intercourse with a man—tradition calls these sins that cause exclusion from caste.*

[69]Killing donkeys, horses, camels, deer, elephants, goats, sheep, fish, snakes, or buffaloes—these should be known as sins that cause a man to be of a mixed caste (10.8 f.).

[70]Accepting wealth from despicable men, trade, serving a Śūdra, and telling lies—these should be recognized as sins that make a man unworthy of receiving gifts.

[71]Killing worms, insects, or birds; eating anything that has come into contact with liquor; stealing fruits, firewood, or flowers; and lack of steadfastness—these make a man impure.

> [72]Listen now attentively to the specific observances
> by which all these sins individually enumerated above
> may be removed.

Penances for Grievous Sins Causing Loss of Caste

Killing a Brahmin [73]A man who has killed a Brahmin should construct a hut and live in the forest for twelve years, eating alms-food and making the head of a corpse his banner, in order to purify himself.

[74]Or, if he so wishes, he may make himself a target for armed men who are cognizant of his state. Or, he may throw himself headlong three times into a blazing fire. [75]Or, he may offer a horse sacrifice, a Svarjit sacrifice, a Gosava sacrifice, an Abhijt sacrifice, a Viśvajit sacrifice, a Trivṛt sacrifice, or an Agniṣṭut sacrifice. [76]Or, to rid himself of the Brahmin's murder, he may walk one hundred leagues* reciting one of the Vedas, eating little, and keeping his organs under control. [77]Or, he may present to a Brahmin learned in the Vedas all his possessions, or wealth sufficient to maintain a person, or else a house with furniture. [78]Or, he may walk upstream along the Sarasvatī,* subsisting on sacrificial food. Or, he may recite three times softly one Collection of the Veda, while limiting his food. [79]Or, after getting his hair shaved, he may live in the outskirts of the village, in a cowshed, in a hermitage, or at the foot of a tree, taking pleasure in doing what is beneficial to cows and Brahmins. [80]Or, he may duly give up his life for the sake of a Brahmin or a cow; one who protects a

cow or Brahmin is freed from the murder of a Brahmin. [81] Or, he becomes freed from it by fighting at least three times in defence of a Brahmin, by recovering all the property of a Brahmin, or by losing his life for the sake of a Brahmin.

[82] Thus always remaining steadfast in his vow, collected in mind, and chaste, he rids himself of the Brahmin's murder at the end of the twelfth year.*

[83] Or, he is freed from his sin by proclaiming it in a gathering of the gods of earth and the gods of men and participating at the bath concluding a horse sacrifice.* [84] The Brahmin is said to be the root of the Law, and the Kṣatriya its crest; therefore, by broadcasting a sin at a gathering of theirs, he becomes purified. [85] By his very origin, a Brahmin is a deity even for the gods and the authoritative source of knowledge for the world; the Veda clearly is the reason for this. [86] When even three of them who know the Veda declare an expiation for sins, it is sufficient for their purification; for the speech of the learned is a means of purification.

[87] By resorting to any one of the above procedures with a collected mind, a Brahmin will rid himself of the sin of killing a Brahmin by means of his self-control.

[88] One must perform the same observance for killing a foetus whose sex cannot be identified, a Kṣatriya or a Vaiśya who is engaged in a sacrifice, or a woman soon after her menstrual period;* [89] for bearing false testimony; for assailing an elder; for stealing a deposit; and for killing a woman or a friend.

[90] This purification is enjoined for killing a Brahmin unintentionally; for killing a Brahmin deliberately, there is no prescribed expiation.

Drinking Liquor [91] If a twice-born man in his folly drinks liquor, he should drink boiling-hot liquor; when his body is scalded by it, he will be released from that sin. [92] Or, he may drink boiling-hot cow's urine, water, milk, ghee, or watery cow dung until he dies. [93] Or, he may eat only broken grain or oil-cake once a day during the night for a full year, wearing a garment of hair, keeping his hair matted, and carrying a banner,* in order to remove the guilt of drinking liquor.

[94] Liquor is clearly the filth of various grains; sin is also called filth.* Therefore, Brahmins, Kṣatriyas, and Vaiśyas must not drink liquor. [95] It should be understood that there are three kinds of liquor:

one made from molasses, another from ground grain, and a third from honey. Just as drinking one of them is forbidden to Brahmins, so are all.* [96] Intoxicants, meat, liquor, and spirits* are the food of demons and fiends; they must not be consumed by a Brahmin, who eats the oblations to the gods. [97] When a Brahmin is intoxicated, he may tumble into filth, blabber vedic texts,* or do other improper things. [98] If the *brahman** resident in a man's body is drenched with liquor even once, his Brahmin nature departs from him and he sinks to the level of a Śūdra.

> [99] I have described above the various expiations for drinking liquor. Next, I will explain the expiation for stealing gold.

Stealing Gold [100] A Brahmin who has stolen gold should go up to the king, proclaim his deed, and say: 'Lord, punish me!' [101] Taking the pestle, the king himself should strike him once. A thief is purified by being put to death or, if he is a Brahmin, solely by ascetic toil.*

[102] If a twice-born wants to rid himself of the sin of stealing gold by means of ascetic toil, however, he should carry out the observance prescribed for killing a Brahmin, living in the wilderness and dressed in tree bark (6.6).

> [103] A twice-born should eliminate the sin resulting from stealing by means of the above observances. The sin of having sexual intercourse with an elder's wife, on the other hand, he should remove by means of the following observances.

Sex with an Elder's Wife [104] A man who had sex with an elder's wife should proclaim his crime and lie down on a heated iron bed, or embrace a red-hot metal cylinder;* he is purified by death. [105] Or, he may cut off his penis and testicles by himself, hold them in his cupped hands, and walk straight towards the south-west until he falls down dead. [106] Or, he may perform the Prājāpatya penance (11.212) for one year with a collected mind, carrying a bed-post, dressed in tree bark (6.6), wearing a long beard, and living in a desolate forest. [107] Or, he may perform the lunar penance (11.217) for three months, keeping his organs under control and subsisting on sacrificial food or barley gruel, so as to remove the sin of sexual intercourse with an elder's wife.

[108] Men guilty of a grievous sin causing loss of caste should eliminate their sin by means of the above observances, but men guilty of a secondary sin causing loss of caste should do so by means of the various observances given below.

Penances for Secondary Sins Causing Loss of Caste

Killing a Cow [109] A man guilty of a secondary sin causing loss of caste by killing a cow should drink barley gruel for a month and live in a cow pen with his hair shaved and wrapped in the skin of that cow. [110] During two months,* he should eat a small amount of food without artificial salt at every fourth mealtime (6.19n.), bathing with cow's urine, and keeping his organs under control [111] During the day, he should follow those cows,* remain standing, and inhale their dust; at night, after attending to them and paying them homage, he should remain seated on his haunches. [112] When they stand, he should stand behind them; when they walk, he should also walk behind them; when they sit down, he should likewise sit down, self-controlled and free from rancour. [113] When a cow is sick, is threatened by dangers from thieves, tigers, and the like, has fallen down, or has got stuck in mud, he should free her with all his strength. [114] When it is hot, raining, or cold, or when the wind is blowing strong, he must never find shelter for himself without first providing it for the cow to the best of his ability. [115] When a cow is eating from his own or another's house, field, or threshing floor, or when the calf is drinking milk, he must not inform anybody of it.

[116] When a man who has killed a cow follows cows in this manner, in three months he rids himself of the sin resulting from killing a cow. [117] After he has duly completed this observance, furthermore, he should give ten cows along with a bull or, if that is impossible, all his possessions to those who know the Veda.

Other Secondary Sins [118] The very same observance should be performed by twice-born men who commit any secondary sin causing loss of caste, with the exception of a vedic student who has broken his vow of chastity, in order to purify themselves; alternatively, they may perform the lunar penance (11.217).

Student Breaking the Vow of Chastity [119] A vedic student who has broken his vow of chastity should offer at night a one-eyed donkey to Nirṛti at a crossroads, employing the ritual procedure of a cooked oblation.*

[120] After offering the oblations in the fire according to rule, he should finally offer oblations of ghee to Wind, Indra, Teacher, and Fire, reciting the verse: 'May the Maruts . . . .' [121] Vedic savants who know the Law declare that when a twice-born votary ejaculates his semen intentionally he breaks his vow. [122] When a votary breaks his vow of chastity, the vedic energy within him enters these four: Wind, Indra, Teacher, and Fire.* [123] When he has committed this sin, he should wear the skin of a donkey and beg food from seven houses, proclaiming his deed. [124] Subsisting on the almsfood obtained from them once a day and bathing three times a day, he is purified in a year.

Penances for the Remaining Categories of Sin

[125] Someone who has committed any of the acts that cause exclusion from caste (11.68) should perform a Sāntapana penance (11.213) if he did it deliberately, and a Prājāpatya penance (11.212) if he did it inadvertently.

[126] For committing acts that cause a person to be of a mixed caste or that make a person unworthy of receiving gifts (11.69–70), the purification is to perform the lunar penance (11.217) for one month, and for those that make a person impure (11.71), the purification is to drink hot barley gruel for three days.

Excursus: Penances for Injury to Living Beings

Homicide [127] One-quarter the penance for the murder of a Brahmin is prescribed by tradition for the murder of a Kṣatriya; one-eighth for the murder of a virtuous Vaiśya; and one-sixteenth for the murder of a Śūdra.

[128] If a Brahmin kills a Kṣatriya unintentionally, however, he should give one thousand cows and a bull to purify himself. [129] Or, he may perform during three years the observance prescribed for killing a Brahmin, keeping himself controlled, wearing matted hair, living far away from the village, and making his home at the foot of a tree. [130] A Brahmin who kills a virtuous Vaiśya should perform the same

observance for one year, or give one hundred cows along with a bull. [131] One who kills a Śūdra should perform the same vow completely for six months, or give ten white cows along with a bull to a Brahmin.

Killing Animals [132] For killing a cat, a mongoose, a blue jay, a frog, a dog, a monitor lizard, an owl, or a crow, a man should perform the observance for killing a Śūdra. [133] Alternatively, he may drink milk for three days, or walk a distance of one league (11.76n.), or bathe in a river, or recite softly the hymn addressed to the waters (8.106n.).

[134] For killing a snake, a Brahmin should give an iron spade; for killing a castrate,* a load of straw and a Māṣa of lead; [135] for killing a boar, a pot of ghee; for killing a partridge, a Droṇa of sesame seeds; for killing a parrot, a 2-year-old calf; and for killing a Krauñca crane, a 3-year-old calf. [136] For killing a ruddy goose, a Balāka flamingo, a Baka heron, a peacock, a monkey, a Śyena hawk, or a Bhāsa vulture, he should give a cow to a Brahmin. [137] For killing a horse, he should give a garment; for killing an elephant, five black bulls; for killing a goat or a sheep, a draught ox; and for killing a donkey, a 1-year-old calf. [138] For killing wild animals, he should give a milk cow if they are carnivorous, and a heifer if they are non-carnivorous; for killing a camel, one Kṛṣṇala. [139] For killing a licentious woman belong to any of the four classes, he should give a leather bag, a bow, a goat, and a sheep, respectively. [140] If a twice-born is unable to expiate the killing of snakes and the rest by giving gifts, to remove the sin he may perform one arduous penance (11.212) for each.

[141] For killing one thousand creatures with bones or a cart-full of boneless creatures, he should perform the observance for killing a Śūdra. [142] For killing creatures with bones, he should give a little something to a Brahmin; when he kills boneless creatures, he is purified by controlling his breath.

Injuring Vegetation [143] For cutting down fruit trees a person should recite softly one hundred Ṛc verses; so also for cutting down shrubs, vines, creepers, or flowering plants.

[144] For killing any kind of creature growing in food stuffs, condiments, fruits, or flowers, the purification is to consume ghee.

[145] For needlessly tearing out cultivated plants or ones that grow spontaneously in the forest, he should follow a cow for one day, subsisting on milk (11.109–15).

[146] Through these observances a man should remove all sins he has committed deliberately or inadvertently by causing injury. Listen now to the observances relating to eating food that ought not to be eaten.

Excursus: Penances for Eating Forbidden Food

[147] When someone drinks Vāruṇī* liquor inadvertently, he is purified only by undergoing vedic initiation. If he drinks it intentionally, no penance is prescribed; its penance ends in death—that is the settled rule. [148] If someone drinks water that has stood in a vessel for keeping liquor or an intoxicant (11.96n.), he should drink milk boiled with Śaṅkhapuṣpī plant for five days. [149] If he touches, gives, or receives according to rule an intoxicant, or drinks water left over by a Śūdra, he should drink water boiled with Kuśa grass for three days. [150] If a Brahmin who has drunk Soma, however, smells the odour coming from a man who has drunk liquor, he is purified by controlling his breath three times while submerged in water and then consuming ghee. [151] Persons of all three twice-born classes ought to undergo re-initiation if they inadvertently consume urine or excrement, or anything that has come into contact with liquor.

[152] Shaving, girdle, staff, begging, and the vows are dispensed with in the rite of re-initiation of twice-born men.

[153] If someone eats the food of individuals whose food is not to be eaten or the leftovers of a woman or a Śūdra, or consumes forbidden meat, he should drink barley gruel for seven days. [154] When a twice-born drinks anything turned sour or pungent decoctions, even though they may be pure,* he remains ritually impure until it has been excreted.*

[155] If a twice-born consumes the urine or excrement of a village pig, a donkey, a camel, a jackal, a monkey, or a crow, he should perform the lunar penance (11.217). [156] He should perform the same observance after eating dried meat, the Bhauma plant, mushrooms (6.14n.), the meat of an unknown animal (5.17), or meat from a slaughter-house.

[157] The hot-arduous penance (11.215) is the purification for eating the meat of carnivorous animals, pigs, camels, cocks, humans, crows, or donkeys.

[158] If a twice-born student who has not performed the rite of

return eats food given at a monthly ancestral rite, he should fast for three days and remain in water for one day. [159] If someone observing the student vow eats honey or meat in any way, he should perform the standard arduous penance (11.212n.) and complete the remainder of his vow.

[160] If someone eats anything that has become impure from the mouth of a cat, crow, rat, dog, or mongoose, or that has been contaminated by hair or insects, he should drink a decoction of the Brahmasuvarcalā plant.

[161] A person who desires to remain pure should never eat unfit food (5.5n.); he should vomit any such thing that he has eaten inadvertently or purify himself quickly with the various methods of purification.

> [162] I have described above the various rules pertaining to the observances for eating food that ought not to be eaten. Listen now to the rules pertaining to the observances that remove the sin of theft.

Excursus: Penances for Theft

[163] A Brahmin who deliberately steals grain, cooked food, or money from the house of someone belonging to his own caste is purified by performing the arduous penance (11.212) for one year. [164] For stealing men, women, a field, a house, or water from a well or a tank, tradition prescribes the lunar penance (11.217) as purification.

[165] If he steals articles of little value from the house of someone else, to purify himself he should return the stolen goods and perform the Sāntapana penance (11.213). [166] For stealing food or delicacies, as also a vehicle, a bed, a seat, flowers, roots, or fruits, the purification consists of consuming the five products of the cow.* [167] For stealing grass, wood, trees, dried food, molasses, clothes, skins, or meat, he should abstain from food for three days. [168] For stealing gems, pearls, coral, copper, silver, iron, brass, or stone, he should subsist on broken grains for twelve days. [169] For stealing cotton, silk, wool, a single-hoofed or double-hoofed animal, a bird, perfume, medicinal herbs, or a rope, he should subsist on milk for three days.

> [170] Through these observances, a twice-born should remove a sin incurred by stealing. The sin incurred

by having sex with a woman with whom sex is forbidden, on the other hand, he should remove by means of the following observances.

Excursus: Penances for Sexual Offences

171 If a man has sexual intercourse with his uterine sisters, the wives of a friend or son, unmarried girls, or lowest-born women, he should perform the observance prescribed for sex with an elder's wife (see 11.58).

172 If he has sex with his sister—the daughter of his father's or mother's sister—or the daughter of his mother's uterine brother, he should perform the lunar penance (11.217). 173 A wise man must not take these three to be his wife. Marriage with them is forbidden because they are blood relatives, and anyone marrying them proceeds downward (6.35 n.).

174 If someone ejaculates his semen in non-human females, in a man, in a menstruating woman, in any place other than the vagina, or on water, he should perform the Sāntapana penance (11.213). 175 If a twice-born has sexual intercourse with a man or a woman in an ox-cart, on water, or during the day, he should bathe with his clothes on.

176 If a Brahmin has sex with Cāṇḍāla or lowest-born women, or eats food or accepts presents given by them, he falls from his caste if he does it inadvertently and becomes equal to them if he does it intentionally.

177 The husband should keep an adulterous wife confined in a single room and make her perform the observance* prescribed for a man who has sex with another man's wife. 178 If she commits adultery again when solicited by a man of the same caste, tradition prescribes an arduous penance (11.212) and a lunar penance (11.217) as the means of her purification.

179 The sin that a twice-born commits in a single night by having sex with a Śūdra woman he removes in three years by living on almsfood and performing soft recitations every day.

180 I have described above the expiation for all four kinds of sinner.* Listen now to the following expiations for those who associate with outcastes.

Association with Outcastes

[181] When someone associates with an outcaste by officiating at sacrifices, by teaching, and by contracting marriages—but not by occupying the same vehicle or seat or by eating together—in one year he himself becomes an outcaste.

[182] When a man forges links (2.40 n.) with any one of these outcastes, he should perform the same observance prescribed for that man in order to purify himself of his linkage with him.

Excommunication [183] In the evening of an inauspicious day and in the presence of his blood relations, officiating priests, and teachers, the rite of offering water to the outcaste should be performed by the relatives belonging to his ancestry (5.60 n.) together with his relatives by marriage. [184] A slave woman* should overturn a pot filled with water with her foot, as for a dead man; and they, along with his relatives by marriage, shall observe a period of impurity for a day and a night. [185] They should suspend conversing or sitting together with him, giving him his inheritance, and even ordinary interaction with him. [186] The rights of primogeniture are also suspended in his case, along with the pre-emptive property owed to the eldest; the pre-emptive share of the eldest should go to a younger brother of his with the highest qualities.

Re-admission [187] After he has performed the penance, however, they should bathe in a sacred body of water and, along with him, throw into it a brand-new pot filled with water. [188] After he has thrown that pot in the water and entered his own house, he should participate in all the activities of the relatives just as he had done before.

[189] These same rules should be adhered to also in the case of women who become outcastes; but they should be provided with clothes, food, and drink, and permitted to live near the house.

[190] No one should transact any business with uncleansed sinners; and under no circumstances should anyone abhor those who have been cleansed.*

Excursus: Miscellanea on Sin and Penance

[191] One must not live together with people who have killed children, women, or those who come to them for protection, or with people who are ingrates, even if they have been purified in accordance with the Law.

[192] When any twice-born men have not been taught the Sāvitrī verse according to rule (2.38 n.), one should make them undergo three arduous penances and have them initiated according to rule. [193] One should prescribe the same when twice-born men who have followed wrong occupations or neglected the Veda seek to perform a penance.

[194] When Brahmins have acquired wealth through a reprehensible activity, they are purified by giving away that wealth and by engaging in soft recitation and ascetic toil. [195] A man is freed from the sin of accepting gifts from a bad individual by softly reciting the Sāvitrī verse three thousand times with a collected mind and by subsisting on milk for a month while remaining in a cow pen. [196] When that man, emaciated by the fast, returns from the cow pen and remains bowing down, they should ask him: 'Friend, do you seek equality?' [197] Saying 'Truly' to the Brahmins, he should scatter some grass for the cows. At that place made holy by the cows,* they should perform his re-admission.

[198] If someone officiates at a sacrifice of Vrātyas (2.39), performs the funeral of outsiders, or carries out a rite of sorcery or an Ahīna sacrifice, he is purified by doing an arduous penance (11.212) three times.

[199] When a twice-born has forsaken someone who has come to him for protection or has misused* the Veda, he removes that sin by subsisting on barley for one year.

[200] When a man has been bitten by a dog, a jackal, a donkey, a carnivorous animal of the village, a man, a horse, a camel, or a pig, he is purified by controlling his breath.

[201] Eating at every sixth mealtime (6.19 n.) for one month, reciting a Vedic Collection, offering daily a Śākalā oblation—these are the means of purification for individuals alongside whom it is unfit to eat.

[202] When a Brahmin deliberately gets onto a camel-cart or a donkey-cart, he is purified by bathing naked and controlling his breath.

203 If someone in distress discharges his bodily waste either without water or in water,* he is purified by bathing with his clothes on outside the village and then touching a cow.

204 For neglecting the daily rites prescribed by the Veda and for breaking the vow of a bath-graduate, the penance is fasting. 205 When someone says 'Huṃ' to a Brahmin or addresses a superior as 'you',* he should bathe, fast the rest of the day, and placate that person by paying him obeisance. 206 If he strikes such a man with even a blade of grass, throttles his neck with a cloth, or defeats him in an argument, he should placate him by prostrating himself on the ground. 207 By wanting to hurt a Brahmin, a man goes to hell—if he threatens him, for one hundred years; if he strikes him, for one thousand years. 208 As many particles of dust as the blood of a twice-born lumps together, for so many thousands of years will the man who spilled it live in hell (4.168). 209 For threatening, he should perform an arduous penance (11.212); for striking, a very arduous penance (11.214); and for spilling a Brahmin's blood, both an arduous and a very arduous penance.

210 For the removal of sins for which no expiation has been specified, one should fix a penance after taking into consideration both the type of sin and the strength of the sinner.

> 211 I will describe to you the means whereby a human
> being may remove sins, means employed by gods,
> seers, and ancestors.

Types of Generic Penance 212 A twice-born practising the *Prājāpatya* penance should eat in the morning for three days and in the evening for three days, eat what is received unasked for three days, and abstain from food during the final three days.

213 Subsisting on cow's urine, cow dung, milk, curd, ghee, and water boiled with Kuśa grass, and fasting during one day*—tradition calls this the Sāntapana penance.

214 A twice-born practising the Atikṛcchra (very arduous) penance should eat as before (11.212) one mouthful a day during the three three-day periods and fast during the final three days.

215 A Brahmin practising the Taptakṛcchra (hot-arduous) penance should drink hot water, hot milk, hot ghee, and hot air during each three-day period and bathe once with a collected mind.

216 When a man, controlled and vigilant, abstains from food for

twelve days, it is called the Parāka penance, which removes all sins.

[217] He should decrease his food by one rice-ball a day during the dark fortnight and increase it likewise during the bright fortnight, bathing three times a day—tradition calls this Cāndrāyaṇa (the lunar penance). [218] This same procedure in its entirety should be followed when a man, with his mind controlled, performs the lunar observance with its middle shaped like a barley corn, beginning it on the first day of the bright fortnight.*

[219] A man practising the lunar penance of ascetics should eat each day at noon eight rice-balls from the sacrificial oblation, controlling himself. [220] A Brahmin should eat four rice-balls in the morning with a collected mind and four after sunset—tradition calls this the lunar penance of children.

[221] If a man eats thrice eighty rice-balls from the sacrificial oblation in any manner whatsoever during one month with a collected mind, he obtains residence in the same world as the Moon.

[222] This observance was practised by the Rudras, the Ādityas, the Vasus, and the Maruts, along with the great seers, to free themselves from all evil.

Observances by the Penitent [223] He should offer a burnt oblation every day by himself, reciting the Great Calls; and he should practise abstention from injuring, truthfulness, abstention from anger, and honesty. [224] He should enter water with his clothes three times during the day and three times during the night, and under no circumstance may he speak with women, Śūdras, or outcastes. [225] He must remain standing during the day and seated at night or, if he is unable, lie down on the ground (6.22 n.). He must remain chaste and devoted to his vow, paying homage to teachers, gods, and Brahmins. [226] He should recite softly the Sāvitrī verse and the purificatory texts* every day to the best of his ability, remaining diligent in this way with respect to all observances carried out for the purpose of a penance.

[227] By these observances should twice-born persons cleanse themselves of public sins; they may cleanse themselves of secret sins, however, through ritual formulas and burnt offerings.

Four Means of Expiation [228] A sinner is freed from his sin by declaring it publicly, by being contrite, by performing ascetic toil, and by reciting the Veda; during a time of adversity, also by giving gifts.

[229] To the extent a man on his own publicly acknowledges an infraction of the Law he has committed, to that extent is he freed from that infraction, like a snake from his slough.

[230] The more his mind abhors that evil deed, the more his body is freed from that infraction; [231] for when a man is contrite about a sin he has committed, he is freed from that sin. 'I will never do so again'—by this forswearing he is purified. [232] Having thus contemplated in his mind the consequences his actions have on his afterlife, he should always pursue wholesome activities with his thoughts, speech, and body. [233] If a man commits a reprehensible act, whether it is inadvertent or deliberate, he must not commit it a second time if he wants to be freed from it.

[234] If someone's mind is not at ease with respect to a particular act he has committed, he should practise ascetic toil for it until his mind is assuaged.* [235] All happiness here, whether divine or human, has ascetic toil as its root, as its middle, and as its end—so have wise men who saw the Veda declared. [236] Knowledge is the ascetic toil for a Brahmin; protection, for a Kṣatriya; trade, for a Vaiśya; and service, for a Śūdra. [237] Solely by ascetic toil do well-disciplined seers, subsisting on fruits, roots, and air, observe the three worlds together with their mobile and immobile creatures. [238] Solely by ascetic toil do medicines, antidotes, spells, and the various divine conditions become effective; for ascetic toil is the means by which they become effective. [239] What is difficult to cross, what is difficult to obtain, what is difficult to enter, what is difficult to do—all that is accomplished by ascetic toil, for it is difficult to prevail over ascetic toil. [240] Persons guilty of a grievous sin causing loss of caste, as also others who have committed misdeeds, are freed from their sins simply by ascetic toil vigorously carried out. [241] Insects, snakes, moths, animals, birds, and immobile creatures attain heaven by the power of ascetic toil. [242] Whatever sin people commit through their mind, word, or body—with ascetic toil as their only wealth, they quickly burn off all that simply by ascetic toil. [243] The denizens of heaven accept the offerings of a Brahmin purified solely by ascetic toil, and they fulfil his desires. [244] Prajāpati, the Lord, created this Treatise solely by ascetic toil; the seers, likewise, obtained the Vedas by ascetic toil. [245] Thus did the gods proclaim this grandeur of ascetic

toil, as they observed the sacred origin of this whole world from ascetic toil.

[246]Reciting the Veda daily to the best of one's ability, performing the great sacrifices, and forbearance quickly destroy sins, even those rising from grievous acts causing loss of caste. [247]As a fire by its energy burns up in an instant a piece of kindling placed in it, so a man who knows the Veda burns up all sins by the fire of his knowledge.*

Further Means of Expiation [249]Controlling the breath sixteen times while reciting the syllable OṂ along with the Calls, when it is performed every day, purifies even the murderer of a learned Brahmin (4.208 n.) within one month.

[250]Even a man who has drunk liquor is purified by reciting softly Kutsa's hymn, 'Burning away our evil . . .', the triple verse of Vasiṣṭha, 'To welcome the Dawn . . .', the Māhitra hymn, and the Śuddhavatī verses.

[251]A man who has stolen gold, on the other hand, becomes instantly stainless by reciting softly the Asyavāmīya hymn and the Śivasaṃkalpa formulas.

[252]A man who has had sex with an elder's wife is freed from his sin by reciting softly the hymns Haviṣpāntīya, 'No anxiety, no danger . . .', and 'This, yes, this is my inclination . . .', and the Puruṣa hymn.

[253]A man who wants to remove grave or slight sins should recite softly during one year the verse 'We placate . . .,' and the verse 'Whatever offence . . .' [254]If a man has accepted a forbidden gift or has eaten reprehensible food, he is purified in three days by reciting softly the Taratsamandī hymn. [255]A man who has committed many sins is purified by reciting the Somāraudra hymn and the three verses 'Aryaman . . .' while bathing in a river. [256]A sinner should recite softly the seven verses 'Indra . . .' for half a year; but if someone commits a reprehensible act* in the water, he should subsist for a month on almsfood. [257]A twice-born removes even a grave sin by offering oblations of ghee during one year while reciting the Śākalahomīya formulas or by reciting softly the verse 'Adoration . . .'.

[258]A man guilty of a grievous sin causing loss of caste should follow cows with a collected mind; he becomes purified by subsisting on almsfood and reciting the Pāvamānī verses for one year (11.109–17).

259 Or, if a man, being ritually pure, recites three times a Vedic Collection in the wilderness and cleanses himself by means of three Parāka penances, he is freed from all the sins causing loss of caste. 260 If a man, self-controlled, fasts for three days while bathing three times a day and reciting the Aghamarṣaṇa hymn three times, he is freed from all the sins causing loss of caste. 261 As the horse sacrifice, the king of sacrifices, removes all sins, so the Aghamarṣaṇa hymn removes all sins.

262 Even if he has slaughtered these three worlds and even if he has eaten food of anyone at all, no sin taints a Brahmin who retains the R̥g-veda in his memory. 263 If a man recites three times with a collected mind the Collection of the R̥g-veda, the Yajur-veda, or the Sāma-veda, along with the secret texts (2.140 n.), he is freed from all sins. 264 As a clod dissolves quickly when it falls into a large lake, so all sins become submerged in the triple Veda. 265 The R̥g verses, the primary Yajus formulas,* and the diverse Sāman chants—these should be known as the triple Veda. A man who knows it is one who knows the Veda. 266 The primary tri-syllabic Veda,* upon which the triple Veda is based, is another secret triple Veda. A man who knows it is one who knows the Veda.

CHAPTER TWELVE

[1]'You have described this Law for the four classes in its entirety, O Sinless One! Teach us accurately the ultimate consummation of the fruits of actions.'

[2]Bhr̥gu, the son of Manu and the very embodiment of the Law, said to those great seers, 'Listen to the determination with respect to engagement in action.'

ACTION

The Fruits of Action

[3]Action produces good and bad results and originates from the mind, speech, and the body. Action produces the human conditions—the highest, the middling, and the lowest.

[4]One should understand that the action of the embodied self—action that in this world is of three kinds, has three bases, and contains ten characteristics—is set in motion by the mind.*

[5]Coveting the property of others, reflecting on undesirable things in one's mind, and adhering to false doctrines are the three kinds of mental action. [6]Harshness, falsehood, slander of every sort, and idle chatter are the four kinds of verbal action. [7]Taking what has not been given, unsanctioned killing, and sex with another's wife are given in tradition as the three kinds of bodily action.

[8]A man experiences the good and bad results of mental actions in his mind alone; those of verbal actions, in his speech; and those of bodily actions, in his body alone. [9]On account of faults resulting from bodily actions, a man becomes an immobile creature; on account of faults resulting from verbal actions, he becomes a bird or an animal; and on account of faults resulting from mental actions, he becomes a man of the lowest caste.

[10]The rod of speech, the rod of mind, and the rod of action—a man in whose intellect these are kept under control is said to be 'triple-rodded'.* [11]When a man has laid down these rods with respect to all creatures and brought lust and anger under control, he thereby secures success.

The Inner Selves [12]The one who makes this body act is called Kṣetrajña, 'the knower of the field'; the one who does the actions, on the other hand, the wise call Bhūtātman, 'the elemental self'. [13]Another inner self innate to all embodied beings bears the name Jīva, 'the individual self', by whom are experienced all the pleasures and pains in succeeding births.*

[14]These two—Mahat,* 'the Great', and Kṣetrajña, 'the knower of the field'—united with the elements, remain pervading the one who abides in creatures both great and small. [15]From his body innumerable forms stream forth, which constantly set in motion the creatures both great and small.

The Process of Rebirth [16]When evil men die, another firm body is produced for them from the same five elemental particles,* a body designed to suffer torments. [17]After experiencing there the torments of Yama with that body, they merge into those very elemental particles, each into its corresponding particle.

[18]After paying for the sins resulting from attachment to sensory objects, sins that lead to misery, he is freed from taint and approaches the same two beings of great power.* [19]Unwearied, these two jointly examine his merits and sins, linked to which one secures happiness or suffering here and in the hereafter.

[20]If he acts righteously for the most part and unrighteously to a small degree, enveloped in those very elements, he enjoys happiness in heaven. [21]If, on the other hand, he acts unrighteously for the most part and righteously to a small degree, abandoned by those elements, he suffers the torments of Yama. [22]After enduring the torments of Yama, Jīva, 'the individual self', becomes freed from taint and enters those same five elements, each into its corresponding particle.

[23]Seeing with his own intellect those transitions of this Jīva, 'the individual self', resulting from righteous and unrighteous conduct, let him always set his mind on righteous conduct.

The Three Attributes [24]One should understand Goodness, Vigour, and Darkness as the three attributes of the body, attributes by which Mahat, 'the Great', remains pervading all these existences completely.

[25]When one of these attributes thoroughly suffuses the body, it makes the embodied self dominant in that attribute. [26]Goodness is knowledge, tradition tells us; Darkness is ignorance; and Vigour is

passion and hatred. These are their pervasive forms that inhere in all beings.

[27] Among these—when someone perceives within himself a condition full of joy, a sort of pure and tranquil light, he should recognize it as Goodness; [28] when it is full of pain and causing anguish to himself, he should understand that it is Vigour, irresistible and constantly drawing embodied beings; [29] when it is full of confusion, with an unclear object, unfathomable by argument, and indiscernible, he should recognize it as Darkness.

> [30] I will explain to you completely the fruits arising
> from all these three attributes—the highest, the
> middling, and the lowest fruits.

[31] Vedic recitation, ascetic toil, knowledge, purification, the control of the organs, righteous activity, and contemplation of the self—these mark the attribute of Goodness. [32] Delight in undertaking activities, resolve, taking up improper tasks, and constant indulgence in sensual pleasures—these mark the attribute of Vigour. [33] Greed, sloth, lack of resolve, cruelty, infidelity, deviation from proper conduct, habitual begging, and carelessness—these mark the attribute of Darkness.

[34] These, in brief and in the proper order, should be known as the marks of all these three attributes located in the three times. [35] An act about which a man is ashamed after he has committed it, while he is committing it, and when he is about to commit it—a learned man should recognize all that as the mark of the attribute of Darkness. [36] An act by which a man seeks to win wide fame in the world and is not disappointed when he fails to win it—one should recognize it as the mark of the attribute of Vigour. [37] What a man seeks to know with all his heart and is not ashamed to perform, at which his inner being rejoices—that is the mark of the attribute of Goodness.

[38] Pleasure is said to be the mark of Darkness; Profit, of Vigour; and Law, of Goodness (2.224 n.). Each later one is superior to each preceding.

> [39] Which of these attributes leads to which types of
> cyclical existence—I will briefly state them in due
> order with respect to this entire world.

[40] Those who possess Goodness become gods; those who possess

Vigour become humans; and those who possess Darkness always become animals—that is the threefold course. [41]One should recognize, however, that this triple course based on attributes is itself threefold, namely, lowest, middle, and highest, depending on the specific type of action and knowledge within each.

[42]Immobile creatures, worms and insects, fish, snakes, creeping animals, farm animals, and jackals—these constitute the lowest course related to Darkness. [43]Elephants, horses, Śūdras, despised foreigners, lions, tigers, and boars—these constitute the middle course related to Darkness. [44]Cāraṇas, Suparṇas, hypocritical men, fiends, and ghouls—these constitute the highest among the courses related to Darkness.

[45]Jhallas, Mallas, Naṭas (10.22), men who live by vile occupations, and people addicted to gambling and drinking—these constitute the first course related to Vigour. [46]Kings, Kṣatriyas, royal chaplains, and professional debaters and soldiers—these constitute the middle course related to Vigour. [47]Gandharvas, Guhyakas, Yakṣas, divine attendants, and all the Apsarases—these constitute the highest among the courses related to Vigour.

[48]Hermits, ascetics, Brahmins, divine hosts in celestial chariots, asterisms, and Daityas—these constitute the first course related to Goodness. [49]Sacrificers, seers, gods, Vedas, celestial lights, years, ancestors, and Sādhyas—these constitute the second course related to Goodness. [50]Brahmā, creators of the universe (1.34–7), Law, Mahat (12.14), and the Unmanifest—the wise call this the highest course related to Goodness.

> [51]I have declared above everything coming from the
> three kinds of action—the entire transmigratory
> cycle affecting all beings, a threefold cycle which con-
> tains a further threefold division.

[52]Vile and ignorant men attain evil transmigratory paths by their attachment to the senses and by their failure to follow the Law.

> [53]Which kind of womb this Jīva, the 'individual self',
> attains in due order within this world through which
> kind of action—listen to all of that.

Sin and Rebirth [54]Those who commit grievous sins causing loss of caste first go to dreadful hells during large spans of years; upon the expiration of that, they reach the following transmigratory states.

[55] A murderer of a Brahmin enters the wombs of a dog, a pig, a donkey, a camel, a cow, a goat, a sheep, a deer, a bird, a Cāṇḍāla, and a Pulkasa.

[56] A Brahmin who drinks liquor enters the wombs of worms, insects, moths, birds that feed on excrement, and vicious animals.

[57] A Brahmin who steals enters thousands of times the wombs of spiders, snakes, lizards, aquatic animals, and vicious ghouls.

[58] A man who has sex with an elder's wife enters hundred of times the wombs of grasses, shrubs, creepers, carnivorous animals, fanged animals, and creatures that commit cruel deeds.

[59] Vicious individuals become carnivorous animals; those who eat forbidden food become worms; thieves become cannibals; and those who have sex with lowest-born women become ghosts.

[60] A man who forges links with outcastes, has sex with someone else's wife, or steals what belongs to a Brahmin becomes a Brahmin fiend.

[61] A man who steals gems, pearls, corals, or any of the various precious substances out of greed is born among goldsmiths.* [62] By stealing grain, one becomes a rat; by stealing bronze, a ruddy goose; by stealing water, a Plava coot; by stealing honey, a gnat; by stealing milk, a crow; by stealing sweets, a dog; by stealing ghee, a mongoose; [63] by stealing meat, a vulture; by stealing fat, a Madgu cormorant; by stealing oil, a cockroach; by stealing salt, a cricket; by stealing curd, a Balāka flamingo; [64] by stealing silk, a partridge; by stealing linen, a frog; by stealing cotton cloth, a Krauñca crane; by stealing a cow, a monitor lizard; by stealing molasses, a flying fox; [65] by stealing fine perfumes, a muskrat; by stealing leafy vegetables, a peacock; by stealing various kinds of cooked food, a porcupine; by stealing uncooked food, a hedgehog; [66] by stealing fire, a Baka heron; by stealing household utensils, a mason-wasp; by stealing dyed clothes, a francolin partridge; [67] by stealing a deer or an elephant, a wolf; by stealing a horse, a tiger; by stealing fruits or flowers, a monkey; by stealing a woman, a bear; by stealing water, a cuckoo; by stealing vehicles, a camel; and by stealing farm animals, a goat. [68] If a man steals anything at all belonging to some one else by force or eats an oblation before the offering has been completed, he inevitably becomes an animal.

69 Women also, when they steal in the above manner, incur guilt; they become the wives of the very same creatures.

70 When people belonging to the social classes deviate from their respective occupations outside a time of adversity, they go through evil cyclical existences and end up as servants of the Dasyu people.* 71 When a Brahmin deviates, he will become an Ulkāmukha ghost eating vomit; a Kṣatriya will become a Kaṭapūtana ghost eating filth and corpses; 72 a Vaiśya will become a Maitrākṣajyotika ghost feeding on pus; and a Śūdra who deviates from the Law proper to him will become a Cailāśaka ghost.

73 The more that people addicted to sensual pleasures indulge in sensual pleasures, the more their proclivity to them grows. 74 By repeatedly engaging in these sinful actions, these men of little understanding undergo torments here in various births—75 tossing about in dreadful hells such as Tāmisra; the hell Asipatravana and the like; being tied up and cut up; 76 various kinds of torture; being eaten by crows and owls; being burnt by hot sand-gruel; the unbearable tortures of being boiled in vats; 77 taking birth constantly in evil wombs full of suffering; being assailed by cold and heat; terrors of various kinds; 78 repeated residence in different wombs; being born agonizingly; being wrapped up in painful ways; doing servile work for others;* 79 being separated from relatives and loved ones; having to live in the company of evil people; earning and losing wealth; winning friends and enemies; 80 old age, against which there is no remedy; being assailed by illnesses; various afflictions; and death itself, which is impossible to overcome.

81 When a man engages in any act with a certain inner disposition, he reaps its fruits with a body corresponding to that disposition.

> 82 I have declared to you above all the fruits arising
> from actions. Listen now to these rules of action for a
> Brahmin, rules that secure the supreme good.

Actions Leading to the Supreme Good

83 Vedic recitation, ascetic toil, knowledge, controlling the senses, refraining from causing injury, and service of the teacher—these are the highest means of securing the supreme good.

84 Among all these splendid activities, a particular activity has been

declared as the best means for a man here to secure the supreme good. [85] Among all these, tradition holds the knowledge of the self to be the highest; it is, indeed, the foremost of all sciences, for by it one attains immortality.

[86] One should understand that acts prescribed by the Veda are always a more effective means of securing the highest good both here and in the hereafter than the above six activities. [87] All these activities without exception are included within the scheme of the acts prescribed by the Veda, each in proper order within the rules of a corresponding act.

[88] Acts prescribed by the Veda are of two kinds: advancing, which procures the enhancement of happiness; and arresting,* which procures the supreme good. [89] An action performed to obtain a desire here or in the hereafter is called an 'advancing act', whereas an action performed without desire and prompted by knowledge is said to be an 'arresting act'. [90] By engaging in advancing acts, a man attains equality with the gods; by engaging in arresting acts, on the other hand, he transcends the five elements.

[91] A man who offers sacrifices within himself attains absolute sovereignty when he sees equally himself in all beings and all beings in himself. [92] Leaving behind even the acts prescribed above, a Brahmin should apply himself vigorously to the knowledge of the self, to inner tranquillity, and to vedic recitation. [93] This, indeed, is the consummation of one's existence, especially for a Brahmin; for only by achieving this does a twice-born accomplish all he has to do, and never otherwise.

[94] The Veda is the eternal eyesight for ancestors, gods, and humans; for vedic teaching is beyond the powers of logic or cognition—that is the settled rule. [95] The scriptures that are outside the Veda, as well as every kind of fallacious doctrine—all these bear no fruit after death, for tradition takes them to be founded on Darkness. [96] All those different from the Veda that spring up and then flounder—they are false and bear no fruit, because they belong to recent times.*

[97] The four social classes, the three worlds, and the four orders of life, the past, the present and the future—all these are individually established by the Veda. [98] Sound, touch, visible appearance, taste, and, the fifth, smell, are established by the Veda alone; their origin is according to attribute and action. [99] The eternal vedic treatise bears

on all beings; it is the means of success for these creatures; therefore, I consider it supreme.

[100] A man who knows the vedic treatise is entitled to become the chief of the army, the king, the arbiter of punishment, and the ruler of the whole world. [101] As a fire, when it has picked up strength, burns up even green trees, so a man who knows the Veda burns up his taints resulting from action. [102] A man who knows the true meaning of the vedic treatise, in whatever order of life he may live, becomes fit for becoming Brahman while he is still in this world.

[103] Those who rely on books are better than the ignorant; those who carry them in their memory are better than those who simply rely on books; those who understand are better than those who simply carry them in their memory; and those who resolutely follow them are better than those who only understand.

[104] For a Brahmin, ascetic toil and knowledge are the highest means of securing the supreme good; by ascetic toil he destroys impurity and by knowledge he attains immortality.

[105] Perception, inference, and treatises coming from diverse sources—a man who seeks accuracy with respect to the Law must have a complete understanding of these three. [106] The man who scrutinizes the record of the seers and the teachings of the Law by means of logical reasoning not inconsistent with the vedic treatise—he alone knows the Law, and no one else.

> [107] This is the totality of activities leading to the
> supreme good as prescribed. The secret doctrine of
> this Treatise of Manu will now be taught.

Excursus: Secret Teaching

[108] If it be asked: what happens in cases where specific Laws have not been laid down? What 'cultured' Brahmins state is the undisputed Law. [109] Those Brahmins who have studied the Veda together with its supplements in accordance with the Law and are knowledgeable in scripture, perception, and inference, should be recognized as 'cultured'.

[110] Alternatively, when a legal assembly with a minimum of ten members, or with a minimum of three members firm in their conduct, determines a point of Law, no one must question that Law.

[111] A man who knows the three Vedas, a logician, a hermeneut, an etymologist, a specialist in Law, and three individuals belonging to the first three orders of life—these constitute a legal assembly with a minimum of ten members.* [112] A man who knows the Ṛgveda, a man who knows the Yajurveda, and a man who knows the Sāmaveda—these should be recognized as constituting a legal assembly with a minimum of three members for settling doubts regarding the Law. [113] When even a single Brahmin who knows the Veda determines something as the Law, it should be recognized as the highest Law, and not something uttered by myriads of ignorant men. [114] Even if thousands of men who fail to follow the observances, who are unacquainted with the Veda, and who merely use their caste to earn a living, come together, they do not constitute a legal assembly. [115] When fools enveloped by Darkness declare something as the Law, though they are ignorant of it—that sin, increased a hundredfold, stalks those who declare it.

> [116] I have explained to you above all the best means of securing the supreme good. A Brahmin who does not deviate from them obtains the highest state.

CONCLUSION

Excursus: Summation

[117] In this manner, the blessed god, desiring to do what is beneficial for the people, revealed to me in its entirety this highest secret of the Law.

[118] With a collected mind, a man should see in the self everything, both the existent and the non-existent; for when he sees everything in the self, he will not turn his mind to what is contrary to the Law. [119] All the deities are simply the self, the whole world abides within the self; for the self gives rise to engagement in action on the part of these embodied beings.

[120] Let him deposit space within his spaces;* the wind within his motion and touch; the highest fire within his digestive organ and eyes; water within his fluids; earth within his physical form; [121] the moon in his mind; directions in his ears; Viṣṇu in his stride; Hari* in his strength; Fire in his speech; Mitra in his organ of evacuation; and Prajāpati in his organ of procreation.

[122] The ruler of all, more minute than even an atom, resplendent like gold, and to be grasped by the sleeping mind—he should know him as the supreme Person. [123] Some call him Fire, some Manu the Prajāpati, others Indra, still others Breath, and yet others the eternal Brahman. [124] This one, pervading all beings by means of the five forms (12.16), makes them go around like a wheel through birth, growth, and death. [125] When a man thus sees by the self all beings as the self, he becomes equal towards all and reaches Brahman, the highest state.

[126] When a twice-born recites this Treatise of Manu proclaimed by Bhr̥gu, he will always follow the proper conduct and obtain whatever state he desires.

APPENDIX I

FAUNA AND FLORA

COMMON fauna and flora that can be readily translated are not listed here; they are found in the Index. For further information on flora, see K. M. Nadkarni, *Indian Materia Medica*, revised edition; 2 vols. (Bombay: Popular Prakashan, 1976). For animals, see S. H. Prater, *The Book of Indian Animals*, Bombay Natural History Society (Reprint. Delhi: Oxford University Press, 1997). For birds, see K. N. Dave, *Birds in Sanskrit Literature*, (Delhi: Motilal Banarsidass, 1985).

Aśmantaka The plant *Bauhinia tomentosa*, whose fibres were used to make the girdle of a student.

Baka This term is applied to a wide variety of water fowl, including heron, ibis, stork, and the common flamingo.

Balāka Flamingo; the term is sometimes applied to other water fowl, such as the egret.

Balvaja A type of coarse grass: *Eleusine Indica*.

Bel (Bilva) The tree *Aegle Marmelos*, as also the fruits of this tree.

Bhāsa The Bearded Vulture (*Gypaetus barbatus*), but often the term may refer to other kinds of vulture.

Bhūstṛṇa The plant *Andropogon Schoenanthus*; geranilum grass; *Ruaghas* in Hindi. A fragrant grass native to central India.

Cakra The ruddy sheldrake called the Brahmani Duck. The fidelity of a mated pair to each other and their grief when separated is celebrated in Indian poetry and folklore.

Darbha A type of grass used for ritual purposes, most commonly the same as Kuśa; specifically the grass *Saccharum cylindricum*.

Dātyūha The Hawk Cuckoo.

Eṇa The black buck (also called *Kṛṣṇasāra*: *MDh* 2.23), an antelope with black hair on the back and sides and white under the belly: *Antilope cervicapra*. About 32 inches at the shoulder and weighing about 90 lbs., it has horns 20–5 inches long.

Haṃsa The ruddy goose, the most celebrated species of Indian goose. The term is often applied to other large geese and swans.

Kākola A kind of raven, although the term may have been used more widely for various species of ravens and crows.

Kālaśāka The plant *Ocimum sanctum*, commonly referred to as Holy Basil or *Tulasī* plant.

Kalaviṅka A species of sparrow, identified as the 'village sparrow' by

Vijñāneśvara on *YDh* 1.174. According to Dave (1985), the word is used for blackbirds, magpies, and finches.

Kataka The fruit of the tree *Strychnos potatorum*, called 'clearing nut tree'; Hindi *nirmalī*.

Khadira The tree *Acacia catechu*, called 'cutch tree'; Hindi *Khair*.

Khañjarīṭaka The yellow wagtail.

Kiṃśuka The tree *Butea frondosa*; called 'bastard teak'; Hindi *palas*.

Koyaṣṭhi The lapwing, also called the paddy-bird. Dave (1985, 358) identifies these as 'the smaller crested Herons and Bitterns which keep standing in shallow waters for hours for prey to come to them'.

Krauñca A species of large water bird, probably the common crane. Haradatta (on *ĀpDh* 1.17.36) says that they travel in pairs, and Bühler identifies the bird as the red-crested crane now called Sāras.

Kubjaka The shrub *Rosa moschata*; called 'musk-scented rose'; Hindi *kujai*.

Kuśa The most common of the sacred grasses (see Darbha) used for rituals purposes; *Poa cynosuroides*.

Madgu The snake fish or a cormorant.

Mahāśalka A kind of large prawn.

Muñja A species of rush belonging to the sugar-cane family and reaching about 10 feet in height and used for basket weaving: *Saccharum Munja*. Its principal ritual use is in the manufacture of the girdle given to a Brahmin boy at his vedic initiation.

Mūrvā A species of hemp used in the manufacture of bow strings and of the ritual girdle given to a Kṣatriya boy at his vedic initiation: *Sansevi-era Roxburghiana*.

Palāśa A variety of fig tree called *Dhak* with a beautiful trunk and abundant leaves: *Butea frondosa*. Incisions produce a red juice used as an astringent. The tree was viewed as sacred in ancient India and its wood used to make ritual implements.

Pāṭhīna A kind of sheat-fish, *Silurus Pelorius* or *Boalis*.

Pīlu The tree *Careya arborea*; Hindi *kumbi*.

Plava A coot or cormorant.

Rājīva Said to be a kind of lotus-coloured fish, or one with stripes.

Rajjuvāla A species of wild fowl.

Rohita A kind of red fish said to feed on moss.

Ruru A species of spotted antelope.

Sāla The tree *Shorea robusta*, called the 'Sal tree'; Hindi *sakhu*, but in other languages *sal*.

Śāli A variety of rice. Commentators call this red winter rice.

Śamī The name covers two plants. First, *Mimosa suma* (Hindi *chikkur*), a thorny shrub. Second, *Prosopis spicigera*.

Śaṅkhapuṣpī The plant *Canscora decussata*.
Sārasa A species of crane, *Ardea Sibirica*.
Saśalka Lit. 'with scales', a kind of fish.
Śelu The tree *Cordia myxa*.
Śigruka The tree *Moringa oleifera* or *pterygosperma*, commonly called 'drumstick' tree (*Murunga*), whose long pods are widely used as a vegetable.
Siṃhatuṇṭa Lit. 'lion-faced', a kind of fish.
Śleṣmātaka Also called *Śleṣmāta* and *Śelu*, the fruit of this small tree is about the size of a cherry. Called *Bhokar* in Marathi, it is used today for making pickles.
Śyena A kind of hawk or falcon, although the term is used for any large bird of prey.
Udumbara A type of fig tree whose wood is used for ritual purposes: *Ficus glomerata*.
Vārdhrīṇasa (lit. 'leather-snouted'). This sometimes refers to the rhinoceros, but in these texts it refers to a type of bird, probably a hornbill. At *BDh* 1.12.6, however, it is classified as a bird that scratches with its feet in searching for food, which would argue against a waterbird.
Vrīhi A variety of long-grained rice different from *Śāli* and ripening, according to commentators, in sixty days.

APPENDIX II

NAMES OF GODS, PEOPLE, AND PLACES

Ādityas Literally the son(s) of Aditi, the term in the plural refers to a group of gods, including some prominent ones such as Varuṇa, Mitra, and Indra. Early texts give their number as eight, but the *Brāhmaṇas* already show their number as twelve, which has remained the norm ever since. Together with the Vasus and the Rudras, they constitute the three major classes of gods. In the singular, the term Āditya refers to the sun.

Agastya The name of an ancient sage, said to be the son of Mitra and Varuṇa. In a later myth he is said to have instructed the Vindhya mountains to remain bowed (not to grow taller) until he returned from southern India.

Agni Fire and the god of Fire.

Agnidagdha The common designation of a class of ancestors (*pitṛ*) who maintained sacred fires while they were on earth.

Agniṣvātta The common designation of a class of ancestors who maintained sacred fires but performed only domestic rites and not vedic sacrifices.

Ajīgarta A sage famous for his story told in the *AitB* 7.13–16. He wanted to sacrifice his son, Śunaḥśepa, to appease the wrath of the god Varuṇa.

Ājyapa Literally, 'ghee drinkers', the name of a class of ancestors descended from Pulastya. They are viewed as the ancestors of Vaiśyas.

All-gods (*viśvedeva*). The name of a class of gods. In the later Dharma texts they are listed as ten in five pairs: Kratu and Dakṣa, Vasu and Satya, Dhuri and Locana, Kāla and Kāma, and Purūravas and Ārdrava. See Kane 1962–75: iv. 457.

Anagnidagdha The common designation of a class of ancestors distinguished from the *agnidagdha;* hence, possibly ancestors who did not maintain sacred fires on earth.

Andha-Tāmisra One of the twenty-one hells. No light of the sun falls into this region. Suicides and adulterers are consigned to this hell.

Aṅgiras Name of a sage. In later mythology, he is viewed as one of the ten mind-born sons of Brahmā.

Āṅgirasa The name of a class of priests closely associated with another group called Atharvan. The name is also used with reference to a group of sundry divine beings and is an epithet of several gods, especially the fire god Agni.

Antyāvasāyin A very low-caste person, even lower than a Cāṇḍāla.

Explained as the offspring of a Niṣāda woman and a Cāṇḍāla man (*MDh* 10.39).

Apsaras A class of female deities connected with water and often regarded as the wives of the Gandharvas.

Asaṃvṛta A name of a hell.

Asipatravana A hell where trees have leaves as sharp as knives. For further Purāṇic descriptions, see Mani 1975: 58.

Asura Although in early Indo-Iranian mythology it was a divine epithet, in Indian myth *asuras* are viewed as demons and opponents of gods.

Aśvin Twin deities described as young, beautiful, fond of honey, and expert in medical knowledge. They are the physicians of the gods.

Atri A famous sage and author of many vedic hymns. Later mythology sees him as one of the ten mind-born sons of Brahmā.

Barhiṣad Sons of Atri, they are the ancestors of various demonic classes of beings. For later descriptions, see Mani 1975: 108.

Bharadvāja An ancient seer to whom the composition of the sixth book of the Ṛgveda is ascribed.

Cailāśaka An evil class of ghosts that feed on moths.

Cāṇḍāla An outcaste person whose mere touch pollutes. He is considered the offspring of a Śūdra father and a Brahmin mother.

Cāraṇa This term can apply to bards, singers, and the like, and also to mythological beings connected with singing.

Daitya A class of demons often associated with Dānavas.

Dakṣa Name of a divine being associated with creation and one of the ten sons of Brahmā. For myths associated with him, see Mani 1975: 192.

Dānava A class of demons often associated with the Daityas.

Dasyu A generic name for degraded persons and outcastes. The name is also applied to ethnic groups outside the four major classes of society (see *MDh* 10.45).

Dhanvantari A god produced at the cosmogonic churning of the ocean, he is the physician of the gods and the divine author of medical science.

Dṛṣadvatī Name of a river flowing into the Sarasvatī from the east.

Gandharva In the early vedic literature Gandharvas appear as a class of divine beings alongside the gods and the forefathers. They are associated with the Soma drink and are said to be fond of females. They are often associated with the celestial nymphs, Apsarases. In later literature, especially the epics, the Gandharvas are depicted as celestial singers and are associated with music.

Guhyaka A class of divine beings; attendants of Kubera.

Havirbhuj Lit. 'eaters of oblations', beings of this class are regarded as the ancestors of Kṣatriyas.

Hiraṇyagarbha Lit. 'golden egg or foetus'. In cosmology, the initial state of the cosmos in the form of an egg (*MDh* 1.9).

Indra The most famous of the vedic gods, Indra is called the king of the gods. He is powerful and loves to drink Soma. His claim to fame is his victory over Vṛtra, a combat that is given cosmogonic significance. Indra is closely associated with rain, and prominence is given to his weapon, the Vajra, conceived of as the thunderbolt in later tradition.

Kālasūtra A hell depicted in the Purāṇas as extremely hot.

Kaśyapa The name of an ancient sage.

Kaṭapūtana An evil class of deceased persons (*preta*) or demons.

Kavi An epithet of Bhṛgu.

Kāvya The name of a class of ancestors.

Kratu One of the mind-born sons of Brahmā.

Kubera God of riches and guardian of the northern quarter.

Kuru Name of a tribe inhabiting the region of between the upper reaches of the Indus and Ganges rivers during vedic times. This tribe became allied with the Pañcālas, who occupied the land to the south-east of the Kurus.

Kurukṣetra The land of the Kurus. In later times, this referred to a stretch of sacred land situated south of the river Sarasvatī and north of Dṛṣadvatī where the epic battle of the *Mahābhārata* took place.

Marīci The first of the mind-born sons of Brahmā.

Maruts A group of gods connected with the wind and the thunderstorm, and thus associated with Indra's exploits.

Matsya Name of a region located to the west of the Pañcālas and south of the Kurus and of the people of that region.

Mitra Name of a vedic god closely associated with Varuṇa.

Nāga A serpent, especially mythical beings viewed as serpents.

Nārada Well known in later literature as a famous sage, he is one of the sons of Brahmā. See Mani 1975: 526.

Nirṛti Goddess personifying death, destruction, and adversity.

Niṣāda A mixed caste considered to be the offspring of a Brahmin father and a Vaiśya mother.

Pañcāla The name of a region in the upper reaches of the Ganges, to the south-east of the Kurus; also refers to the people of this region.

Piśāca An evil supernatural being; a goblin.

Pracetas One of the sons of Brahmā.

Prajāpati Literally 'lord of creatures', he is the creator god *par excellence* in the Brāhmaṇas and the Upaniṣads. He is the father of the gods and the demons (*asura*), as well as of all creatures.

Prayāga The sacred city at the confluence of the rivers Ganges and Yamunā; present-day Allahabad.

Pulkasa An outcaste individual viewed as particularly impure; the son of a Niṣāda man and a Śūdra woman (*MDh* 10.38).

Rudra Generally regarded as a storm god, Rudra has an ambivalent personality. He is fierce and feared. He is also a healer, the one who averts the anger of gods. In his benign aspect he is referred to as *śiva*, 'the benign one', an epithet that becomes the name of the later god Śiva, with whom Rudra is identified.

Rudras In the plural, the term refers to a group of eleven gods, who, together with the Ādityas and the Vasus, constitute the three classes of gods. The Rudras are associated with the Maruts; both of these groups are ruled by Rudra.

Sādhya A group of somewhat ill-defined deities, said to occupy a region above that of the gods.

Sarasvatī The most celebrated river of the vedic age, it is personified as a goddess. In the Brāhmaṇas she becomes identified with speech and the goddess of speech, and in later mythology Sarasvatī is the goddess of eloquence and wisdom. This river flowed between the Indus and Ganges river systems. Its disappearance in the desert became the focus of myths and folk tales.

Sarpa A serpent; also mythical beings in the shape of serpents.

Saumya A class of ancestors.

Śaunaka A famous vedic sage to whom various vedic texts, as also works on Law, are ascribed.

Soma A sacrificial drink pressed from a plant with apparently mind-altering qualities, it was personified as a god and later identified with the moon. Thus the term often simply means the moon.

Somapa Lit. 'Soma-drinker', a class of ancestors.

Somasad A class of ancestors.

Sukālin A class of ancestors.

Suparṇa Generally referring to any large bird, the term is used with references to bird-shaped mythical beings.

Śūrasena(ka) The name of a region somewhat to the south of Matsya; also the appellation of the inhabitants of this region.

Ugra A mixed class considered to be the offspring of a Vaiśya father and a Śūdra mother.

Utathya Name of an authority on Law.

Varuṇa One of the great gods in the early vedic literature, he is viewed as the grand sovereign and upholder of the natural and moral order. He becomes increasingly associated with the waters and the west, and his residence comes to be located within the ocean.

Vasiṣṭha One of the most important seers of the Ṛgveda. Many stories surround his personality, and he is credited with the authorship of numerous texts, including the seventh book of the Ṛgveda and a treatise on Law. His hostility to Viśvāmitra is a recurrent theme in the stories.

Vasus A group of eight gods distinguished from the Ādityas and Rudras, although their general character and specific identities remain rather vague.

Vinaśana The place where the river Sarasvatī is believed to disapper into the ground.

Vindhya The major mountain range in north-central India dividing north India from the Deccan.

Virāj Literally 'the wide-ruling one', he is presented as the first creature in the Ṛgvedic creation story in the Puruṣa hymn (*ṚV* 10.90). In the *MDh* (1.32) also he is presented as the first creature to emerge from the union of the primeval pair.

Viṣṇu The great god of later Hinduism. He is a somewhat minor solar deity in the vedic literature and is especially celebrated in his two human incarnations, Rāma and Kṛṣṇa.

Viśvāmitra An important seer of the Ṛgveda. Stories depict his hostility towards Vasiṣṭha. In later legend, he is viewed as a Kṣatriya who transformed himself into a Brahmin by means of austerities.

Vrātya The term is used in ancient literature to refer to groups of people, at least some of whom appear to have led a wandering or a nomadic life. Already in some vedic texts, however, the Vrātya is presented as a mysterious, powerful, and even divine person. In later times the term is used to refer to either mixed-caste people or to Brahmins who have not undergone vedic initiation.

Yama The Indian god of death from the most ancient period of vedic mythology until contemporary times. In ancient myths he is called king and divine characteristics are ascribed to him, but he comes to be identified with death itself and many of the negative aspects of death become associated with Yama. Later myths associate him with judgement and punishment of the dead.

Yavana The Indian designation of Greeks and Greek-speaking peoples in the north-western parts of the subcontinent. A mixed class considered to be the offspring of a Kṣatriya father and a Śūdra mother.

APPENDIX III

RITUAL VOCABULARY

1. Names of Rites, Priests, and Ritual Objects

Abhijit A particular sacrifice that is a component part of the major sacrificial session (*sattra*) lasting twelve months known as Gavāmayana.

Adhvaryu One of the four principal priests at a vedic sacrifice. He belongs to the Yajurveda and is responsible for most of the sacrificial actions, including the offerings made in the sacred fire.

Agniṣṭut A particular form of Soma sacrifice lasting a single day.

Ahīna A particular kind of Soma sacrifice at which the pressing lasts between two and twelve days.

Bali The offering of cooked food to various deities, spirits, and animals.

Brahman One of the four principal priests at a vedic sacrifice.

Camasa A square ladle made of banyan wood and used for a variety of purposes in a sacrifice, including serving as a container or a drinking vessel for Soma.

Caru A porridge prepared from rice or barley and cooked in water with butter or milk.

Gosava A one-day Soma sacrifice. It is recommended for people aspiring to sovereignty. See Kane 1962–75: ii. 1213.

Graha A ladle used to take Soma out of a larger container.

Horse sacrifice (*aśvamedha*) One of the most important vedic sacrifices, it is perfomed by a king to demonstrate his sovereignty and ritually to enhance his dominion. A horse is set free to roam at will for a whole year, during which time it is guarded by the king's troops. At the end of the year it is brought back and sacrificed.

Hotṛ One of the four principal priests at a vedic sacrifice. He belongs to the Ṛgveda and is responsible for all the recitations during a sacrifice.

Sacrifice of first fruits An oblation consisting of the first fruits of the harvest offered at the end of the rainy season.

Sacrificial cake (*puroḍāśa*). A cake made with rice or barley flour and baked in potsherds.

Seasonal sacrifice Four sacrifices, each performed at the end of the four seasons.

Śākalā An oblation accompanied by the eight verses of *VS* 8.13.

Śakaṭa A cart used to carry Soma plants and for other ritual purposes.

Sāvitra Commentators take this to be an oblation offered to the god Savitṛ or an oblation using the Sāvitrī verse.

Sphya A wooden sword made of Khadira wood and used within the vedic ritual for a variety of ritual purposes.

Sruc The common name for ladles (including Juhū, Upabhṛt, and Dhruvā) used for pouring ghee into the sacred fire.

Sruva Distinguished from the Sruc-type ladles, this is a smaller spoon used mainly for spooning out ghee or milk into the Sruc. The Sruva has a long handle at the end of which there is a small globular spoon without a spout. It is made of Khadira wood.

Śūrpa A winnowing basket made of bamboo or reeds and used to winnow grain for the ritual.

Trivṛt An oblation with the chanting in 'triplicated' form of three verses, especially the verses of *ṚV* 9.11.

Udgātṛ One of the four major priests in a vedic ritual. He belongs to the *Sāmaveda* and performs the chanting of Sāmans.

Vaiśvānara A sacrifice to the 'Fire present in all men' generally cooked on twelve potsherds.

Viśvajit A sacrifice at which one gives away all one's possessions. It is also a particular sacrifice that is a component part of the major sacrificial session (*sattra*) lasting 12 months known as Gavāmayana.

2. *Names of Ritual Formulas and Texts*

Aghamarṣaṇa This is the hymn *ṚV* 10.190 used in a particular ritual to efface sins.

Asyavāmīya This the rather long hymn *ṚV* 1.164.

Calls (*vyāhṛti*) These are the names of the seven worlds in ascending order: *bhur* (earth), *bhuvaḥ* (mid-space), *svar* (sky), *mahar* (great), *janas* (people), *tapas* (austerity), *satya* (truth). These names are considered sacred and powerful. The first three are generally referred to as simply Calls, whereas all seven are called Great Calls (*mahāvyāhṛti*).

Gāyatrī Another name for Sāvitrī.

Great Calls See Calls.

Haviṣpāntīya This is the hymn *ṚV* 10.88.

Jyeṣṭha Sāmans Haradatta (on *ĀpDh* 2.17.22; *GDh* 15.28) identifies this as *SV* 1.31 (= *ṚV* 1.24.15), while Govinda (on *BDh* 2.14.2) identifies it as *SV* 1.67 (= *ṚV* 6.7.1) and (on *BDh* 3.10.10) as *SV* 1.33 (= *ṚV* 10.9.4) and *ṚV* 1.115.1. Commentators of the *MDh* identify these as Sāmans sung in the wilderness. Obviously, there is a lot of confusion regarding these Sāmans.

Kutsa's hymn The hymn with eight verses *ṚV* 1.97.

Kūṣmāṇḍa The four formulas *TĀ* 2.3; sometimes identified with the formulas at *TĀ* 2.6.

Māhitra The hymn *ṚV* 10.185.

Pāvavmānī Opinions are divided about the identity of these verses. Some identify them as *ṚV* 9.67.21–27. Medhātithi (on *MDh* 11.258) takes them to be *ṚV* 9.1–114 (that is, the entire ninth Maṇḍala), whereas Bhāruci identifies them as *ṚV* 9.14–67.

Puruṣa hymn The creation hymn *ṚV* 10.90.

Ṛc The sacred verses found in the Ṛgveda.

Śākalahomīya These are the eight verses of *VS* 8.13 = *TS* 3.2.5.7.

Sāman A verse generally taken from the *ṚV* and sung to a particular melody. The Sāmans are contained in the Sāmaveda.

Sāvitrī Also called Gāyatrī, this is the most sacred of ritual formulas: *ṚV* 3.62.10 (see App. III.3: 'That excellent . . .'). Sometimes the term is used with reference to vedic initiation, because teaching this verse to the initiated boy forms a central part of that rite.

Śiras formula 'OṂ the Waters, the Light, the Taste, the Immortal, Brahman! Earth, Atmosphere, Sky! OṂ!', *Mahānārāyaṇa Upaniṣad* 342.

Śivasaṃkalpa The first six verses of *VS* 34.

Solar formulas According to Medhātithi (on *MDh* 5.86), they are the verses beginning with *ṚV* 1.50.1. According to Govinda (on *BDh* 3.8.14), *ṚV* 1.50.10; 1.50.1; 1.115.1.

Somāraudra This is the hymn with four verses *ṚV* 6.74. Bhāruci (on *MDh* 11.255), however, identifies them as the verses to Rudra at *ṚV* 2.33.4 and to Soma at *ṚV* 9.96.5.

Śuddhavatī The three verses *ṚV* 8.95.7–9.

Svadhā The exclamation accompanying the offering of an oblation to ancestors.

Svāhā The exclamation accompanying the offering of an oblation to gods.

Taratsamandī The hymn *ṚV* 9.58.

Vaṣaṭ A ritual exclamation uttered by the Hotṛ priest at the conclusion of the sacrificial verse as the Adhvaryu priest puts the oblation into the sacred fire.

Yajus A ritual formula in prose contained in the Yajurveda. These formulas accompany the ritual offerings into the fire.

3. *Formulas Cited in the Translations by the First Words*

'Adoration . . .'. Commentators identify this variously. Medhātithi and Bhāruci take it to be 'Adoration to Rudra, to the strong one, to the one with braided hair . . .' I have not been able to identify this verse.

'Aryaman, Varuṇa, and Mitra, Indra and Viṣṇu among these, Maruts and Aśvins . . .' This is *ṚV* 4.2.4. Some commentators think that the three or two verses beginning with this are meant.

'Indra, Mitra, Varuṇa, Agni, the host of Maruts, and Aditi—we invoke for assistance . . .' The 7 verses beginning with this are *R̥V* 1.106.1–7. Bhāruci (on *MDh* 256), however, takes this to be *R̥V* 1.7.1.

'May the Maruts pour upon me, may Indra and Br̥haspati; and may this fire pour upon me long life and strength. May they make me live long.' *TĀ* 2.18.

'May the virile strength return again to me, may long life and prosperity. May goods return to me again, may the Brāhmaṇical state.' *ĀśGr̥* 3.6.8. Variants of this verse are found in *AV* 7.67; *BāU* 6.4.5.

'No anxiety, no danger, . . .' This is the hymn *R̥V* 10.126.

'That excellent glory of Savitr̥, the god, we meditate, that he may stimulate our thoughts.' *R̥V* 3.62.10.

'This, yes, this is my inclination . . .' This is the hymn *R̥V* 10.119.

'To welcome the Dawn the inspired Vasiṣṭhas did first awaken with songs and praises . . .' This is the hymn *R̥V* 7.80 containing three verses.

'Untie, Varuṇa, from us the bond at the top, at the middle, and at the bottom, so that in your commandment, Āditya, we may remain sinless for Aditi.' *R̥V* 1.24.15.

'Waters, you are refreshing. Further us to strength, to see great joy. The auspicious flavour that is yours, accord to us here, like eager mothers. To him may we come with satisfaction, to whose dwelling you quicken us, O waters, and propagate us.' *TS* 4.1.5.1. These are the Abliṅga formulas.

'We placate your anger, Varuṇa, with obeisances, sacrifices, and oblations. Wise Lord, ruling king, loosen from us the sins we have committed.' *R̥V* 1.24.14. Bhāruci, however, identifies this as *R̥V* 10.59.9.

'Whatever offence that we humans commit against the race of gods, Varuṇa, if by inattention we have violated your institutes, O god, may you not punish us because of that evil.' *R̥V* 7.89.5.

APPENDIX IV

WEIGHTS, MEASURES, AND CURRENCY

NB: weights, measures, and coins have varied over time in India. The values given below are approximations. In coins the weight of each measurement differed for gold, silver, and copper. See *MDh* 8.132–7.

Bow A measurement of length; approximately 6 feet or 1.82 metres.

Dharaṇa A measure of weight; approximately 377.6 grams; a silver dharaṇa, however, is said to weigh only 3.776 grams.

Droṇa A measurement of capacity especially of grains: probably about 5 litres. When it is a measure of weight, it is approximately 9.6 kg.

Gaurasarṣapa 'White mustard seed'; a minute measure of weight equal to three Rājasarṣapas.

Kārṣāpaṇa Also known as Paṇa, this basic copper coin weighed approximately 9.33 grams. A silver kārṣāpaṇa weighed 3.76 grams.

Kārṣika A copper coin, the same as Kārṣāpaṇa or Paṇa.

Kṛṣṇala A measure of weight approximately 0.118 grams.

Kumbha A measure of capacity: about 105 litres.

Likṣā 'Egg of a louse'; a very minute measure of weight equal to eight Trasareṇus.

Māṣa 'A bean'; a measure of weight; approximately 0.59 grams.

Māṣaka A silver māṣaka weighed approximately 0.25 grams; a gold coin of this name is mentioned at 8.393.

Niṣka A measurement of weight said to be four suvarṇas, i.e. 37.76 grams.

Pala A measure of weight; approximately 37.76 grams.

Paṇa Same as Kārṣāpaṇa.

Purāṇa A silver weight said to be sixteen silver Māṣakas, i.e. 3.776 grams.

Rājasarṣapa 'Black mustard seed'; a minute measure of weight equal to three Likṣās.

Rod's throw It is unclear whether this is an actual measurement or the distance that a rod can be thrown.

Śatamāna A silver śatamāna weighed approximately 11.66 grams.

Suvarṇa A measure of weight; approximately 9.44 grams.

Trasareṇu A particle of dust seen in a sunbeam; smallest measure of weight.

Yava A measurement of weight; 0.039 grams

NOTES

For more detailed and technical notes on the translation, the diverse interpretations of commentators and scholars, the explanations of the choices I have made, and the variant readings and additional verses found in manuscripts, see the notes to the translation in my critical edition (Olivelle forthcoming *c*).

CHAPTER ONE

1.2 *those born in between*: namely, the mixed classes dealt with at 10.8–73.

1.3 *ordinance*: although commentators give diverse interpretations of this term (*vidhāna*), it probably refers to the 'treatise' (*śāstra*) on Law that the Creator composed and taught to his son, Manu: see 1.58.

1.5 *pitch-dark*: this may also be a reference to the cosmic attribute (*guṇa*) of darkness (*tamas*) within Sāṃkhya philosophy (see 12.24–49). There is, however, a clear resonance with the Nāsadīya hymn of the Ṛgveda (1.129), which also describes the initial state of the cosmos as 'darkness hidden by darkness'.

1.11 *Brahmā*: the sandhi in the Sanskrit *brahmeti* makes it difficult to decipher whether the original is the masculine *brahmā* as a personal god or the neuter *brahman* as the impersonal ground of creation. See the similar ambiguity at 1.50.

1.13 *place of the waters*: the reference is probably to the Milky Way, which is regarded also as the bright ocean of heaven in vedic cosmology. See Witzel 1984.

1.16 *these six*: the exact meaning of 'six' remains unclear, but the great self and the five sensory organs mentioned in the previous verse (so Hacker 1959), or the mind and the five elements referred to in verse 18, are the best candidates.

1.19 *seven males*: the term 'male' (*puruṣa*) is used metaphorically, possibly echoing the image of the body of Puruṣa in the Ṛgvedic hymn (10.90). The meaning of 'seven', once again, is unclear. It probably refers to the six already mentioned, with the addition of the Creator, particles of whose body combine with those six to create the world (verses 16–17). Or the seven may be the great self, the mind, and the five sensory organs (Hacker 1959).

1.20 *Of these . . . in the series*: the order of the series is: ether, air, fire, water, and earth. The distinctive quality of each is sound, touch, visibility, taste, and smell. Ether has only the first; air has the first two (its own and that of ether); fire the first three; water the first four; and earth all five. See 1.75–8.

1.21 *stations*: the meaning of this term is unclear. I detect a contrast between 'specific activities' and 'specific stations', the former referring to ritual obligations and the latter to worldly or professional activities.

1.25 *he brought forth . . . these creatures*: these words conclude the creation of the physical universe and they echo nicely the beginning of the story at 1.8.

1.32 This second account of creation (1.32–41), the classification of fauna and flora (1.42–50), and the description of cosmic cycles (1.51–7) are, in all likelihood, additions resulting from later redactorial activities. The original discourse on creation ended at verse 31 with the creation of the four social classes. In the original text, verse 31 was immediately followed by the section on transmission (1.58–60).

1.39 *pseudo-humans*: mythical animals/humans, sometimes depicted as having the body of a man and the head of a horse. The term is also connected to the older *kiṃpuruṣa*, possibly relating to barbarians in the jungle or 'wild men'. See Smith 1994: 255–6.

1.51 *disappeared . . . with time*: the reference is to the end of time, when the Creator withdraws everything into himself; and 'striking down time with time' means destroying the time of creation with the time of dissolution. These two periods are conceived as the times when the Creator is awake and asleep.

1.56 *When . . . bodily frame*: the subject of this verse, as also that of the preceding one, is unclear. If we take it to be the individual human self, then these verses would describe the re-emergence of individual humans after their dissolution at the end of time.

1.58 *treatise*: clearly a reference to the primordial form of Manu's own treatise, which was introduced at 1.3.

Marīci: he is the first of the ten seers that Manu procreated, listed at 1.35, Bhṛgu being the ninth in the list. They are viewed here as both his sons and his pupils.

1.61–2 *six further Manus*: in the Indian cosmological tradition, each Kalpa, which is the largest time span and is considered a day of Brahmā, contains fourteen units called Manvantara ('Manu interval' or epoch), each presided over by a different Manu. Within each Manvantara there are other units called Yuga (Age). The seven Manus listed here are the first seven; the other seven are given diverse names in the Purāṇas. See Kane 1962–75: v. 686–93. The temporal extents of a Kalpa, Manvantara, and Yuga are given at 1.68–73, 79–80.

1.64 *Muhūrta*: this is the basic division of a 24-hour day. It is 48 minutes long. Kalā, the Indian minute, is therefore 1.6 minutes; and a Kāṣṭha, approximately 0.05 seconds. In legal and ritual literature, however, the term Muhūrta is frequently used with a more generic meaning and refers to a specific time during the day or the night. Auspicious times for significant activities, such as marriage, are also called Muhūrta.

1.66 *For ancestors . . . sleeping*: the day and night are here inverted, as are most things relating to ancestors, the bright constituting the night and the dark the day. The reason is purely ritual, because offerings to ancestors are offered during the dark half of the month (waning moon) when the ancestors are awake.

1.70 *For each . . . by one*: Tretā: 3,000 years, with twilights of 300 years each; Dvāpara: 2,000 years, with twilights of 200 years each; Kali: 1,000 years, with twilights of 100 years each. The total for all four Ages thus comes to 12,000 years.

1.81 *four feet*: tradition offers various identifications of the four feet. 'Four' is clearly a whole and sacred number, and here it may also refer to the four feet of an animal (bull at 8.16), indicating firm footing and stability.

1.83 *by a quarter*: note that in Sanskrit both quarter and foot have the same word *pāda*. So we have a clear parallel between the loss of a foot (Law) and the loss of a quarter of the life span (humans).

1.85 *progressive shortening . . . Age*: the meaning is not altogether clear. The meaning could be 'in keeping with the progressive shortening of the human life span in each Age'. Alternatively, the 'shortening' or decrease may have a broader meaning, including the Ages themselves, the human life spans, as well as the feet of the Law.

1.92 *A man . . . part*: the reason for the relative impurity of the lower half is given at 5.132.

1.93 *retains the Veda*: the Sanskrit term *dhāraṇa* means both carrying and retaining in memory. This statement is more powerful than it may first appear, because at a time when the Veda did not exist externally in manuscript form it could only exist in the world within the memory of Brahmins who had learnt it. The Brahmin is thus the receptacle of the Veda in the world.

1.96 *those who subsist by intelligence*: the reference here is to higher animals, such as dogs and jackals, who know to take shelter when it rains and to go after food and water.

1.99 *a ruler . . . of Laws*: the parallel with the birth of a king is obvious. A king is born in a particular region to protect the treasures of a particular people. A Brahmin, on the other hand, rules over all and the treasure he protects is Law (*dharma*) itself.

1.101 *The Brahmin . . . people eat*: if the whole world belongs to the Brahmin *de jure*, then whatever he eats cannot but be his own. So, even when a Brahmin eats someone else's food as a guest, he is actually eating his own food. A principle such as this is invoked as a justification for stealing or taking forcibly the property of Śūdras, or even of other individuals, in order to perform a sacrifice: see 11.11–15. This ideology appears to be based on the principle that property is intended to be sacrificed. Indeed, the transaction between humans giving to the gods in sacrifice and the gods sending rain to produce crops is embedded in vedic thought. Given that Brahmins are closely connected with the offering of sacrifice, they can claim ownership of all property—at least at the level of ideological rhetoric.

1.114 *Renunciation, Retirement*: the Sanskrit term *mokṣa* literally means liberation. Manu, however, attaches a technical meaning to the term, using it as a synonym of renunciation and the fourth order of life dedicated exclusively to the search after personal liberation. The term *mokṣa* has the same meaning when used in the common compound *mokṣadharma* ('laws pertaining to renunciation'), which is a section of the *MBh* and a distinct topic in medieval legal digests. Manu makes a clear distinction between this renunciatory asceticism and the life of a vedic retiree which he designates as *saṃnyāsa* (see 6.86). This term, which is the common word for renunciation in later literature, is never used by Manu with that meaning. For a more detailed study, see Olivelle 1981.

1.117–18 *Examination of the good . . . and guilds*: these three topics are not found at the end of the *MDh*, although aspects of these topics are dealt with in different parts of the treatise. Their absence raises significant questions about the relationship of the synopsis to the text. The synopsis was clearly written at a later date and inserted into the *MDh*; but the lack of these topics indicates that the author of the synopsis may have been working with a somewhat different text than the extant version of the *MDh*.

CHAPTER TWO

2.13 *authority*: the Sanskrit term *pramāṇa* has epistemological implications. Beyond mere authority, it indicates the means of cognition. There are other meanings of knowing the Law, such as observing the conduct of virtuous people (perception); and even logical argument (inference: see 12.106). Among all these means, scripture, which falls under 'verbal authority' in the enumeration of the means of knowledge, is the highest.

2.14–15 *When there . . . a vedic scripture*: here we have a basic principle of vedic exegesis. When two vedic injunctions contradict each other, both are authoritative; such a contradiction gives rise to an option. An example of such an option is given in verse 15. Some vedic passages prescribe the morning fire offering (*agnihotra*) to be performed just before sunrise, and others after sunrise. One has, therefore, the option to follow either rule. A contradiction, however, gives rise to an option only when the two injunctions are of equal force (see *GDh* 1.4). If one of them is weaker (e.g. a traditional text) and the other stronger (e.g. an explicit vedic text), then the stronger prevails.

2.16 *A man . . . this treatise*: the implication of this rule is to exclude all women, as well as Śūdras and other lower castes. The significant expression here is 'with the recitation of vedic formulas', because women's rites of passage are performed without the recitation of mantras: see 2.66–7.

2.17–23 *The land . . . land of foreigners*: this section contains elaborations and further classifications of the original concept of Āryāvarta first encountered within the legal tradition in *BDh* 1.1.2.9 and *VaDh* 1.8–12, and recorded also by the grammarian Patañjali (commenting on Pāṇini's grammatical *sūtras* 2.4.10 and 6.3.109). There the extent of the Āryāvarta corresponds to the 'middle region' of Manu (1.21), and this region coincides with the natural range of the antelope known as the 'black buck'.

2.23 *foreigners*: often translated as 'barbarians', the Sanskrit term *mleccha* refers to individuals and groups that do not belong to the mainstream of society as envisaged by the Brahmanical theologians. They include foreigners, as well as tribal and other groups not forming part of the accepted society. Their speech is different (see 10.45), they tend to live in geographically distinct areas (see 2.23), and sometimes they are coupled with Śūdras (12.43).

2.27 *tying of the Muñja-grass cord*: the reference is to vedic initiation (2.36 ff.), at which the tying of the girdle around the boy's waist is a central ritual element (2.43).

2.28 *body is made 'brāhmic'*: the term *brahma* in this expression probably means the Veda. The meaning is that the man's body is made fit for reciting the Veda, or a fit receptacle for the Veda (see 1.93 n.).

2.29 *male child*: the specification relates to the phrase 'to the accompaniment of vedic formulas'. For girls, the same ceremony is performed without such formulas (cf. 2.16 n.; 2.66). The specification of 'male' also excludes children of indeterminate sex, such as hermaphrodites.

fed gold, honey, and ghee: clearly, the baby is too young to feed him these things. A small mixture is placed within the mouth. Further, gold is obviously not fed to the child. Either a piece of gold is placed in the mouth or, as some commentators explain, the ghee and honey are touched with gold before being placed in the baby's mouth. Some Gṛhyasūtras (*ŚāṅGṛ* 1.24.3; *PārGṛ* 1.16.4) state that these are fed with a golden spoon or from a golden vessel, while others include gold dust in the mixture (*ĀśGṛ* 1.15.1).

2.30 *time*: for the meaning of this term (*muhūrta*), see 1.64 n. Although it refers to a specific length of time, when dealing with astrologically auspicious times it means a more specific time of the day.

2.38 *Sāvitrī*: the Sāvitrī verse is frequently used as a metonym for the rite of initiation ; the imparting of this verse constitutes a central element of it. 'Fallen from Sāvitrī', therefore, means 'not undergoing vedic initiation at the proper age'.

sixteenth year: we must assume on the basis of the statement in verse 36 that all ages are counted from conception rather than birth.

2.40 *vedic . . . links*: these refer to any type of ritual relationship, such as officiating at an initiation or a sacrifice, teaching, studying, and the like.

2.43 *When Muñja . . . Balvaja grass*: according to the traditional interpretation, the three substitutes are meant for the three classes, respectively: Kuśa for a Brahmin, Aśmantaka for a Kṣatriya, and Balvaja for a Vaiśya. According to this interpretation, the statement 'When Muñja grass is unavailable' must implicitly mean when any of the standard material for the three classes is unavailable.

One should wrap . . . five knots: the Sanskrit is very terse and elliptical. In the second half of verse 43, Manu is making a transition from the girdle's manufacture to the way it is worn; hence the mention of the knots. Within this context, 'three times' probably refers to the number of times the cord is wrapped around the waist before tying the knots. For the custom of wrapping the girdle three times, see *ŚaṇGṛ* 2.2.1; *ĀpGṛ* 4.10.11.

2.49 *placing . . . at the end*: the set formula for requesting almsfood is: 'Madam, give food' (see *BDh* 1.3.16), which is how a Brahmin would say it. A Kṣatriya would say 'Give, Madam, food', and a Vaiśya, 'Give food, Madam'. The formula implies that it was the housewife who normally distributed food to students and mendicants.

2.53 *orifices*: they are eyes, ears, nose, and mouth. For the procedure, see 2.60.

2.56 *eat between meals*: the meaning is that he should not eat between the two main meals taken in the morning and in the evening. Another interpretation is that one should not eat again after interrupting the meal by getting up.

sullied with remnants: this is a technical term (*ucchiṣṭa*) for the state of impurity resulting from the remnants of food attached to lips and fingers after eating. The same term is used for remnants of food after someone has eaten (leftovers), which are also impure because they have come into contact with one's saliva. The extended meaning of the term covers also impurities caused by other bodily functions, such as after voiding urine or excrement. See Olivelle 1998.

2.58 *part of the palm . . . ancestors*: the area of the palm used to pour water into the mouth during sipping bears the technical name *tīrtha*, literally a sacred ford or bathing place on a river. As a *tīrtha* on a river is where water comes into contact with the body, so the various parts of the palm are the *tīrthas* through which water enters the mouth and the body.

2.59 *beneath these two*: that is, at the bottom of the thumb and the index finger.

2.63 *When the right . . . cord down*: the sacred cord is worn over the left shoulder and under the right arm for rites connected with gods and on most other occasions. To wear it in this manner, one raises the right hand to pass the cord under it. It is worn over the right shoulder and under the left arm (a pattern called *prācīnāvīta* involving the raising of the left arm) at ancestral rites, and over the neck like a garland (a pattern called *nivīta*) in rites involving humans, such as sexual intercourse, sacramental rites, and going to the toilet.

2.65 *shaving ceremony*: this rite of passage consists of the first shaving (*keśānta*) of the beard of a teenage boy. The rite is also known by the name Godāna ('gift of cow'), because it involved giving a cow to the teacher.

2.75 *cleansed . . . grass*: these are blades of grass carried in the hands or twisted around the fingers to form a purificatory ring. The *GDh* (1.48) specifies that the various organs are touched with blades of Darbha grass.

76–7 *The phonemes . . . Sāvitrī verse*: these phonemes are the constituent parts of the syllable OṂ, the initial 'o' being dissolved into the two simple vowels 'a' and 'u'. The three terms for the three spheres of the cosmos are considered sacred sounds. Each of these triads, as well as each foot of the three-footed Sāvitrī verse, is viewed as the essence squeezed out from each of the three Vedas, respectively.

2.82 *highest Brahman*: here we have a subtle, and in Sanskrit imperceptible, transition from *brahman* as Veda (in verse 81) to *brahman* as the absolute being or state (in verses 82–4), here identified with OṂ.

2.84 *Offering ghee . . . standing*: the reference is to a twofold division of rites within the vedic exegetical tradition indicated here by the use of two technical terms. The term *juhoti* refers specifically to the offering of ghee in the sacred fire carried out while the priest is seated on his haunches. The term *yajati* refers to the offering of other substances in the fire (*yāga*) while the priest remains standing.

The syllable . . . imperishable: here we have a play on the double meaning of the Sanskrit term *akṣara*, which can mean both a syllable and something imperishable. The *akṣara* par excellence in both senses is the syllable OṂ, which is both a syllable and the absolute Brahman.

2.86 *four types of cooked oblations*: probably four of the five great sacrifices that involve cooked food: offerings to gods, ancestors, beings, and human guests (3.70).

2.87 *Maitra*: this term in its usual sense refers to a man who does good to all and harms none. There is, however, another interpretation that fits the context better. The term *mitra* (friend and the deity Mitra) is the sun, and *maitra* is a man devoted to the sun, that is, to the Sāvitrī verse, whose deity is the sun. Thus *maitra* means a man who constantly recites the Sāvitrī, an interpretation fitting the context, which is a eulogy of this verse.

2.99 *foot of a skin*: the simile is a water bag made of an animal skin. If any one of its feet is not properly sealed, water will spill through it, just as one's wisdom will slip away through a single organ that is not properly mastered.

2.105 *Vedic Supplements*: there are six such supplementary sciences: pronunciation, metre, grammar, etymology, astronomy, and ritual.

2.106 *The daily . . . Vaṣaṭ*: this verse is a very brief allusion to a long passage in *ŚB* (11.5.6.8) and cited in *ĀpDh* 1.12.3, where this theme is fully developed. A sacrificial session (*sattra*) is a sacrifice where the officiating priests and the patron are the same individuals and which lasts a long period of time.

2.108 *rite of returning home*: this rite, which includes a ritual bath, concludes the period of studentship (see 2.245; 3.4). For a description of this rite, see Kane 1962–75: ii. 405–15; Heesterman 1968.

2.109 *an honest person* this term (*śuciḥ*): could also mean a pure person (Olivelle 1998). Given that all the terms in this verse refer to internal dispositions or relationships to the teacher, honesty fits the context better.

someone close to him: this term (*āptaḥ*) indicates a close, often blood, relationship. See 5.101; 11.171.

one who is his own: (*svaḥ*) either a relative or someone close to the teacher due to some other relationship, such as a boy at whose initiation he has officiated.

2.123 *When greeting . . . simply say 'I'*: the reference may be to people who do not know Sanskrit and are thus unable to grasp the meaning of such an elaborate greeting. In such cases, one simply says 'I greet you', the word 'I' in the verse being an allusion to this form of greeting.

2.124 *'bho'*: this is an interjection commonly used in addressing someone. It is especially common in greetings between teacher and pupil, both using this particle to address each other. It connotes both respect ('Sir') and endearment ('my dear'). It is viewed as containing the essence of all names, because it can be used in place of any proper name.

2.125 *he should say . . . prolate the previous syllable*: the meaning is that the final vowel of the name is lengthened to three morae.

2.132 *paternal and maternal relatives*: the distinction between the Sanskrit terms *jñāti* and *sambandhin* (also *bāndhava*) is not always clear. Sometimes the terms refer in general to relatives; but when they are used together the terms appear to have technical meanings. The latter term can also refer to relatives by marriage. See 4.179, 5.74.

2.140 *secret texts*: (*rahasya*) the reference is probably to the Upaniṣads.

2.142 *'Elder'*: the term (*guru*) here is clearly applied to one's own father. For other meanings of this term, see Note on the Translation, p. xlvi.

2.145 *greater*: the Sanskrit term *gaurava*, literally 'heaviness' or 'gravitas', also refers to the state of being a *guru* ('elder'). At one level then, the meaning is that the mother is a thousand times more a *guru* than the father, who was presented as the *guru* par excellence in verse 142.

2.185 *heinous sinners*: this technical term (*abhiśasta*) probably refers to public sinners or socially ostracized people. Acts making someone a heinous sinner are given at *ĀpDh* 1.24.6–9 and *VaDh* 23.14.

2.193 *right arm uncovered*: literally, the meaning of *uddhṛtapāṇiḥ* is that he should raise his hand or arm. Raising here, as in the context of wearing the sacrificial cord (cf. 2.63n.), means raising the (right) arm when wearing the upper garment or shawl. It goes over the left shoulder and under the right arm, thus leaving the right arm and shoulder uncovered. Incidentally, this is precisely the way Buddhist monks are depicted as wearing their robes when they were in presence of the Buddha. Uncovering the right shoulder appears to have been a mark of respect.

2.195 *standing*: if we take this literally and in conjunction with not sitting or lying down, then the student can never speak with the teacher! The meaning may be that the student should not speak to the teacher standing still. This agrees with the statement in verse 196 that when the teacher is standing the student should walk towards him when he wants to speak.

2.207 *Ārya sons*: in all likelihood 'Ārya' here refers to the three twice-born classes. This would exclude any son born to a Śūdra wife of the teacher, something implied here in spite of its condemnation at 3.14–19. On the number of wives permitted to a Brahmin, see 9.149–51.

2.224 *triple set*: Law (*dharma*), Wealth (*artha*), and Pleasure (*kāma*) form the triple set (*trivarga*), the three aims or goals of human existence, later expanded to four with the addition of liberation. For a study of the aims of human existence, see Malamoud 1982.

2.229 *other rule of conduct*: the meaning is not altogether clear. It appears to be that the student should not undertake any religious activity that would hinder his service to his parents and teacher. Examples include going on pilgrimage and fasting. Manu may also have in mind a student becoming an ascetic before getting married, a common theme in Brahmanical literature.

2.231 *The householder's . . . offertorial fire*: the three fires mentioned here are the three principal ritual fires used in major vedic sacrifices. The first is on the western side of the ritual enclosure, the second towards the south, and the third, in which divine offerings are placed, is on the eastern side.

CHAPTER THREE

3.11 *A wise man . . . in force*: for the institution of the 'female-son', see 9.127–40. The absence of either a brother or the father can give rise to the fear that one's wife is so designated by the father. The first is obvious. When the father is absent it is not possible to find out whether the girl has been appointed as a female-son. This custom was very old and discussed at length with Iranian parallels by Schmidt 1987.

3.14 *story*: the reference must be to stories of ancient people, the behaviour of whom may be viewed as providing legitimation for taking a Śūdra wife. For such stories, see 7.41; 10.105–8.

3.19 *begets himself*: vedic texts often present the son as the reborn self of the father. The husband, then, begets himself through his wife as his son: see Olivelle 1993, 41–6.

3.26 *conjointly*: that is, when the two have become lovers first according to the Gāndharva mode, and then the man abducts the willing girl from her father's house.

3.45 *during her season*: the 'season' for the wife is the days of the month when she is fertile, which were thought to be the days immediately following her menstrual period. During that time a husband was obligated to have sexual intercourse with his wife. *ĀpGṛ* 3.9.1 recommends even days from the fourth day (that is, the day when the period of menstrual impurity ends with the wife's bath) to the sixteenth following the start of the menstrual flow. See also 3.46–8.

moon's change: the new moon, the eighth day after the new moon, the full moon, and the fourteenth day after the full moon. See 4.128.

3.46 *together with the other four days*: these days probably fall outside the sixteen days mentioned in the second foot. Interpreted this way, the season lasts for twenty days.

3.47 *Of these . . . recommended*: this verse is obscure. The sixteen days, as we saw, exclude the days of menstruation. The first four must refer to the first four nights after the menstrual period. So, the prohibited nights are the four days of menstruation, the first four days after that, and the eleventh and thirteenth days of the menstrual cycle. For other forbidden days of the month, see 4.128.

3.49 *When the man's . . . takes place*: this statement supports the previous one that a man should have sex on even nights. The female seed is considered to diminish during even nights and increase during odd nights.

3.50 *during the other eight nights*: these eight nights are contrasted with the preceding twenty of the woman's season. Then the rule is very simple. A man who has sex with his wife only to produce offspring and not for lust should be considered a celibate. During the last eight days of the menstrual cycle (outside the above twenty) the wife is infertile. During the four days of menstruation, she is both infertile and unclean. During the first four days after menstruation and on the eleventh and the thirteenth, he is forbidden to have sex. All this accounts for eighteen days. He should have sex outside these eighteen days; that is, during the ten days, which is precisely what is stated in verse 49. This interpretation has the added benefit of accounting for the twenty-eight-day menstrual cycle.

3.52 *relatives*: relatives are the woman's father and the like, and not her in-laws. The context is the prohibition of a bride-price.

3.53 *At a 'Seer's' . . . a sale*: verses 51–4 appear to constitute a single argument against bride-price. Verses 51 and 52 lay down Manu's point of view. In verse 53 we have a possible argument against such a view. The opponent cites the example of the Seer's marriage where a bride-price in the form of a cow and bull is clearly recognized. Manu rejoins, saying that this is untrue. That gift does not constitute a true bride-price. The reason is spelled out in the next verse (54): when the relatives do not keep the bride-price for themselves, then it does not constitute a sale; so it is not really a bride-price. That the bride-price was a common practice in ancient India is evident even from Manu's own statements elsewhere in his treatise. For example, at 8.204–5 the giving of a girl to her husband is viewed as a sale, and it is indeed listed under the third 'Ground for Litigation', sale without ownership (see also 8.224). At 9.93, 97 also the bride-price is presupposed, although at 9.98, 100 he again condemns it.

3.76 *from food, offspring*: this passage relates to the chain of causation that brings about children. The main source of this image, I think, is the doctrine of five fires found in the Upaniṣads (*BāU* 6.2.9–16; *ChU* 5.4–10). This verse appears to have combined the view that fire sacrifices reach the sun and bring down rain, thus assuring prosperity, and the more specific doctrine of the re-birth process entailed in this passage to the sun and back to the earth: the dead person when cremated goes to the sun as smoke, returns to earth as rain, becomes absorbed into plants, and when eaten becomes semen and finally a child.

3.78 *most senior order of life*: Manu is here playing with the word senior (*jyeṣṭha*), which is also the term for the oldest brother (see 9.105–10). The oldest is supposed to look after his younger siblings like a father. Manu applies this image to the orders of life. The householder supplies food and knowledge to the others; so he is comparable to the oldest brother.

3.83 *at this*: namely, at the daily ancestral offering forming part of the five great sacrifices. At other types of ancestral rites, such as the monthly ancestral offerings, Brahmins are invited to represent the All-gods (3.209). See Kane 1962–75: iv. 403.

3.91 *In the back house*: this expression must be an euphemism for the lavatory, just as the English 'out-house'. In the context of this rite, *ŚāṅGṛ* 2.14.15 clearly refers to the 'privy', supported by *GobhGṛ* 1.4.10.

3.97 *equivalent of ashes*: sacrifices are offered in a fire set ablaze. The mouth of a Brahmin is often compared to such a fire, and his fire is ablaze only through vedic knowledge (3.98). Feeding an ignorant Brahmin is like offering a sacrifice in ashes; both are equaly futile. See 3.168, 181; *VaDh* 3.10.

3.102 *He is called . . . is brief*: here we have a phonetic etymology of 'guest' (*atithi*) derived by combining '*a*' from *anitya* ('brief') and '*tithi*' from *sthiti* ('stay'). Identical verse at *VaDh* 8.7.

3.107 *accompanying them as they leave*: the host is expected to accompany the guest from his house some distance as he leaves. Āpastamba (*ĀpDH* 2.9.2–4) is specific: 'If a guest has come in a carriage, he should follow him as far as the carriage; others he should follow until they give him leave to return. If a guest forgets to do so, he may turn back at the village boundary.'

3.108 *he need not . . . offering*: the assumption is that the guest has arrived after the family members have eaten and the food is over. Fresh food has to be cooked for the guest. Generally, after cooking food one has to perform the All-god (Vaiśvadeva) and Bali offerings. This provision calls for the omission of these offerings in the event of a second cooking of food.

3.111 *fulfilling the conditions of a guest*: namely, that he has exhausted his provisions; that he lives in another village; and that he arrives at mealtime.

3.119 *honey-mixture*: *madhuparka*, a drink presented to an important guest made by mixing honey into curd, milk, or water. See *ĀpDh* 2.8.5–8.

3.122 *sacrifice to ancestors*: this is a vedic (*śrauta*) sacrifice called Piṇḍapitr̥yajña: cf. *ĀśŚr* 2.6–7.

supplementary offering of rice balls: this refers to the monthly ancestral offering (*śrāddha*), which is not a vedic (*śrauta*) but a traditional (*smārta*) rite, that is, a rite that is only enjoined in the traditional texts, especially the Gr̥hyasūtras, and not the vedic texts.

3.127 *This rite . . . him always*: this verse is very obscure. It may be that 'rite for the deceased' (*pretakr̥tyā*) of the first line refers to the vedic (*śrauta*) offering for the dead, whereas the 'non-vedic (lit., 'worldly') rite' refers to the traditional ancestral rite (*śrāddha*): see 3.122 n.

3.130 *search far and wide*: some interpret this statement to mean that one should look into even the remote ancestors of that person. It is more likely, however, that it refers to distance rather than to kinship. The meaning is that it is not necessary to invite Brahmins living near by if they are ignorant; one should rather invite learned men from far away. See the obligation to invite neighbours at 8.392.

3.136–7 *Between a man . . . as superior*: one interpretation takes these two somewhat elliptical verses as referring to a father–son pair. In one case the father is learned and the son ignorant, and in the other the son is learned and the father is ignorant. The conclusion is that the son whose father is learned is superior to the learned son with an ignorant father. But this would contradict the statement of verses 133 and 142 that one should not invite an ignorant man (here the son) to a rite. The more plausible explanation is that the verses are speaking about two men who are assumed to be learned. The question is who is better: the one whose father is learned but whose son is ignorant, or the one whose father is ignorant but whose son is learned? Manu comes down in favour of the former.

3.141 *Such a sacrificial . . . single stall*: older versions of this interesting verse are found in *ĀpDh* 2.17.8 and *MBh* 13.90.39. The simile is also different in these sources; instead of a blind cow in the same stall, the point of which is unclear, we have a cow who has lost its calf roaming around the corrals. The meaning appears to be that the cow remains in the corral and does not go out to the pastures. Comparing the sacrificial fee (*dakṣiṇā*) to a cow is common in the vedic literature, principally because the paradigmatic sacrificial fee is a cow.

3.150 *impotent*: this term (*klība*) has been subject to widely different interpretations. It probably did have a range of meanings, and in different contexts may have assumed somewhat different connotations. In general, the term refers to males who are in some way sexually dysfunctional or deviate from the culturally constructed notions of masculinity. Such individuals include the impotent, the effiminate, transvestites, hermaphrodites, and the like. This term does not refer to castrated eunuchs. A verse of Kātyāyana cited in the *Dāyabhāga* (5.8, tr. Rocher) gives a definition of *klība*: 'If a man's urine does not foam, if his stool sinks in water, if his penis has no erection or sperm, he is called *klība*.'

3.151 *bald-headed*: this term (*durvāla*) is often interpreted to mean bad skin. Bad skin, however, does not fit with the rest of the terms; they all refer to classes of people. 'Bald-headed' here may refer to kinds of ascetic, just like 'matted hair'.

3.154 *linked to an association*: the precise meaning is unclear. Interpretations include: 'village headman' and 'a man who has embezzled money from a corporation'. The term literally means 'one who is within (or intimately connected with) a corporate body'. No other legal treatise has this term; the closest parallel I have come across is *GDh* 15.18, where, within a similar list of people unfit to be invited, it lists 'a servant of a corporation'. A similar person may be intended here.

3.159 *evil disease*: the term *pāparoga*, which recurs frequently in Manu, does not simply refer to a serious sickness. The disease is regarded as the consequence of sins committed in previous lives (see 11.48–53). Evil diseases are generally viewed as skin diseases of various types.

poison vendor: in the term (*rasavikrayin*) *rasa* may refer to any liquid, such as milk and sugar-cane juice, and also to poison, generally also a plant extract. The context supports poison.

3.163 *breaches . . . obstructing them*: the meaning is that such a person cuts the side of a public water course to divert water to his own field. Obstructing it may have the same purpose or, because he 'delights in' it, may indicate a man who takes perverse delight in obstructing the free flow of water.

3.171–5 *When someone . . . hereafter*: it is likely that these verses, which constitute a commentary on five technical terms used in verses 154–69, are a later interpolation. At the very least, they constitute a parenthetical remark. Their intrusion also breaks the natural continuity between verses 170 and 176–82.

3.184 *expository texts*: probably the Vedic Supplements (2.105 n.).

3.185 *three Nāciketa*: Bodewitz (1985: 8–10, 25) has shown that this term refers not to particular fires but to the building of a special fire-altar bearing the name of Naciketas, the central figure in the *Kaṭha Upaniṣad*.

five sacred fires: besides the three mentioned at 2.231, there are the hearth fire (*āvasathya*) and the hall fire (*sabhya*).

3.186 *a thousand*: when the number is unspecified, cows, the paradigmatic gift, are understood. For fines with simply numbers, see 8.120 n.

3.192 *primeval deities*: from the statements in verses 194–9 it is apparent that these 'ancestors' are not the immediate forefathers of a person but mythical ancestors who originated at the very beginning of creation, identical with the great seers of the creation account (1.34–7; see also 3.201). Gods themselves are the creation of these seers. In verse 201, however, ancestors are called the sons of seers, but there 'ancestors' may be used more restrictively with reference to the specific ancestors of various beings spelled out in verses 196–9.

3.202 *with a generous spirit*: the Sanskrit terms *śraddadhāna* and *śraddhā* are often taken as referring to 'faith'. But in the early literature these terms are closely associated with hospitality and generous giving. Greed and envy are given as the opposites of *śraddhā* at *VaDh* 6.8; 8.9. See also *MDh* 4.224–5 where the *śraddhā* of the generous ursurer is contrasted with the *aśraddhā* of the miserly scholar. For *śraddhā* as generosity, see Jamison 1996: 176–84; Hara 1979; Köhler 1973.

3.214 *end in the south*: this is an obscure expression. It probably refers to the performance of any series of actions so as to terminate towards the south.

3.216 *those who partake of leavings*: these are the three ancestors beyond the third generation: the great-great-grandfather and his father and grandfather.

3.220 *If his father . . . Brahmins*: why would the son perform an ancestral offering if his father is alive? The father would normally do this. Here perhaps we have evidence of retirement, when the property is divided during the father's lifetime and the son becomes the head of household and the chief ritual performer.

3.230 *ghosts*: this term (*preta*) generally refers to newly deceased persons, but here probably has an extended meaning of malevolent spirits.

3.232 *ancillary texts*: the meaning is unclear, but the probable reference is to ancillary texts of the Veda, such as Śrīsūkta, legends, etc.

3.247 *Sapiṇḍa*: this is a rite, usually performed on the twelfth day after death, at which the newly deceased person is ritually united with his ancestors. See 5.60 n.

3.248 *above manner*: verse 247 dealing with the newly deceased is a parenthetical comment. Manu now picks up the thread of his argument by saying that subsequent to the Sapiṇḍana rite ancestral offerings are carried out precisely in the manner described before the interruption.

3.251 *'Please, stay around!'*: this is a polite invitation to leave. In polite discourse you do not ask a guest to leave; so we have the euphemistic 'stay', which really means 'go'. A similar example is found in my mother tongue, Sinhala. When guests leave, they say 'we'll come'.

3.254 *cow-pen offering*: generally called Goṣṭhīśrāddha, this is one of the twelve types of ancestral offerings listed in medieval sources. Kane (1962–75: iv. 381–2) gives the following description: 'The Goṣṭhīśrāddha is one which is performed when a man becomes enthusiastic owing to talk about śrāddha or when many learned men gather together at a sacred place and, finding it impossible to have separate cooking arrangements for each, pool their resources for collecting śrāddha materials and perform simultaneously śrāddha for the pleasure it affords to themselves and for the gratification of the pitṛs [forefathers].'

offering for prosperity: called Abhyudayaśrāddha, these ancestral offerings are performed on joyous occaions, such as the birth of a son.

3.257 *Food of sages*: the designation for a variety of food items that are in some way uncultivated (see 6.12–21), the most common being *nīvāra*, a kind of wild rice.

3.273 *Magha*: this is the tenth of the fifteen constellations (*nakṣatra*). The term may refer to the Māgha month, roughly corresponding to January–February, or more specifically to the thirteenth day of the dark half of the month of Bhādra (August–September) within the rainy season, when a particularly important ancestral offering named Mahālayaśrāddha is offered. The legal literature developed intricate rules regarding the dates and times for the performance of ancestral offerings. For details, see Kane 1965–75: iv. 369–77.

3.274 *elephant's eastern shadow*: this day is also called Gajachāyā. Medieval authors interpret this word differently, some even taking it literally: one should perform the offering in the shadow of an elephant. Generally, it is considered the thirteenth day of Bhādrapada (August–September) when the moon is in the Magha constellation and the sun in the Hasta constellation.

3.277 *later fortnight, earlier fortnight*: the first or earlier fortnight is when the moon is waxing, and the latter is the fortnight of the waning moon.

CHAPTER FOUR

4.1 *After spending . . . at home*: see parallels at 5.169; 6.1, 33.

4.5 *Gleaning and picking*: gleaning (*uñcha*), according to the traditional explanation, is gathering up ears of corn that have fallen on the ground when farmers take their harvest to their homes or granaries. Picking (*śila*) is gathering up ears of corn that have fallen to the ground from the plants in the field either before or after the harvest. The major difference is that the former is collected along the road and the latter in the field.

4.7 *to fill a granary . . . jar*: traditionally, these are viewed as individuals who have grain sufficient for a certain period of time, just like the last two kinds of persons. One who has a granary-full is viewed as a man who has grain sufficient to last three years, one year, or twelve days, and one who has a jar-full as a man who has grain sufficient to last one year, six months, or six days.

4.9 *One of these . . . of the Veda*: these relate to the six occupations of a Brahmin (see 10.75). Three activities are studying, offering sacrifices, and giving gifts; 'two' are the first two of these; and 'one' is studying, which is here referred to as 'sacrifical session of the Veda': see 2.106n.

4.19 *treatises*: the term (*śāstrāṇi*) may refer also to the Veda, which is often referred to simply as the *śāstra*, and this interpretation is supported by the use of the singular in verse 20. But it may also refer to other treatises, including epics, Purāṇas, Dharmaśāstras, and treatises on logic, grammar, Mīmāṃsā, astrology, medicine, and the like.

ancillary texts: (*nigama*) these are texts that facilitate the understanding of the Veda, such as etymologies, grammar, and exegesis.

4.22–4 *Some individuals . . . rooted in knowledge*: the ritual tradition, often under the influence of ascetic ideologies, reinterpreted ritual activities providing many substitutes for actual ritual acts. The offering of food in the breaths (*prāṇāgnihotra*) in the act of eating is one of them. See *ChU*, 5.19–24.

4.31 *after completing . . . vedic vows*: the first refers to those who have only learned the Veda by heart; the second to those who have mastered its meaning; and the third to those who have completed the vows associated with vedic study, such as living with the teacher for a certain number of years, even if they have not mastered the Veda.

4.32 *those who do not cook*: namely, vedic students and ascetics.

4.39 *mound of earth*: the meaning is obscure. The reference may be to some type of memorial mound.

4.55 *take off his own garland*: a man should get someone else to remove a garland from his neck. The reason is unclear; it may have been thought to be inauspicious to remove it by oneself.

4.57 *awaken a sleeping superior*: this verse was, in all likelihood, an ancient proverbial saying already recorded in vedic texts. See Jamison's (2000) detailed analysis of this expression derived from the *Maitrāyaṇī Saṃhitā* 3.4.5.

4.69 *never cut his nails or hair*: the meaning is unclear, but it appears that what is prohibited here is the cutting of hair and nails by means other than the proper tools (nail clippers, scissors).

4.72 *wear a garland outdoors*: the prohibition relates to wearing these ostentatious adornments in public. See the very similar prohibition at *ĀpDh* 1.32.5. See also *BDh* 2.6.9.

4.83 *refrain from . . . striking the head*: given the context, which deals with one's own body, the prohibition probably relates to one's own hair and head. Pulling the hair of others and striking their head is, of course, forbidden by other injunctions. The meaning, then, is that one should not pull one's hair or strike one's head in anger.

4.92 *time sacred to Brahman*: this is the last watch of the night (about three hours).

4.103 *lightning, thunder, and rain*: the suspension takes place only when these three occur together (see verse 106). During the rainy season, it is likely that one or the other of these may occur every day.

4.106 *When lightning . . . during the day*: this and verse 104 appear to be commentaries on verse 103. The expression 'as long as the heavenly lights are visible' (see also 5.82 and *GDh* 16.31; *VaDh* 13.37), means that the suspension lasts as long as the sun is visible (i.e. until nightfall) if the event happened during the morning twilight, and as long as the stars are visible (i.e. until daybreak) if the event happened during the evening twilight. The expression 'the other event' refers to the third event listed in verse 103, namely, rain. The meaning is that if all three occur together, then irrespective of whether it happens during the day or the night the provision of verse 103 applies and the suspension lasts until the same time the following day.

4.112 *squatting . . . knees*: the reference is to the band of cloth tied around the waist and over the knees so as to make it easier for a person to remain in the squatting position. It is unclear why this position is forbidden, but it may have something to do with a similar custom among ascetics. The band used by them is called *yogapaṭṭa*, and, as the name suggests, it was used during yogic practice.

4.123 *conclusion of a Veda*: the meaning is unclear. It may refer to the Upaniṣads, which is supported by the mention of *Āraṇyaka*, or to the end of any vedic text.

4.125 *Knowing . . . then the Veda*: the 'extract' probably refers to the first lines of each Veda. These are recited first before the actual recitation of the particular Veda of one's own vedic branch.

4.126 *passes in between*: the meaning is that an animal passes either between the teacher and the pupil, or between a circle of reciters, while they are engaged in vedic recitation.

4.127 *These alone . . . purified*: this refers to the suspension of the daily vedic recitation, which is one of the five great sacrifices. At 2.105 we have the statement that 'Rules regarding the suspension of vedic recitation have no bearing . . . on daily vedic recitation'. Thus all the rules given above apply only to vedic study and recitation that are outside the daily recitation. This verse, however, specifies that on these two occasions even the daily recitation is to be suspended.

4.129 *with his clothes on*: bathing with one's clothes on is prescribed for particular observances and as a purification for various types of offences (11.174, 123). Here the prohibition pertains to doing it on a regular or daily basis.

4.130 *god*: this must surely refer to the shadow cast by an image of a god.

4.139 *He should call . . . 'Lucky'*: this half-verse is very obscure, with a difficult and possibly elliptical syntax. What is clear is that the context of this verse is the advice in verse 138 that one should not say something unpleasant even though it may be true. This is basic politeness and underlies several of the rules in *GDh* 9.19–22 and *ĀpDh* 1.31.11. I think the sentence can be interpreted rather simply by taking the second expression as universalizing the previous statement that required a person to call a lucky thing lucky. So, one is exhorted to say 'Lucky' (which must have been a common exclamation) not only when someting is actually lucky but also in other contexts, that is, even when confronted with unlucky and inauspicious situations.

4.156 *unlucky marks*: an example is a black mark on the shoulder that foretells poverty and other such misfortunes.

4.172 *Like the earth*: (*gaur iva*: lit. 'like a cow') there appears to be a double simile here, the one based on similarity and the other on dissimilarity. In the latter case, the comparison is with a cow; in the former, it is with the earth (also bearing the epithet cow). Like the earth—and unlike a cow—unrighteous conduct does not bear fruit immediately but only with the passage of time.

4.174 *root*: 'root' may refer to home, fields, wealth, family, and progeny. The meaning, obviously, is that his destruction is total and leaves no trace behind.

4.190 *with his stone float*: the donor is here compared to a float or raft made of stone; both sink to the bottom. See the same simile in verse 194, and also 11.19.

4.200 *insignia of a religious profession*: the Sanskrit term *liṅgin* is ambiguous. It refers to a person who bears a distinguishing mark or emblem. Generally, this refers to the emblems of a religious professional, such as a vedic student, a forest hermit, or an ascetic.

4.203 *natural ponds*: literally, ponds 'dug by the gods', so as to distinguish them from the reservoirs built by humans and forbidden in verse 201.

4.204 *central virtues . . . secondary observances*: these two are technical terms (*yama* and *niyama*) denoting the first two steps in the eightfold path of Yoga. It is, however, more likely that the terms here refer to two sets of observances, *yama* being central virtues such as non-injury and *niyama* being outward religious rites such as twilight-worship. Virtues and observances falling under these two categories are spelled out in verses added in some manuscripts. See also *YDh* 3.312–13.

4.205 *A Brahmin must never partake of food*: here begins Manu's discussion of 'unfit food', as well as persons whose food is unfit to be eaten, both of which are technically called *abhojyānna* (4.221): see 5.5n.; Olivelle 2002*a*.

4.208 *murderer of a Brahmin*: the Sanskrit term *bhrūṇahan* has two meanings: a killer of a foetus (abortionist) and a killer of a learned Brahmin. The Dharma literature uses the term with both meanings. At *GDh* 21.9 it means an abortionist, while at *BDh* 1.18.13 it clearly refers to a murderer of a Brahmin. At other places it is impossible to tell which meaning is intended. Indeed, both meanings may be intended in many of these passages; *VaDh* 20.23, in fact, gives both definitions of the term. This term appears also at *MDh* 8.317 and 11.248. For a detailed discussion of this term, see Wezler 1994.

4.228 *from all*: the meaning of 'all' is unclear. Traditional interpreters propose sins, suffering, hell, and faults.

4.236 *lie about a sacrifice*: the whole point of this verse is that people should not boast about or exaggerate religious activities they have undertaken. The meaning is that one should not tell a lie about a sacrifice one has performed, most probably by exaggeration.

4.253 *a person . . . himself*: possibly a Śūdra who has fallen on hard times and has voluntarily entered another man's service. It is unclear whether such a man becomes a slave or merely a servant or worker.

4.257 *debts*: fundamental religious obligations of a Brahmin were presented within Brahmanical theology as 'debts'. The theology of debts arose quite early, and three debts are recorded already in the *TS* 6.3.10.5: 'A Brahmin, at his very birth, is born with a triple debt—of studentship to the seers, of sacrifice to the gods, of offspring to the fathers. He is, indeed, free from debt, who has a son, is a sacrificer, and who has lived as a student.' The *ŚB* (1.7.2.1–6) adds the debt of hospitality to men, bringing the theology of debts into closer alignment with the five great sacrifices. The obligation to marry, to perform sacrifices, and to beget offspring was used by Brahmanical theologians against the ascetic ideals of anti-ritualism and celibacy (6.35). For a detailed discussion of the debts and their relationship to asceticism, see Malamoud 1980; Olivelle 1993: 46–53.

CHAPTER FIVE

5.1 *born from the fire*: although Bhṛgu is said to be a son of Manu (1.34), other accounts of his origin record his birth from the fire. See *AitB* 3.34; *MBh* 1.5.216*.

5.5 *forbidden*: the Dharma literature makes a clear distinction between *abhakṣya*, foods forbidden because of their very nature, and *abhojya*, foods that have become unfit for a variety of reasons: given by an unfit individual, touched by an impure person or animal, contaminated by an impure substance, or gone stale or bad due to time (see 4.205 n.). I translate the former as 'forbidden' and the latter as 'unfit'. On this distinction, see Olivelle 2002*a*. For a detailed discussion of food prohibitions in the legal texts, see Olivelle 2002*b*.

5.7 *Kṛsara porridge, Saṃyāva cake*: Kṛsara appears to be a dish made with milk, rice, and sesame seeds. Saṃyāva is a sweet cake made with flour, milk, and ghee.

5.11 *single-hoofed . . . permitted*: there is no text that permits the eating of any single-hoofed animal. It may well be that this exception is made in view of the horse-sacrifice during which horse meat is consumed by the priests. Such an exception, however, would be unique in the Dharma literature.

5.17 *animals with five nails*: this is an ancient and widespread rule forbidding the eating of animals with five nails or claws, with the exception of some. Here seven such exceptions are listed, whereas the standard rule contains only five exceptions. The general formulation of this rule is: 'The five five-nailed animals may be eaten', meaning that five-clawed animals other than those enumerated are forbidden. The forbidding of animals with five 'nails' may indeed be a residue of a proscription of cannibalism, since human beings are among animals with five nails. See *ĀpDh* 1.17.37; *GDh* 17.27; *BDh* 1.12.5; *VaDh* 14.39. For a detailed study, see Jamison 1998.

5.18 *animals with incisors in only one jaw*: the reference is to animals that have incisor teeth only on the lower jaw; cows, goats, and sheep are examples. These are the paradigmatic farm animals whose meat may be eaten. The opposite of these are animals with incisor teeth on both jaws. Examples include horses, donkeys, and mules, as well as dogs, cats, and most carnivorous animals.

5.24 *infused with oil*: the meaning appears to be that food prepared with oil, such as fried foods, does not become stale; leftovers of a sacrificial oblation, on the other hand, even if it is not made with oil, is by definition not subject to becoming stale. The parallel passages in *YDh* 1.169 and *ViDh* 51.35 support this interpretation.

5.27 *He may . . . at risk*: this verse opens the discussion on eating meat with a broad and general statement giving four occasions for eating meat. The discussion ends with verse 56, which is again a broad statement attempting to reconcile the opposing viewpoints given earlier. These two verses bracket the discussion, which contains two views. The first (28–30) defends the traditional position regarding meat-eating; that is the natural order of creation established by the Creator himself. The second position (31–55) proposes the ethic of vegetarianism and non-injury, strongly condemning killing and eating meat outside very restrictive parameters established by the needs of the vedic sacrifice. See the nice contrast between verses 28 and 39. Manu does not tell us explicitly his own view. It is, however, the traditional method to give the view of an opponent or the view to be refuted first and the view of the author himself last. If this holds good here, then Manu must have favoured the restriction of meat to sacrificial occasions. This is supported by the fact that Manu disposes of the first view in three verses, whereas he devotes twenty-five verses to defending the second view.

5.31 *rule of gods . . . rule of fiends*: possibly, we have here a *double entendre*. On the one hand, saying that the rules are divine or fiendish indicates the goodness of the one and the evil of the other. On the other hand, we can take 'rule' as the manner of acting: thus, gods eat meat only during vedic sacrifices, whereas Rākṣasas are well known as always relishing blood and meat.

5.39 *The Self-existent . . . for sacrifice*: this statement appears to refute the claim made by the defenders of meat eating in verse 28 that Prajāpati created the whole world as food for living beings.

5.55 *Me he . . . nature of 'meat'*: the belief that the food a person eats may in turn eat him appears to have been old. Such sentiments are expressed in the vedic literature with reference not only to animals but also to plants and grains: *JB* 1.43; *ŚB* 12.9.1.1. Here Manu gives a phonetic etymology of the Sanskrit term for meat *māṃsa*, the two syllables of which mean 'me' (*mām*) and 'he' (*sa*).

5.58 *Someone who has teethed . . . of hair*: the meaning of 'younger' (*anujāte*), literally 'born after', is unclear. A possible clue to the meaning may be found in verse 70 where a child who has teethed is juxtaposed with a child whose naming ceremony has been performed. If the naming ceremony is considered some kind of birth, then the unusual term *anujāta* may refer to it. The full ten-day period of impurity is observed only when someone who has undergone vedic initiation dies. At the death of a child who has undergone the hair-cutting ceremony, the period is three days; for a child who has teethed, one day; and for a baby who has not teethed, purity is restored immediately.

5.59 *until the collection of bones*: according to the *ViDh* 19.10, this takes place on the fourth day after death.

5.60 *common ancestry*: the Sanskrit term *sapiṇḍa* refers to a group of close relatives, but there is great controversy in the tradition with regard to both its meaning and the extent of the group covered. One interpretation takes *piṇḍa* (lit. 'round lump') to mean a bodily particle and *sapiṇḍa* to mean people who through birth have bodily particles in common. Another interpretation takes *piṇḍa* to mean the balls of rice offered to ancestors and *sapiṇḍa* to mean people who are connected through these ancestral offerings. In general, the relationship extends to six generations before and after the father (seven generations, if one includes the father in the enumeration) and five generations before and after the mother. See *BDh* 1.11.9; Jolly 1885: 168–74; Kane 1962–75: ii. 452–78; iii. 735.

relationship based on offering libations: the Sanskrit term *samānodaka* refers to a broad and ill-defined group of extended relatives based on the offering of water to the same ancestors. Some take it as comprehending the seven generations of ancestors beyond the seven comprising 'common ancestry'.

5.61 *The same . . . by bathing*: the critical edition has here only a single verse, which has been expanded to two verses in the vulgate and in most manuscripts. This verse records three differing opinions regarding the period of impurity caused by childbirth: (1) birth impurity is the same as death impurity; (2) after a birth only the parents are subject to impurity; and (3) only the mother is subject to impurity, while the father is purified by simply bathing. According to the vulgate reading the translation is: 'As this period of death-impurity is prescribed for those who belong to the same ancestry, so the same holds true at a birth for those who desire perfect purity. Death-impurity affects all, but birth-impurity affects only the mother and the father. The mother alone is subject to the period of birth-impurity; the father becomes pure by bathing.'

5.63 *On the contrary . . . three days*: the meaning of this verse and its connection to the rest of this section is quite unclear. This verse should be understood within the context of the differing opinions regarding the impurity affecting a father and mother mentioned in the previous verse. This verse appears to be contradicting the view expressed in the final phrase of the previous verse, namely, that after a birth the father is purified by bathing. The opponent here says that a father is purified by bathing alone only after having sex; when a child is actually born, he has to observe a period of impurity lasting three days. This interpretation makes sense of the otherwise incongruous insertion of sexual intercourse within a passage dealing with birth and death. The author may also be alluding to the view expressed in the *Aitareya Upaniṣad* (2.1–3) that the emission of the semen by the man into the woman constitutes his first birth, and the actual birth of the child constitutes the second. If this holds true, then the author of this view is arguing against the earlier view, saying that a bath alone purifies after his first birth (emission of semen) but not the second, which is the topic of discussion here.

5.64 *Those who touch . . . three*: 'Those who touch the corpse' probably refers to those close relatives who actually participate in the funeral, rather than to any person who may happen to touch a corpse, because of the context; this also parallels the statement about the pupil in the very next verse. The expression 'those who offer libations' refers to the class of relatives who are required to offer water to the deceased: see 5.60 n.

5.68 *lay it down*: the meaning is not altogether apparent. Some commentators interpret the expression to mean 'bury'; this is also the understanding of *YDh* 3.1. The image of leaving the body behind like a piece of wood found in the very next verse, however, raises the possibility that, according to Manu, the body was actually left on the ground rather than buried. Customs, of course, may have changed over time.

5.72 *The relations . . . prescribed rule*: the verse is quite obscure and a slightly variant version occurs in *BDh* 1.11.5. It is possible that the verse is taken from a source which may have provided a different context for understanding the verse. So, for example, the context here or in *BDh* does not permit us to understand the exact meaning of 'according to prescribed rule'. Here the straightforward meaning is that when an unmarried woman dies, her relatives (maternal and paternal) are impure for three days, whereas her siblings, and one must assume also her parents, remain impure for the standard statutory period of ten days.

siblings: (*sanābhayaḥ*) literally, 'those connected by the same navel', probably referring to either the 'uterine' (brothers and possibly sisters) or, more likely, to the immediate family, including the parents.

5.74 *kinsmen and relatives*: these two terms (*sambandhi bāndhavaiḥ*) have wide applications, although in their restrictive usage, the former refers to relatives by marriage and the latter to maternal relatives (see 2.132n.).

5.82 *someone who is . . . or an elder*: the expression 'living near by' must be understood here from the preceding verse. This is somewhat problematic because two half-verses intervene, but without that term this injunction would require a period of impurity whenever anyone who is not a vedic scholar dies, which is absurd.

5.84 *while performing . . . to impurity*: for the view that ritual and royal obligations take precedence over the observance of impurity, see 5.93–7; and also *GDh* 14.45–6; *YDh* 3.27–9.

5.85 *Divākīrti*: the meaning of this term (literally 'calling or declaring during the day') is unclear. Most commentators take it to mean a Cāṇḍāla: see *MBh* 12.136.106, where its meaning is clearly a Cāṇḍāla (see also *MBh* 12.136.110). The term may refer to the fact that these individuals were expected to go about only during the day and to announce their presence.

5.88 *votary*: this (*ādiṣṭī*) is a hapax legomenon in the ancient Dharma literature, except for the citation of this very verse in *ViDh* 22.87. All commentators take this as a synonym of *brahmcārin* ('vedic student'). See the similar use of *vratin* ('man engaged in a vow') at 2.188; 5.91, 93; 11.121, 224.

5.89 *born through capricious caste mingling*: the meaning of the original Sanskrit is obscure. The contrast may be to caste mingling that is approved, such as hypergamous marriages (see 3.13).

5.92 *as appropriate*: all commentators interpret this to mean that a Vaiśya is carried through the western gate, a Kṣatriya through the northern, and a Brahmin through the eastern.

5.93 *for they . . . with brahman*: commentators, rightly I think, see an implied 'respectively' in the second half-verse. The meaning is that the king is seated on Indra's throne; whereas vedic students and those performing sacrificial sessions are united with *brahman*. The meaning of *brahman* is also unclear. Given the context of a student and a sacrificer, it is likely that *brahman* here refers to the Veda and vedic rites in which these two are immersed.

5.95 *for anyone the king wants*: the meaning is that a person delegated by the king to carry out his duties, such as his chaplain or judge, is also subject to instant purification in order for him to carry out his official functions. This appears to be an extension of the king's own instant purification. The principle articulated here is that rules of impurity and the like are overridden by the requirements of public office and ritual obligations.

5.105 *Knowledge . . . time*: 'food' refers to special penitential foods, such as milk and roots, or possibly to fasting (cf. *YDh* 3.31); 'time' means the passage of the statutory period of impurity discussed earlier.

5.108 *What needs . . . renunciation*: a point worth noting in this proverbial saying is that all the instruments of purification (muddy water, fast current during the rains, menstrual flow, and the ochre garment of a renouncer) are dirt-coloured. This verse recurs with some variations in *VaDh* 3.58; *ViDh* 22.91; *YDh* 3.32.

5.111–12 *anything lapidary . . . unembellished*: the two verses, 111 and 112, are related; the first telling us how to clean certain articles when they are stained, and the second when they are unstained. We should expect to find the same or similar articles in the two lists; and we do. Stone implements would be out of place here amidst precious articles. Of the metal objects in 111, gold and unembellished silver are singled out in 112; and I think 'aquatic' (*abja*) and 'lapidary' (*aśmamaya*) of 112 parallel 'jewels' (*maṇi*) and 'lapidary' (*aśmamaya*) of 111. That the tradition recognized two types of precious stones, the one aquatic (e.g. pearls, corals) and the other stone (e.g. sapphire, ruby, diamond), is clear from what Manu says at 8.100.

5.122 *Grass . . . again*: verse 123 of the vulgate has been expunged from the critical edition. It is found in the vast majority of the manuscripts. Evidence, however, strongly suggests that it is an interpolation. One can see clearly how this verse migrated into the text of Manu. The verse is cited by the commentator Medhātithi at the very conclusion of his commentary on verse 122; scribes may have mistaken it for a verse of Manu. The migration of verses cited in commentaries into the root text via the misperception of scribes is a common phenomenon. The verse is actually *VaDh* 3.59.

5.133 *droplets of water*: the meaning is not altogether clear. The reference is probably to droplets of spit coming from the mouth (2.141).

5.135 *marrow*: the inclusion of marrow in this list is anomalous. All others are substances that commonly ooze out of the human body; it is hard to imagine marrow oozing out unless someone is seriously wounded. Could *majjan* refer here to oily residue on the skin after sweating?

5.136 *on one hand*: within the context the meaning is clear. 'One hand' refers to the left hand, with which the person applied the earth and water to the penis and anus. All purifications below the navel are carried out using the left hand.

5.143 *If a sullied . . . thing down*: the context is a meal, and the man is carrying dishes for serving the guests. During this time if one of the diners, who is by definition sullied with remnants of food on his hand, happens to touch the man serving, the latter need not put the dish down (which he carries in his left hand) but simply sip some water.

5.147 *Even in their . . . independently*: this and the following verse have become a *cause célèbre* in anti-Manu rhetoric, even though these or similar provisons are encountered in numerous other legal texts: *GDh* 18.1–2; *BDh* 2.3.44–6; *VaDh* 5.3; *ViDh* 25.13; *YDh* 1.85–6. Similar sentiments are expressed later by Manu (9.2–3). Clearly, Brahmanical law saw women as eternal minors to be guarded and protected by their male relatives. Other and more positive depictions of the role of women and their relationship to males, however, are often ignored by critics. The term *svatantra* ('independent') also has specifically legal connotations and is used with reference to a person who can act independently to enter a legally binding contract.

5.149 *both families*: that is, her natal family and that of her husband. See 9.5.

5.152 *act of giving away*: this is a significant observation about the centrality of the giving away (alienation) by the father with respect to the husband's authority over his wife. The term *svāmya*, which I have translated with the broad 'lordship', can also mean ownership; this term is regularly used with regard to someone's legal ownership of property (see 8.197–205). A factor that is implicit in this statement regarding 'giving away' may be the ancient custom of bride purchase, alluded to at 8.204. If marriage is a sale, then ownership is transferred from the previous owner (father) to the new owner (husband).

5.160 *Just like . . . death*: this and the following verses are clearly directed both against the custom of levirate (see 9.57–70) and against the woman's own desire to have children, perhaps through re-marriage. The term 'good woman' (*sādhvī*) is probably used with a pregnant meaning: a woman who is *always* faithful to her husband (see verse 165).

5.169 *In accordance . . . of his life*: this concluding verse of the section on the householder who is a bath-graduate nicely recapitulates the subject. Note that the last half-verse here is identical with the second half-verse of 4.1, thus bracketing this section with this repetition. See parallels at 6.1, 33.

CHAPTER SIX

6.1 *After living . . . his organs*: see parallels at 4.1; 5.169; 6.33.

6.10 *constellation-sacrifice*: a sacrifice, called Nakṣatreṣṭi, offered to the lunar mansions and described in the *TB* 3.1.

Turāyaṇa: the first of a series of yearly sacrifices performed on the full-moon day of Phālguṇa (February–March) or Caitra (March–April). See *ĀśŚr*, II.14.

Dākṣāyaṇa: another in the series of yearly sacrifices. This sacrifice is performed both on the full-moon and the new-moon.

6.14 *Bhauma plant*: the meaning of *bhauma* is uncertain. The commentator Medhātithi identifies the plant as *gojihvikā*, which Jha (1920–39) calls cabbage and the lexicons identify variously as *Anisomeles malabarica*, *Premna esculenta*, *Coix barbata*, and *Elephantopus scaber*.

6.18 *clean up immediately*: the meaning is that the hermit cleans his bowl immediately after eating, leaving nothing for the next time. Such a man does not maintain a store of provisions, but lives from day to day.

6.19 *he may . . . eighth mealtime*: the standard mealtimes for a normal human being are twice a day, once in the morning and once in the evening. Eating only at night (i.e. evening) or during the day implies that he skips one meal. Eating every fourth mealtime means that he skips three meals; when one eats every eighth mealtime, one skips three days and eats in the evening of the fourth.

6.21 *Vaikhānasa doctrine*: the term Vaikhānasa is frequently used to refer to forest hermits. The term also refers to the doctrine or treatise of the sage Vikhanas (see *BDh* 2.11.14).

6.22 *spend the day standing and the night seated*: this refers to a religious observance during which the person has to remain standing during the day (without sitting down) and seated during the night (without lying down). The *VaDh* (24.5) clearly specifies that this observance involves standing during the day and sitting at night. See *ĀpDh* 1.25.10; *GDh* 22.6; *BDh* 2.2.10; 4.7.17. The same expression recurs in Manu at 11.224. For this ascetic/penitential practice, see 11.111.

6.23 *the five fires*: the hermit sits in the middle of four blazing fires at each cardinal point, with the summer sun scorching overhead as the fifth fire. For the five sacred fires, see 3.185n.

6.25 *depositing his sacred fires in his body*: Brahmanical theology of renunciation represents the abandonment of rites and ritual fires as a process of internalization. The technical expression for the ritual process by which this internalization is accomplished is called 'depositing the fires in one's body/self'. This procedure is patterned after the vedic custom of depositing the fires either in the fire-drills or in the body when a sacrificer has to undertake a journey. He brings back his fires either by producing a fire using the fire-drills or by blowing onto an ordinary fire. The *BDh* (2.17.26) gives a simple form of this rite: the ascetic breathes in the smell of each fire, reciting the vedic formula 'With that body of yours worthy of sacrifice' (*TB* 2.5.8.8). After this rite the ascetic carries the fires in the form of his breaths.

6.33 *After spending . . . during the fourth*: see parallels at 4.1; 5.169; 6.1.

6.35 *proceed downward*: going downward here and in other similar contexts (see 6.37; 7.53; 11.173) probably implies both a fall from caste (sociologically, going down the social ladder) and going down to the netherworlds (cosmologically). See the similar expression at 11.153, where it means that the food eaten has gone down (i.e. been excreted).

6.39 *freedom from fear*: the meaning is that the ascetic assures all creatures that no harm will come to them from him. This is commonly referred to as the 'gift of safety', and it is also associated with a king after his conquest of a new region (see 7.201). He is supposed to assure the safety of the people living there. Verse 40 picks up this theme of 'fear' with reference to the ascetic's afterlife.

6.44 *renouncer*: although the term (*mukta*) means literally 'a liberated man', it is used to refer to a wandering ascetic. The discussion here is about asceticism and ascetics, not about liberation and liberated individuals (see 1.114n.).

6.46 *purified by his sight*: the meaning is that he should look at the spot where he is about to place his foot, lest he trample to death any living creatures such as ants and worms (see 6.68). This must have been a value and custom common to most ascetic communities; Jain ascetics carry a broom to sweep the ground in front of them lest they step on any tiny insect unintentionally.

6.48 *seven gates*: the meaning is unclear. They probably refer to the seven openings of the head: two eyes, two nostrils, two ears, and mouth, which are the major organs of perception and communication.

6.49 *Taking delight . . . felicity*: a contrast is drawn here between being seated and walking. The first refers to the yogic posture and meditation. The life of the ascetic is split between sitting in meditation and walking about, especially to beg for food, which is the very next topic.

6.50 *palmistry*: the Sanskrit term (*aṅgavidyā*) is broader than palmistry, although this must have been the principal form. It can include the interpretation of other physical characteristics and marks.

6.58 *with a show of reverence*: it is unclear who shows the reverence. Native interpreters are divided, some thinking that it is the donor, and others that it is the ascetic himself who shows reverence to the giver. Ascetic literature warns the ascetic to fear honours bestowed on him by ordinary people and to shun such honours as if they were poison, and recommends that he welcome disrespect as if it were ambrosia: see 2.162 with reference to a student.

6.66 *an emblem . . . Law*: the meaning appears to be that wearing an ascetic emblem does not *ipso facto* mean that the man is following the Law. In the very next verse the emblem appears to be compared to a Kataka fruit, which is believed to have the property of making turbid water clear. But the fruit has to be immersed in the water for this to happen. Likewise, an emblem itself will not make an ascetic virtuous; he must live according to the Law of which the emblem is merely an outward sign.

6.75 *that state*: the meaning is not altogether clear. In all likelihood, it refers to the highest state of the liberated self, namely the state of Brahman (see 6.79, 81, 85).

6.76–7 *Constructed . . . ghosts*: the human body is here compared to a house, a common image in ascetic literature. The ascetic has, of course, abandoned his house, but he still carries his body with him. The imagery here invites the reader to regard the house, commonly perceived as offering safety and shelter, as a place of torment and danger. The expression 'dwelling place of ghosts' (*bhūtāvāsa*) carries a double meaning; *bhūta* can mean both ghost and element. Indeed, the body is composed of elements, but it is, at another level, the abode of impure and dangerous ghosts. See *Maitrī Upaniṣad*, 3.4.

6.78 *When a tree . . . painful grasp*: commentators and translators alike have failed to understand this simile, which, I must admit, has been cast in turbid syntax. All take the tree falling from the bank and the bird leaving the tree as two independent similes. That is very unlikely. Further, they take *grāha* (which I think means alligator rather than shark) only with the giving up of the body in the second half of the verse. I think the last foot is connected to both the simile and the ascetic giving up the body. The meaning then seems to be that a bird flying off before the fall of the tree escapes the alligator's grasp in the river. Likewise, when an ascetic abandons the body before its natural fall at death (which is here compared to the fall of the tree), he escapes the grasp of the alligator, probably Yama (6.61). This fits nicely with the theme of the preceding verse, namely, that an ascetic must abandon the body.

6.80 *by the passion . . . object of passion*: Manu is clearly playing with the double meaning of the Sanskrit term *bhāva*, which is both the inner disposition of the spirit and the external object, especially those that are the object of passion.

6.90 *end up*: most commentators take this as a reference to the fact that persons in the other orders of life must get their sustenance from the householder, even though this is not strictly true in the case of a forest hermit. The image of the rivers flowing into the ocean, however, evokes another image: that of the rebirth process as described in the *BāU*

(6.2.9–14) and the *ChU* (5.1–9). After death all beings go through the transformations of smoke, rain, and plants, and finally end up as the semen of a householder before taking birth in the womb of his wife (see 3.76 n.).

CHAPTER SEVEN

7.2 *vedic consecration*: (*brāhmaṃ saṃskāram*) although all commentators take this as a reference to vedic initiation, it is clearly the royal consecration that is intended here. It is this consecration that makes him a king along with the obligation to protect his subjects.

7.4 *Indra . . . Lord of wealth*: these are the eight guardian deities of the cardinal points, beginning with Indra in the east and ending with Kubera, the lord of wealth, in the north.

7.10 *every aspect*: the aspects (*viśvarūpam*) he assumes are indicated in the next verse: benevolence, valour, anger. I also think that, in light of his comparison to the sun in verse 6, the old meaning of *viśvarūpa* (Bodewiz 1985) as dazzling or brilliant (like gold and the sun) may resonate here also.

7.11 *of them all*: namely, the eight gods from whose particles he was created.

7.13 *When the king . . . that Law*: the verse is not altogether clear. 'Law' here is probably a royal decree or edict. The commentator Medhātithi gives examples of such decrees: 'There is a wedding in the minister's house, and all should gather there.' Against those in disfavour: 'No one should associate with this man.'

7.14 *Punishment*: it appears that Manu begins the discussion of punishment by personifying it. Punishment is the son of the Lord made from Brahman's energy. But by verse 32 he passes on to its common meaning of punishment imposed by the king.

7.15 *accede to being used*: verses 22 and 23 make the meaning of this unusual expression clear. Different beings open themselves to being used (literally 'enjoyed') by others; one can think of the chain of food and eaters. In a socio-political context, moreover, 'being used' may refer specifically to the king's enjoyment of his subjects' wealth through taxes and duties.

7.16 *the place and the time*: that is, when and where the crime was committed.

7.19 *after careful examination*: the reference is probably to a judicial inquiry. This phrase relates to what was said in verse 16. The two verses bracket this brief discussion of the proper way to inflict just punishment.

7.35 *The king . . . to them*: this verse concludes the section on the creation of the king to be the protector of people, a section that began with verse 3. The connection of verses 35 and 3 is clearly established by the use here of the word 'was created' (*sṛṣṭaḥ*) that connects with '(Lord) created' (*asṛjat*) of verse 3.

7.37 *After getting up in the morning*: note that the entire section on the duties of the king is structured according to a day in the life of the king. Other materials, such as the appointment of officials, organization of the state, and political strategies, are all presented, sometimes quite artificially, within that overall structure. The artificiality of the structure is apparent, because at 7.145 Manu returns to the morning duties of the king, possibly because so much material (108 verses) had intervened. This is followed by the afternoon routine (7.216–22) and the evening (7.223–6). See the similar division of a king's day and routine in the *AŚ*, 1.19.6–25.

7.40 *those residing in the forest*: the reference is probably to the Pāṇḍava brothers of the *MBh*. They recovered their kingdom after the great war. I thank Professor Albrecht Wezler for this insight. Commentators ignore this point and take the term as referring simply to poor persons.

7.41–2 *Vena came . . . Gādhi*: these are well-known stories from ancient lore. Vena is a king notorious for his evil conduct. He prohibited sacrifice and, consequently, was killed by Brahmin ascetics with their spells. Among the many legends surrounding the figure of King Nahuṣa is one where he wanted to obtain Indra's wife and was therefore cursed to become a snake. Sudās Paijavana (the son of Pijavana) is a king named in the *Ṛgveda*. The famous seers Vasiṣṭha and Viśvāmitra were his priests. Sudās killed Vasiṣṭha's son and, abandoned by Viśvāmitra, came to ruin. No information appears to be available on Sumukha. Nimi, too impatient to wait for Vasiṣṭha, started a sacrifice on his own and dies under a curse by Vasiṣṭha. Pṛthu is the son of Vena produced posthumously by Brahmins by churning Vena's body. He ruled the earth justly, and for this the earth is named Pṛthvī, the wife of Pṛthu. Both Kubera and Viśvāmitra (the son of Gādhi) came to their respective positions because of ascetic toil (*tapas*). Kubera, the guardian of the north, became the lord of wealth, and Viśvāmitra, originally a Kṣatriya, rose to the rank of a Brahmin.

7.54 *counsellors*: this term (*sacivān*) occurs only once elsewhere in Manu (7.120), where also it refers to a very high official. In the *MBh* (15.14.11) Yudhiṣṭhira's four brothers are called his *sacivas*, indicating the high rank of officials bearing that name.

natives of the land: this is a difficult term (*maulān*). Commentators take it to mean people whose ancestors were in royal service. The term *maula* is used by Manu in two other places (8.62, 259) both in the context of competent witnesses. The meaning of 'hereditary' makes no sense within those contexts. In all three instances *maula* probably refers to native or original inhabitants of the locality as opposed to newcomers; that is, people with deep roots in the region. In this sense, it may also imply 'hereditary', because the ancestors of these people were inhabitants of the region.

7.60 *officials*: this is a generic term (*amātyān*) used with reference to all high-ranking government officials (see Scharfe 1993: 132), especially those below the level of *mantrin* ('counsellor'). Revenue collection is, of course, one of the principal duties of officials. Within the state organization envisaged in *AŚ*, there was a special official called Samāhartṛ (precisely the word used here by Manu) who was the revenue collector: see Scharfe 1993: 157–9. Note the parallel between this verse on the appointment of *amātyas* and verse 54 on the appointment of counsellors.

7.63 *hint, bearing, or gesture*: the *AŚ* (1.15.7–9) gives only 'hint' and 'bearing' and defines the former as non-normal movement or gesture, and the latter as 'putting on an expression', explained by commentators as unnatural facial expressions, such as paleness. All three terms clearly refer to the ability of the envoy to interpret properly the signs that may betray the inner thoughts of the rival kings.

7.68 *he should take*: the subject of the verb is unclear. Is it the ambassador, whose activities were the focus of the preceding verses, or the king? Commentators are divided. I think that the context favours the ambassador.

7.70–1 *A fortress . . . a hill fortress*: on the different kinds of fortresses and their relative merits, see *AŚ* 2.3.1–35.

7.75 *conveyances*: this term (*vāhanāni*) is difficult to translate because it includes vehicles (carts, carriages, chariots), as well as draught animals, beasts of burden, and riding horses (cavalry).

7.78 *domestic rites . . . fires*: the distinction here is between the domestic rites (*smārta*) that are described in the *Gṛhyasūtras*, and the solemn vedic rites (*śrauta*) that require the three vedic fires (2.231).

7.90 *treacherous*: for example, a weapon concealed in a wooden exterior.

7.91 *a man standing on the ground*: the implication is that the soldier, in this case the king, is fighting on a chariot or a mount.

7.97 *pre-emptive share*: the same term (*uddhāra*) is used with reference to the extra share reserved for the oldest brother in partitioning ancestral property (see 9.112–17). It appears also that in the division of war booty the king, as the chief, received a share of the best pieces before the rest was divided among the soldiers, as also the best item from the booty won by an individual.

7.99 *The king . . . worthy recipients*: this has the hallmarks of a proverbial saying. In the *Pañcatantra* (I, verse 2) there is a very similar statement with regard to a merchant and his ambition to become rich. See the parallel in *AŚ* 1.4.3; Scharfe 1993: 46.

7.100 *goals of man*: (*puruṣārtha*) same as the triple set (*trivarga*): 2.224n. Often a fourth, liberation (*mokṣa*), is added, giving a quadruple set.

7.105 *hide his limbs like a tortoise*: a variant of this verse is cited in *AŚ* 1.15.60. The simile may be a comparison of the five limbs of counsel (*mantra*) to the five limbs (four feet and head) that the tortoise withdraws into the shell. The five limbs of counsel are given as: means for commencing operations, provision of men and material, distribution of place and time, remedies for setbacks, and success of the undertaking. See *AŚ* 1.15.42.

7.107 *strategies beginning with conciliation*: the four strategies are conciliation, gifts, fomenting dissension, and war. See 7.198–200.

7.119 *'family'*: (*kula*) many divergent interpretations are offered by commentators. This was probably a technical term referring to a segment of a village from which the official derives his benefits in terms of taxes and duties.

7.121 *high stature*: (*uccaiḥsthānam*) although traditionally interpreted as an eminent person coming from a high-ranking family, the term may well refer to the physical stature or height rather than the social or moral stature of the individual, especially in juxtaposition with his fierce appearance.

7.124 *people who have business*: commentators generally take this to mean people who have lawsuits pending. The reference is then to the bribery of judges. The term could also have a wider meaning, including other matters requiring official sanction. In that context the provision may include bribery and kickbacks.

send them into exile: this term (*pravāsanam*) can also mean the infliction of capital punishment (see 8.123 n.).

7.144 *specified rewards*: the reference is to the taxes a king collects, which are considered to be payment for the protection provided by the king.

7.153 *tying up . . . undertakings*: the reference is to past activities where some aspects may not have been completely carried out and need further attention. See 7.179.

7.154 *eightfold agenda*: there is no consensus among the commentators as to the identity of these eight. Many cite a verse that lists eight activities of a king: income, expenditure, dismissal (e.g. of bad officials), preventing (e.g. wrong activities on the part of officials), propounding the correct meaning, resolving lawsuits, punishment, and prescribing penances. The commentator Medhātithi offers two other possible meanings of the eight. First: undertaking what has not been done, carrying out what has been done, enhancing what has been carried out, reaping the fruit of the activity, conciliation, sowing dissension, bestowing gifts, and using force. Second: trade, building bridges and dykes, building forts, keeping them in repair, trapping elephants, constructing mines, settling uninhabited lands, and clearing forests.

set of five: most commentators explain this as a reference to the five kinds of spy employed by a king: deceiver, fallen ascetic, householder in distress, trader in distress, and a person wearing the insignia of a hermit. For a discussion of the various types of spy, see Scharfe 1993: 204–39.

circle of neighbouring kingdoms: (*maṇḍala*) ancient Indian political science envisaged, perhaps somewhat artificially and geometrically, kingdoms to form circles around any given kingdom. The neighbouring kingdoms constitute natural enemies; the kingdoms beyond the immediate neighbours constitute the enemy's enemy, and thus one's own natural allies; the kingdoms beyond these constitute the ally's natural enemies, and therefore one's own enemies; and so on. See Scharfe 1993: 105–17.

7.155 *buffer king*: this is a king whose realm stands between the king and the kingdom he intends to attack.

7.156 *The above constituents . . . twelve*: the constituents must be four in order to come up with the total of twelve. Scharfe (1993, 108) appears to take the constituents as the seven listed in *AŚ* 6.1; but it is likely that Manu considers them to be the four encircling kingdoms listed in verse 155. On the 'root' of the circle, called 'womb' (*maṇḍalayoni*) in the *Arthaśāstra*, see Scharfe 1993: 107–8. The 'eight others' are identified by the commentators as the eight other kinds of surrounding kingdom listed by Kāmandaki (*Nītisāra*, 8.16–17). Four in front beyond the enemy: ally, enemy's ally, ally's ally, enemy's ally's ally. Four in the rear: foe at the heel, rescuer from the rear, supporter of foe at the heel, and supporter of rescuer from the rear. For these terms, see 7.207 n.

7.157 *There are also . . . coming to seventy-two*: each of the twelve listed in the previous verse has five constituents, thus bringing the total to 60 (see *AŚ* 6.2.28, which calls these sixty 'material constituents'). Together with the previous twelve (called 'constituents of kings' in *AŚ* 6.2.28), the total comes to seventy-two.

7.160 *double strategem*: the meaning is unclear. The explanation given in verse 167 indicates that the strategy consists of separating the army from the king. How this was carried out and the strategy behind it are unclear. Most commentators say that the king divides his army in two, which is also the explanation given in 7.173. It is more likely that this strategy calls for pursuing war and peace at the same time. The king pursues peace and diplomacy, while surreptitiously preparing for war. That may be the reason for separating the army (or part of the army) from the king, so he can give the appearance that he is not preparing for war. In verse 167 the meaning may not be that the army stops in one place and the king in another, but that the king remains stationary, while the army is on the march (or vice versa). The division of the army into two (7.173) may also envisage such a strategy: one part remaining stationary, giving the impression that war in not imminent, while the other launches a surprise attack.

7.185 *three types of road*: most commentators explain this as dry land, wet land, and forests.

six divisions: most commentators list elephants, horses, chariots, infantry, general, and workmen. Nandana prefers the sixfold division given by Kāmandaki (*Nītisāra* 16.6): hereditary troops, hired troops, troops from guilds, ally's troops, enemy's troops (?), and foresters. This same list is given in *AŚ* 9.2.1.

and only then . . . enemy's fort: note that the last foot of this verse is identical with the final foot of verse 181, which opened this section on preparations for a military expedition. This repetition indicates the close of this small sub-section.

7.187 *staff . . . eagle*: in the staff formation the army is arranged in a line with the field general (*balādhyakṣa*) in the front, the commander-in-chief (*senāpati*) at the rear, and the king in the middle, with the flanks protected by elephants and horses. This is used when danger is expected from all sides. In the wagon formation, used when there is a threat from the rear, the front is narrow like a needle and the rear is broad. In the boar, used when danger is perceived from the flanks, the front and the rear are narrow and the middle broad. In the crocodile, used when danger is expected from the front and the rear, the front and the rear are broad and the middle is narrow. In the needle, used when an attack is expected from the front, the army is arranged in a thin and long formation. The eagle formation is similar to the boar, except that it has longer wings extending outwards on the flanks. For a detailed discussion of these and other military formations, see *AŚ* 10.5–6.

7.188 *lotus formation*: in this formation the king is placed in the middle for protection, and the various units spread out in semicircles extending from the centre in all directions.

7.189 *post . . . in every direction*: since this is physically impossible, commentators explain that by the commander-in-chief and the general are meant all their subordinates. In other words, these two chief officers are responsible for guarding all the directions.

7.191 *thunderbolt*: in this formation, the army is deployed in three separate units.

7.196 *launch surprise assaults*: the meaning of this term (*samavaskandayet*) is not altogether clear. Most commentators appear to indicate something like commando raids, perhaps on sleeping troops.

7.201 *After the victory . . . amnesty*: all these activities refer to what the king must do within the conquered territories. So the gods and Brahmins are those local to those territories. 'Exemptions' refer to tax holidays of varying lengths granted to Brahmins and other significant individuals of the conquered lands. Amnesty is the freedom from fear (*abhaya*): see 6.39n.

7.205 *All activities . . . to the human*: this philosophy is clearly opposed to the 'passive' ideology insisting that everything is determined either by fate (*daiva*) or by one's own previous actions (*karma*). See *AŚ* 6.2.6–12, which is a close parallel to this verse.

7.206 *alliance with him*: given that this strategy is an alternative to war, the alliance must be with the enemy king.

7.207 *the foe at his heel . . . rear*: these are technical terms for certain kingdoms constituting the circle (see 7.154n.). 'The foe at his heel' is the king to his immediate rear, who by definition is an ally of his enemy, whom he is attacking and therefore is located to his front. The enemy can call on the foe at his heel to attack him from the rear. When this happens, the attacking king can call on the king located to the rear of the foe at his heel; this king, being the immediate neighbour of his foe, is his natural ally. He is called 'rescuer from the rear'. This term literally means 'cry for help'; evidently, when a rear attack took place, the king could send word (cry for help) to this ally, who would attack the former from his rear. On these terms, see the detailed study by Scharfe 1993: 111–16.

7.216 *After conferring . . . in this manner*: these words connect this section on the afternoon routine with the section on the king's morning routine and his conferring with his counsellors (7.147). It is to be assumed that the intervening sections on political strategies and war constituted the topics of the king's consultations with his counsellors.

7.224 *escorted by women*: the reference is probably to female guards rather than to servants. For a description of the various female guards posted around the king especially when he is in his private quarters, something already noted by Megasthenes, see Scharfe 1993: 152–3.

CHAPTER EIGHT

8.6 *sexual crimes against women*: usually this expression (*strīsaṃgrahaṇam*) means adultery. I have given it a broader definition, because under this ground for litigation are included a wide variety of crimes against women, including rape.

8.12 *pierced by Injustice*: the image here is of Justice that is pierced by a dart, which is Injustice itself, and which the court is obliged to remove. Commentators provide a different explanation. Justice is pierced by a dart when a judge decides wrongly and permits a miscarriage of justice to occur in his court. If the other officials of the court let it go unchallenged, then they are themselves wounded by this dart.

8.17 *Justice . . . with the body*: here the meaning of *dharma* shifts imperceptibly from justice to merit. See the more explicit image of relatives who abandon the dead man at 4.238–43.

8.27 *no longer a minor*: males reach majority at 16 and females at 12: see *AŚ* 3.3.1; *NSm* 1.31.

8.45 *appearance*: (*rūpam*) the meaning is unclear and commentators offer educated guesses. One interpretation takes it to mean the nature of the lawsuit; the judge should see whether it is serious or not. This interpretation is reasonable, although in a very similar passage of *AŚ* 3.1.15 *rūpa* is used with regard to the appearance of an item subject to a legal transaction (e.g. debt) noted in the document drawn up for the transaction.

8.49 *by traditional strategies*: an example is the custom of the creditor fasting at the door of the debtor until he pays up.

8.52–7 *When the debtor . . . these very reasons*: for the explanation of these verses and the technical vocabulary in them, especially the term *deśa* for document, found also in the *Arthaśāstra*, see the critical edition: Olivelle forthcoming *c*.

8.66 *a single person*: (*ekaḥ*) the reference within this context is probably not to a single witness (permitted in verse 77) but to what we would call a 'single person', that is, an individual who lives on his own and is not part of a larger household, either his own or an extended family.

8.72 *investigate*: the meaning is that the judge should not look into factors that would disqualify a witness (see verses 64–7) in these kinds of cases. Anyone is permitted to testify.

8.76 *not listed as a witness*: this term (*anibaddha*) probably refers to witnesses not listed in the original plaint and response by the plaintiff and the defendant. In later legal texts, listed witnesses are called *kṛta* ('appointed'), whereas those called later as witnesses are called *akṛta* ('unappointed'). See *NSm* 1.129.

8.78 *anything different . . . no validity*: the meaning is that such people tell a lie for a higher purpose. See this point spelled out in verses 103–4, where also we have perjury committed for the sake of the Law. Such false statements are made, for example, if the life of the defendant is at stake.

8.87 *In the presence of gods and Brahmins*: commentators and translators alike take 'god' (*deva*) here to mean images of gods. This may well be the case. But *deva* can also refer to the king (see 7.8; 11.83), and we have an exact parallel in 8.60 where the questioning of the witness is done in the presence of the king and Brahmins.

8.88 *with a reference to cows, seeds, and gold*: the Vaiśya is made to touch these substances before testifying; and this is precisely what is stated in verse 113. Alternatively, the judge may have uttered an imprecation about the man's cows etc.

8.92 *then you do not . . . Kuru land*: if the witness has no quarrel with Yama, the god of death and the judge of the dead, then there is no need for him to visit the Ganges or the land of the Kurus to expiate his sin.

8.97 *kills*: the term is probably used metaphorically here. Some take it to mean that he sends the relatives to hell. According to another view, the man incurs a sin equal to his killing a certain number of his relatives.

8.100 *concerning water*: the reference is probably to aqueducts, reservoirs, and the like. See the reference to breaking and obstructing water courses at 3.163.

8.106 *addressed to water*: these are the three verses (*R̥V* 10.9.1–3): 'Waters, you are refreshing . . .'. See Appendix III.

8.107 *of the total*: the meaning is unclear. It could be of the total amount under litigation, the total fine that would be owed to the king by the losing party, or the entire debt.

8.109 *oath*: Manu uses this term (*śapatha*) for both an oath and an ordeal. In later legal texts, such as *YDh*, *ViDh*, and *NSm*, we find the technical term *divya* for an ordeal. This term must have entered the legal vocabulary somewhat late, because it is not found in any of the *Dharmasūtras*, in Manu, or in the *Arthaśāstra*.

8.110 *Vasiṣṭha*: the story probably refers to a verse in *R̥gveda* 1.104.15. Vasiṣṭha was accused of being a fiend who had eaten his own sons. He cleared himself by an oath that if it were true he should die that very day.

8.113 *He should make . . . of caste*: see 8.88n. and the parallel prescriptions for the four classes within the context of purification at 5.99.

8.115 *When the blazing . . . strikes him*: the procedures for various ordeals are described in *NSm* 20. In the fire ordeal, eight circles are drawn on the ground. Seven banyan leaves are tied to the palms of the person undergoing the ordeal and a hot iron ball is placed in his hands. He must carry it through the circles and drop the ball at the designated place. If his palms are unburnt, he is declared innocent. In the water ordeal, an arrow is shot from a medium-sized bow. The person undergoing the ordeal must remain submerged in the water until a fast runner brings back the arrow. The third ordeal listed here is actually an oath; if his family does not suffer any mishap soon (during fourteen days, according to commentators), he is innocent.

8.116 *Long ago . . . told the truth*: Vatsa was accused by his brother of being the son of a Śūdra woman and thus not a pure Brahmin. Vatsa went through fire to prove his pedigree. See *Pañcaviṃśa Brāhmaṇa* 14.6.6.

8.120 *fined 1,000*: when the number alone is stated, the term Paṇa is understood within the context of fines (see 8.138; and Appendix IV). See also 3.186n.

8.123 *execute*: the term *pravāsayet*, which normally means 'sending into exile', here has the same meaning as parallel statements in the *AŚ* (1.18.16; 11.1.33, 47; 12.3.4; 12.4.4; 12.5.23; 13.4.29); it refers to execution. Like the modern military-inspired term 'liquidate' or the more common 'get rid of', *pravāsayet* may have been an euphemism for imposing the death penalty.

8.132 *Trasareṇu*: the term *trasa* means something moving or quivering, and *reṇu* means a grain of dust or pollen. The term refers to the smallest visible particle of matter, often regarded as having the mass of three atoms. See App. IV.

8.143 *nor shall the pledge . . . time has lapsed*: the meaning appears to be that the time for redeeming the loan has passed. This can happen when the interest on the loan equals the amount of the loan (payment due then is double the original loan). Ancient Indian law stipulated that when this happens the interest on the loan stops (see 8.151; this rule is called *dāmdupaṭ* in modern times). Even when this happens a pledge cannot be alienated.

8.148 *within his own locality*: traditional interpretations take this (*viṣaye*) to mean within one's sight or in one's own country or region.

8.151 *Interest . . . five times*: 'twice the principal' means that the interest should not exceed the amount of the loan, so that the repayment (loan plus interest) is twice the original amount of the loan. Likewise, for grain etc., the interest would be four times the loan; the repayment then being five times. The phrase 'when fixed at one time', according to some, means that the whole of the interest is payable at the end of the loan period; this would then not apply to loans where the interest is paid in instalments, for example every month.

8.153 *He must not charge . . . manual labour*: the cyclical rate is a kind of compound interest calculated, for example, monthly, but payable only at the end of the loan period together with the principal. The periodic rate is generally payable each month. The contractual rate is variable, either above or below the normal rate of interest, depending on the reliability of the person taking the loan. Manual labour is probably connected with indentured labour, the interest on the loan being deducted from the daily wages. On the question of debts in ancient India, see Kane 1962–75: iii. 414–61; Chatterjee 1971.

8.154–5 *When someone . . . as is due*: these two verses probably refer to cyclical interest. When at the end of the loan period the debtor is unable to repay the debt along with the accrued interest, he has the option of paying the accrued interest and renegotiating the contract for the principal. Verse 155 is somewhat obscure; it appears to be a rider on the previous verse providing a remedy when the debtor is unable to pay even the accrued interest. The intent appears to be that the new debt instrument must include both the principal and the accrued interest, if the debtor cannot pay off at least part of the interest at the time of the new loan.

8.158 *here*: given that the literary setting of this entire section is the court, it makes sense to take 'here' to mean 'here, in this court'.

8.159 *vain gifts*: these may refer to money promised to others either frivolously or for illegitimate purposes (to prostitutes, for example). The Sanskrit expression, however, may also be interpreted to mean loans taken out for illegitimate purposes.

8.160 *The above rule . . . to pay it*: there are three kinds of sureties: for appearance, namely that the man will appear either at the time stipulated to pay the debt or in court; as a guarantor of the debtor's trustworthiness; and as a guarantor of payment (see *YDh* 2.53). This rule exempts the heirs of only the first two kinds of sureties from the obligation to repay the debts for which the latter stood as surety.

8.161–2 *When someone . . . his own funds*: these two verses are rather obscure. The question-and-answer format is also quite unusual for Manu, leading to the possibility that these verses have been taken over from a different source and context. A likely interpretation is that the debtor has given a collateral to the surety as assurance of payment. This collateral may have become part of his wealth that the heirs inherited. In this case, the heirs are bound to repay the debt from their inheritance.

8.172 *by bringing together the social classes*: this Sanskrit expression (*varṇasaṃsargāt*) has caused enormous problems for the understanding of the verse. Commentators give diverse and contradictory explanations. Given that the two other activities are duties performed by the king, I think this also should be something that the king does. On the face of it, *varṇasaṃsarga* means confusion of classes, something the king is sworn to prevent. I think *saṃsarga* here may be used in close to its etymological meaning: combining and bringing together, not in a sexual sense which would cause the intermixing of classes, but in a broader sense. Here we can take it either as supporting the proper functioning of classes within the broader social structure, or more restrictively, as referring to the cohesiveness of each class within itself.

8.181–2 *When a man . . . request it*: the syntax of these two verses is quite confused, which must be one of the reasons for the rearrangement of verses by several commentators. I follow the commentator Medhātithi in rearranging the verses to give some syntactic coherence by placing verse 182 after the first half of 181, and placing the second half of 181 last.

8.184 *both*: namely, the gold that was deposited by the judge and the original deposit that resulted in the lawsuit.

8.185 *In the event . . . they do not perish*: 'both' here refers to sealed and open deposits. The point of the second half of the verse is unclear. We can readily understand the risk the man takes, because if the next-of-kin dies without delivering the deposit, the original depositor has the right to claim it. The last statement 'and if there is no mishap, then they do not perish' is so obvious, I cannot understand why it needs to be stated, especially because the second half of the verse is intended to give reasons why the deposit should not be given to a next-of-kin. Stephanie Jamison (personal communication) thinks that this half-verse may be a proverbial saying that has lost some of its punch in this context.

8.188 *That is the rule . . . from it*: the phrase 'That is the rule' clearly cannot refer to the previous verse. This verse refers back to verse 180, which states that a deposit should be returned in the same state in which it was deposited. An exception is made in the case of sealed deposits, because the man holding the deposit has no way of knowing what the original condition of the deposit was.

8.195 *as the delivery, so the recovery*: note that this phrase, occurring also in verse 180, brackets nicely the entire discussion of deposits.

8.197 *the king should not . . . offer testimony*: the meaning of this half-verse is not altogether clear. Most commentators say that such a man should not be permitted to become a witness in any lawsuit. This seems somewhat of a strange beginning to the section of sale without ownership; we would have expected a statement about what concrete steps should be taken regarding such a person, as indeed stated in the very next verse. One commentator takes this to mean that in a court case on the matter this man should not be allowed to call witnesses in his defence; in other words, the king can issue a summary verdict. This is quite an appealing interpretation. Professor Wezler (personal communication) has suggested an alternative. In any lawsuit filed by the original owner to recover his property from the current owner, the man who sold the article without ownership cannot be permitted to testify; he is after all a thief, though he may not consider himself to be one. Clearly, this is a very pithy statement with a whole lot left unsaid.

8.210 *Among all the priests . . . to a quarter*: the principal priests are the four mentioned in the previous verse. Next in rank are Maitrāvaruṇa, Pratiprasthātr̥, Brāhmaṇacchaṃsin, and Prastotr̥; then come Acchāvāka, Neṣṭr̥, Agnīdhra, and Pratihartr̥; and finally, Grāvastotr̥, Netr̥, Potr̥, and Subrahmaṇya. According to the commentator Medhātithi, assuming the total to be 112, the shares distributed are: 56, 28, 16, and 12. According to others, assuming the total to be 100, the shares distributed are: 48, 24, 16, and 12. See Kane 1962–75: v. 1329–30.

8.219 *When a man . . . from his realm*: the contract dealt with here is not private but within a corporate body. When a contract is made with the stipulation that all those who belong to that corporate entity will do something, then each individual is bound by it. Here the corporate entities are village, region (group of villages), and a corporation (traders, artisans, sect). See *NSm* 10.1; *YDh* 2.190f. The term 'truthfully' is interpreted by some to mean an oath: see 8.113 where a Brahmin has to swear by the truth.

8.227 *seventh step*: the reference is to the seven steps that the bride and groom take around the sacred fire during the marriage ceremony. The implication in all these verses coming within the context of the cancellation of a sale or purchase is that marriage is precisely such a transaction where the bride is sold by the father and bought by the future husband (see my note on bride-price at 3.53). The reasoning here appears to be that once the seventh step is taken, the transaction is ritually complete and cannot be annulled.

8.237 *one hundred . . . throws*: for these measurements, see Appendix IV.

8.242 *Manu has . . . herdsman or not*: the bulls meant here are probably those released at certain festivals or rituals, such as the Vr̥ṣotsarga. Animals dedicated to gods are temple cattle and the like. It is unclear whether the punishment concerns the animals themselves (beating, impounding) or their owners. Possibly the former, because at least in the case of temple cattle there are no human owners.

8.243 *For an offence . . . of the owner*: this appears to involve a dispute between an owner of a field and his tenant farmers. If the owner damages the crops, then he is fined ten times his share of the crop; and if his servants do the damage unknown to the owner, then the fine is half that amount.

8.245 *when landmarks . . . visible*: during this month, which is between spring and the rains, the land is parched and the grass is dried up. The hidden landmarks can be seen most clearly during this time of the year.

8.265 *on the basis of utility*: commentators point out that a smaller piece of land may be more productive than a larger parcel. Likewise, a reservoir may be more useful to one village (for example, it has no other water source) than to the other (which may have other sources).

8.270 *If a once-born . . . lowest part*: a once-born man is a Śūdra. The implied background of this harsh punishment is the creation myth of the Puruṣasūkta (*ṚV* 10.90), which has become a root metaphor in the Dharma literature. The twice-born here probably refers specifically to Brahmins, who were born from the mouth (speech). When a man born from the feet uses speech to abuse a man born from the mouth, he loses his right to the tongue, the organ of speech.

8.277 *exactly the same punishment*: when a Vaiśya abuses a Śūdra or vice versa, the punishment is the same as for a Brahmin abusing a Kṣatriya or vice versa.

8.284 *sent into exile*: this term (*pravāsyaḥ*) can also mean imposing capital punishment (see 8.123 n.).

8.287 *total fine*: (*sarvadaṇḍam*) commentators offer diverse explanations. The most obvious interpretation is that all his wealth is assessed as a fine, possibly when the man is too poor to shoulder the full medical expenses of his victim.

8.303 *his sacrificial session*: (*sattra*) see 2.106 n. Here the reign of a king is compared to a sacrificial session of long duration at which the gift of safety (6.39 n.) to his subjects is considered equal to the sacrificial fee. See also 8.306.

8.320 *corporal punishment*: the Sanskrit term *vadha* in the legal literature is used both for corporal punishment, including mutilation and amputation, and for capital punishment. It is often difficult to tell from the context which is meant. In this verse, given the amount stolen, I think corporal punishment is meant. In the next verse, on the other hand, capital punishment is clearly meant, because verse 322 gives lesser forms of corporal punishment.

8.324 *time and purpose*: the meaning appears to be this. If an article was stolen when it was urgently needed (e.g. stealing a weapon during a time of war), the theft becomes more serious. Likewise, the purpose served by the article may make the theft more severe, such as stealing the medicine of a sick man (cf. 9.293 n.).

8.325 *in the case . . . of the heel*: this half-verse has been subject to much misunderstanding. One interpretation takes *sthūrikā* as the nose. Following several commentators, Bühler translates: 'for piercing (the nostrils of) a barren cow.' I think this interpretation is mistaken; within a section dealing with stealing, there is no reason to introduce the mutilation of animals. Lariviere (see his translation of *NSm* 1940) has correctly identified *sthūrā* as the Achilles tendon; and *sthūrikā* cannot be other than a synonym for it. See Olivelle forthcoming *c* for further comments on this reading.

8.332 *in the presence . . . outside his presence*: this verse is clearly a versification of *AŚ* 3.17.1–2: 'Violence is a forcible act in the presence (of the owner). In the absence (of the owner) it is theft'. It appears that the *Arthaśāstra* tradition coined the technical terms *anvayavat* and *niranvaya* for thefts and robberies committed in the presence or outside the presence of the owner. The term *sānvaya* used by Manu in 8.198 and 331 appears to be a synonym of *anvayavat* created possibly for metrical exigencies. Although robbery is more serious than theft, yet in 331 theft (in the presence of the owner) is considered the lesser offence, possibly because it may imply an implicit consent, especially if the person taking the article is known to the owner. These two technical terms appear to have fallen into disuse within the later Dharma tradition.

8.336 *In a case . . . fixed rule*: this is quite a significant rule. If taken at its face value, it implies that even the king was not above the law! Commentators point out that in the case of the king, the fine should be thrown into water (9.245).

8.337–8 *With respect . . . good or bad*: the penalty is calculated on the basis of the value of the stolen goods. In general, the principle is that lighter penalties are assessed for people of higher classes. But here a different principle is enunciated, more in keeping with the penances, where the severity of the penance for the same offence increases for those of higher classes.

8.342 *When someone ties . . . as for theft*: clearly these acts must have been viewed as not real theft, otherwise there is no reason to insist that they should be viewed as theft. The first two acts fit this category well; the reference is probably to untying someone else's cattle so they may get lost, or tying up (i.e. impounding) another's cattle in one's own property, possibly to make use of them.

8.344 *violence*: the distinction between violence and physical assault (8.279–301) is not readily apparent from their treatment in Manu. In the *AŚ* (3.17), on the other hand, *sāhasa* (violence) is clearly defined as forcible seizure of property, including robbery; whereas physical assault does not involve taking the other's property.

8.345 *someone who is . . . with a rod*: these three individuals refer to the previous three grounds for litigation.

8.366 *bride-price*: it is unlikely that this provision forces the man to marry the girl he has violated. It simply means that he should pay reparation to the father in the form of the bride-price that he would have otherwise received at her wedding. See verse 369 where even another woman who violates a virgin has to pay a similar price.

8.367 *two of his fingers*: the cutting of two fingers is prescribed for any deflowering of a virgin short of sexual intercourse. The reason is probably that the violator used his fingers for the sexual act. See verse 370 where a similar punishment is prescribed also for a woman who violates a virgin.

8.374 *loses everything*: that is, he loses all his property, as well as his life.

8.386 *The king . . . world of Indra*: the five crimes referred to here are actually the five grounds for litigation (11–15), all involving some degree of violence.

8.396 *He must not . . . wear those clothes*: the point of this verse is to lay down minimum ethical standards on washermen. They are not to tie up a load of clothes within a cloth that has been given for washing (e.g. a large piece of cloth such as a sari). The meaning of the final phrase is that he should not rent out clothes that have been given for washing.

8.397 *A weaver . . . fine of 12*: the weight of the yarn would have increased in the process of making the cloth, with the addition of starch. The fine of twelve is interpreted either as money (Paṇa), twelve times the weight of the cloth, or a twelfth part of the yarn.

CHAPTER NINE

9.1 *when they are together . . . apart*: Manu provides here different rules by which married people should live when they live together and when they are somehow apart, either temporarily, as when the husband is away, or permanently, as when the husband or wife dies. See 9.74 for rules when the husband is missing.

9.8 *The husband . . . again in her*: this is a variant of a verse in *AitB* 7.13. For a discussion of the son as one's very self born again in the wife, see Olivelle 1993: 41–46. My translation of *jāyātvam* (lit. 'state of being a wife') is non-literal; but the abstract noun in Sanskrit does carry a pregnant and multi-valent meaning, indicating both the nature of a wife and the etymology of 'wife'.

9.17 *Bed . . . to women*: note the close parallel between this verse and the assigning of the various duties to different classes at 1.87–91.

9.18 *'Without strength . . . untruth'*: this may have been viewed by the author as a vedic citation; see the beginning of the very next verse. In the *TS* 6.5.8.2 we have a very similar passage: 'Therefore, women are without strength, do not inherit, and speak more submissively than even a poor man.' See also *BDh* 2.3.46.

9.20 *Here is . . . of it*: this text is found in *ŚāṅGṛ* 3.13; variant in *Āpastamba Śrautasūtra*, 1.9.9. The exact reference of 'of it' is unclear, but the likelihood is that it refers to the true character (8.19) of women, of which the cited text is illustrative.

9.23 *Akṣamālā . . . respect*: Akṣamālā, better known as Arundhatī, was the wife of the sage Vasiṣṭha. Although textual sources give her a high pedigree, the commentators state that she was born in a low caste but attained a high status because of her marriage. Mandapāla was an ascetic who was barred from celestial worlds because he had failed to father sons. He then became a Śārṅgi bird and mated with the female Śārṅgī, Jaritā. The children born from this union excelled in their knowledge of the Veda (*MBh* 1.220–5).

9.28 *obedient service*: this term (*śuśrūṣā*) usually refers to the service rendered by a person of lower rank to one of higher rank, especially by a pupil to his teacher. The meaning here is uncertain, some taking it as referring to hospitality and others to taking care of the husband's physical needs. The latter is supported by the more explicit statement in 9.86.

9.32 *It is acknowledged . . . of the field*: the question centres on what happens when the sire (*kartṛ*) is different from the husband (*bhartṛ*). The first half-verse is rather elliptical: the first foot gives the consensus opinion that a son belongs to the husband; the second foot introduces the dispute, which centres around the man who fathers the son; and the second half of the verse spells out the two positions in this dispute briefly. Arguments in support of the first position are given in verses 36–40, and arguments for the second position in verses 41–55.

9.40 *For one kind . . . sprouts forth*: there seems to be a lacuna here. The argument for the dominance of the seed should have included sociological conclusions from the biological observations. See, for example, *VaDh* 6.8–9, where precisely such conclusions are drawn. The suspicion of a lacuna here is strengthened by the beginning of the second argument; this verse begins with 'therefore', but the statement in it is unrelated to the previous verse, which supported quite the opposite view.

9.43–4 *When someone shoots . . . owns the arrow*: the examples reinforce the notion that a virgin belongs to the person who first deflowers her, assumed here to be her husband. This is true with a virgin field as with a virgin girl. So, the first king, Pṛthu (after whom is named *pṛthivī*, Earth; cf. 7.41–2 n.), who tilled the ground, took possession of the entire earth; kings coming after him do not have such a claim. So also a man who first clears the forest has claim to it. The image changes with the hunt, but here too the one who first wounds the unwounded (virgin) animal lays claim to it. The Sanskrit term *kha*, which I have translated 'vitals', literally means hole; Bühler translates as 'wound'. I want to thank Professor Wezler for suggesting that the meaning might be the vital or mortal parts of the animal, the parts at which a hunter will shoot an arrow. Shooting another arrow at the wound created by the first arrow does not make much sense. Note also the interesting parallel between the arrow, the implied plough, and the penis.

9.52 *agreement*: beyond the agreement that the owners of the field and the seed may reach, the reference here is to leviratic union, where the biological father is officially appointed (*niyoga*) to raise a son for the woman's husband, a topic that immediately follows (8.57–70).

9.54 *When a seed . . . its fruit*: the simile here is of a sower in a neighbouring field. If some of the seeds he sows are carried by the wind or by a stream of water (probably in a paddy field) to an adjacent field, the crop that is produced from those seeds belongs to the owner of that field.

9.55 *This is the Law . . . buffaloes*: this is a rather strange and unexpected ending to the argument. It elevates a simile, already given in verse 48, to the level of a proposition. See my earlier comments about possible lacunae in this section: 9.40n.

9.57 *wife of an elder*: it may well be that here the term 'elder' (*guru*: see Note on the Translation, p. xlvi) refers specifically to the father, because in the absence of the father the eldest brother becomes a surrogate father to his younger siblings (9.108).

9.61 *Some who . . . such women*: commentators cite a proverb: 'A man who has one son is a sonless man.' The reason clearly is the danger that a single son may die before he himself can father a son to continue the line, which was the very purpose of the appointment.

9.64 *Twice-born men . . . eternal Law*: this and the following verse contradict the opinion on levirate just expressed in verses 57–63. I think that here also Manu may be engaging in an argument with an opponent, whose view is given first and then refuted. Manu's own view appears to be that levirate is morally reprehensible in the case of a widow; the only allowance he makes is when the husband dies after the betrothal (8.69–70).

9.70 *dressed in white*: the social meaning of colours is one area where cultural perceptions may be diametrically opposed. White may indicate the colour of the wedding dress in the West, but in India it is the colour of mourning prescribed for the girl who has lost her husband.

9.88 *not attained the proper age*: the probable meaning is that the girl has not reached puberty (supported by its mention in the very next verse). I think the first half of the verse implies that a suitor has come asking for the girl's hand. Within this context one can understand the second half: one should give the girl to such a suitor even if she is below age.

9.104 *have passed on*: the ambiguity of this expression has given rise to different interpretations. That the reference is clearly to the death of the parents is indicated by the last foot of the verse: 'they are incompetent while those two are alive.'

9.120–1 *If a younger . . . in accordance with the Law*: the issue here is the share of a son born through a leviratic union. Should he, as the heir of the eldest brother, receive the pre-emptive share reserved for the eldest? The answer given is no; and the argument is that the biological father of the son is the 'principal' and not the biological mother, through whom the son's connection to the eldest brother is established. Therefore, the leviratic son (i.e. the nephew) should receive the same share as all brothers. See a similar situation in 9.134 with regard to the 'female-son'.

9.126 *Subrahmaṇyā*: this is the name of a ritual invocation addressed to Indra inviting him to partake of the Soma. See *AitB* 6.3.

9.127 *'female-son'*: the term *putrikā*, which is a feminine construction of *putra* ('son'), has generally been translated as 'appointed daughter', an institution that is also found in other Indo-European cultures. This translation is somewhat misleading, because, as Jolly (1885: 147–9) has pointed out, she is not merely the one who produces a son for her father but is actually a 'son' in her own right. Many legal texts list her immediately after the natural son and before other kinds of sons (see 8.158–60) within the context of inheritance. See also verse 130 about her right to inherit the paternal estate. Although somewhat awkward, I have opted for 'female-son' to highlight the fact that she is truly a son who is female. For an examination of this institution in India and elsewhere, see Schmidt 1989.

9.128–9 *In ancient times . . . King Soma*: this story of Dakṣa's daughters is told in *MBh* 1.70.7–8.

9.150 *ornament*: the exact reference is unclear, given that a family would have more than one ornament. The commentator Medhātithi gives the example of the father's ring.

one share from the best property: the meaning is unclear. Some commentators say that the property is divided into shares and the most excellent of these shares is given to the eldest, while others take it to mean that the most excellent items of the property are divided into shares and the best of these given to the eldest.

9.154 *Whether he has . . . no son at all*: if we take 'proper son' as a son by a Brahmin wife, then the man may have sons by other wives. In this case also, the son by a Śūdra wife must get only one-tenth of the property. If the man has no son at all, that is, no son from a wife of an upper class, and the son from a Śūdra wife is the only son he has, then too he must give that son only one-tenth of the property. The rest of the property should be divided by the next-of-kin, following the method for a man who dies without issue.

9.156 *When all the sons . . . equal shares*: this appears clearly to be an alternative (preferable?) to the intricate rules spelled out earlier.

9.162 *If a natural son . . . not the other*: the verse is obscure. Some commentators assume this situation. A husband who is impotent gets a son through appointment (*niyoga*); after that his impotency is cured and he fathers a natural son. In this case, the natural son inherits the entire estate of his father, not the son begotten on the wife. Something like this appears to be the intent of the verse, especially in light of what is said in verses 163 and 164. Other commentators contemplate a situation where one of two brothers dies while the estate is undivided, and the living brother produces a son for the deceased brother by appointment on his widow. The question is whether the latter son can claim more than one share, because he is the leviratic son of the dead brother and the biological son of his uncle. This is an attractive interpretation; but what is said in the subsequent verses appears to contradict it. See the parallel at 9.191.

9.165 *but the other ten . . . and the estate*: this verse is once again not altogether clear. Many interpretations are offered by commentators. The meaning appears to be that the sons enumerated later inherit the estate in the absence of those enumerated earlier (9.184). This appears to be a version of the so-called obstructed inheritance (*sapratibandha*): Jolly 1885, 176. See *YDh* 2.132.

9.166 *principal son*: the meaning here is that the natural son is the standard son, the son in the true sense of the term, whereas other sons are in some way secondary or substitutes. Indeed, in verse 180 the eleven other sons are in fact called substitutes. See the identical wording with regard to principal and secondary rules at 11.30.

9.179 *The son . . . settled Law*: the expression *dāsadāsī* (lit. 'slave woman of a slave') has been subject to much misunderstanding. Rocher (2002) has demonstrated conclusively that *dāsa* and *dāsī*, although literally 'slave man' and 'slave woman', refer in fact to a Śūdra man and woman, respectively. In other words, *dāsa* here is a synonym for Śudra. In the present context, the Śūdra has fathered a son either by an unmarried Śūdra woman (*dāsī*) or by a Śūdra woman married to some other Śūdra man (i.e. not to the father of her son).

9.182–3 *If among several brothers . . . women who have sons*: variants of these provisions occur also in *VaDh* 17.10–11 and *ViDh* 15.41–2. The connection between the two verses is not altogether clear. The second clearly refers to a polygamous marriage. According to Wezler (1991–2), when one brother has a son all his other brothers also become 'men who have sons' because through that son they all are freed from the debt to their father of bearing a son to continue the line. Likewise, the common wives are relieved of the burden of bearing a son for their common husband. At a linguistic level, moreover, a man can claim 'I have a son' when his father gets a grandson, just as a woman can claim 'I have a son' when her husband gets a son.

9.186 *To three . . . for a fifth*: the three are father, grandfather, and great-grandfather. These are the three to whom the standard monthly ancestral offering is offered. The person who is obliged to make the offering, that is the son, is the fourth. A fifth individual whether grandson or great-great-grandfather does not enter into this ritual picture. When the grandson becomes the offerer, his father becomes one of the three and the father's grandfather falls out of the picture.

9.191 *When two . . . of the other*: at issue here is a woman married consecutively to two men who have each fathered a son. The men are dead and their estates are in the hands of their common wife. In this case, each son inherits the estate of his biological father. See the parallel at 9.162 and the note to it.

9.211 *his share is not lost*: that is, his share has to be reserved for his own heirs; it cannot be divided among themselves by his brothers.

9.216 *A son born . . . with them*: the context is a child born to the father after he has partitioned his estate among his sons. That child will inherit the father's portion of the divided estate and any other property the father may have acquired after the partition.

9.220 *ritual procedure for sons*: that is, the ritual procedures for establishing these kinds of sons. We can thus understand why the natural son is left out, because he is not created by any ritual procedure as in the case of the leviratic or adopted sons.

9.227 *In a former age*: this may be a reference to the calamities that struck the epic heroes Yudhiṣṭhira and Nala as a result of their addiction to gambling.

9.231 *inflamed by the heat of money*: the image is of passion for money through bribes.

9.232 *constituents of the realm*: (*prakṛti*) see 9.292 for the six constituents. In the present context, however, the reference may be more specifically to the ministers.

9.233 *not bring it back again*: the meaning appears to be that the king should not retry cases that have already been settled; this may also refer to matters settled by the former administration in territories he conquers.

9.242 *to be executed*: (*pravāsanam*) could also mean exile or banishment (8.123n.). I think the argument here goes something like this. A Brahmin should be given the middle fine of 500 Paṇas (if he does it thoughtlessly?) or sent into exile without property confiscation (if done deliberately?). In the case of others, property is confiscated if done thoughtlessly (and then exile as in the case of the Brahmin?) and they are executed if done deliberately.

9.251 *Carrying out . . . been acquired*: this verse takes us right back to the section on the king's duties of Chapter 7. Manu has clearly embedded his section on legal procedure squarely within this treatment of the duties of a king, which concludes at verse 324.

9.252 *eradication of thorns*: the word 'thorns' here is a technical term for every type of criminal and social parasite (9.259–60) within the kingdom. Here Manu returns to the theme of the general duties of the king, after the long disquisition on legal procedure that occupied all of Chapter 8 and much of Chapter 9.

9.266 *patrolled by . . . agents*: mobile and stationary squads refer to regular police and army units employed in internal security. Mobile agents work for the secret service, which employs besides the mobile agents also agents resident in spy establishments that are stationary. For a detailed study of secret agents, see Scharfe 1993: 204–39.

9.279 *clean execution*: (*śuddhavadha*) this is another instance of Manu employing *Arthaśāstra* terminology. This expression is not found in any other Dharma text. It occurs only in the *AŚ* 4.9.2; 4.10.16; 4.11.2, 15, 26. What is meant is a neat and clean execution, probably decapitation. Such an execution would be different from a 'colourful execution' involving various forms of torture and impalement. See 9.291 n.

9.280 *elephants, horses, or chariots*: in all likelihood, the reference is to those owned by the king. A parallel passage in *AŚ* 4.11.7 explicitly refers to king's elephants, horses, and chariots.

9.287 *If a man deals . . . middle fine*: the meaning appears to be that the man barters commodities that should be bartered as equal (e.g. one measure of rice for one measure of sesame seeds; see this principle articulated in 10.94) in an unequal manner either directly or in terms of price. That is, he buys one commodity at one price and sells the other at a different price.

9.291 *jacks up the price of seed corn*: the reference is probably to price-gouging during sowing time when there may be a shortage of seed corn.

executed with mutilation: such an execution preceded by torture and mutilation is opposed to the clean execution consisting of decapitation (see 9.279 n.).

9.293 *the time and the purpose*: stealing agricultural implements, for example, is more serious during times of cultivation; likewise medicine when someone is sick, and weapons during a time of war (cf. 8.324 n.).

9.303 *The king . . . and Earth*: these eight guardian deities of the directions are the gods from whose particles the king was initially created (see 7.4); the only difference is that Earth is here substituted for Kubera. He must, therefore, imitate their activities.

9.304–5 *four months . . . eight months*: in northern India, the monsoon rains come during the summer season; ideally the rainy season is depicted as lasting four months. Here Indra, the god of rain, is said to rule over these months. The remaining eight months constitute the dry season when the sun shines and extracts water from the earth.

9.312 *In this and . . . in others*: clearly, this concluding verse is directly connected with verse 293 and what preceded it. The intervening sections had little to do with the eradication of thorns. I suspect that they are an interpolation; so also, in all likelihood, the section on Brahmins that follows (9.313–23).

9.314 *They made the fire ... wane and wax*: these are well-known legends recorded in the epic *Mahābhārata* concerning great Brahmin sages. Bhr̥gu cursed Fire to be an omnivore when he claimed to have the right to take Bhr̥gu's wife (*MBh* 1.6; 12.329.43). When the Ocean refused to come when called, Vaḍavāmukha cursed him to become undrinkable and made him salty with his sweat (*MBh* 12.329.48). Because Moon, to whom he had given twenty-seven of his daughters in marriage (see 9.129), favoured one and neglected the others, Dakṣa cursed him to wane and wax (*MBh* 9.34.40–67; 12.329.45–6).

9.321 *Kṣatriya from Brahmin*: this doctrine is articulated already in the *BāU*, 1.4.11, which calls *brahma* (the priestly power) the womb of the *kṣatra* (the ruling power).

CHAPTER TEN

10.5 *in the direct order of class*: given that the wife belongs to the same class as the husband, this specification makes little sense within the context of this verse. It may well be stated here, in the manner of *sūtra* texts, so as to govern what is stated in the verses that follow (6–10), namely the marriage of higher-class men to lower-class wives.

10.16–17 *From a Śūdra ... a Sūta*: these verses and this entire second discourse on mixed classes is suspect. They basically repeat what has been stated in verses 11–12. Further, the term *apasada* ('low-born') is defined here as sons born in the inverse order, whereas earlier in verse 10 it is defined as sons born in the direct order. The last phrase here is elliptical. From a Vaiśya man by Kṣatriya and Brahmin girls are born Māgadha and Vaideha, respectively; and from a Kṣatriya man by a Brahmin girl is born a Sūta (see verse 11).

10.21–3 *From a Vrātya ... Sātvata*: many of these are ethnic and tribal names. This passage appears to be an attempt to account for ethnic groups within the ideology of caste intermixture (see 10.43–5). See a similar attempt in *GDh* 4.21.

10.24 *By adultery ... classes*: here we begin yet another discourse on mixed classes, a section that is also quite suspect. Note the final foot of this verse 'originate the intermixture of classes', which parallels the final foot of the closing verse of the first discourse (10.12).

10.28 *As from two ... excluded men*: once again we have an elliptical verse. The meaning appears to be this. From a woman of two of the three upper classes (that is, from a Brahmin and a Kṣatriya woman), a Brahmin begets a son that is his own self (9.8n.).

10.36 *From a Niṣāda ... a Meda*: the women from whom these are begotten are not mentioned. In the case of a Kārāvara, commentators say that the mother is a Vaideha; in the case of an Andra, a Kārāvara; and in the case of a Meda, a Niṣāda.

10.38 *Sopāka*: this term may be a Prakr̥tic form of the Sanskrit Śvapāka (10.19, 51).

10.44 *Puṇḍrakas . . . Daradas*: these are clearly ethnic names. Coḍas and Draviḍas were ethnic groups of the south (Dravidians). Kāmbojas were a group in what is today north-western Pakistan. Pahlavas (Parthian) = Persians; Yavana = Greeks; Cīna = Chinese.

10.46 *low-born . . . delinquent-born*: the distinction between these two categories (*apasada* and *apadhvaṃsaja*) is not altogether clear. In this verse, the low-born appear to indicate mixed-caste individuals born in the proper order of classes (higher man and lower woman). This is also the meaning of the term in verse 10. In verse 17, however, those born in the inverse order (lower man and higher woman) are designated low-born. The delinquent-born here appear to indicate precisely such individuals born in the inverse order.

10.50 *well-recognizable*: the meaning is that these people should wear certain kinds of clothes and other marks that would identify their castes. See the punishment of low-caste men wearing the marks of Āryas at 9.260.

10.51 *Apapātras*: it appears that this term in its early usage referred to certain individuals excluded from society because of some serious lapse. One interpretation of the term is that when an Apapātra eats food from someone in a vessel, that vessel should be thrown away. See also the mention of broken vessels in verses 52 and 54. Another interpretation is that the food should not be placed in vessels that they hold in their hands but either placed on the ground or held by someone else.

10.57 *without the proper complexion*: all commentators and translators take this compound (*varṇāpetam*) to mean a man who is outside the social classes. This makes little sense, because the question at issue is how to identify a man who looks more or less like an Ārya. I think *varṇa* here means colour or complexion rather than caste or social class. That colour of skin and hair was used as an identifier of a Brahmin is evident from the interesting remarks of the grammarian Patañjali (second century BCE; on Pāṇini 2.2.6), who describes a Brāhmaṇa as 'white in colour, of pure conduct, with hair that is yellowish or reddish brown'.

10.62 *without artifice*: the expression clearly refers to anything that is not overly crafted (in cooking, in embellishment, etc.); and here it means that the man does this with a pure and simple heart, without expectation of any reward.

10.65 *so does a Brahmin the rank of a Śūdra*: the meaning is not altogether clear. One possible meaning is that the offspring of a Brahmin man from a Śūdra woman (i.e. a Pāraśava) will become a pure Śūdra in the seventh generation by marrying Śūdra women.

10.74 *that whose source is the Veda*: the meaning of this expression (*brahmayonisthāḥ*) is quite uncertain and commentators offer diverse interpretations: persons devoted to the contemplation of Brahman, persons born from a Brahmin father and mother, persons devoted to the activities proper to them. The most cogent explanation is that *brahmayoni* ('that whose source is the Veda') refers to *dharma* (see 2.25). So the expression refers to a man who is firmly established in the Law.

10.83 *dependence on others*: the reference may be to the condition of a tenant farmer. If a Brahmin or a Kṣatriya has fallen on hard times, it is unlikely that he has his own farm to cultivate.

10.103 *like fire and water*: water (specifically flowing water in rivers) and fire are viewed as pure by definition. See 9.318 where fire is said to be undefiled by burning a corpse. The *VaDh* 28.1 cites a proverb: 'A woman is not polluted by a lover, a Brahmin by vedic rites, water by urine and faeces, and fire by the act of burning.'

10.105–8 *Ajīgarta . . . hand of a Cāṇḍāla*: the story of Ajīgarta is told in the *AitB* 7.13–16, although there the father did not intend to eat the son. The story must have changed over time. The story of Vāmadeva eating dog's meat is told in the *MBh* 13.94–5. The story of Bharadvāja is told in Sāyaṇa's commentary on the *R̥V* 6.45.31. Viśvāmitra's story is the most famous and is told in the *MBh* 12.139.

10.122 *when he has the name 'Brahmin' attached to him*: the meaning appears to be that when a Śūdra serves a Brahmin, that name attaches to him; e.g. 'he is a Brahmin's servant'. By some extension of the name, he can call himself a Brahmin!

10.124 *They*: the antecedent is not certain, but it must refer to Brahmins who employ Śūdras.

10.126 *he is not prohibited . . . the Law*: commentators explain that Śūdras are not prohibited from doing some acts prescribed by Law, such as bathing, performing the five great sacrifices, and the like.

CHAPTER ELEVEN

11.1–2 *A man seeking . . . in vedic learning*: Manu ended the last chapter saying: 'Next, I will explain the splendid rules pertaining to penance.' Instead of penance, however, he spends forty-three verses on unrelated topics, turning to the subject of penance only in verse 44. I believe that the first forty-three verses represent the work of redactors.

11.3 *sacrificial arena*: techincally this is the area measured out and consecrated for a vedic sacrifice and containing the three vedic fires. The meaning appears to be that if these individuals come to beg while a sacrifice is taking place, they should be given food and a sacrificial fee, as if they were priests.

11.5 *When a married man . . . expenses*: after this verse the vulgate gives here the following as verse 6, which is eliminated in the critical edition: 'A man should give wealth to Brahmins who know the Veda and live in solitude according to his ability; he will thus attain heaven after death.'

11.11–12 *While a righteous . . . complete the sacrifice*: opinion is divided over who actually takes the property from the Vaiśya: the sacrificer himself or the king on behalf of the sacrificer. For a justification of such an act, see 1.100–1.

11.16 *the rule . . . next day*: the meaning is that he should take only sufficient food to last just that day. This rule is often associated with certain types of ascetics: 4.7.

11.19 *both*: that is, the man from whom he takes and the man to whom he gives.

11.21 *such a man*: that is, the man referred to in verses 16–17. This reference makes the authenticity of the intervening verses suspect.

11.27 *turn of the year*: the new year begins on the first day of the bright fortnight of Caitra (March–April).

11.41 *killing a hero*: in *GDh* 15.6 and *VaDh* 1.18 a man who extinguishes his sacred fires is called 'a killer of a hero'. The meaning clearly is that by extinguishing the fire he has killed a hero, fire being the hero among the gods. This is clearly spelled out in *TS* 1.5.2: 'Clearly, he is a slayer of the hero of gods who extinguishes the fire.' Manu, however, says that extinguishing the fire is *equal to* the killing of a hero. Within this context, the hero may not be the fire itself but some other man. Most commentators take it to be the son.

11.47 *When a twice-born . . . that penance*: this appears to be a verse introducing verses 48–53 that deal with evil diseases and deformities believed to be caused by either fate or by sins committed in a past life. Such 'sins' are different from the sins actually committed that were the subject of verses 45–6.

11.51 *steals speech*: this appears to be an early indictment of plagiarism. It is interpreted as plagiarism by several commentators, one stating that the man actually writes his name as the author of a book written by someone else. Other interpretations include a man who steals books and a man who steals the Veda by eavesdropping on someone reciting it.

lame legs: additional verse given as 52 in Bühler's translation but omitted in the critical edition: 'A man who steals a lamp becomes blind; and a man who extinguishes one becomes one-eyed. By causing injury, a man becomes frequently sick; and by not causing injury, a man becomes free from sickness.'

11.55 *drinking liquor, stealing*: it appears that drinking liquor becomes a grievous sin only when done by Brahmins: see *GDh* 2.20. Stealing is also a grievous sin when it involves the gold of Brahmins: see 11.57, 100.

11.56 *A lie concerning one's superiority*: that is, falsely claiming a superior status either by birth or with respect to other attributes such as learning and virtue.

11.57 *killing a friend*: the Sanskrit term *vadha* can mean both killing and causing physical hurt (8.320 n.). Here killing is probably intended, in light of verse 89, where the term most probably means killing.

11.62 *breaking the vow*: given the seriousness of the offence, the reference is probably to the breaking of the vow of chastity by a vedic student. This is confirmed by its inclusion in the section on penances for these sins (11.119ff.).

11.64 *root-witchcraft*: the meaning of this expression (*mūlakarma*) is quite unclear. The commentators are unanimous in taking it to mean some kind of witchcraft by which another person is brought under one's power : see 9.290 where the meaning is clearly some form of witchcraft. In *Av* 4.28.6 *mūlakṛt* ('root-cutter') also refers to some kind of witchcraft.

11.68 *cause exclusion from caste*: it is unclear how exactly this differs from 'falling from caste'. Clearly it is a lesser sin than the latter. The commentators offer no help. It is possible that this sin did not result in the formal excommunication of the sinner (see 11.183–6); it may have resulted merely in social ostracism within the caste.

11.76 *league*: (*yojana*) this is a distance of approximately 9 miles or 14.5 kilometres. The total distance he walks comes to about 900 miles.

11.78 *walk . . . Sarasvatī*: one commentator says that the penitent starts from Prabhāsa and goes up along the river bank to Plakṣasravaṇa.

11.82 *Thus . . . twelfth year*: this verse is directly connected with verse 73 and appears to ignore verses 74–81, casting doubt on their authenticity.

11.83 *by proclaiming . . . horse sacrifice*: 'gods of earth' are Brahmins, and 'gods of men' are kings or, more generally, Kṣatriyas. Commentators believe that the gathering is for the purpose of a horse sacrifice.

11.88 *One must . . . menstrual period*: the implicit understanding here is that the foetus is that of a Brahmin (see *GDh* 22.13). The argument is that a foetus without developed sexual organs will turn out to be a male. The *VaDh* 20.24 says that the foetus can be turned into a male through the power of pre-natal rites such as the *puṃsavana* ('quickening a male child'). Aborting such a foetus, therefore, is equivalent to murdering a Brahmin (always assumed to be male, because the murder of a female does not carry the same sanction). A Kṣatriya or a Vaiśya, when they have been consecrated for a sacrifice (*dīkṣita*), is considered a Brahmin at least in some ritual traditions: see *Āpastamba Śrautasūtra* (10.11.5–6): 'A man who is consecrated for a sacrifice is indeed born from the Veda (*brahman*). Therefore, even a Kṣatriya or a Vaiśya, it has been taught, is a Brahmin.' A woman soon after her menstruation is called by the technical term *ātreyī*, which is given an interesting etymological spin in *VaDh* 20.35–6. The woman is then in her fertile period (3.46–50) and killing her is tantamount to killing a future Brahmin. In this case there is the added possibility that the woman is pregnant. For a detailed study of this provision, see Jamison 1991: 213–23.

11.93 *banner*: in *BDh* 1.18.18 the banner is specified as 'liquor banner', probably a banner that advertised a tavern. Commentators specify a drinking cup.

11.94 *filth*: Manu plays on the word *mala*, which can mean any filthy or putrid substance (here fermentation being equated with putrefaction) and also the filth of sin (see 11.72, 102, 107 for the latter meaning).

11.95 *It should . . . so are all*: the issue here appears to be whether all kinds of liquor are forbidden or only certain kinds. Liquor made from grain was explicitly forbidden in verse 94; this verse extends that prohibition to all three kinds. The *VaDh* 20.19 appears to single out liquor called *surā* as particularly pernicious and prescribes a lighter penance for drinking non-*surā* kinds of liquor (see note to next verse). Commentators are divided about the meaning of *mādhvī*, the third type of liquor. Some take it as derived from honey (a kind of mead), whereas others think that it is made from a flower of the Madhuka tree (see next note).

11.96 *Intoxicants, liquor, and spirits*: there appears to be a distinction made here between liquor (*surā*) and intoxicant (*madya*). The latter has probably a broader meaning, whereas *surā* is more specific and viewed as more pernicious (see previous note). The meaning of 'spirit' (*āsava*, literally 'pressing') is unclear; commentators call it a variety of *madya;* given its name, it may refer to some type of wine.

11.97 *blabber vedic texts*: most commentators take this to mean that an intoxicated Brahmin may not be able to pronounce vedic texts correctly or recite them when he is impure. The text, however, does not specify this. The likely meaning is that an intoxicated Brahmin would recite the Veda in the presence of people who are forbidden to hear it.

11.98 *brahman*: the term is used with a *double entendre* here. On the one hand, *brahman* is the Veda residing in the Brahmin's memory; on the other hand and closely related to the first meaning, it is his Brahmanical nature (*brāhmaṇya*) that makes him a Brahmin (see 1.93 n.).

11.100–1 *A Brahmin who . . . ascetic toil*: there is something amiss in these two verses. The king takes the pestle, which has not been introduced in the first verse. Traditionally, the thief was supposed to take the pestle with him (see 8.315). Then, in the last half verse, the thief is purified by being killed. Given that the thief is a Brahmin, we must assume that the king kills him. But this would go against the general prohibition of the death penalty in the case of Brahmins. Finally, a Brahmin is said to be freed from the sin by ascetic toil alone. The verses are garbled; I assume that sections of these verses have been taken from different sources and condensed here.

11.104 *metal cylinder*: the meaning of the Sanskrit term *sūrmī* is not altogether clear. It is certainly a cylindrical object made of metal. Most commentators take it to be a metal image of a woman. At *ĀpDh* 1.28.15, however, the criminal is said to enter it, which points to something, such as a column, that is hollow. The recent study by Falk (2001) has cast much light on the history of the term *sūrmī*. Falk demonstrates that originally the term referred to a clay cylinder with openings at both ends for casting metal, that is, a primitive furnace. Such a cylinder was about the size of a human being; it could be both embraced and entered. The obsolescence of this kind of metal casting and the subsequent loss of the original meaning may have changed the term's meaning to that of a female figure, especially within the context of this penance for sexual misconduct.

11.110 *During two months*: although the connection between this and the preceding verse is not altogether clear, it appears that the two months mentioned here are in addition to the one month mentioned in the previous verse. Thus, the entire penance lasts for three months, as made clear in verse 116.

11.111 *follow those cows*: much is implied here. The vow consists of attending to cows during three months. During the day the man follows the cows into the pasture or the forest; brings them back to the cow pen in the evening; attends to all their needs; and sits in the cow pen by their side during the night. For a literary description of this observance, see Kālidāsa's *Raghuvaṃśa* (1.88–95; 2.1–75). On the ascetic practice of standing during the day and remaining seated at night, see 6.22 n.

11.119 *cooked oblation*: the procedure for cooked oblations (*pākayajña*) is given at the very beginning of most *Gṛhyasūtras*: see *ŚāṅGṛ* 1.1.

11.120–2 *After offering . . . and Fire*: 'Teacher' is an epithet of Bṛhaspati, the teacher of the gods, also identified with the planet Jupiter. The parallel passage in *GDh* 25.1–2 reads: 'So, they ask: "Into how many does a student who has broken his vow of chastity enter?" Into the Maruts with his breaths; into Indra with his strength; into Bṛhaspati with the splendour of his vedic learning; and into just the Fire with everything else.'

11.134 *castrate*: all the commentators appear to take this provision as referring to humans. Coming, as it does, right in the middle of a list of animals, in this verse the term certainly could refer to a castrated ox.

11.147 *Vāruṇī*: commentators take this to include liquor made from honey (*mādhvī*) and molasses (*gauḍī*) and to exclude that made from grain: see 11.95 n., 96 n.

11.154 *even though they may be pure*: (*medhyāni*) that is, even though the substances in their natural state may be fit for eating.

until it has been excreted: the *GDh* 23.23 and *VaDh* 23.30 use this expression for the total evacuation of the bowels. According to *GDh* 23.24, this happens in three days, whereas the *VaDh* implies seven days.

11.166 *five products of the cow*: milk, curd, ghee, urine, and dung.

11.177 *observance*: adultery by a man is counted among the secondary sins causing loss of caste in 11.60. The penance for such sins is given in 11.118: either the lunar penance (11.217) or the cow-vow described in 11.109–17. For adultery as a crime, see 8.332–59.

11.180 *I have . . . four kinds of sinner*: if my hypothesis that the previous four sections (11.127–79: which I have called 'Excursus') are interpolations is right, then the four sinners refer to the categories mentioned in 11.55–71. The problem is how we come up with four. The grievous and secondary sins causing loss of caste make two. I think the third is sins that cause exclusion from caste (11.68). Three other sins are enumerated in 11.69–71; but I think Manu thinks of these three as a single large category, because when dealing with the penances for them he deals with them together in a single verse (11.126).

11.184 *A slave woman*: the term *dāsī* here may also refer simply to a Śūdra woman: see 9.179n.

11.190 *No one . . . cleansed*: this verse appears to conclude Manu's discussion of penance. The excursus on miscellaneous matters relating to penance (verses 191–247) appears to be an interpolation.

11.197 *made holy by the cows*: the verse is elliptical. The place is made holy only if the cows actually eat the grass given by the penitent. The acceptance of the grass by the cows is viewed as a sign that the man has freed himself from his sin.

11.199 *misused*: this term (*viplāvya*) has a very broad meaning. Most commentators take it to mean that the man has divulged the Veda to an inappropriate person. Several possibilities are given: reciting the Veda at a time when recitation is forbidden (4.101 ff.), interfering with someone who is properly reciting it, and reciting the Veda uninvited for monetary gain.

11.203 *without water or in water*: 'without water' means that the man did not have water with him to perform the normal purification after voiding urine or excrement; and 'in water' means that he voided it into water.

11.205 *'Huṃ' . . . 'you'*: it appears that 'Hum' was an exclamation or curse hurled at someone in anger. When addressing a superior one should not use the informal singular *tvam* (literally, 'thou'; much like the *tu/vous* of French and other Romance languages) but the honorific plural *yūyam*.

11.213 *Subsisting . . . one day*: commentators point out two procedures. The man may subsist on the listed substances during one day and fast the next; or he may subsist on one of the six substances for a day during six days and fast on the seventh.

11.217–18 *He should decrease . . . first day of the bright fortnight*: the standard lunar penance begins on the full-moon day, when the penitent eats fourteen mouthfuls. He decreases the food by one mouthful a day, fasting on the new moon day. The intake of food is similarly increased during the fortnight of the waxing moon. Here the month is shaped with the middle narrow (fasting on the new moon) and the two ends are broad (fourteen mouthfuls at the beginning and the end). The alternative procedure with the middle broad and the ends lean (like a barley corn) begins on the new-moon day with a fast; the quantity of food is increased during the first fortnight until the full moon, and then decreased during the second fortnight. For a detailed description, see *BDh* 3.8.

11.226 *purificatory texts*: commentators identify these variously as the Aghamarṣaṇa, the Pāvamānī verses, the Puruṣa hymn, the Asyavāmīya, and the like. Clearly the term referred in general to vedic texts viewed as particularly purifying.

11.234 *If someone's mind . . . assuaged*: the meaning is somewhat unclear. The meaning may be that if after someone has performed a penance for a particular sin, he still has a heavy heart, he may continue to perform the same penance until his mind is at ease.

11.247 *As a fire . . . knowledge*: the vulgate editions and most manuscripts add here a verse, which is 248 in Bühler's translation: 'Thus I have described to you above penances for sins in accordance with the rules. Listen next to the penances for secret sins.' This verse is omitted in the critical edition.

11.256 *a reprehensible act*: the reference is probably to sexual intercourse. This may be carried out in water or on water, that is, in a boat. See 11.174–5.

11.265 *primary Yajus formulas*: the reference is probably to formulas found in the *Yajurveda Saṃhitā* as opposed to those given within the Brāhmaṇas.

11.266 *tri-syllabic Veda*: that is, the syllable OṂ, which consists of the phonemes 'a', 'u', and 'm'.

CHAPTER TWELVE

12.4 *One should . . . by the mind*: 'three kinds': highest, middling, and lowest; 'three bases': mind, speech, and body; 'ten characteristics' are the three kinds of mental action, the four kinds of verbal action, and the three kinds of bodily action listed in 5–7.

12.10 *The rod of speech . . . 'triple-rodded'*: rod means the use of mental, verbal, and physical actions to harm other creatures. 'Triple-rodded' (*tridaṇḍin*), or triple-staffed, is an allusion to a Brahmanical renouncer who carries a triple staff or a tripod. This verse also occurs in ascetic literature and is probably borrowed by Manu from such a source.

12.12–13 *The one who . . . succeeding births*: these verses contain several technical terms: Kṣetrajña refers to the spirit that observes the body and its activities as if they were a field (*kṣetra*); Bhūtātman is a term that is less clear (see also 5.109), but probably refers to a self made of material elements but which acts as a centre of consciousness; Jīva generally refers to the individual self within the body and identical with Kṣetrajña. Here Manu appears to be making a distinction between the two.

12.14 *Mahat*: in Sāṃkhya philosophy this term refers to the intellect, which is a material product, but reflects the conscious light of the self and thereby becomes conscious itself and able to cognize. Many commentators take it as a synonym of Jīva. They may be right, because the opening words 'these two' appear to refer to the two entities listed in the previous verses, and the only candidates are Kṣetrajña and Bhūtātman.

12.16 *five elemental particles*: earth, water, air, fire, and ether, which constitute the normal earthly body of a human being.

12.18 *two beings of great power*: commentators identify these differently: Great One (*mahat*) and the Knower of the field; individual soul and the Highest Self; Great One and Highest Self. I favour the first interpretation, because those two are mentioned in verse 14.

12.61 *goldsmiths*: some commentators interpret the Sanskrit term *hemakartṛ* as referring to a particular species of bird.

12.70 *Dasyu people*: this term can refer to a particular ethnic group (10.32), or barbarians (10.45), or simply bandits (7.143).

12.78 *being wrapped . . . for others*: the second half of this verse deals with childhood, as the first half did with birth; the following two verses likewise deal with various vicissitudes of life and finally with old age, sickness, and death. The wrapping must refer to the swaddling of infants, and servile work to serving the teacher during studentship.

12.88 *advancing . . . arresting*: this is a well-known division of activities enjoined by the Veda. The advancing (*pravṛtta*) acts prolong saṃsāric existence by procuring heaven or better births. These activities include all rituals and moral/immoral acts. The arresting (*nivṛtta*) acts, on the other hand, are intended to suppress the advance of saṃsāric existence and to bring about liberation. These include the pursuit of knowledge, meditation, and renunciation.

12.95–6 *The scriptures . . . to recent times*: the reference here must be to scriptural texts of traditions such as Buddhism and Jainism, which were gaining in popularity and power during the time when the *MDh* was composed.

12.111 *A man who . . . ten members*: the difference between logician and hermeneut is unclear. Commentators take the latter to mean a Mīmāṃsika, that is, an expert in interpreting the Veda. The first three orders, according to most commentators, are student, householder, and hermit. Some, however, think that they are student, householder, and wandering ascetic, both because a hermit is not allowed to enter a village and because in Gautama (*GDh* 3.2) the hermit is listed last.

12.120 *spaces*: the reference probably is to bodily cavities.

12.121 *Hari*: generally, this is an epithet of Viṣṇu. Given that Viṣṇu is already mentioned, the epithet may refer to Indra.

INDEX

abattoir 4.84–6
abduction 8.323
Ābhīra 10.15
abuse 7.48, 51
Ācārya 10.23
acid 5.114
action (activity) 1.18, 21, 22, 26, 28, 30, 41, 42, 49, 53, 55, 65, 66, 87, 91, 102, 107, 117; 2.4; 6.74; 7.205; 10.74, 76, 80–1, 96, 99–100, 117; 11.44, 65–6, 100, 126, 188, 194, 232–5, 246, 256; 12.2–116
  mental 1.104; 12.5, 8, 9
  oral 1.104; 12.6, 8, 9
  physical 1.104; 12.7, 8, 9
actor 4.214
Adhvaryu 3.145; 8.209
Ādityas 3.284; 11.222
adoption 9.141–2, 159–60, 168
adornment 3.55, 59; 4.152; 9.129
adulteration 11.50
adultery 3.156, 158, 174; 8.356–9, 371–86; 10.24; 11.60, 177–8
adversity, time of 1.116; 2.40, 113, 241; 3.14; 4.100; 5.33; 7.213–14; 9.56, 58, 103, 168, 313, 336; 10.1–131; 11.27–30, 34, 228; 12.70
afternoon 3.277
Agastya 5.22
age 2.136, 154–5; 4.18; 9.14
  old 6.62, 77
Age 1.68, 70, 71, 72, 73, 79, 82, 83, 84, 85
  Dvāpara 1.85, 86; 9.301–2
  Kali 1.85, 86; 9.301–2
  Kṛta 1.69, 81, 83, 85, 86; 9.301–2
  Tretā 1.83, 85, 86; 9.301–2
Aghamarṣaṇa 11.260–1
Agnidagdha 3.199
Agniṣṭoma 2.143
Agniṣvātta 3.195, 199
agriculture 1.90; 3.64; 4.5; 8.410; 10.79, 82–4, 90, 116
Āhiṇḍika 10.37
air 3.77, 90; 6.31; 11.215, 237
Ajīgarta 10.105
Ājyapa 3.197–8
Akṣamālā 9.23
alkali 5.114
All-gods 3.83–5, 90, 108, 121
alliance 7.160–3, 169, 206
alligator 6.78
ally 7.158, 164–6, 177, 180, 186, 206–9; 9.294
almsfood 2.51, 108, 183, 188; 3.94–6; 4.5, 248–9; 5.129; 6.7, 27–8, 34, 50, 55; 8.93; 11.73, 124, 256, 258
ambassador 7.153
Ambaṣṭha 10.8, 13, 15, 19, 47
ambrosia 2.162, 239
amnesty 7.201
Anagnidagdha 3.199
ancestors 1.37, 66; 2.58–9, 176; 3.37–8, 74, 80–1, 91; 3.146; 4.124, 249, 257; 8.37; 9.28, 106; 10.91; 11.211; 12.49, 94
  classes of 3.192–202
  worship of 4.150
ancestral offering 1.94–5, 112; 2.189; 3.18, 70, 72, 81–3, 97, 122–284; 4.31, 109–11, 116–17, 131; 5.16, 32, 41, 52; 6.24; 9.127
  food 3.266–72
  invitees 3.150–91, 187–91; 4.110
  time for 3.273–81
ancestry 2.247; 3.5; 5.59–60, 78, 100–1; 9.59, 187; 11.183
Andha-Tāmisra 4.88
Andhra 10.36, 48
anger 1.25; 2.214; 3.192, 213, 229–30, 235; 4.163–4, 166; 6.92; 7.11; 8.118, 121, 173, 280; 10.63; 11.223; 12.11
Aṅgiras 1.35; 2.151; 3.198
animals 7.72, 149; 8.44, 146, 242, 286, 296–7, 328, 404; 9.43; 10.32, 49, 72; 11.12, 132–42, 157, 200, 241; 12.9, 40, 68
  aquatic 1.44; 12.57
  carnivorous 12.58–9
  classification 1.43–5
  creeping 12.42
  domestic 5.39–40
  double-hoofed 11.169

MORE ABOUT **OXFORD WORLD'S CLASSICS**

American Literature

British and Irish Literature

Children's Literature

Classics and Ancient Literature

Colonial Literature

Eastern Literature

European Literature

History

Medieval Literature

Oxford English Drama

Poetry

Philosophy

Politics

Religion

The Oxford Shakespeare
